PRAISE FOR
PROFESSIONAL STANDARDS FOR EDUCATIONAL LEADERS

"The effectiveness of the new Professional Standards for Educational Leaders *depends upon both their quality and their ability to be used to frame educational leader practices and the policies that inform their work. This book provides an excellent foundation to understand their nature and to promote their active use in leader practice and policy. The book lays out a clear, current empirical and intellectual foundation, while strengthening the field's commitment to its moral purposes of leading schools of care and effective learning for all children."*

—Margaret Terry Orr
Bank Street College of Education

"This book is a thorough exposition of foundational evidence and argument for effective educational leadership. It establishes a well-supported rationale for the new Professional Educational Leadership Standards 2015 and goes further to help readers clearly understand the elements of educational organization and practice—key foci of leadership work—most conducive to student success. Particularly important is the way that this book integrates the essential elements of ethics and equity. When we are tempted to reduce educational leadership to a set of technical elements, this book rightly reminds us that it is a deeply moral and human enterprise."

—Mark A. Smylie, PhD, Professor Emeritus
College of Education, University of Illinois at Chicago

"Murphy leaves behind the superficial propaganda of 'leadership matters' to offer an exploration of the kind of leadership that matters most for each and every student. Let us hope the thinking reflected in this book and the new PSEL standards redirects our attention to what it really means to lead in education."

—Michelle D. Young, UCEA Executive Director, Professor of Leadership
University of Virginia

"Joseph F. Murphy debunks myths about standards for educational leaders and skillfully unpacks the moral, foundational, and experiential basis for the revised professional standards to guide effective leadership of our nation's schools. He does a masterful job of depicting how the ten standards reflect academic press and caring support and are driven by mission, vision, and core values; ethics and professional norms; equity and cultural responsiveness; and school improvement. This book is a must read for those interested in leadership for learning and the academic success and wellbeing of students, because these standards will shape our field for the next quarter century as the ISLLC standards have done since 1996."

—Martha McCarthy, Presidential Professor
Loyola Marymount University

To Mark Smylie, the tugboat captain
who, with some friends, brought the
USS PSEL down the harbor
and safely to dock.

Professional Standards
for
Educational
Leaders

The Empirical, Moral, and
Experiential Foundations

Joseph F. Murphy

CORWIN
A SAGE Publishing Company

A SAGE Publishing Company

FOR INFORMATION:

Corwin
A SAGE Company
2455 Teller Road
Thousand Oaks, California 91320
www.corwin.com

SAGE Ltd.
1 Oliver's Yard
55 City Road
London, EC1Y 1SP
United Kingdom

SAGE Publications India Pvt. Ltd.
B 1/I 1 Mohan Cooperative Industrial Area
Mathura Road, New Delhi 110 044
India

SAGE Publications Asia-Pacific Pte. Ltd.
3 Church Street
#10-04 Samsung Hub
Singapore 049483

Executive Editor: Arnis Burvikovs
Senior Associate Editor: Desirée A. Bartlett
Senior Editorial Assistant: Andrew Olson
Editorial Assistant: Kaitlyn Irwin
Production Editor: Veronica Stapleton Hooper
Copy Editor: Janet Ford
Typesetter: Hurix Systems Pvt. Ltd.
Proofreader: Dennis W. Webb
Cover Designer: Anupama Krishnan
Marketing Manager: Anna Mesick

Copyright © 2017 by Corwin

Printed in the United States of America

Library of Congress Cataloging-in-Publication Data

Names: Murphy, Joseph, 1949-

Title: Professional standards for educational leaders : the empirical, moral, and experiential foundations / Joseph F. Murphy.

Description: Corwin Thousand Oaks, California : Corwin, 2017. | Includes bibliographical references and index.

Identifiers: LCCN 2016037642 | ISBN 9781506337487 (pbk. : alk. paper)

Subjects: LCSH: School principals—United States. | Educational leadership—Standards—United States. | School management and organization—United States.

Classification: LCC LB2831.92 .M87 2017 | DDC 371.2/012—dc23 LC record available at https://lccn.loc.gov/2016037642

This book is printed on acid-free paper.

SFI Certified Sourcing
www.sfiprogram.org
SFI-00453

17 18 19 20 21 10 9 8 7 6 5 4 3 2 1

Contents

About the Author

 **Joseph F. Murphy** is the Frank W. Mayborn Chair and associate dean at Peabody College of Education at Vanderbilt University. He has also been a faculty member at the University of Illinois and The Ohio State University, where he was the William Ray Flesher Professor of Education.

In the public schools, he has served as an administrator at the school, district, and state levels, including an appointment as the executive assistant to the chief deputy superintendent of public instruction in California. His most recent appointment was as the founding president of the Ohio Principals Leadership Academy. At the university level, he has served as department chair and associate dean.

He is past vice president of the American Educational Research Association and was the founding chair of the Interstate School Leaders Licensure Consortium (ISLLC). He is coeditor of the *AERA Handbook on Educational Administration* (1999) and editor of the National Society for the Study of Education (NSSE) yearbook, *The Educational Leadership Challenge* (2002).

His work is in the area of school improvement with special emphasis on leadership and policy. He has authored or coauthored twenty-three books in this area and edited another twelve.

Introduction

This introduction first appeared in the *Journal of Educational Administration* in 2015. It is used with the permission of Emerald Group Publishing Limited. Additional members of the writing team were Jacquelyn Wilson, Co-Chair, Erin Anderson, Beverly Hutton, Mark Smylie, Susan Printy, and Jonathan Supovitz.

In this introduction, we explore the foundations of the Professional Standards for Educational Leaders (PSEL). We begin by uncovering the purpose dimensions of the Standards, what they are designed to influence. We undertake this initial assignment through a brief historical discussion, by highlighting core design principles, and with an analysis of the importance of the Standards. In the balance of the introduction, we examine the two intellectual pillars on which the Standards rest: academic press and caring support.

HISTORICAL DEVELOPMENT

The vision for national standards for school leaders took shape inside the National Policy Board for Education Administration (NPBEA) and bears the fingerprints of its executive director in the mid-1990s, Scott Thomson. The NPBEA was formed in response to recommendations contained in the 1987 report of the University Council for Educational Administration (UCEA)-sponsored National Commission on Excellence in Educational Administration (NCEEA) (Griffiths, Stout, & Forsyth, 1988; Thomson, 1999). It is a hallmark document in the history of school leadership that provided bridging from the forty-year post-WWII era to new conceptions about what educational administration might become (Forsyth, 1999). It was the NPBEA that secured the funding to develop national standards for school leaders, although in 1994 in an effort to prevent duplication, the grant application to the Pew Trusts for creation of "common and higher standards . . . was amended to designate the Council of Chief State School Officers (CCSSO) as assuming primary responsibility for this work" (Thomson, 1999, p. 107). Over eighteen months, the newly formed Interstate School Leaders Licensure Consortium, which encompassed twenty-four states and members from the associations in the NPBEA, crafted the

1

first set of national standards for school administrators (Forsyth, 1999) that came to be known as the ISLLC Standards for School Leaders (Interstate School Leadership Licensure Consortium, 1996).

As we report below, the ISLLC Standards quickly began to influence the profession of school administration in both direct and indirect ways. Some of this influence can be traced to the timing of their development. During the decade from 1985 to 1995, there was growing acceptance that the field was in need of major overhaul (Griffiths, 1988). Central here was the belief that the profession required a stronger and more unified center of gravity, and that the profession was more than a conglomerate of varied holding companies (Campbell, Fleming, Newell, & Bennion, 1987; Murphy, 1999a). The national standards also drew strength from a growing concern with the quality of leadership preparation throughout the nation, angst carefully delineated in a wide range of critical reviews of the profession beginning with Bridges (1977) and Erickson (1977, 1979) and running through the years of the NCEEA and its aftermath (Murphy, 1990b, 1992a; National Commission for the Principalship, 1990, 1993). Interest was also galvanized by the fact that the Standards captured a vision of school administration that was beginning to take hold across the four spheres of the profession—research, development, policy, and practice. Using a macrolevel prism and employing the language of Boyan (1963), the profession was moving from its long history of administration as a subfield of management to administration as a subfield of education. Using a more fine-grained lens, a shift from leading organizations to leading learning was unfolding (Hallinger & Murphy, 1985). The long period of neglect of the technical core of education (Bates, 1984; Callahan, 1962; Evans, 1991; Greenfield, 1988; Murphy, 1992a) was coming to a close, and the newly crafted Standards captured changing formulations of the profession (Murphy, 2005b).

As expected, the release of the Standards in 1996 and their expanding importance in the profession catalyzed a good deal of scholarly critique. Almost all of the concerns fell into two categories. Some analysts addressed shortcomings in the content of the Standards. These, in turn, focused on both omission of content (e.g., insufficient attention to matters of social justice) (see, for example, Davis, Leon, & Fultz, 2013; Hess, 2003; Leithwood & Steinbach, 2005; Young & Liable, 2000), and the incorporation of questionable content (e.g., the inclusion of nonempirical material) (see, for example, English, 2000; Hess, 2003; Leithwood & Steinbach, 2005). Other scholars were concerned that the Standards could be (would be) misused.

For an incongruous set of reasons that can best be described as political in nature, the struggle to democratize the Standards and extend ownership on the one hand, and to solidify control on the other, the 1996 Standards were revised in 2008. The initial process of developing the ISLLC Standards was transparent, but relatively low-keyed and largely contained within the development team of state and association participants. By 2008, the climate surrounding the Standards had changed considerably. The Standards had become a very important part of the profession, to a much greater extent than even the developers imagined. Consequently, nearly everyone who had a stake in the profession desired a stronger and more direct voice in recrafting the Standards. At the same time, the official guardians of the Standards, especially CCSSO, demanded a more visible role than they had in 1996. In the process, the 2008 Standards became both more widely owned and more tightly controlled. On the substantive side of the revision ledger, there was little appetite for major changes. The dominant stance was that the Standards were just beginning to become infused throughout the profession (e.g., in preparation programs, in principal evaluation systems). Any recasting that significantly altered the Standards was viewed as problematic, carrying with it the probability that progress since 1996 would be rolled back. Concomitantly, there was general agreement that the expansion of the knowledge base in school leadership in the decade in question did not warrant a need for major alterations. The decision was made to keep the original six standards. Revisions would occur through additional and stronger crystallization of the subdomains that defined each of the standards. These "functions" replaced the long lists of knowledge, skills, and dispositions that defined the 1996 Standards (ISLLC, 1996). As such, they brought greater meaning to the Standards while honoring the principle that the Standards were directional in nature, not immediately measurable (Murphy, 2005b). In 2013, CCSSO decided that it was time to revise the Standards for a second time. The seven-member team responsible for rewriting the Standards arrived at three important decisions at the start of their work. First, they decided that the foundation on which the Standards stood, leadership for learning, was solid; that is, it provided the correct architecture for understanding and defining school administration. Second, they concluded that some of the scaffolding, leadership of the core technology, leadership of the school culture, and leadership of diverse communities required significantly more attention. Third, the team agreed that the bands that held the platform together (community, social justice, and school improvement) (Murphy, 1999a) needed to be strengthened and made more visible. We examine these substantive issues below. Before we do so, however, we explore some of the core design principles of the Standards.

DESIGN PRINCIPLES

There are a number of essential understandings about the Standards that merit attention, often because they have been misunderstood. Much of this confusion can be traced to insufficient explanations by the developers of the Standards. Some can be explained by insufficient attention on the part of reviewers (Murphy, 2005b).

The Standards are based only on empirical evidence. The reality is that the Standards were never designed to be constructed using only empirical research findings. To be sure, a large portion of the Standards rest on the best available empirical evidence. This is appropriate. At the same time, the creation of the Standards was predicated on the conclusion that other materials need to be employed in the building process (Murphy, 1992a). The Standards acknowledge and honor the reality that educational administration is and should be a profession of values, of ethics, and of professional norms (Beck & Murphy, 1994; Foster, 1988; Greenfield, 1988). For example, there is no empirical ground for the claim that leaders should be stewards of public resources. Nor is there any empirical evidence that school administrators should disproportionately allocate human and social capital to care for marginalized children and their families. Yet it would be an impoverished profession if we failed to underscore such norms and values. The Standards also include craft knowledge of colleagues in the practice of administration, what scholars often refer to as the wisdom of practice (Murphy, 2005b).

The Standards are primarily for preparation programs. The Standards were never intended to be limited to (or primarily focused on) the preparation of school administrators. This misunderstanding grew from a number of converging dynamics. To begin with, the NPBEA in the mid-1990s decided to feature preparation as the most viable approach to improve the profession (Thomson, 1999). Second, the ISLLC leadership team design strategy to bring the Standards to life called for a first move into program accreditation, i.e., the creation of ELCC (Educational Leadership Constituent Council) Standards. The next move targeted state laws and regulations in the area of licensure of program graduates, including the development with ETS of the School Leader Licensure Examination. All of these forces combined to create a tight bond between the ISLLC Standards and preparation programs (Murphy, 1999b).

At the same time, the leadership team understood that these first two strategies would prove insufficient to the task of widespread infusion of the Standards. The team design called for strong connections to be formed between the Standards and the full array of "leverage points" that could influence the definition and practice of school administration (e.g., preparation, professional development, leader evaluation) (Murphy & Shipman, 2003; Murphy, Yff, & Shipman, 2000).

The Standards are measurable. The Standards are directionable, they push and pull the profession in well-specified pathways (e.g., ethical behavior, vision development work). By design, they rest at a level above measurement. They provide a framework that underscores issues meriting operationalization. To move the Standards onto measurement terrain, three additional issues must be addressed. To begin with, the appropriate leverage point needs to be made explicit. Are the Standards being applied to principal evaluation? To professional development? To program accreditation? Administrative roles also need to be specified. There likely will be, for instance, different quality points for principals and superintendents within a specific leverage point (e.g., licensure). Third, indicators need to be created. What, for example, would we need to see to determine if a principal were creating meaningful parental engagement?

IMPORTANCE

An essential question is why the profession writ large and professors in particular should attend to national standards for school leaders (Young, 2014). At one level, the answer is that the PSELs represent consensual agreement across all the professional associations about the grounding for school administration. At a more concrete level, investment is important because the Standards exert considerable influence on the shape and texture of the profession of school administration. For example, we know that the PSELs are welded into the framework of school leadership at the state level. Indeed, forty-five states have laws and regulations that infuse the Standards into core understandings and actions in the domain of school administration (McCarthy, Shelton, & Murphy, 2014). More concretely, via the Educational Leadership Coordinating Council, the PSELs have become the foundation for preparation programs across the nation.

INTELLECTUAL FOUNDATIONS

The Standards are scaffolded on the two pillars of academic press and caring support. In this section, we unpack these core constructs. In the process, we reveal a good deal about three crosscutting themes that bind the PSELs together: culture, school improvement, and justice.

ACADEMIC PRESS: LEADING LEARNING

If there is anything approaching a law in education, it is that teacher quality is the most critical factor in explaining student learning (Hughes, 2003; Lewis, 2008). That is, "the achievement of school children depends substantially on the teachers they are assigned" (Wayne & Youngs, 2003, p. 89), more so than the school that they attend (Hattie, 2009). Who teachers are and the values, knowledge, and skills that they bring to teaching are critical to school and student success. Equally important, what they do matters a good deal (Darling-Hammond & Post, 2000; Hattie, 2009).

Scholars over the decades have labored to determine the size of teacher effects on student learning. Bryk, Sebring, Allensworth, Luppescu, and Easton (2010) found that students with more effective teachers learn more than twice as much as students assigned to less effective teachers. Weak teachers in schools with a poor work orientation represent a particularly troubling condition for student learning. Smerdon, Borman, and Hannaway (2009) found that more effective teachers produce about 1.5 years in student achievement while less effective teachers add only 0.5 years growth. Nye, Konstantopoulos, and Hedges (2004) conclude that

> the difference in achievement gains between having a 25th percentile teacher (a not so effective teacher) and a 75th percentile teacher (an effective teacher) is over one third standard deviation (0.35) in reading and almost half a standard deviation (0.48) in mathematics. (p. 253)

Equally important, researchers consistently find that the effects of having a series of weak or strong teachers are cumulative. They also document that the effects of ineffective teachers linger on and that it is difficult to recover from having weak teachers, especially in consecutive years (Hattie, 2009; Smerdon et al., 2009). Thus we close with the law we introduced above. Instruction trumps programs, student grouping patterns, choice arrangements, and all other school factors (Supovitz & Turner, 2000; Wahlstrom & Louis, 2008). We also close with the central message of the Standards: "An examination of instruction must be at the heart of the question of leadership" (Louis, Dretzke, & Wahlstrom, 2010, p. 321).

If indeed teachers and teaching is a critical theme in the school improvement narrative, we should not be surprised that in good schools the administrators are leaders of the learning process (Hallinger, 1992, 2003; Robinson, 2008; Siu, 2008). Robinson, Lloyd, and Rowe (2008, p. 668) document this finding in their study, concluding "that a school's leadership is likely to have more positive impacts on student achievement and well-being if it is able to focus on the quality of learning, teaching, and teacher learning." We also discover from the research that instructionally focused leadership fosters loyalty and satisfaction among teachers (Blase & Kirby, 2009); an increase in professional capacity (Geijsel, Sleegers, Leithwood, & Jantzi, 2003); and more collaboration among staff (Blase & Blase, 2000). The mediating variable is, of course, more effective teaching practices. What this means is that the principal touches student performance indirectly by influencing teacher's instructional strategies (Hallinger & Heck, 1996, 1998; Heck & Hallinger, 2014; Supovitz, Sirinides, & May, 2010). On one hand, they do this by modeling instructional practices, or providing feedback on lessons. They also shape instruction in classrooms indirectly by molding the settings and environments in which teachers work (Hayes, Christie, Mills, & Lingard, 2004), e.g., their relationships and opportunities to work with their colleagues and by forging a positive climate in which to teach (May & Supovitz, 2011; Supovitz et al., 2010).

The essential ground to learning-centered leadership is a deep connection to the core technology. Learning becomes one of the two cardinal dimensions in the work of leaders. Structures, operations, procedures, and practices are more consciously and adeptly constructed on and linked to learning (Barnett, McCormick, & Conners, 2001; Dinham, 2005; Stein & Coburn, 2008). A long line of empirical inquiry reveals that this centrality is defined in four spheres: commitment to, knowledge of, involvement with, and responsibility for learning and teaching (see Beck, Murphy, & Associates, 1997; Hallinger & Murphy, 1985; Murphy, in press; Murphy, Elliott, Goldring, & Porter, 2007, for reviews).

We know from the research that learning-centered leaders are more interested in the core business of schooling, what Sweeney (1982, p. 347) early on labeled "concern for instruction and achievement." They are less likely to move away from or abandon their identities as teachers (Bryk et al., 2010). For example, Louis and team (2010), Nelson and Sassi (2005), Robinson (2007), and Southworth (2002) all found that instructional leaders have considerable understanding of curriculum, pedagogy, and assessment.

Researchers have also documented that effective principals translate this interest in, commitment to, and knowledge of learning and teaching into more "personal involvement in planning, coordinating, and evaluating teaching" (Robinson, 2007, p. 13). Overall, they are engaged in issues of teaching and learning (Walker & Slear, 2011). They are also more involved in "teachers' advice networks" (Robinson et al., 2008) and learning communities and in building instructional capacity in schools (Hallinger & Murphy, 1985; Murphy, 2016). Principals make themselves available to work on these matters (Cotton, 2003; Hallinger, 1992). They are in classrooms frequently and are adept at enriching the instructional program by providing detailed feedback (Wahlstrom & Louis, 2008), and they model instructional expectations (Walker & Slear, 2011). In short, researchers consistently conclude that principals spend considerable time engaged with learning and teaching and are "less distracted by the day-to-day demands of their jobs" (McDougall, Saunders, & Goldenberg, 2007). Effective principals "spend more time than their counterparts in low-performing schools in working with teachers to coordinate the school's instructional program, solve instructional problems collaboratively, [and] help teachers secure resources" (Hallinger & Heck, 1998, p. 176).

Finally, scholars over the last thirty-five years have found that effective principals are more likely than their less effective colleagues to take responsibility for instruction (Robinson et al., 2008; Wellisch, MacQueen, Carriere, & Duck, 1978). They do not deflect blame onto others or justify failure. Indeed, as Sweeney (1982, p. 348) concluded in one of the first reviews of effective schools, "schools where teachers attributed more responsibility to the principal in a greater number of areas were significantly more likely to be successful."

CARING SUPPORT

At the heart of the PSELs is the empirical conclusion that schools that serve children and young people well are defined by two anchoring pillars, strong academic press and caring support. Ancess (2000, p. 595) refers to this as "a combination of nurture and rigor or affiliation and intellectual development" and Bryk and team (2010, p. 74) characterize it as "a press toward academic achievement . . . coupled with personal support from teachers." In the last section, we examined the research on academic press. Here we analyze what is known about caring community, highlighting community for students. We begin with the conclusion that focusing primarily on the academic dimension of school improvement is insufficient (Bryk et al., 2010; Newmann, Rutter, & Smith, 1989; Shannon & Bylsma, 2002), especially for students placed in peril by poverty (Becker & Luthar, 2002; Murphy, 2010; Noddings, 1992; Rumberger, 2011). Academic press alone "does not attend sufficiently to the quality of social relations required for effective teaching and learning" (Goddard, Salloum, & Berebitsky, 2009, p. 293). That is, schools with strong press can still prove inadequate if they provide little attention to the social and relationship dimensions of education (Crosnoe, 2011; Felner, Seitsinger, Brand, Burns, & Bolton, 2007; Murphy & Torre, 2014; Quint, 2006).

At the same time, we know that nearly exclusive attention to culture is problematic as well, that it is a "necessary but not sufficient factor in promoting worthwhile forms of student achievement" (Newmann et al., 1989, p. 225). A number of landmark studies have revealed how overemphasis on culture can lead to a lowering of academic expectations (Cusick, 1983; Powell, Farrar, & Cohen, 1985; Sedlak, Wheeler, Pullin, & Cusick, 1986). Too great an emphasis on providing nurture and support can constrain educators from promoting serious academic engagement (Farrell, 1990). The concern is that students may "be exposed to socially therapeutic rather than intellectually demanding values and activities, and that their schools' efforts to build supportive and cohesive communities may actually help divert attention from academic goals" (Shouse, 1996, p. 52). Communal support for students, separate from focus on achievement, creates distinct complications for students (Newmann & Wehlage, 1994). When this occurs, "there [does] not seem to be any subject matter other than . . . cordial relations" (Cusick, 1983, p. 53), and caring separated from challenge contributes to student disengagement (Page, 1991). Research confirms that community is best conceptualized as in the service of learning (Ancess, 2003; Antrop-González & De Jesús, 2006; Shouse, 1996). The evidence is also clear that press and support work best when they are viewed as an amalgam (Murphy, 2013) or conceptualized as two strands of DNA that wrap around each other (Dinham, 2005; Kruse, Seashore Louis, & Bryk, 1995; Strahan, 2003). "Rigor and care must be braided together" (Fine, cited in Antrop-González, 2006, p. 274) to work best.

According to Sweetland and Hoy (2000, p. 705), culture is a "concept used to capture the basic and enduring quality of organizational life." It encompasses the values and norms that define a school (Dumay, 2009; Franklin & Streeter, 1995; Rossmiller, 1992). It is "those facets of organization that reflect underlying assumptions guiding decisions, behavior, and beliefs within organizations" (Scribner, Cockrell, Cockrell, & Valentine, 1999, p. 155). It can be thought of as the personality of the school (Hoy, Hannum, & Tschannen-Moran, 1998).

In the PSELs, school culture is defined in terms of community, a construct that is defined in a variety of overlapping ways (Beck & Foster, 1999). Battistich, Solomon, Kim, Watson, and Schaps (1995, p. 628) use community to capture "the psychological aspects of social settings that satisfy group members' needs for belonging and meaning." It consists of ingredients such as membership, support, care, integration, and influence (Baker, Terry, Bridger, & Winsor, 1997; Murphy & Torre, 2014; Osterman, 2000). Community stands in juxtaposition to institutionalism and hierarchy as an organizational frame of reference (Beck & Foster, 1999; McLaughlin & Talbert, 2001; Murphy, 1991; Scribner et al., 1999).

> Communally organized schools are marked by three *core components:* (1) a set of shared and commonly understood organizational values and beliefs about institutional purpose, what students should learn, how adults and students should behave, and students' potential as learners and citizens; (2) a common agenda of activities that defines school membership, fosters meaningful social interaction among members, and links them to school traditions; and (3) the distinctive pattern of social relations embodying an ethic of caring visible in both collegial and student-teacher relationships. (Shouse, 1996, p. 51)

Here, we illustrate the concept of community as it applies to students, what is characterized in the PSELs as communities of pastoral care. The explanatory narrative begins with this essential reality: "It is students themselves, in the end, not teachers, who decide what students will learn" (Hattie, 2009, p. 241) and students do not volunteer effort when they are detached from school (Crosnoe, 2011; Murphy & Torre, 2014; Newmann, 1981; Weis, 1990). Schooling for students is profoundly voluntary. Children have to "go to school." The decision to "do schooling" is substantially their own. This means, of course, that they are key decision makers in the learning production. The major purpose of supportive learning community is to positively influence students' willingness to learn what the school believes they require to be successful in life, to cause students to embrace academic challenges, and to help them reach those ends (Baker et al., 1997; Joselowsky, 2007; Newmann, 1992).

Educators in general and leaders in particular have three options at this point: ignore this reality, fight to change it, or use it as a platform for action. The first and second options have been the tools of choice for education historically. This is hardly surprising given the institutional nature of schooling and the managerial logic of school leadership (Callahan, 1962; Cuban, 1988). The problem is, however, that these choices have not been especially effective (Boyer, 1983; Crosnoe, 2011; Cuban, 1988; Eckert, 1989; Farrell, 1990; Goodlad, 1984; Newmann, 1981; Noddings, 1992; Patterson, Beltyukova, Berman, & Francis, 2007; Sizer, 1984; Weis, 1990), especially for students placed in peril by society and schooling (Alexander, Entwisle, & Horsey, 1997). Supportive learning community for students as defined in the PSELs moves the profession to option three: weaving the wisdom, needs, concerns, interests, and worries of students deeply into the "doing of schooling" without sacrificing academic press. Or more globally, it requires educators to acknowledge that achieving valued outcomes for students "involves, as a first step, recognizing that school culture is the setting in which [students] are being educated" (Crosnoe, 2011, p. 40). For example, research confirms that social concerns form the caldron of interest for students in schools (Crosnoe, 2011; Newmann, Wehlage, & Lamburn, 1992). It also shows us that to reach working-class youngsters, we need to address social connections beyond the schoolhouse (Eckert, 1989; Farrell, 1990; Stinchcombe, 1964). The charge for school leaders according to the PSELs is to work these and related realities productively in the service of helping students master essential academic goals.

On the research front, a deep line of empirical findings concludes that school communities in which many young persons find themselves, especially older students and youngsters in peril (Adams, 2010; Baker et al., 1997; Murphy, 2016; Quint, 2006), do not exert the positive influence and support necessary for them to commit to "do schooling" (Balfanz, Herzog, & MacIver, 2007; Croninger & Lee, 2001; Newmann et al., 1992). While this is not the place to examine this line of analysis in detail, we need to point out that student disengagement, often passive, sometimes active, is common in schools (Conchas, 2001; Murphy & Torre, 2014; Patterson et al., 2007; Quint, 2006). This is hardly surprising given that one of the pillars of institutions and bureaucracy is impersonality (Weber, 1978). As Ancess (2003, p. 83) reminds us, because of this "schools are conventionally organized as though relationships are not only unimportant and irrelevant, but an obstacle to efficient operation" (see also Noddings, 1992).

Analysts have uncovered a good deal of knowledge about what supportive communities of pastoral care for students look like and how they function. The PSELs are anchored on that research. Supportive learning community is defined by essential norms (care, support, safety, and membership). These norms combine to produce intermediate outcomes, such as student learning dispositions and psychological states which, in turn, lead to academic engagement. All of this powers student learning (Murphy & Torre, 2014).

Communities of pastoral care emphasize two strategies, one working to overcome liabilities and the other to build up assets. To begin with then, communities of pastoral care "foster productive learning by removing developmentally hazardous conditions" (Felner et al., 2007, p. 210). They suppress factors that undermine hopes for success, such as the formation of dysfunctional and oppositional peer cultures. Personalization damps down aspects of schooling that push students away from engaging the work of "doing school" well. A supportive learning community provides a "protective power" (Garmezy, 1991, p. 427) while attacking social problems that place students in peril (Christle, Jolivette, & Nelson, 2005; Crosnoe, 2011; Murphy, 2010; Murphy & Tobin, 2011b). It helps create a "social environment that neutralizes or buffers home stresses" (Alexander & Entwisle, 1996, p. 77) and community problems and individual characteristics that foster social marginalization and academic disengagement (Demaray & Malecki, 2002a; Garmezy, 1991). Concomitantly, scholars document that caring and supportive learning environments create assets, social and human capital, to draw youngsters into the hard work that is required to be successful in school (Ancess, 2003; Dinham, Cairney, Craigie, & Wilson, 1995; Goddard, 2003; Supovitz, 2002, 2008). They transform schools into places "where the social and pastoral environment nurture[s] a desire to learn in students" (Blair, 2002, p. 184). Assets, such as care and warmth, are stockpiled to assist in helping students reach ambitious learning targets (Demaray & Malecki, 2002a, 2002b; Quint, 2006; Roth & Brooks-Gunn, 2003; Yu, Leithwood, & Jantzi, 2002).

CONCLUSION

The ongoing work to update the PSELs has been subject to a number of powerful forces and dynamics. One of the most important was the history of the creation (1996) and the initial revision (2008) of the Standards. Organizational and political sediment demanding attention had built up over 20 years. Second, the reality that the Standards had become a high impact platform was inescapable. They had and most likely would continue to cascade over professional organizations, states, and districts in highly influential ways. They had signaled that important changes in the work of academics, practitioners, policy makers, and program developers were unavoidable. Most significantly, the knowledge base on which the Standards were scaffolded, academic press and caring support, demanded an enlarged treatment of what leaders should be doing to create schools where inside an environment of care, all youngsters reach ambitious targets of academic learning.

1

Mission, Vision, and Core Values

We learn from the broader literature on leadership that vision routinely surfaces in studies of effective organizations. We see this logic in studies of school improvement and of the leaders in improving schools and districts. School success and vision for learning are empirically linked. As we note throughout the book, vision is especially critical in periods of major transitions in education.

Researchers also report that the leader is generally the essential figure in ensuring that a school or district vision is created. Or in alternate form, vision focus distinguishes more effective from less effective leaders. It is hardly surprising then that vision work is a hallmark component of every important school leadership framework beginning in the 1980s.

We unpack vision into three distinct, but related domains: mission, which addresses overarching values and purpose; goals, which provides direction; and expectations, which establishes specific targets. All three seem to be required for vision to impact student learning.

VALUES AND MISSION

At the broadest level, vision is about moral purpose and possibilities, concepts forged from values and beliefs on which school improvement is scaffolded. As Fullan (1982, 1993, 2002) has reminded us numerous times, values are the bedrock of school improvement. Schools and districts do not progress well without it. Additionally, mission rarely evolves without the guiding hand of leadership.

Researchers have also harvested important clues about how mission serves school improvement. Mission influences the instructional program and the learning climate that in turn shape the behaviors of teachers and students. Because schools and districts are loosely coupled systems, they often lack clear goals. In such situations, there is a natural tendency for effort to splinter, an effect only exacerbated by the frenetic nature of schooling. Mission begins to tighten systems by establishing the boundaries in which "schooling" occurs. Mission coheres means and ends around shared values and beliefs.

It is important to note that not all school missions harness equal amounts of energy. From our analysis, we distill eight core values that anchor stronger missions, those that consistently direct the school into productive channels of work, that is, school improvement. To begin with, the mission needs to convey a sense of hope, to open the door of possibility. Missions should be inspirational. They need to convey a palpable sense that conditions (e.g., low levels of success, disaffiliation) are malleable and that improvement is possible, even likely.

In addition, missions should address commitment to success and to the effort that such commitment entails. This encompasses the understanding that second best is insufficient and the conviction that the school can and will improve. In a related vein, mission should reflect the belief that all students will be successful. That is, no one is permitted to fail. The embedded understanding is that schooling is the game changer for students, a conviction and moral imperative about success.

Relatedly, mission should reflect asset-based thinking about students and the larger community. As Edmonds (1979) and Brookover and colleagues (1977, 1978, 1979) reported at the beginning of the modern era of school improvement, this third core idea pushes back against the deficit-based thinking often found in struggling or failing schools and schools with large numbers of students placed at risk. It is anchored on the belief that all students are capable of learning, that the school does not underestimate the abilities and efficacy of children. Asset-based thinking means not accommodating instruction to preconceived assumptions of limitations, but rather conducting schools in ways that change students' abilities and interests. Optimism rather than pessimism holds the high ground. Problems and failure are not attributed to children and their families. Deficiencies are not assumed. Negative attitudes are conspicuous by their absence. Constraints are recognized, but they are challenged as impediments to success. Schools push back on resistance to norms of success proactively not reactively.

Student focus is the fourth core element/value in mission. Student-centered values hold the high ground. The spotlight is on children and youth—what is in the best interests of students. Effective leaders run child-centered schools and districts. Concretely, that means developing structures, policies, operating systems, and budgets around a learner-centered ideology and the specific youngsters in the school.

Fifth, the mission in improving schools is academically anchored. It highlights student learning and academic success. An academically focused mission targets the instructional program. Teaching and learning hold center stage and better instruction is job one. Sixth, effective leaders also develop outcome-focused missions. These outcomes feature measures of student learning in general and provide markers of student achievement in particular. Seventh, missions in effective schools carry the value of continuous improvement. Norms of complacency are challenged. Risk taking is promoted and there is an appetite for change. Finally, missions in improving schools are characterized by a norm of collective responsibility. A culture of accountability emerges, replacing traditions of externalizing responsibility. Success is a collective endeavor.

ESTABLISHING GOALS AND EXPECTATIONS

Goals

Five storylines in the area of goals merit attention. To begin with, goal setting is seen as one of the most influential roles that leaders can undertake to promote school improvement. Second, districts and schools are often found to have vague goals, ones that lack the power to direct action, especially teacher behavior. Third, even when there are clear goals they are often developed in ways that do not encourage ownership by school staff. Fourth, districts and schools that are effective in helping all students reach ambitious targets of performance have widely shared and clearly formed academic goals, goals that are "both a property of leadership and a quality of school organization" (Robinson, Lloyd, & Rowe, 2008, p. 659). Fifth, in "getting goals right" considerable attention needs to be devoted to the content of the goals as well as the goal development process. We explore both of these issues—content and processes—below.

Nature of the Goals

Our analysis of research over the last thirty-five years leads us to conclude that goals that function well can be identified by critical markers. The most essential of these is a focus on the academic domain in general and on student learning in particular. We know that goals are most productive when they are specific, not generic. Supovitz and Poglinco (2001, pp. 3–4) make this point as well, concluding that while generic goals can be a starting point, the "exponential value of instructional leadership comes from a marriage of intensive organizational focus on instructional improvement with a clear vision of instructional quality." Barnett and McCormick

(2004) call this a "task focus," and Strahan (2003) refers to it as a specific "stance about learning." Thus "academic focus" and "learning stance" are essential. They positively impact student achievement.

Implicitly and explicitly, other cardinal elements can be discerned in an analysis of academic learning focus. We discover, for example, that goals are best when the spotlight is on students, when there is a children first perspective, and when student achievement is the central theme. Researchers also inform us that the goals that are found in improving schools are challenging, but achievable and apply to all students. They direct activity, but are not rigid. Goals that work well are meaningful to school staff. Meaningfulness includes knowledge of, internalization of, and ownership of goals.

Almost every study of leadership for school improvement has concluded that goals need to be clear and concrete, not abstract or subject to interpretation. They should provide "stakes in the ground" indicating the destination and the way to travel. Parsimony and simplicity are desirable. Scholars also report that goal clarity in improving districts and schools directs the allocation and development of human and financial resources. Recent studies have also identified the importance of tailoring goals to context—the specific needs of students in a given school at a given time. Short-term goals that move the school to larger ends are desirable as they permit staff to experience reinforcing, short-term wins. It is important, however, that these short-term wins derive from and support the more encompassing mission of the district and school.

Developing and Communicating Goals

Analyses across time also reveal important insights about the ways in which effective districts and schools forge goals. One critical discovery is the importance of a process that fosters staff ownership of goals. The literature highlights both the personal engagement of leaders and collaborative work of teachers. What is particularly important is the creation of ownership of the work to reach goals and responsibility for the results of those efforts. Wide participation of community stakeholders and reliance on hard data to arrive at decisions also define goal development in high-performing schools and districts.

School improvement leadership is also about ensuring that school goals are important, importance nurtured by discussing and reviewing them with staff periodically during the school year, especially in the context of instructional, curricular, and budgetary decisions. Both formal communications (e.g., goal statements, staff bulletins, articles in the principal or site-council newsletter, curricular and staff meetings, parent and teacher conferences, school handbooks, assemblies) and informal interactions (e.g., conversations with staff and students) are used to communicate the school's mission.

Not only do effective leaders spend more energy than their peers in communicating goals, they also appear more successful in getting their messages across. For example, researchers conclude that teachers in schools with robust school improvement leadership are more aware of and can clearly communicate the school's mission and goals. Their counterparts in schools with less effective instructional leadership lack a common understanding of schoolwide goals and expectations.

The emerging theme from the research runs as follows: the development and inculcation of widely shared, ambitious, and unambiguous learning goals is one of the most valuable instruments in the school improvement toolbox. We close this part of our analysis with a note on what that research tells us about how goals function to fuel school improvement. At a fundamental level, goals adhering to the description above provide tangible meaning to the district and school mission. In so doing, they solidify action around shared values and purpose. They signal importance to all stakeholders. As such, they help people see more clearly. They keep staff from becoming distracted by separating the really important work from the balance of activity. Effort becomes more focused and more productive. Goals also serve as a powerful mechanism for organizational cohesion, helping leaders with the essential role of coordinating action in complex organizations (Murphy, 2015b).

On the personal side, strong goals can be powerful motivators for staff, encouraging educators to reach for higher standards. Goals have been shown to have an energizing effect. They also have the potential to bring about cooperative work and to help dismantle the wall between teaching and school administration. Shared work, in turn, can strengthen commitment and responsibility.

Expectations

Expectations are the third layer of school vision. They make even more concrete the understandings of performance for members of the school community. They create a platform to bring goals to life. They are both a measure of and a method to develop academic press and productive culture in the school.

Over the last four decades, researchers have shown that expectations have important organizational consequences. Most importantly, they differentiate between more and less effective schools, with higher academic expectations linked to better outcomes, outcomes defined in terms of student learning. They work in part by helping to shape school culture and by promoting organizational learning. Expectations have their largest impact on children on the wrong side of the achievement gap, especially children from low-income families.

On the teacher front, expectations help define in concrete terms understandings of quality. According to Leithwood, Jantzi, and Steinbach (1999, p. 69), who have examined this issue in considerable depth, expectations of this sort help teachers see the challenging nature of the goals being pursued in their school. They may also sharpen teachers' perceptions of the gap between what the school aspires to and what is presently being accomplished. Done well, expressions of high expectations also result in perceptions among teachers that what is being expected is also feasible.

High expectations convey in tangible fashion the hard work required to create a school where all youngsters reach ambitious targets of performance. They can energize faculty to work collectively, assume leadership responsibilities, and keep student improvement in the spotlight. At the heart of the success equation here are consistency and repetition of shared expectations.

VISION-IN-ACTION

Operationalization: The Possibilities

So far, we have constructed a scaffold for school vision, one highlighting three domains: mission, goals, and expectations. Our remaining assignment is to review the research on how leaders help keep vision vibrant and at the center of school improvement work. We know that schools are shaped by context, highly complex, and deeply human enterprises. They are also layered over with a wide assortment of demands from a diverse array of stakeholders. Under these conditions, it is not unusual for vision to fall by the wayside or to lose its directive power. Vision often becomes simply another item on an extensive list of important things. A meaning-infusing tool is transformed into a "bureaucratic necessity" (Leithwood et al., 1999, p. 60). The specific implications for work are often undeveloped. Even when they are forged, they often "go missing."

> Because considerably more happens in schools than the pursuit of explicit goals, even the most goal-focused leaders will need to skill-fully manage the constant distractions that threaten to undermine their best intentions. Such distractions, in the form of new policy initiatives, school crises, calls for goal revision or abandonment, and the need to maintain school routines that are not directly goal related, all threaten to undermine goal pursuit. (Robinson et al., 2008, p. 667)

Thus we know that considerable effort is required to keep vision in a starring role, to ensure that "the mission serves constantly as the criterion and desideratum for everything" (Raywid, 1995, p. 70). For this to occur, the school needs to go beyond developing mission, goals, and expectations, beyond articulation. Everyone needs to be committed to the vision. The staff, with leaders on point, need to refresh and reinforce school vision, consciously working to maintain it as a driving force. Trust is a key leavening agent in most school matters, but never more so than in building commitment to the school's mission, goals, and expectations for children. Trust is central to Timperley's (2009, p. 220) concept of "vision in action."

As was the case with the formulation and dissemination of vision, the leader's actions are critical in bringing vision to life and to keeping it healthy. Leaders' actions foster the commitment of others, nurture needed workplace trust, and steer improvement work—or not. Or as Kruse, Seashore Louis, and Bryk (1995, p. 39) so aptly note, "What leaders say and do expresses what they value for the organization, and the behavioral expectations that they communicate on a daily basis either reinforce or call into question these basic values."

Elsewhere we have made the empirical case that forging consistency, coordination, coherence, and alignment is one of the three or four most critical, cross-domain functions of school leaders (Murphy, 2015b). Given the truism that "you get what you work on in schools" (Louis & Miles, 1991, p. 77), nowhere is that responsibility more essential than in the operationalization of school vision, pushing, pulling, and carrying vision into the workflow of the school. We know that in more effective schools, vision acts as the "organizing principle" (Desimone, 2002, p. 451) for work. Vision encourages aligned actions in the service of school improvement. It becomes infused into key organizational activities, such as operating procedures, structures, policies, and budgets and is the cardinal leitmotif of school culture. Challenges are addressed and problems attached less on an ad hoc basis and more within the guidance of a master road map. As a consequence, there is less organizational drift and better uptake of organizational values.

Communicating and Consensus Building

Beginning with the studies on school and teacher effects in the 1970s, investigations have been adding to our understanding of how leaders work to operationalize vision. Two themes from our analysis, consensus building and communication, were introduced above in our discussion of the goals aspect of vision. We expand on them here. Researchers show us that ongoing, coherent communication around school mission and goals is a hallmark dimension of school improvement. It is, to use a metaphor, the fuel needed to power school vision. Researchers also unpack the variety of ways communication in the service of operationalizing vision occurs: through (1) the use of stories, symbols, rituals, and slogans; (2) the ways that resources are committed; (3) conspicuous displays of mission, goals, and expectations, including achievements, throughout the school; (4) providing information on mission, goals, and expectations, including news of progress, in all oral and written communications; (5) the clear linkage of vision to educational programs; and (6) acknowledging progress and celebrating success. All of these strategies are enhanced to the extent that the focus is on the specific youngsters in a given school, that is, that context is taken into consideration.

Earlier we explained that consensus in mission and goal development promotes a variety of important conditions (e.g., commitment) that mediate school improvement. Here we deepen that narrative to collective action in operationalizing vision, to ownership of the full staff for school improvement work. Collective work around a shared vision nourishes commitment and efficacy and promotes personal and organizational learning needed to fuel continuous school improvement.

Modeling and Monitoring

Research affirms that leaders infuse vision with meaning by the ways in which they act, by modeling. In effective districts and schools, leaders demonstrate commitment through how they allocate their time, where they spend time, what they place on agendas, and how they accept responsibility for school success. They "carry the torch" for the school and its values, ensuring tight alignment between their behaviors and the school vision. Through modeling, they become catalysts of school improvement.

Colleagues from the earliest studies of school effects have shown the keystone position that monitoring occupies in the improvement algorithm. Here we highlight its position in relation to the vision dimension of highly productive schools and districts and effective leadership. On that score, there is abundant evidence that rigorous assessment and monitoring of mission, goals, and expectations is an important part of the vision implementation playbook for leaders. More importantly, studies reveal that this monitoring occurs in improving schools, while it is not highlighted in reports of stagnant schools. The core elements of this monitoring parallel those found in the general literature on assessment.

2

Ethics and Professional Norms

Joan Poliner Shapiro and Steven Jay Gross

INTRODUCTION

This chapter focuses on the 2015 Standard 2: Ethics and Professional Norms. Standard 2 is considered to be one of the four "driver" standards along with Standard 1: Mission, Vision, and Core Values, Standard 3: Equity and Cultural Responsiveness, and Standard 10: School Improvement.

Prior to the acceptance of the 2015 standards, a very real concern for those of us who teach ethical educational leadership to aspiring educational leaders was that Ethics and Professional Norms would not be included as a separate standard. Apparently, we were correct to have this concern as some of the designers of the 2015 Standards felt that Standard 2 was a "given" and as such was so overarching that it should be included in the introduction of the standards, but not as a separate entity. However, others on the working group realized that, without the creation of a separate standard, this important and flourishing area would not be treated with the gravitas it deserved. Additionally, since many of us believe that professional ethics is needed if educational leadership is to be called a profession, then it is truly important that it be seen as a field that deserves to be taught as a separate course or unit in graduate programs and should be a discrete entity of faculty development programs in schools and in central offices.

In this chapter, we will provide some background to the new scholarship of ethical educational leadership and for the need of teaching this burgeoning field to educational leaders. We will also describe an assignment regarding personal and professional codes as well as offer an introduction to paradoxes. Then we will turn to ethical decision making. This is a way to put educational leaders' professional beliefs into practice by dealing with paradoxical situations and by making hard choices. The ability to make wise, intelligent, and thoughtful decisions is extremely important for educational leaders in these very challenging times.

While discussing ethical decision making, a few ethical decision-making models will be mentioned. Two models in particular, the multiple ethical paradigms and turbulence theory, will be introduced and described. Following the description of the two models, ethics standards from 1996 and 2008 will be briefly reviewed. Then the 2015 Standard 2 itself and its functions will be deconstructed, utilizing the multiple ethical paradigms and turbulence theory to determine if the ethics of justice, critique, care, and the profession are part of this standard. Finally, to help make this standard more accessible, exemplars will be described to enable an educational administrator to determine how a particular aspect of a standard can be actualized.

Ethical Educational Leadership: The New Scholarship

Just a glance at the Table of Contents of the *Handbook of Ethical Educational Leadership* (Branson & Gross, 2014) clearly shows the growth of scholarship in this field both nationally and internationally. Shields (2014) makes a strong case that this new knowledge is essential for educational leaders to study. She challenges the assumption of one senior colleague who said to her some years ago that "ethics has nothing to do with educational administration" (pp. 24, 41). Instead, her argument places ethics at the center of learning in this current era of diversity and interdependence globally.

The flourishing of ethical educational leadership can be traced back to the early 1990s. Previously, as Farquhar (1981) pointed out, after surveying the University Council for Educational Administration (UCEA) member institutions, there was a paucity of ethics courses or units in educational administration programs. It was not until 1992 that Beck, Murphy, & Associates (1997) saw marked progress in ethics being taught either as a separate course or in an infused manner in educational leadership. In particular, in 1995, the UCEA Center for Values and Leadership Education, originally housed at the University of Toronto and the University of Virginia, helped to move ethical leadership into the curriculum for educational administrators. Later on, the Consortium for the Study of Leadership and Ethics Education (CSLEE) was developed, encompassing a number of global centers and institutions, and this organization helped to make ethical educational leadership an international field. These centers and institutions place ethics and values at the forefront of their educational leadership curriculum.

Today, to be effective, an educational administrator needs to have knowledge of this growing field of ethical educational leadership. This field encompasses values, virtues, decision making, and standards (Shapiro, 2015). Ethical educational leadership expects K-12 administrators to think rationally, empathetically, and comprehensively before making an important ethical decision that may affect faculty, staff, parents, and especially students.

Values, Virtues, and Standards: Different Ideals

Early on, educational ethicists turned to diverse values that they believed were essential for leaders to possess in education. For example, Branson (2009, 2010; Branson & Gross, 2014) highlights wisdom and moral integrity; Haiyan and Walker (2014) focus on empathy; Begley (2006) and Begley & Johansson (2003) stress self-knowledge and sensitivity; Gross (2014a; Gross & Shapiro, 2016) turns to exemplars who exhibit a wide range of salient qualities; and Bredeson (2005) encompasses values when he describes ethical architects as school leaders. Some of these writers emphasize the need to teach values to future educational leaders through moral literacy (Tuana, 2007). Others, such as Starratt (2004), do not turn to values. Instead, Starratt does advocate the importance of specific virtues. His foci are: responsibility, authenticity, and presence.

Another major way that educational ethical values are gleaned is through the various standards designed by professional organizations. They include, for example, the past National Policy Board for Educational Administration's ISLLC Standards (1996, 2008) and the current National Policy Board for Educational Administration's Professional Standards (2015), the American Association of School Administrator's Statement of Ethics for Educational Leaders (2007), and the University Council for Educational Administrators' Code of Ethics for the Preparation of Educational Leaders (2011). Many other local, national, and international organizations have designed their own codes, focusing frequently on important values and virtues that educational leaders should possess. Above all, it is important for educational leaders to develop their own codes consisting of values and even behaviors.

Personal Versus Professional Ethics Codes:
The Importance of Reflection

A number of us who teach ethics usually give an assignment asking our graduate students, who are aspiring educational leaders, to create two codes. One of these is a personal code that lists the values and behaviors of their interactions with their families and friends. The other code, the professional one, asks them to develop a list of values and behaviors that they turn to when they are in their work environments. For some students, the codes are similar. While for others, they are very different. Discussing the similarities and differences in small groups becomes a worthwhile and fascinating activity. Some students are so affected by the codes that they place them nearby at home and at work so that they can remember to read them each day. The importance of reflection cannot be underestimated. There is so little time in the busy life of an educational leader to actually carry out the reflective process. When given the opportunity, developing ones' own personal and professional codes can be of great importance to educational leaders as they are intrinsic and authentic. They can prepare educational administrators for the challenges ahead.

Being an Ethical Person Versus Acting Ethically: Dealing With Paradoxes

Developing ones' own personal and professional ethical codes is an excellent start to becoming an ethical educational leader; however, it is only a beginning. In an era of wars, terrorism, hurricanes, volcanoes, tornados, financial uncertainty, and high-stakes testing, educational leaders face a myriad of complex problems. They need to take into account evacuation plans, lockdowns, immigration issues, psychological problems, and even global events. Each day, educational leaders face paradoxes that often challenge their own values. These paradoxes can be categorized, for example, as security versus civil liberties, community standards versus individual rights, equality versus equity, accountability versus responsibility, and many more. Thus, it is important to prepare educational leaders for some of the paradoxes they will have to face while providing them with time to think through their values and explore their possible reactions to the situations in safe spaces.

Ethical Dilemmas: Educational Leaders' Challenges

There are many kinds of dilemmas that educational leaders face today. For example, they must deal with not only the bullying that occurs frequently in the playground or lunch room, but also now there are cases of cyberbullying and sexting. They have to take into account the problems that come from the carrying of guns and the difficulties of immigration. The variety of ethical dilemmas that they face are many and varied. Here is one example of an ethical dilemma that an educational leader might face in this era of high-stakes testing.

TEST ROOMS VERSUS RESTROOMS

It's time for standardized test week at the Wonderbrook Middle School. State testing regulations say that students cannot use the restrooms during tests. Leaving a proctor to watch the rest of the class, the teacher, Ms. Smith, escorts a student who urgently needs to use the bathroom. Ms. Smith's action is reported to the principal by another teacher who fears that the rules were broken and that Ms. Smith might have placed the reputation of the school in jeopardy. You are the principal, what do you do? On the one hand, should Ms. Smith and the student be reprimanded for breaking a testing regulation? On the other hand, is it really right to not allow a student to go to the bathroom, even during tests?

The above example is only one of the many cases that educational leaders face today. In this instance, the ethic of justice (rules and regulations) is pitted against the ethic of care (concern for others) and the profession (best interests of the student). Additionally, because of the pressure related to standardized testing placed on schools today, the turbulence level is bordering on severe. To help leaders deal with these problems, a number of models are now part of the new scholarship in ethical educational leadership. The next section discusses briefly some of the models in the literature and focuses on two models, the multiple ethical paradigms and turbulence theory.

Ethical Decision Making: The Multiple Ethical Paradigms and Turbulence Theory

In the literature, not only are values and virtues emphasized, but also the actual process of ethical decision making is highlighted. There are numerous ways to approach educational ethical decision making. Strike, Haller, and Soltis (2005), for example, focus on evidence-driven decision making. They believe that a decision should be "supported by evidence" and that the decision should be "implemented morally" (pp. 111–113). Cranston, Ehrich, and Kimber (2014) propose a different ethical decision-making model. Their five-part model contains:

> the critical incident, individual decision makers and their personal values; the factors or forces that illuminate the ethical dilemma; the choices available in resolving the dilemma; the action that is taken; and the implications of the decision or action for the individual, the organization and the community. (p. 243)

Another model for ethical decision making has been developed by Starratt (2004). He focuses on ethical decision making using three lenses—the ethics of justice, care, and critique. Shapiro and Stefkovich not only utilize the three lenses, but they add a fourth—the ethic of the profession.

Starratt's work provided a foundation on which Shapiro and Stefkovich (2001, 2005, 2011, 2016) were able to create their multiple ethical paradigms for ethical decision making. When faced with an ethical decision, Shapiro and Stefkovich ask educational leaders to turn to the multiple ethical paradigms of justice, critique, care, and the profession.

Let's take a look at the multiple ethical paradigms in more detail. Although there is no expectation that the ethic of justice will be turned to by educational leaders, frequently, in a litigious society, they consider this lens to be the first step in the decision-making process. The ethic of justice (e.g., Beauchamp & Childress, 1984; Sergiovanni, 2009; Strike, 2006; Yodof, Kirp, & Levin, 1992) is concerned with the legal system, fairness, and freedom. It takes into account questions, such as: Is there a law, right, or policy that relates to a particular case? If there is a law, right, or policy, should it be enforced? Is the law enforced in some places and not in others? Why or why not? And if there is not a law, right, or policy, should there be one?

The ethic of critique (e.g., Apple, 2003; Freire, 1970; Giroux, 2006; Portelli, 2007; Reitzug & O'Hair, 2002; Shapiro, 2009; Shapiro & Purpel, 2005), inherent in critical theory and critical pedagogy, is aimed at awakening educational leaders to inequities in society and, in particular, to injustices in education at all levels. It asks leaders to deal with the difficult questions regarding social class, race, gender, and other areas of difference such as Who makes the laws, rules, and policies? Who benefits from them? Who has the power? Who is silenced?

The ethic of care (e.g., Beck, 1994; Ginsberg, Shapiro, & Brown, 2004; Marshall & Gerstl-Pepin, 2005; Marshall & Oliva, 2006; Noddings, 2003) directs educators to contemplate the consequences of their decisions and actions. It asks them to consider questions such as Who will benefit from what I decide? Who will be hurt by my actions? What are the long-term effects of a decision I make today? And if someone helps me now, what should I do in the future about giving back to this individual or to society in general?

Finally, the ethic of the profession (e.g., Beck, Murphy, & Assocs., 1997b; Beckner, 2004; Begley & Johansson, 2003; Greenfield, 2004; Normore, 2004; Murphy, 2005b; Strike et al., 2005) expects educational leaders to formulate and examine their own professional as well as personal codes of ethics in light of standards set forth by educational leadership, and then place students at the center of the ethical decision-making process. It also asks them to take into account the wishes of the community. It goes beyond the ethics of justice, critique, and care to inquire What would the profession ask me to do? What do various communities expect me to accomplish? What about clashes of codes—does this exist, and is there a problem? And what should the professional educator take into account to consider the best interests of the students, who may be diverse in their composition and their needs (Frick, Faircloth, & Little, 2013; Stefkovich, 2006, 2014).

There is another ethic that is currently included under the ethic of the profession in the Shapiro and Stefkovich model, but it is considered to be a separate ethic by Furman (2004; Furman-Brown, 2002). She expands on what she characterizes as the "ethic of the community" and defines it as a process. Furman asks leaders to move away from heroic (solo) decision making and to reach conclusions with the participation of the community or communities.

Another model, turbulence theory (Gross, 1998, 2000, 2004, 2006, 2014b; Shapiro & Gross, 2013), while not an ethic, is very much related to the multiple ethical paradigms. When combined with the multiple ethical paradigms, turbulence theory helps to identify the emotional intensity of a given ethical dilemma.

The origins of turbulence theory came from a study of ten schools and districts in the United States and Canada that were engaging in successful and sustained innovation in curriculum, instruction, and assessment (Gross, 1998). Ironically, these schools and districts were also faced with various levels of disturbance, sometimes threatening the innovation that made them so attractive in the first place. This paradox led to a comparison of four levels of turbulence experienced by pilots (Braybrook, 1985; Lester, 1994). During light turbulence, there is little or nearly no movement of the aircraft. In moderate turbulence, there are clearly noticeable waves of motion. In severe turbulence, strong gusts threaten control of the craft, and during extreme turbulence, the structural integrity of the aircraft itself is damaged or destroyed. By comparing disturbances in school settings to each of these levels, Gross was able to better describe specific situations, such as the severe turbulence experienced in Verona, Wisconsin, when one faction of the community supported a progressive approach to curriculum and instruction while an equally powerful faction favored a traditional approach. Building on the initial work, a system of turbulence gauges was developed to help educators and researchers identify current levels of turbulence as well as where the turbulence level might go in the future (Gross, 2004).

Knowing that there are multiple levels of turbulence and that these levels altered up or down depending on specific actions of school and district leaders led to reflections on the underlying forces of turbulence itself. Three such integrated forces that work as a combined system have been identified (Gross, 2006, 2014; Shapiro & Gross, 2013). These drivers of turbulence include positionality, cascading, and stability. They provide critical context with which to understand and work with the inevitable turbulence that comes with educational leadership at all levels.

Positionality explains why one feels a specific way about a turbulent event depending on the position she or he has vis-à-vis that event (Alcoff, 1991–1992; Collins, 1997; Hauser, 1997; Kezar, 2000; Maher & Tetreault, 1993). Students may feel very different than faculty or community members for instance. Even in one specific group, there are going to be differences. All students are not alike, therefore there will be differing levels of turbulence felt among them. Educational leaders need to empathize and put themselves in the place of the varied individuals involved in any turbulent situation. Constructing multiple turbulence gauges from different vantage points in a given dilemma is suggested for that very reason.

The second underlying force driving turbulence is cascading. Since no challenging situation in schools exists in isolation, events preceding a turbulent incident are important to take into account. A teacher strike, previous problems with high-stakes testing, a failed school budget, a recent incident of violence all could cause the current turbulence to escalate to higher levels, just as the cascade of rapidly flowing water speeds up as it tumbles over vertical drops on its way. At times, this works as a positive feedback loop (Senge, 1990), similar to the firebombing of Dresden in World War II, where the very intensity of the attack led to fire storms that built one atop the other (McKee, 1984). At other times, unrelated but mutually stimulating events spur on a cascade. Similar to the use of empathy to better understand the range of positions during turbulence, educational leaders who reflect on the potential of cascading events to escalate turbulence will be better prepared to guide their schools.

Finally, the perceived stability of an organization, such as a school, will influence the degree to which it is impacted by turbulence. Consider two schools. One has a reputation for high achievement, good community relations, and a strong bond among students, faculty, staff, and administration. The second school has none of these advantages and suffers from poor morale, frequent faculty and administrative turnover, and a poor record of achievement. Now imagine that both schools experience a negative community response to a new social studies curriculum where topics such as the constitutionality of flag burning are debated. The stability of the first school would likely lead residents to feel this topic, while not comfortable, could probably be handled well. Yet in the second school, reaction could be very different. Families and community members could simply regard this as just another misstep by a school administration and faculty that they do not trust. A similar case of community division was kept from escalating beyond control due to the perceived traditional quality of the school system's work (Gross, 2001).

These three drivers of turbulence work as a combined system. At the most extreme cases, positionality among the parties seems mutually exclusive, cascading events bound one to another in escalating fury, and stability seems to have vanished, leading to ever higher, damaging levels of turbulence. History gives us examples such as the year 1968, where this was the case around the world (Kurlansky, 2004). More recent international contexts like the Arab Spring, or even certain of our election cycles, demonstrate similar levels of volatility. This situation calls to mind the metaphor of a seesaw where for one side to be up, the other must be down. Put into organizational language, there is no overlap in the Venn diagram of interests between the parties. For balance and shared experience to be regained, some common ground for outcomes needs to be developed.

It would be wrong to conclude that a leader's only reaction should be to diminish turbulence. In fact, many situations call for ratcheting up turbulent levels to initiate constructive change (Gryskiewicz, 1999). The use of action research (Lewin, 1947) to experiment with new strategies in real time offers just one well-documented case in point. A school community, for example, might innovate by creating deep structural changes to its instructional program, simply because it felt stuck in outdated patterns. Large-scale historical examples such as F.D.R.'s New Deal show the possibilities of initiating turbulent new programs to confront the dynamic challenge of the Great Depression (Grafton, 1999).

The overarching lesson to be learned from turbulence theory is that turbulence is a constant in our organizations just as it is in the physical world. Change simply is a part of our universe (Hegel, 1892). Therefore, educators need to learn to work with the inevitable turbulence that comes with their jobs.

The multiple ethical paradigms (MEP) and turbulence theory can combine to help educators think through ethical dilemmas in a systematic way. First, we encourage those facing ethical dilemmas to consider which of the ethical paradigms best informs their approach to the dilemma at hand. Next, we suggest that they measure the turbulence level now facing their school. Third, after considering the ethical dimensions and turbulence level, educators need to make a plan of action. As mentioned above, this might include a strategy that will escalate turbulence or diminish it. Finally, after deciding on a plan, they should attempt to predict the level of turbulence that may result. We believe that this approach will help educators navigate through the challenges of ethical dilemmas and possibly avoid misjudgments that have upended leadership engaged in educational reform (Sarason, 1990).

Ethics Standards 1996, 2008, and 2015: A Brief Comparison

In this section of the chapter, we will briefly compare and contrast the 1996, 2008, and 2015 ethics standards. This comparison will highlight the positive changes made in the new version of the ethics standard, indicating its driver status and its infusion into other standards.

In the 1996 version, Standard 5 focused on ethics. The overarching statement read:

> A school administrator is an educational leader who promotes the success of all students by acting with integrity, fairness, and in an ethical manner.

What followed this statement were lists of knowledge, dispositions, and performances that a school administrator should uphold. The lists were long and comprehensive.

While very well intentioned, the standard's expectations were spelled out in such a way that they conveyed a prescriptive approach, holding administrators accountable for a great deal of knowledge and a myriad of dispositions and performances. It is important to keep in mind that this was only one standard, among five others, that was described with such specificity.

Turning to the ISLLC Standards of 2008, in the introduction, it was stated that the structure or "footprint" of the six original ISLLC Standards was retained, but that they were written for new purposes and audiences. The authors said that these standards reinforced the proposition in the original ISLLC Standards that leaders' primary responsibility was to improve teaching and learning for all children. But the 1996 standards were so prescriptive that it was hard to discern this focus. By 2008, the National Policy Board and others who designed the standards appeared to understand that an educational administrator would do better with less detail than in the 1996 version.

Thus, while ethics continued to be Standard 5, it was developed as more of a synthesis of what was expected of an educational leader, providing only functions rather than dispositions and performances. Somehow, these standards appeared to be more manageable and appeared to show more confidence in the educational leader by not being so specific. The 2008 Standard 5 read:

> An education leader promotes the success of every student by acting with integrity, fairness, and in an ethical manner.

Functions

A. Ensure a system of accountability for every student's academic and social success

B. Model principles of self-awareness, reflective practice, transparency, and ethical behavior

C. Safeguard the values of democracy, equity, and diversity

D. Consider and evaluate the potential moral and legal consequences of decision making

E. Promote social justice and ensure that individual student needs inform all aspects of schooling

Schooling

In this new version, not only is ethics an independent and "driver" standard, but it is also infused in a number of other standards. In those infused instances, however, ethics is sometimes explicitly stated while at other times, it is more implicit. For example, in Standard 1, core values are explicitly emphasized. While in Standard 3, the ethic of care is implicit as it focuses on equity and cultural responsiveness. Standard 5 also threads in an ethic of care, while emphasizing community and the support of students. Standards 6 and 7 turn to the ethic of the profession while supporting school personnel and community.

The Deconstruction of Standard 2: Using the Multiple Ethical Paradigms and Turbulence Theory

One way to understand Standard 2 is to deconstruct it. This can be accomplished by turning to different models. For example, using the multiple ethical paradigms of justice, critique, care, and the profession and by also adding the ethic of the community, we can determine if all of the ethics are covered in this new standard. Then we will turn to turbulence theory to see if the new standard makes sense using this model.

Using the multiple ethical paradigms, we have placed in bold the ethics that Standard 2 and its various subcategories describe.

Standard 2. Ethics and Professional Norms

Effective educational leaders act ethically and according to professional norms to promote each student's academic success and well-being. (Ethics of the Profession and Care)

Effective leaders:

A. Act ethically and professionally in personal conduct, relationships with others, decision making, stewardship of the school's resources, and all aspects of school leadership. (Ethics of the Profession and Community)

B. Act according to and promote the professional norms of integrity, fairness, transparency, trust, collaboration, perseverance, learning, and continuous improvement. (Ethics of the Profession and Justice)

C. Place children at the center of education and accept responsibility for each student's academic success and well-being. (Ethics of the Profession and Care)

D. Safeguard and promote the values of democracy, individual freedom and responsibility, equity, social justice, community, and diversity. (Ethics of Justice, Critique, and Community)

E. Lead with interpersonal and communication skill, social-emotional insight, and understanding of all students' and staff members' backgrounds and cultures. (Ethic of Care)

F. Provide moral direction for the school and promote ethical and professional behavior among faculty and staff. (Ethic of the Profession)

After deconstructing Standard 2 using the multiple ethical paradigms, it is clear that all of the ethics are covered when describing the criteria for effective leaders. Most noticeable is that the Ethic of the Profession appears in most of the listed functions. The Ethic of Care is also very prominent. However, the Ethics of Justice, Critique, and the Community are not neglected. Above all, the best interests of the student is at the center of this standard (Stefkovich, 2014). Thus, it is clear that this is a very comprehensive standard focusing on student learning and on leaders who are professional and who care.

In all six areas of this standard, educational leaders are likewise challenged to work with the turbulence surrounding their positions in order to act ethically. For instance, in a time of scarce resources, leaders must anticipate potentially divisive conflicts (A). This in turn will challenge relationships and the trust in fairness needed to sustain them (B). Parties may argue and confront one another over who exactly is working for the best interests of the students (C). Depending on how these debates are handled they may enhance or diminish the pursuit of equity and social justice (D). Again, depending on the skill with which this tension is dealt with, it will impact the goal of having an inclusive school community (E and F).

Additionally, it is important to note that unlike the 2008 ethics standard, in sections C and D of this version, the term *responsibility* and not *accountability* is used. By moving away from accountability, which is often perceived as a term of blame (Gross & Shapiro, 2016, pp. 15–18; Shapiro, 1979; Shapiro & Gross, 2013, pp. 107–109; Shapiro & Stefkovich, 2016, pp. 148–150), the drafters of this current ethical standard appear to understand that outstanding and effective educational leaders truly care about and feel responsible for their students' academic success and well-being and do not need punitive directives, conveyed in the term accountability. However, they perceive, like Starratt (2004), that responsibility is a virtue and worthy of attention.

Educational Exemplars of Standard 2: Providing Standard Bearers

We believe that the use of illustrative exemplars is important in rounding out the meaning of this standard by providing critical context. We have written an exemplar for each of the categories included in Standard 2. Our exemplars are taken from actual cases from our book, *Democratic Ethical Educational Leadership: Reclaiming School Reform* (2016). Please note that each case involves a leader facing a critical incident. We consider this to be important since the challenge of the incident in question reveals this leader's values as they are played out in action.

Below are the subcategories of Standard 2 along with the exemplar case.

Act ethically and professionally in personal conduct, relationships with others, decision making, stewardship of the school's resources, and all aspects of school leadership. **(Ethics of the Profession and Community)**

Lisa Kensler and Cynthia Uline (2016) depict the leadership of Superintendent Curt Dietrich who faced a critical financial challenge in the aftermath of the Great Recession. Rather than the budget-slashing measures that others took, this leader decided to find a creative solution based on savings in energy. He established an energy policy for the district and a management structure to assure results, including hiring a manager of energy and operational facilities. Using a shared governance strategy, Dietrich led the effort of converting his district from being an energy waster to achieving an Energy Star rating. The money saved was sent to support classroom instruction, thereby modeling ethical, educational, and environmental leadership (pp. 54–58).

Act according to and promote the professional norms of integrity, fairness, transparency, trust, collaboration, perseverance, learning, and continuous improvement. **(Ethics of the Profession and Justice)**

Donnan Stoicovy (2016) is an elementary principal in central Pennsylvania. Her school enjoys a fine reputation in the community. However, when her school narrowly missed its achievement target, it was placed on warning by the state. Donnan led her school through this process by challenging the state's evaluation on the one hand and increasing dialogue within the school and the community it served. The idea in both cases was to make sure that the state and the school community kept their focus on children and their learning. Her work helped to ensure that facts were not trumped by accusations. In the end, the school weathered the storm. By her hands-on response, Donnan is an exemplar of this element of Standard 2 (pp. 21–25).

Place children at the center of education and accept responsibility for each student's academic success and well-being. **(Ethics of the Profession and Care)**

Susan Shapiro (2016) wrote a vivid description of an early childhood director she calls Tammy who dramatically exemplified these qualities on 9/11. Tammy's school was very close to the World Trade Center towers, placing all of her school's small children at risk. Thanks to her practice of distributive leadership she kept the children safe. Most parents were able to pick up their children, but some could not. Tammy collected the children and with the help of a parent evacuated them to New Jersey.

There, she made sure that parents knew their young ones were safe. After sleeping over at the home of a parent alum, the children returned to their homes back in New York. Tammy's quick thinking and effective outreach to those around her helped to reduce the extreme turbulence of that tragic day to a manageable level. Children's well-being were clearly taken as a profoundly serious priority (pp. 49–53).

> Safeguard and promote the values of democracy, individual freedom and responsibility, equity, social justice, community, and diversity. **(Ethics of Justice, Critique, and Community)**

Roger Barascout's (2016) account of Kevin Jennings demonstrates these qualities in action. Growing up as a gay person in an intolerant community, Jennings had to face homophobia, isolation, and oppression. This did not stop him. As a teacher he started the Gay Lesbian and Straight Education Network (GLSEN) to support teachers, students, and administrators who wanted to build an inclusive school community. GLSEN raised awareness of bullying and harassment facing LBGT students and its tragic consequences. This work led to policies to protect these students, widen the support of allies, and educate schools and communities. Eventually Jennings's work moved to the national level where he became an Assistant Deputy Secretary in the U.S. Department of Education. His example shows the power of building a democratic community that welcomes rather than fears diversity and supports all of its members (pp. 144–148).

> Lead with interpersonal and communication skill, social-emotional insight, and understanding of all students' and staff members' backgrounds and cultures. **(Ethic of Care)**

Lynne Blair's (2016) story of Rachel Scott hits particularly hard at a time when random gun violence seems to have a permanent place in our world. Rachel was one of the victims at Columbine High School. Rachel had reached out to those in her school who were marginalized and ignored. After the tragedy, Rachel's father, Darrell Scott, was left with a choice. He could mourn privately, something that everyone would understand. Or he could use Rachel's example as a foundation with which to respond. He took the second path and started Rachel's Challenge, a program that reaches high school students across the country with inspiring accounts and training. Cutting across boundaries with sensitivity and effective action, this is an example of leadership that turned a personal nightmare into an example of hope (pp. 103–106).

> Provide moral direction for the school and promote ethical and professional behavior among faculty and staff. **(Ethic of the Profession)**

Peter Brigg (2016) provides a clear example in the case of James Murray, a successful building leader. At the end of one school year, principals were told about a pay for performance plan meant to motivate teachers to boost test scores. Others in the room were silenced but Murray spoke out, urging the superintendent and school board to reconsider. He argued that the plan was a poor fit with district's values. Unmoved, the superintendent insisted that the plan would go forward, but he also offered Murray a place on the planning committee. Murray accepted. He studied the research behind similar plans, listened to all points of view and quietly built up the reputation as a respected expert in the field. Murray's careful work enhanced his image as an ethical leader who placed students and faculty at the center. His presentations to the school board were so compelling that a majority were convinced to put the plan on hold (pp. 116–120).

CONCLUSION

We believe that the Standard 5 in the 2015 Standard on Ethics is a marked improvement from those in the 1996 and 2008 editions. This current version considers ethics and professional norms to be one of four driver standards, placing this category and subcategories at the very center of the work of educational leaders. Ethics and professional norms are also infused into Standards 1, 3, 5, 6, and 7.

In this chapter, we strived to explain the use of the Standard on Ethics and Professional Norms. We indicated how it could be used for decision making and also showed how the standard could be deconstructed. In the latter case, it is clear that this standard includes both the multiple ethical paradigms of justice, critique, care, and the profession as well as community. We also know that it incorporates turbulence theory or the emotional context for making ethical decisions.

Additionally, we have added to this chapter exemplars to illustrate the subcategories of Standard 2. Educators can choose to emulate some of the exemplars who are described. More than simply words, these exemplars indicate how to actually make a positive difference in the lives of students and staff.

Chapter 2

3

Equity and Cultural Responsiveness

In this chapter, we expose the foundations of Standard 3, Equity and Cultural Responsiveness. Because of the overlap between these two concepts, we intertwine them in the analysis below; that is, we treat them as two strands in a model of DNA. We begin with the picture of cultural marginalization and inequity in the instructional programs for children of color and students from low-income homes. We end with an in-depth discussion of solution strategies that district and school leaders can put into play to address these two dimensions of Standard 3.

CULTURAL MARGINALIZATION AND INEQUITY

Teachers and Teaching

Roscigno (1998) informs us that "the institution of education shapes achievement through the stratifying and segregating of students, through the placement of expectations, and through the allocation of resources" (p. 1051). And it is here that we find the pathway by which schools contribute to or fail to offset patterned learning differentials by race and social class (Conchas, 2001; Kleinfeld, 1975; Ladson-Billings, 1994). On the general front, "American public schools [do] not provide equitable and excellent education for all children" (Shannon & Bylsma, 2002, p. 33). There are "pointed differences in resources and quality between schools" (Stiefel, Schwartz, & Ellen, 2006, p. 10; Lee & Burkam, 2002). Specifically, students of different social classes and races often "experience dramatically different learning environments" (Stiefel et al., 2006, p. 19), "receive dramatically different learning opportunities" (Darling-Hammond & Post, 2000, p. 127), and are exposed to "dramatically different learning experiences" (Raudenbush, Fotiu, & Cheong, 1998, p. 254). "Given that blacks and whites have little overlap in the schools they attend, differences in school quality are plausible explanations for why black students are losing ground" (Fryer & Levitt, 2004, p. 456).

Poor and minority youngsters often have "unequal access to key educational resources" (Darling-Hammond & Post, 2000, p. 128). Black and low-income students are often underserved in the schools they attend (Hughes, 2003; Murphy, 2010; Norman, Ault, Bentz, & Meskimen, 2001). As Haycock (2001) asserts, "we take the students who have less to begin with and then systematically give them less in school" (p. 8). Analysts regularly confirm "that low-income and minority students encounter less opportunity to learn, inadequate instruction and support, and lower expectations from their schools and teachers" (Shannon & Bylsma, 2002, p. 9).

Teachers

One of the most important lines of research on equity focuses on "distributional equity" (Bali & Alvarez, 2003, p. 487) in the assignment of qualified teachers to students from different races, ethnicities, and social classes. The issue here is about "the distribution of assignment of teachers" (Thompson, 2002, p. 16) to youngsters in schools (Clotfelter, Ladd, & Vigdor, 2005; Rumberger & Gandara, 2004). The findings are highly consistent. "On virtually every measure, teacher qualifications vary by the status of the children they serve" (Darling-Hammond & Post, 2000, p. 138): "The poorest, least prepared minority children systematically are assigned to the least prepared instructors in the poorest quality schools" (Mickelson, 2003, p. 1073); "schools with particularly disadvantaged students are likely to have less-educated and less-experienced teachers" (Hertert & Teague, 2003, p. 19). More forceful versions of this narrative maintain that these youngsters are routinely exposed to "underqualified" (Uhlenberg & Brown, 2002, p. 502), "not qualified" (Padron, Waxman, & Rivera, 2002, p. 71), "weak" (Balfanz & Byrnes, 2006, p. 144), and "unqualified" (Barton, 2003, p. 10; Haycock, 1998, p. 14) teachers.

On the issue of degrees earned, similar patterns are evident. "Students in high-poverty schools are . . . least likely to have teachers with higher levels of education—a master's, specialist, or doctoral degree" (Darling-Hammond & Post, 2000, p. 138). For example, Stiefel and team (2006) using New York City data reveal that while 80 percent of white eighth graders had teachers with master's degrees in the 2000 to 2001 school year, only 68 percent of black students did so. And on this measure of preparation, there is a positive association between master's degrees and student achievement scores, at least through the middle school grades (Ferguson, 1991).

Likewise, the California Center for the Future of Teaching and Learning reports "that in schools with the highest percentages of minority students, more than 20% of teachers are underqualified as compared with less than 5% of teachers in schools serving the lowest percentage of minorities" (Hertert & Teague, 2003, p. 20). And Scales and colleagues (Scales, Roehlkepartain, Keilsmeier, & Benson, 2006) find that "in elementary, middle, and high schools . . . [disadvantaged] children are twice as likely to attend schools with less-qualified and less-experienced teachers" (p. 401; see also Haycock, 1998).

It is also important to remind ourselves that "teachers matter" (Ferguson, 1991, p. 7)—teacher quality is crucial for student learning (U.S. Commission on Civil Rights, 2004). Indeed, "recent studies have found that differences in teacher quality may represent the single most important school resource differential between minority and white children" (Darling-Hammond & Post, 2000, p. 128). Teacher quality is a keystone plank in the effort to narrow social class and racial learning differentials (Lubienski, 2002; Myers, Kim, & Mandala, 2004).

When we examine *licensure/certification*, similar results surface. We discover that low-income and children of color are disproportionately taught by non-certified teachers or "teachers who are not fully credentialed" (Rumberger & Gandara, 2004, p. 2037; also Bol & Berry, 2005; Land & Legters, 2002; Spradlin et al., 2005; Velez, 1989). For example, Hertert and Teague (2003), relying on data from the California Center for the Future of Teaching and Learning, show that "in schools where 76%–100% of students are poor, 19% of teachers are not fully credentialed. In contrast, in schools with the lowest percentages of poor students, on average only 8% of teachers are not fully credentialed" (p. 20). They also report that "in the lowest-performing schools, as ranked in the Academic Performance Index (API), on average 21% of teachers are not fully credentialed" (p. 20). Darling-Hammond and Post (2000), in turn, reveal that "in schools with the highest minority enrollments, students had less than a 50 percent chance of getting a science or mathematics teacher who held a license and a degree in the field he or she taught" (p. 138).

Given everything that we have observed to this point in the area of teacher qualifications, it will come as no surprise to learn that children of color and low-income youngsters often receive less-experienced teachers than white and middle-class children (Irvine, 1990; Thompson & O'Quinn, 2001; Uhlenberg & Brown, 2002), what is referred to by Hughes (2003) as "the practice of first-year teacher student assignments" (p. 300).

Some examples from the research on teacher experience are informative. Barton (2003) confirms this assessment for low-income students, reporting that these children are also twice as likely to have teachers with three or fewer years of experience—20 percent of teachers in high-poverty schools versus 11 percent in low-poverty schools (p. 13). Clotfelter and team (2005) find that "black 7th graders in North Carolina are far more likely to face a novice teacher in math and English than are their white counterparts. The differences are about 54 percent in math and 38 percent in English for the state as a whole, over 50 percent in some of the large urban districts (p. 391).

Also emerging as one dimension of experience is an understanding of the deleterious impact of teacher turnover on student achievement and knowledge about the types of students most likely to be effected by this turnover. Research confirms, for example, that teacher turnover is more pronounced in schools with high concentrations of minority and low-income children (Harris & Herrington, 2006; Williams, 2003). Analysts regularly conclude that teachers "tend to transfer out of low-income minority schools as they gain experience. Excessive test pressure tends to accelerate this process, compounding the schools' problems since experienced teachers are a precious resource for schools" (Lee, 2006, p. 7). For example, in his work Barton (2003) observes that "fourth-grade students who are Black are much less likely to be in schools where the same teachers who started the year were there when the year ended" (p. 12). He unearths similar findings with students from low-income families as well.

Assessments of teacher qualifications in the domain of performance come in five forms that cluster into three categories: inputs, processes, and outputs. Across all forms and categories, researchers consistently document that teachers working with children from low-income homes and minority youngsters score less well than colleagues teaching more-advanced children (Darling-Hammond & Post, 2000). To begin with, we know that teachers who work in schools with concentrations of minority and poor students, on average, attend less selective colleges and earn lower grades while there (Reynolds, 2002; Wayne & Youngs, 2003). Second, researchers confirm that "teachers with high test scores are . . . quite unequally distributed" (Jencks & Phillips, 1998, p. 49) and that children from low-income homes and children of color "are far more likely to be taught by teachers who scored poorly" (Haycock, 1998, p. 16) on end-of-program licensure examinations (Ferguson, 1991). Furthermore, "the average scores of white teachers who teach in proportionately more black districts tend to be lower than the scores of white teachers in white districts (p. 15). Thus, "where the percentage of black children in a Texas school district is higher, the average score on the TECAT is typically lower for each race of teachers—black, Hispanic and white" (p. 2). Borman and Kimball (2005) also unearth evidence showing that "Classrooms with high concentrations of minority students [are] taught by teachers with lower evaluation scores than classrooms with low concentrations of minority children" (p. 10). Teachers who instruct low-income and minority children are more likely to be absent from school than peers teaching other youngsters. For example, Barton (2003) explains that "Black twelfth-grade students are more than twice as likely as White students to be in schools where 6 to 10 percent of their teachers are absent on an average day" (p. 12). Finally, "there is strong evidence that minority students are assigned to the least effective teachers, as measured by value added" (Harris & Herrington, 2006, p. 224) to student achievement.

What is important to remember is that these measures of performance have power in the student achievement equation. For example, Borman and Kimball (2005) inform us "that fourth-grade teachers with higher evaluation scores made some progress in closing the achievement gap separating poor and nonpoor children in reading and, to a lesser extent, in math" (p. 16). And perhaps most importantly, researchers confirm "that students learn more from teachers with higher test scores" (Wayne & Youngs, 2003, p. 100). As Ferguson (1991) notes in general, "the fact that teachers in Texas who instruct children of color tend to have weaker language skills appears, other things equal, to account for more than one quarter of the reading and math score differential between black and white children in Texas" (p. 1).

Teaching

In the previous section, we explored the topic of equity through teacher qualifications. We saw how these qualifications influence student learning and how greater exposure to teachers with more limited qualifications disadvantages students of color and students from low-income homes. Here we introduce our discussion of patterns of instructional practices often found in schools and classrooms heavily populated by minority and poor children.

Research in the area of instruction based on race and social class clusters into four categories: anemic instructional designs, inordinate focus on lower-level skills, inappropriate learning contexts, and low teacher expectations for students (Alder, 2000; Ladson-Billings, 1994; Murphy, 2010). On the first two issues (design and focus), analysts suggest that classrooms dominated by students from low-income homes and students of color are marked by a heavy emphasis on "passive instruction." In some cases, this is defined by an inordinate amount of didactic instruction, or more accurately teacher-centered instruction in which students are passive rather than active participants (Hattie, 2009), a pattern that Gamoran (2000) labels "repetitive teaching" (p. 103). Culpability here is linked less to teacher centeredness than to student inaction.

Critics find that disadvantaged youngsters receive a disproportionate amount of worksheets and drill-based skill work (Bennett et al., 2007; Lubienski, 2002; Strutchens & Silver, 2000), often decontextualized assignments with little relevance to either the academic goals of the class or the lives of the students (Bempechat, 1992; Stevenson, Chen, & Uttal, 1990). The focus is often on memorization and low-level skills (Lubienski, 2002), what Irvine (1990) calls "rote learning" (p. 7). Students "work at

Chapter 3

a low cognitive level of boring tasks that are not connected to the skills they need to learn" (Darling-Hammond & Post, 2000, p. 142). Students of color and poor children are "typically given more routine highly structured class work focused on low-level intellectual activities" (Shannon & Bylsma, 2002, p. 33). Low-level assessments are commonplace (Entwisle, Alexander, & Olson, 2000; Strutchens & Silver, 2000). The center of gravity is "lecture, drill and practice, and remediation, and student seatwork consisting mainly of worksheets" (Padron et al., 2002, p. 70). Undifferentiated whole-class instruction dominates (Cooper, 2000; Hattie, 2009; Shannon & Bylsma, 2002). Students are often in classes where "the skills tested on the assessments become the entire curriculum" (Murnane & Levy, 1996, p. 408). The DNA of instruction here becomes behavioral control rather than intellectual engagement and mastery (Cooper, 2000; Murphy & Torre, 2014): "Consequently, teachers spend more time controlling students and trying to neutralize potential behavior problems than in [real] teaching" (Shannon & Bylsma, 2002, p. 32). Orderliness displaces the goal of learning (Irvine, 1990; Murphy, 2015a; Norman et al., 2001). Students are occupied in "routine busywork," although they remain "intellectually unengaged" (Shannon & Bylsma, 2002, p. 33). Teachers act as "custodians or referral agents" (Ladson-Billings, 1994, p. 23).

This "drill and practice," it is argued, "may be particularly damaging to minority students" (Learning Point Associates, 2004, p. 9). The focus "retards their learning and their development of higher cognitive skills" (Shannon & Bylsma, 2002, p. 29). Indeed, missing in this framework of "inappropriate teaching practices" (Waxman, Padron, & Garcia, 2007, p. 134), "low level intellectual activity" (Shannon & Bylsma, 2002, p. 33), and "steady diet of worksheets and rote learning" (Darling-Hammond & Post, 2000, p. 142) is any commitment to mastering higher-level skills. Conspicuous by their absence are topics, such as "nonroutine problem solving" (Strutchens & Silver, 2000, p. 47) and reasoning (Raudenbush et al., 1998). Thus, "low-achieving students continue to fall behind their high-achieving counterparts" (Shannon & Bylsma, 2002, p. 33).

Studies confirm the conclusion that the instruction provided to students in lower-track classes is of a lesser quality than that provided to their peers in more academically oriented groups (Irvine, 1990; Murphy, 2015a; Oakes, 1985). At the secondary level, one of the reasons for this is the implicit assumption that teachers who must teach outside of their areas of expertise can more easily handle lower-level courses. As we reported above, such classes are often assigned to the least well-prepared teachers. Teachers also report less interest in working with lower-track students (Cooper, 2000; Heyns, 1974), and they frequently confess to a lack of knowledge about how to prepare and conduct classes for both "general" and lower-track students (California State Department of Education, 1984). Also, they spend less time preparing for nonacademic classes (Gamoran, 2000). At the elementary level, students in lower-ability compensatory education classes sometimes receive a large amount of their instruction from aides rather than regular classroom teachers (Brookover, Brady, & Warfield, 1981). Finally, there is evidence that teachers use less demanding standards to judge their own performance with nonacademic track students and lower-ability groups (Gamoran, 2000; Schwartz, 1981).

Students in lower-ability curricular tracks also seem to be disadvantaged in the type of instruction they receive (Ferguson, 1998; Irvine, 1990). The following teaching activities have been shown to be associated with student achievement: (a) providing the class with an overview of the lesson; (b) reviewing lesson objectives; (c) spending time actively teaching new content; and (d) maintaining an academic focus (Hattie, 2009). Evertson (1982) found that objectives were explained and materials introduced more clearly in higher-ability classes. In an effort to get students working, there is some evidence that teachers are more likely to skip important introductory learning activities in lower-track classes (Page, 1984; Schwartz, 1981).

Moreover, teachers often engage in less interactive teaching in their lower-track classes. In lower-track classes, face-to-face interactions within a group context are often threatening to teachers. To avoid these exchanges, teachers use films and worksheets in lieu of direct instruction and dialogues with students (Irvine, 1990; Shannon & Bylsma, 2002). In addition, other important instructional resources that are associated with student learning, such as teacher clarity, provision of work standards, teacher efforts to hold students accountable for their work, emphasis on higher-order cognitive skills, and teacher enthusiasm and warmth, seem to be disproportionately allocated to higher-ability groups (Cooper, 2000; Shannon & Bylsma, 2002).

Finally, a number of authors have concluded that lower-track groups are characterized by limited "task orientation" and "academic focus" (Downey, von Hippel, & Broh, 2004; Evertson, 1982; Mickelson, 2003). In her classic study of lower-track classes at a college-preparatory high school, Page (1984) reported that teachers and students often appear "to go through the motions of teaching and learning" (p. 18). She noted that "genuine academic encounters" (p. 18) are rare in these classes (Murphy, 2015a).

Four aspects of academic focus differentiate lower- and higher-ability tracks. First, the content of lower-track classes is less academically oriented (Gamoran, 2000; Irvine, 1990). Teachers tend to talk of meeting the personal and social needs of students rather than academic goals; they use more "relevant" subject matter, and they tend to blur academic content by trying to present it in an entertaining manner. Therapeutic goals often displace academic ones. There are also fewer task-related interactions between teachers and students in lower-track classes (Irvine, 1990; Powell, Farrar, & Cohen, 1985). Second, teachers of lower-track classes and groups, even after controlling for ability, require less academic work of students. Material is covered at a slower pace, lower-level objectives are emphasized, fewer academic standards are specified, fewer reports and projects are assigned, less academic feedback is provided, and fewer tests are given (Gamoran, 2000; Strutchens & Silver, 2000). Third, work within individual classes in lower-ability tracks is less sequential and integrated than in the academic streams. In addition, because the assorted activities on which lower-track students work are often unrelated, there is a lack of coherence and meaning to their learning (Page, 1984, Powell et al., 1985). Finally, while teachers in higher-track classes stress achievement more than behavior, the situation is often reversed in lower-ability classes. For example, in higher-ability classes, teachers use selected teaching functions within lessons to promote academic objectives, while these same functions (e.g., asking questions, providing feedback) are often directed toward the control of student behavior in lower-ability classes (Allington, 1983; Murphy, 2015a).

Time is another instructional variable that has been correlated with student learning. Students who spend more time on academic tasks and are more actively engaged with these tasks learn more than their non-engaged peers (Hattie, 2009). Yet it appears that students in nonacademic curricular tracks are discriminated against in the distribution of this critical condition of learning (Hallinan, 2001; Meehan, Cowley, Schumacher, Hauser, & Croom, 2003; Strutchens & Silver, 2000). Within individual class periods, instruction in low groups tends to start later and end earlier than in high-ability classes. Students in low-ability groups lose more time during transitions and experience more "dead time," or time with no work assignment, than their peers in more academically oriented classes. More time is lost due to student and teacher interruptions in low-ability groups. Homework is also more likely to be assigned as an in-class activity in low groups, thus encroaching on rather than extending learning time (Hall, 2001; Neuman & Celano, 2006). Finally, students in lower-ability groups are generally off task more, or less actively engaged with their work, than pupils in higher-track groups.

Several factors contributing to the poorer use of time in low groups have been identified, including an instructional milieu that lacks an academic focus and the failure to differentiate learning activity formats in an appropriate way. Researchers have noted that students in lower-ability groups can benefit from exposure to a greater variety of learning activities of short duration and fewer sustained periods of seatwork. Yet students in those groups often receive fewer learning activities and are expected to maintain attention on each one for longer periods of time than pupils in other groups. Periods of uninterrupted seatwork are as long or longer than those experienced by higher-ability students. Page (1984) has attributed the higher rates of off-task activity in low-ability groups to the blurred and confused participation structures that often characterize nonacademic tracks in American schools. Whereas the structures that establish how students in high-ability groups are to participate in classes tend to be clear and stable, students in lower-track classes experience "ambiguous classroom situations, generated by frequently shifting and unclearly marked participation structures" (Eder, 1981, p. 160). In a similar vein, Allington (1983) and Eder (1981) argue that higher rates of off-task activity in elementary reading groups may be due to weaknesses in the instructional environment and inappropriately differentiated instructional treatments. Eder (1981) noted in her study that the higher number of student disruptions in lower-ability groups was due to the fact that the teacher created many more opportunities for disruption in these groups.

"Established structure," the patterned set of rules and procedures that guide classroom interactions, is also an important variable for which we find inappropriate differences between high and low learning groups in classrooms. Where such structure exists and is internalized by students, on-task student behaviors increase, interactions between teacher and students on behavioral matters decrease, and student learning is enhanced. Evidence confirms that "established structure" characterizes more academically oriented groups, while a more chaotic condition is often found in low-ability classes and groups. More important in terms of equity, it appears that this condition is often attributable not to the characteristics of students, but to the instructional environment of the classroom and the specific practices and behaviors of teachers (Murphy, 2015a, b). Thus a number of studies have found that teachers in low-ability groups invest considerably more time than teachers in high-ability groups in controlling and managing student behavior (Downey et al., 2004; Eder, 1981; Oakes, 1985). This has often been attributed to the characteristics of students in low-ability groups, for example lack of motivation and a short attention span. While there is merit to the argument that students in low groups often make it difficult to develop and maintain "established structure," research suggests that a combination of classroom conditions and teacher behaviors characterizes low groups and makes the situation especially problematic: lower teacher expectations for student behavior, greater willingness on the part of teachers to trade structure for student compliance, greater confusion about appropriate modes of student participation, and undifferentiated instructional forms (Evertson, 1982; Page, 1984; Powell et al., 1985; Reeves, 1982; Schwartz, 1981). In addition, there is evidence that tracking at all levels of schooling often promotes the formation of lower stream peer groups that actively resist institutional norms and subvert classroom educational encounters (Good & Marshall, 1984; Murphy, 2010, 2016; Oakes, 1985). Rather than passively accepting the negative messages of schooling, students in lower-ability groups often "act back" on the expectations embedded in the fabric of educational institutions (Weis, n.d., p. 8).

Interpersonal relations comprise a final area in which conditions that are positively related to important student outcomes are inequitably distributed across instructional groups. There is often a lower quality of student-teacher interactions in low tracks (Conchas, 2001; Goodlad, 1984; Oakes, 1985). Teachers of lower-track classes tend to distance themselves from their students. Teachers rely heavily on student feedback, especially evidence of student achievement, as a basis of personal rewards (Lortie, 1975). Since such rewards are generally less evident in low-ability classes, teachers tend not to form close relations with students in these groups. Second, as noted earlier, within low groups, teachers are more likely to trade behavioral and academic performance expectations for student goodwill. Goodwill, however, is not a strong base for forming meaningful relationships. Third, since teaching higher-track classes is often considered more prestigious, teachers tend to invest more time working with students in these classes. Finally, teachers often find it easier to form relationships with those who share backgrounds and aspirations that are similar to their own.

There is some research that suggests that the context or environment in which learning occurs may be connected to inequitable outcomes. Specifically, it is maintained that certain contexts hinder efforts to close gaps. Most generally, the problem is traced to a system of education in which minority children are forced to fit into a design developed for white and more affluent youngsters (Ladson-Billings, 1994; Seiler & Elmesky, 2007). Scholars expose several dimensions of learning context that are in play. First, they find that a key element of traditional learning environments—competitive individualism (Jagers & Carroll, 2002)—is often inconsistent with, if not oppositional to, the more communal dynamic of the lives of children of color (Irvine, 1990). These analysts maintain that teachers of black youngsters "need to design classroom activities and promote students' intellectual camaraderie and attitudes toward learning that build a sense of community and responsibility for each other" (Bennett et al., 2007, p. 261).

Second, these analysts also show that classroom "participation structures—the interactional arrangements and rules operating in the learning environment" (Norman et al., 2001, p. 1108)—are often at odds with accepted patterns in minority and low-income communities. They find that the well-grooved structures common in most schools are "more problematic for Black students than for White students" (p. 1108).

Third, reviewers here condemn schools for the near absence of culturally relevant environments and culturally responsive instruction (Hughes, 2003; Norman et al., 2001; Steele, 1992, 1997), for their failure to "attempt to identify the distinctive cultural retentions of black students and to develop teaching strategies that are compatible with them" (Irvine, 1990, p. 93). According to Hughes (2003), in the instructional domain "ineffective teachers tend to use the most common pedagogy in U.S. schools, which assumes that the dominant White middle-class cultural way of schooling is universal, or should be universal and most appropriate for all" (p. 302). According to Norman and team (2001), in the learning environment domain, teachers of children of color are often found to be ill-prepared to "navigate the complexities of cultural interface zones" (p. 1107) that ribbon classrooms, thus dumbing down learning (Kleinfeld, 1975).

The larger context of this chapter posits that "schools often collaborate in the maintenance of poverty, inequality, and the unequal status of black people" (Irvine, 1990, p. 9), other children of color, and people from the bottom rungs of the social class ladder. The mechanism engaged is the unequal treatment of certain children based on biosocial markers, such as race and class (Ferguson, 2003; Miller, 1995). The result then is differential outcomes, especially academic success, for students in these groups. The particular theme in this larger narrative that occupies us here is teacher expectations.

To begin with, there is considerable evidence that socioeconomic conditions and racial status have bearing on the expectations and beliefs that teachers form about children (Hertert & Teague, 2003; Miller, 1995). "Teachers' expectations of students indeed are often influenced by student characteristics, such as social class" (Becker & Luthar, 2002, p. 202). The logic here is "that part of the reason some students do not excel academically is that schools do not ask them to" (Reynolds, 2002, p. 12).

More importantly, these differences in expectations are tilted against minority children (Burns, Keyes, & Kusimo, 2005; Darity, Castellino, Tyson, Cobb, & McMillen, 2001; Ferguson, 2003; Hale-Benson, 1990; Irvine, 1990; Stinson, 2006) and youngsters from poor families (Baron, Tom, & Cooper, 1985; Hallinan, 2001; Haycock, 2001; Lewis, 2008). That is, "many teachers internalize negative assumptions about the intellectual competencies of low-income African American students. More specifically, "teachers expect poor students to do less well than their middle- and upper-class counterparts regardless of ability" (Roscigno, 1998, p. 1035). And, according to Irvine (1990), teachers have more positive expectations for white students than for minority students. "Disadvantaged and minority youth are more commonly expected to do poorly" (Becker & Luthar, 2002, p. 202).

The essential point here is that expectations are consequential (Ferguson, 2003; Fryer & Levitt, 2004; Land & Legters, 2002; Peng, Wright, & Hill, 1995). "Teacher expectations are crucial to student performance" (Roscigno, 1998, p. 1039); they "affect how much black youngsters learn" (Wilson, 1998, p. 504)—they are a "contributing factor in student achievement" (Spradlin et al., 2005, p. 21). At a minimum, they "sustain differences in student performance levels" (Irvine, 1990, p. 54). In the worst case, they exacerbate learning problems and gaps (Bol & Berry, 2005; Ferguson, 2003; Irvine, 1990), especially as they are cumulated across a school career (Ferguson, 2003). On the other hand, when set more appropriately, that is, higher, expectations "can improve learning and reduce inequality" (Gamoran, 2000, p. 114): "High expectations disproportionately lead to high self-efficacy and high subsequent performance among Black students" (Hughes, 2003, pp. 301–302).

It is important to start by reminding ourselves that teacher expectations are mediated by teacher actions and student responses to those actions (Murphy, 2016). According to Farkas, Grobe, Sheehan, and Shuan (1990), "teacher's reduced expectations lower students' self-image and effort and lead the teacher to present less-demanding material, resulting in reduced cognitive achievement" (p. 128). Alternatively, low expectations can lead to teacher behaviors that lower motivation and effort thus reinforcing low teacher expectations about the academic potential of low-income and African American students (Reynolds, 2002): "Low expectations that teachers have of poor and minority students . . . affect teachers' determination to help students and also affect students' determination to succeed" (Reynolds, 2002, p. 11).

CURRICULUM

Access

In this chapter, we are exploring the equity and cultural responsiveness between the instructional program in the school and learning. And, as the structure of the chapter conveys, instructional program is composed of two overlapping components, teachers and teaching and curriculum. Our conclusion on the first element presented above (teachers and teaching) is that high teacher qualifications and effective instructional practices are allocated inequitably (less favorably) to minority and low-income students. Our position here on the second element (curriculum) is that poor children and black students score worse on academic measures of performance "because they have not been exposed to the curriculum that would best prepare them to be successful on tests" (Darity et al., 2001, p. 17); that is, they "encounter a weaker curriculum" (Reynolds, 2002, p. 14) than their more advantaged peers.

We show that the major engine that produces this condition is curricular ability grouping/tracking, demonstrating that low-SES (socioeconomic status) children and black youngsters are clustered together and "taught a less demanding curriculum" (Farkas, 2003, p. 1123). We present evidence that this effect unfolds on three levels. First, we show that these students are disproportionately found in schools where, on average, this weaker curriculum dominates the educational program (Raudenbush et al., 1998). Second, we document that "minority and low-income students are [also] . . . disproportionately placed in lower-ability groups and that these assignments seriously reduce their opportunities for learning" (Farkas, 2003, p. 1126). Third, we review findings exposing that what transpires in these lower-level classes and groups is of significantly less quality than what takes place in higher-track classes.

Student exposure to academic content in schools is influenced by a variety of factors—teacher qualifications, parental expectations, counselor efforts, student motivation and career plans, and so forth. But no factor is more critical, especially for students of color and from low-income homes, than the way students are sorted into curricular-focused programs of study (Conchas, 2001). The first thing we need to remember about curriculum tracking is that it is a direct proxy for one of the two most critical elements in the student learning algorithm, opportunity to learn (Murphy & Hallinger, 1989). On this point, we know that "tracking functions as a major source of unequal opportunities to learn" (Mickelson & Heath, 1999, p. 569; O'Connor, 1997). It is also an indirect proxy for the second critical element, quality of instruction. On this point, we will see that tracking serves as a conduit to differentiated instructional quality, both in terms of teacher qualifications and instructional effectiveness. Earlier we examined some of the instructional aspects of tracking. Here we explore the curricular dimensions of tracking.

The second acknowledgment to be made about tracking is that "track placements are strongly correlated with students' race and social class" (Mickelson & Heath, 1999, p. 567). The "assignment process . . . favors whites over blacks of equal ability" (Thompson & O'Quinn, 2001, p. 13) and affluent children over children from low-income homes of similar abilities (Conchas, 2001; Miller, 1995). On this front, we know that these assignments have deep historical roots, beginning in the early 20th century with the inculcation of the social efficiency philosophy into education (Murphy, Beck, Crawford, & Hodges, 2001). Under this banner, schools became places in which youngsters were tapped and then educated to fill slots in the larger economy, a process notoriously decoupled from merit and laced with both classism and racism (Kliebard, 1995; Krug, 1964, 1972; Wraga, 1994). Thus, "from the early beginnings of 'tracked' educational programs to contemporary schools, white and more affluent students have had opportunities and access to an education that differs markedly from the education provided for students of color and poverty (Conchas, 2001; Shannon & Bylsma, 2002, p. 29). We also know that for all the "research demonstrating the ineffectiveness of low-track classes and of tracking in general, schools continue the practice" (Burris & Welner, 2005, p. 595).

The third point to be made about curriculum tracking/ability grouping is that it is highly consequential. It "can reproduce or even exacerbate inequality" (Downey et al., 2004, p. 615) and translate into lower-income and "Black student disadvantage" (Roscigno, 1999, p. 161). Here we concentrate our attention on the link between tracking and learning outcomes. However, it is important to acknowledge that tracking is associated with other outcomes as well (Murphy & Torre, 2014; Rosenbaum, 1980). For example, research informs us that track placements "affect students'

Chapter 3

self-concepts" (Irvine, 1990, p. 15) and self-esteem (Alexander & McDill, 1976; Land & Legters, 2002) as well as exposure to "friendship networks" (Lucas & Gamoran, 2002, p. 175) in general and to motivated (or unmotivated) peers in particular (Berends, Lucas, Sullivan, & Briggs, 2005).

Track curriculum assignments also shape an especially key variable in the student success storyline, "aspirations for the future" (Lucas & Gamoran, 2002, p. 175). There is considerable evidence that track membership has marked consequences for the development of academic orientations and for aspirations for continued education, and particularly post-high-school education plans (Alexander, Cook, & McDill, 1978; Murphy, 2010; Oakes, 1985). Alexander and Cook (1982) and Heyns (1974) suggest that schools exercise their primary influence over pupil socioeconomic attainment through their role in helping students establish orientations toward educational goals. As Heyns (1974) notes, "it is possible that schools play a more decisive role in the stratification system through encouraging and implementing aspirations than through altering patterns of achievement" (p. 1445). Work on the reproduction of cultural inequalities in American education through differential teaching of both the formal and the "hidden curriculum" at different track levels and at schools with students of varying biosocial backgrounds lends support to this position. Since they cluster students of color, track placements and ability groupings have also been implicated in the resegregation of education, this time within schools, by race and class (Irvine, 1990; Rumberger & Palardy, 2005), what Mickelson and Heath (1999) call "second-generation segregation within schools" (p. 577). As such, it is held, "tracking policies and practices serve as the major vehicle to institutionalize and perpetuate racial divisions" (Cooper, 2000, p. 620) among school-age youth and adults (Land & Legters, 2002).

Turning to student learning outcomes, research confirms that sorting students into curricular tracks is associated with high school graduation (Camara & Schmidt, 1999) and degree completion in college (Singham, 2003): "The academic rigor of the courses taken in middle school and high school not only affects students' current achievement, but also is the single most important predictor of college success" (Kober, 2001, p. 27). Studies also reveal the linkage between track assignment and measures of academic achievement (Alexander et al., 1978; Gamoran, 2000; Hallinan, 1984; Roscigno, 1998; Strutchens & Silver, 2000; Tate, 1997; Weinstein, 1976). Here we find that students in the lower-level track with the "less challenging courses do less well on standardized examinations" (Hall, 2001, p. 227). Overall, Gamoran (2000) concludes, "Grouping and tracking not only magnify the differences between high and low achievers, they expand inequality of achievement among students of different social class backgrounds" (p. 104).

The critical issue here is that group placements and track assignments provide a direct measure of opportunity to learn, one of the most important causes of student achievement (Murphy & Hallinger, 1989). More specifically, we will see that students at the lower end of these arrangements are often provided with "a substandard education" (Land & Legters, 2002, p. 18). They are "taught less" (Uhlenberg & Brown, 2002, p. 503)—they receive less rigorous and less challenging material (Murnane & Levy, 1996; Spradlin et al., 2005). They are denied the "opportunity to learn the more advanced material available to students in higher groups" (Thompson, 2002, p. 29). The consequence is "a qualitatively different schooling experience" (Cooper, 2000, p. 601), inequality in access to knowledge and less opportunity to learn (Mickelson & Heath, 1999; Peng et al., 1995).

Four summary findings are of interest here. First, at the broadest level there is evidence that schools heavily populated with children from low-income homes and children of color have access to a less rigorous curricular program, fewer mathematics and science courses for example than what is generally found in schools serving more advantaged youngsters (Gamoran, 2000; Raudenbush et al., 1998). And although course enrollment not offerings is the critical issue (Gamoran, 2000), students cannot enroll in courses that are not offered (Norman et al., 2001).

Second, there is evidence that minority youngsters and children from low-income homes enroll in fewer semesters of coursework in the core academic subjects (Haycock, 2001; Strutchens & Silver, 2000), although there has been some significant improvements here since 2000. Barton (2003) reports that while 46 percent of white high school graduates in 1998 completed four years of English, three years of social science and mathematics, and two years of foreign language, only 40 percent of black students did so (p. 9).

Third, children of color and low-income students are much more likely to be found in lower tracks and lower-track classes than are their white and more affluent peers. Children from the wrong side "of the street" are dramatically overrepresented in special education, remedial, compensatory, general, and vocational tracks, or their modern-day equivalents (Cooper, 2000; Miller, 1995; Oakes, 1985)—in the "nonacademic tracks" (Mickelson & Heath, 1999, p. 569) and in the "non-college preparation programs" (Peng et al., 1995, p. 73). On the special education front, Bingham (1994) reports that "black students are approximately three times as likely to be in a class for the educable mentally retarded" (p. 5) as whites—and alternatively only "half as likely to be in a class for the gifted and talented" (p. 5). Mickelson and Heath (1999) in a district that they were examining found that "special education classes are overwhelmingly Black" (p. 572). Researchers also routinely conclude that minority students are overrepresented in remedial tracks and remedial classes (Clotfelter et al., 2005). On the vocational track front, Bempechat and Ginsburg (1989) report enrollments of 51 percent for blacks and 34 percent for whites. Finally, turning to the general track, Peng and team (1995) find that about 40 percent of black 10th graders are in general mathematics courses as compared to about one-fourth of white students (p. 50), a finding echoed by Mickelson and Heath (1999).

Chapter 3

Fourth, low-income and "black students are underrepresented in higher-track classes" (Land & Legters, 2002, p. 18) and "high-level courses" (Spradlin et al., 2005, p. 3). In particular, researchers document "the underrepresentation of the children of the poor and several minority groups in the college preparatory track in secondary school" (Miller, 1995, p. 330), in "gifted and talented classes [and] enrichment classes" (Shannon & Bylsma, 2002, p. 29), and in more advanced and challenging courses in general, such as advanced placement offerings (Mickelson & Heath, 1999).

Turning to gifted and talented coursework, there is a discernible sense in the research that "one factor that . . . contributes to the Black-White . . . gap is the inequitable selection of students into gifted programs" (Hughes, 2003, p. 301). Mickelson and Heath (1999) in their research find that "elementary gifted and talented students [are] overwhelmingly white" (p. 576). According to Ford, Grantham, and Whiting (2008) "Black students are underrepresented by as much as 55% nationally in gifted education; although Black students compose 17.2% of school districts, they represent 8.4% of those identified as gifted" (p. 217). Studies in North Carolina add to the evidence, noting and quantifying underrepresentation: "African-American students are sharply underrepresented in programs for academically and intellectually gifted (AIG) students. During the 1999–2000 school year, black students represented about 30% of the overall student population, but only about 10% of the enrollment in AIG programs" (Thompson & O'Quinn, 2001, p. 12). And Burns and team (2005) reveal similar patterns in honor society membership.

Relevance

Cultural relevance is an important curricular topic as well. At a minimum, culture responsiveness and cultural congruence means "creat[ing] a schooling environment that is not in conflict with the student's cultural background" (Howard, 2001, p. 145). More forcefully, it means nurturing "an environment that respects students cultural background" (p. 145). The starting point is that "students bring certain human characteristics that have been shaped by their socializing group to the classroom. . . . The cultural, social, and historical backgrounds of children have a major impact on how they perceive school and the educational process" (Shade, Kelly, & Oberg, 1997, p. 11). Authentic school work is work that honors students' cultures, that reinforces cultural identity (Murphy, 2015a, b) "in a manner compatible with academic pursuit" (Fordham & Ogbu, 1986, p. 203). Before delving into the concept of culturally relevant academic work, we pause to remind ourselves that this hallmark aspect of curricular authenticity has been honored more in the breech than in action. That is, "delegitimizing" (Zanger, 1993, p. 184) is more common, as is disregard for intellectual-cultural capital that rests outside the mainstream culture (Alder, 2000; Murtadha, 2009).

Using culture as a way of interpreting children's behavior and learning style is not an approach to which teachers are accustomed. Up to this point, the students are judged by the cultural norms of the school or the teacher and are expected to learn in the same way. Any variation is considered inappropriate or deficient. This is a typical response for people who are not acquainted with other ways of functioning or who see the world only from their perspective. (Shade et al., 1997, p. 19)

We also remind ourselves of a key conclusion noted earlier, that is, this deficit-based understanding of knowledge and the resultant marginalization place students at academic peril.

Culturally congruent academic focus on the other hand is an attempt to create a schooling experience that enables students to pursue academic excellence without abandoning their cultural integrity. Thus, the ways of communicating conceptions of knowledge, methods of learning, and the overall context of the educative process are situated within a framework that is consistent with the students' cultural background. (Howard, 2001, p. 136)

It is constructed learning designed "to meet the challenge of teaching to individual differences with a particular emphasis on the variation that occurs because of a student's cultural background" (Shade et al., 1997, p. 9). "Cultural integrity and support for academic excellence" (Lipman, 1995, p. 205) are ribboned together. "Features of the students' cultural capital are incorporated into pedagogical practices" (Howard, 2001, p. 145). The pathway from "acknowledging the culturally constituted nature of students' lives" (O'Loughlin, 1995, p. 111) to culturally relevant learning has been well laid out for children of color by Howard (2001, p. 147).

Teachers need to abandon the deficit-based thinking about the cognitive capacity, sociocultural backgrounds, and overall learning potential of students. Second, there must be a willingness on behalf of teachers to make modifications in their teaching styles to align them more closely with students' ways of knowing, communicating, and being. Finally, teachers must have the will and the courage to learn about the culture, life, and history of African-American people. The acquisition of this knowledge requires more than reading various literature about the African-American experience. It entails talking to parents, students, and community members and immersing oneself in various facets of the day-to-day environment that students experience.

More tangibly, three avenues of effort are viable: recognizing and understanding ways of knowing of non-mainstream "children; build[ing] cultural bridges between the school culture and the culture of the community from which children come" (Shade et al., 1997, p. 81); and using materials that reflect the contributions of diverse cultures.

On the first point, we know that what is appropriate at home in some cultures is inconsistent with the norms of conducting the business of learning in classrooms (Shade et al., 1997). Authenticity is nurtured when both congruencies and differences between home cultures and school cultures are acknowledged, respected, and employed in the learning process (Tyson, 2002; Zanger, 1993), "when cultural communication styles are incorporated into instruction" (Shade et al., 1997, p. 92). The second point links authenticity to a framework that seeks to establish cultural continuity between home and the school (Antrop-González & De Jesús, 2006) "using various directives, monitoring, interactional styles, and participation structures within the classroom that were congruent with the interaction and learning situations commonly found in the students' homes" (Howard, 2001, p. 135).

> The litmus test for the accessibility of an educational system is the degree to which the instructional language and teaching practices match the unofficial teaching practices and informal communication systems of the students' homes and communities. It would appear that if we are to hear students' voices, we must be willing to explore culturally relevant forms of teaching. (O'Loughlin, 1995, p. 110)

The third point shows us that authenticity is deepened when "culture specific" (Shade et al., 1997, p. 120) artifacts and materials, "cultural specific information" (p. 90) and "students' cultural capital or funds of knowledge" (Antrop-González & De Jesús, 2006, p. 412) are employed to "ensure that the curriculum and materials reflect contributions of a variety of people" (Cabello & Terrell, 1994, p. 22), when educators "privilege the funds of knowledge that students and their respective communities bring to the school" (Antrop-González & De Jesús, 2006, p. 409) and "transcend the boundaries of traditional schooling and create social conditions and relationships that are aligned with students' cultural orientations" (p. 421). The major conclusion of the analysis in this section is that differences among student outcomes are, to a small but important extent, the result of differences in access to knowledge and culturally responsive education. The available evidence indicates that curriculum assignment, in addition to its sorting function, is an institutional mechanism for the systematic and selective allocation of important learning resources; systematic in that the allocation occurs in regular patterns and selective in that the resources are distributed in a different manner to various curricular groups. Students in lower-ability groups and nonacademic tracks are systematically discriminated against vis-à-vis their peers in more academically oriented groups. Even after controlling for ability and biosocial background factors, students in these less academically oriented groups perform less well than academic-track students.

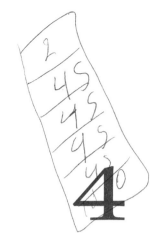

Engaged Teaching

4

While the focus of our attention in this chapter is on the behavioral aspects of engaged teaching, we also provide insights as well about the more global dimensions of effective teachers. Four issues merit attention. The first is what Mergendoller and Packer (1985, p. 595) call "appealing temperament." Students describe such teachers as "enthusiastic and proactive" (Rudduck & Flutter, 2004, p. 78). They have appealing personalities (Beishuizen, Hof, Putten, Bouwmeester, & Asscher, 2001). Second, students see good teachers as "knowledgeable and experienced" (Flutter & Rudduck, 2004, p. 47). They possess robust content knowledge and they employ it well (Hoge, Smit, & Hanson, 1990). Third, they enjoy and take great pride in their work, that is, teaching (Thompson, 2004; Wentzel, 2002), what Moos (1979, p. 188) calls "love of learning," enthusiasm and love of work (Burke & Grosvenor, 2003): "They care about learning and model the behaviors they wish to see in their students" (Davis, 2003, p. 227). Fourth, good teachers take a strong interest in their students (Mergendoller & Packer, 1985; Miron & Lauria, 1998).

The above four points capture research views on "types" of teachers. For the balance of the chapter, we attend to the practices good teachers undertake. We remind ourselves that our interest in this section is on the pedagogical aspects of the core technology of schooling. In the following chapter, we attend to the curriculum, although by necessity there is considerable overlap between the two themes of the narrative. Our point of commencement is that how teachers teach and the "instructional style has a significant impact on who learns, what they learn, and how much they learn" (Wilson & Corbett, 2001, p. 61). We are attentive here to how teachers "encourage and enable to define themselves as learners, thinkers, and doers" (Davis, 2003, p. 221).

55

CREATING A SENSE OF VALUE AND POSSIBILITY

An analysis of the literature leads to a number of salient aspects of engaged teaching. We learn, for example, the importance of creating learning goals in terms of values and practices (Kershner, 1996). At the broadest level, this is about helping students internalize the values of lifelong learning (Brewster & Fager, 2000; Cooper, Ponder, Merritt, & Matthews, 2005). It is also about instilling a sense of confidence that students can be successful (Rudduck & Flutter, 2004), a sense of optimism "about their potential for further growth" (Weinstein, 1983, p. 302). It is about forming an intrinsic orientation (Harter, 1996) and "intrinsic value for schoolwork" (Pintrich & DeGroot, 1990, p. 37). It is about helping youngsters see "the relevance of education to future endeavors" (Lehr, Sinclair, & Christenson, 2004, p. 282).

At the mid-level, the spotlight is on purposeful work (Davis, 2003), an understanding of the importance of work undertaken, instilling meaning to what is often seen as empty routines (Murphy, 2016; Newmann, Wehlage, & Lamburn, 1992; Warrington & Younger, 1996). At the micro-level, research underscores the importance of "target setting" (Flutter & Rudduck, 2004, p. 122), "explicit learning expectations" (Thomson & Gunter, 2006, p. 853) for student work or "lessons that have a clear focus" (Rudduck, Chaplain, & Wallace, 1996, p. 174). The research also emphasizes clarity in reaching learning expectations (Quiroz, 2001): "Outlining in clear terms a set of steps for getting on to an answer" (Wilson & Corbett, 2001, p. 82).

Research forcefully and eloquently illuminates the place of positivism in creating a sense of future (Flutter & Rudduck, 2004). They are prone to do this by calling out negative actions that they view as crippling. Of particular concern to youngsters are deficit-based school learning climates and negatively orientated teacher behaviors (Miron & Lauria, 1998; Nieto, 1994). As we see in the work of Weinstein (1983, p. 294), "youngsters themselves are aware of differences in teacher treatment within classrooms." They speak openly and negatively of teacher expectations formed on the basis of race, class, immigrant status, and language (Hamilton, 1983; Slaughter-Defoe & Carlson, 1996), as well as school policies, practices, and routines that disempower and marginalize certain students (Hamilton, 1983). Students tell us that in many cases schools simply mirror the devaluation and negativism found in the larger society in which they live (Flutter & Rudduck, 2004; Nieto, 1994). There is a palpable sense of anger and disillusionment in their eyes that possibilities are equated with academic achievement levels (Chaplain, 1996a, b).

From the research, we learn that the day in and day out work of forming a sense of possibility and future-oriented values has much to do with the concept of expectations discussed throughout this volume. The overall storyline has been wonderfully described by Weinstein (1983, p. 302).

The research to date has also pointed out that students are enormously sensitive to the differential behaviors that teachers might display toward various groups of students. Students sense highly subtle differences in interaction patterns and are responsive as well to nonverbal messages conveyed. Through differential treatment, students can infer teachers' expectations for their academic performance. In classrooms where students were aware of the teachers' differential treatment of high and low expectations, the students' own expectations for themselves more closely matched the teachers' expectations, and the teachers' expectations for their students were powerful predictors of student performance.

Turning to students again, they tell us that even though "they want teachers who care about them and demand rigorous work" (Fine, Torre, Burns, & Payne, 2007, p. 803), they feel locked out of possibilities—either because such hopes and possibilities for the future are not communicated or because teachers communicate the perspective that for many of them they are unattainable. They feel as if "adults have given up on them" (Lee, 1999, p. 230). Not surprisingly, researchers consistently report that classroom policies and practices are formed on the scaffold of inadequacy (Brattesani, Weinstein, & Marshall, 1984).

The first link in the expectation-possibility chain is the well-documented process of low expectations being translated into differential treatment and minimal demands (Oakes & Guiton, 1995; Page, 1991). This is accomplished in both subtle and not so subtle ways (Saunders, Davis, Williams, & Williams, 2004; Shade, Kelly, & Oberg, 1997). Indeed, "there is evidence that, consciously or unconsciously, teachers project through procedures, interactions, body language, and classroom management techniques the idea that some children are not worthy of being taught by them" (Shade et al., 1997, p. 47). More specifically, Shade and colleagues (1997, pp. 46–47) note that teachers

- demand less of low-expectation than high-expectation students
- give low-expectation students the answer and call on someone else rather than try to improve their response through clues or new questions
- criticize low-expectation students more often than high-expectation students for failure
- pay less attention to low-expectation students and interact with them less frequently
- seat low-expectation students farther away from the teachers than high-expectation students
- accept more low-quality or more incorrect responses from low expectation students

Chapter 4

- give high-expectation students rather than the low-expectation students the benefit of the doubt in borderline cases when administering or grading tests or assignments

The second link is that these transmitted expectations come to be accepted by students (Chaplain, 1996b). We see students molding themselves to those expectations (Slaughter-DeFoe & Carlson, 1996). Students ratchet down their own expectations and sense of efficacy (Eccles-Parsons et al., 1983; Thompson, 2004), putting in their time and doing just enough "to get by or pass" (Miron & Lauria, 1998, p. 1971). They develop a more negative perception of classroom climate, negative responses to the teacher, and reduced motivation. Or as Brattesani and colleagues (1984, p. 246) summarize it,

> teachers behave in ways that communicate their achievement expectations to their students, that students perceive these expectations from their teachers' behavior, and that these expectations influence students' own expectations.

The final link is rampant disengagement, often passive, sometimes aggressive, and reduced learning (Murphy & Torre, 2014; Silverstein & Krate, 1975). That is, there is abundant evidence "that teacher expectations and teacher treatments of youth are critical predictors of academic performance" (Fine et al., 2007, p. 816). Brattesani and team (1984, p. 245) provide us our conclusion here, documenting "that teachers do not merely sustain pre-existing differences in student achievement, but can also increase these differences."

TURNING ON TO LEARNING

Over the years, a variety of analysts have shown that good teachers turn students on to learning (Larkin, 1979). "Students' accounts underscore the importance of intellectually stimulating and engaging learning environments wherein students are actively connected to what is being taught" (Howard, 2001, p. 145), where there is "exciting and pleasurable work" (Cruddas, 2001, p. 66), where teachers "make the lesson interesting and link it to life outside the school" (Flutter & Rudduck, 2004, p. 78). Turning onto learning also includes the ability of teachers to ensure that lessons are not a haphazard rush to the finish line (Flutter & Rudduck, 2004), that teachers take the time required for "students to grasp the material" (Wilson & Corbett, 2001, p. 82).

When schools fail to entice students into learning, classrooms are dominated by teacher monologues, when "lacklustre lessons" (Chaplain, 1996b, p. 122), "the dry, sterile subject-driven version [of schooling]"

(Burke & Grosvenor, 2003, p. 58), and days dominated with textbooks and blackboards (Nieto, 1994). "Irrelevant knowledge [and] pointless activities" (Arnot, McIntyre, Pedder, & Reay, 2004, p. 68) lead to boredom (Howard, 2001; Steinberg, 1996), often mediated by anger and resistance (Chaplain, 1996a; Wilson & Corbett, 2001).

> Of course, one reason why pupils turn to disruptive behaviour is that they are bored; their attention is not focused on learning and there is a dangerous circularity in that disengaged pupils' behaviour leads others to switch off learning because they feel that there is little point in trying to work under these conditions. (Flutter & Rudduck, 2004, p. 116)

When teaching is boring "nearly all other characteristics of the [teacher] as well as the curriculum elude discernment" (Mergendoller & Packer, 1985, p. 597). Relationships wither (Johnson, 2009). Students themselves are also quite vocal about the positive dimensions of engagement for learning. They maintain, not surprisingly, (1) need for sufficient time to process material and engage with their teachers (Burke & Grosvenor, 2003; Flutter & Rudduck, 2004), (2) preference for "varied classroom activities" (Wilson & Corbett, 2001, p. 3), and (3) the importance of non-isolating, collective ways to tackle those activities (Alvermann et al., 1996). Students also report that "the process of disengagement can be reversed if [they] feel that significant others in the school are able to see and acknowledge some of their strengths" (Rudduck & Flutter, 2004, p. 70).

Turning onto learning is also defined by "responsive teaching." Responsive teaching at the broadest level is "demanding, critical, and expansive" (Fine, 1986, p. 407). The "emphasis is getting across to pupils the message that learning is for them rather than something 'done to them'" (Fine et al., 2007, p. 808). One element of responsive teaching is teachers' use of "different ways of showing and trying to get [lessons] across" (Arnot et al., 2004, p. 11). For example, Lee (1999, p. 232), tells us that students learn the most when "teachers take the time to present concepts in multiple ways." In their studies, Wilson and Corbett (2001, p. 83) found that "students lauded teachers who employed multiple ways of understanding a problem or completing an assignment. . . . Teachers who taught a concept in alternative words to the textbook's explanation were labeled as particularly helpful."

Research confirms the importance of "learning-focused dialogue" (Flutter & Rudduck, 2004, p. 8). "When such a learning dialogue is in place, pupils will begin to gain a sense of competency and self-worth, not through cajoling or threatening, but by recognizing and responding to the evidence of their own efforts and achievements" (Doran & Cameron, as cited in Flutter & Rudduck, 2004, p. 9). Research also underscores the importance of pacing and organization in responsive teaching. Here,

Chapter 4

students emphasize the skills of teachers in breaking down "assignments into manageable steps" (Dillon, 1989, p. 250) and "explain[ing] material at varying paces depending on student comprehension" (Lee, 1999, p. 232). The skills of individualization and differentiating instruction are visible here as well (Burke & Grosvenor, 2003; Davis, 2003), a "flexible pedagogy that understands the complexity of students' lives" (Smyth, 2006, p. 282), "allowing and helping students learn at their own pace" (Rudduck & Flutter, 2004, p. 116). Indeed, research consistently reports that individualization and sensitivity are critical ingredients in responsive teaching (Goldstein, 1999; Penna & Tallerico, 2005). As Wallace (1996a, p. 42) confirms, "the chorus of need that we see in the [student] interviews is for more individualized support alongside clear and well-structured whole-class 'exposition.'" The individual assistance theme ranged between contrast poles describing inadequate and adequate instructional resources. "At one end of the continuum we see teachers who are not available to students or who refused to answer individual questions" (Mergendoller & Packer, 1985, p. 586). These "impersonal strategies can leave students feeling vulnerable and may cause them to question a teacher's fairness" (Davis, 2003, p. 213). Many students describe their "teachers as impatient with their lack of understanding because instructors often failed to take the time to provide needed individual attention" (Lee, 1999, p. 225). The question we are left with for school leaders then is: "Are there any ways in which [we] can make space for more individual consultation about learning?" (Wallace, 1996b, p. 47). How can we promote "jointness" between teachers and students (Davis, 2003; Goodenow & Grady, 1993)?

Research also equates responsive teaching with "teachers asking questions in a way of sustaining deeper levels of active engagement" (Arnot et al., 2004, p. 18). Effective teaching features what Davis (2003, p. 220) describes as "scaffolding techniques, . . . matching the demands of each task and the instrumental support to students' abilities." As we discuss in the next chapter, scaffolding concepts and materials are often linked with the construct of cultural responsiveness (Natriello, McDill, & Pallas, 1990; McQuillan, 1998). Finally, analysts conclude that responsive teaching also has to do with the willingness of teachers to take risks (Wallace, 1996b), to provide students with autonomy and responsibility (Davis, 2003), and to reflect the seriousness with which learning should be engaged (Flutter & Rudduck, 2004).

GETTING TO UNDERSTANDING

Although all the ideas in this chapter on engaged teaching share common space, four stand out sufficiently to be collected into this section on "getting to understanding." Wallace (1996a, p. 38) sets up the narrative here as follows, underscoring "not" understanding.

More common was the experience of being 'lost' and this usually went beyond the confines of a single concept or topic and could attach to the subject as a whole—or even the curriculum as a whole. There are different reasons why pupils have such a feeling of being lost or not being able to get a grip on what is puzzling them. A common response in such a situation is to blame someone else, usually the teacher. Pupils talk about whole-class teaching with teachers who 'go too fast' or who 'don't explain things properly' and who, when pupils say they don't understand, blame them for 'not listening' or for 'being stupid.'

The first of the four concepts is that understanding depends greatly on the robustness of teacher explanations, "teachers going to great lengths to explain assignments and concepts" (Wilson & Corbett, 2001, p. 3), and the "ability to make course context comprehensive" (Phelan, Davidson, & Cao, 1992, p. 700). "When teachers provide clear explanations this may improve students' perceptions of the meaning of schoolwork" (Bru, Stephens, & Torsheim, 2002, p. 290).

Students' comments focused repeatedly on the clarity with which teachers explained new material and corrected students' confusions regarding the assignments they were expected to complete. . . . Students expected their instructors to be teachers in the root sense of the word: persons who *show* others how to master a subject. From the students' point of view, an instructor who abandoned students in the face of ambiguous worksheets and confusing lectures was cheating students of the high quality of instruction to which they felt entitled. Students seemed to consider the interactive processes of teaching and learning to be two parts of a bargain; they were willing to learn the assigned material as long as teachers' instructional practices facilitated their learning. When teachers did not keep up their part of the classroom contracts, but continued to assess and reward student performance, mutterings of "foul" appeared in the transcripts. (Mergendoller & Packer, 1985, pp. 586–587)

Wilson and Corbett (2001, p. 64) corral all this quite eloquently. Understanding means "the teacher explained things until the 'light bulb went on' for the whole class."

A teacher's being willing to help meant that the teacher found a way for the student to get continued explanations of a concept, problem, or assignment until the student understood it. . . . The important point was that the help had to result in the students' understanding. Students praised the teacher who "makes sure that I got it," who "makes sure I understand," who "teaches me so I can do it," who "makes it easier to understand," who "makes it clear," who will "actually teach." That was the sole criterion of effectiveness. (Wilson & Corbett, 2001, p. 23)

Our analysis suggests that students were in agreement about significant aspects of teaching and learning, such as having the teacher make explicit the learning expectations and explaining things clearly. (Thomson & Gunter, 2006, p. 853)

Research reveals that the best explanations are "clear and incorporate plenty of examples and involve concrete demonstrations of new concepts and ideas" (Arnot et al., 2004, p. 11).

Taken as a whole, the definition statements concerning instructional facility suggested that students wanted to learn the material they were assigned and sought to complete their academic tasks competently. Students expressed disappointment and anger when they perceived teachers' instructional behaviors as impeding their understanding and completion of their assigned work. Conversely, the seventh graders seemed quite appreciative when teachers helped students to learn by giving clear explanations of the material they were expected to master and by being responsive to each student's questions and problems. (Mergendoller & Packer, 1985, p. 587)

The second element of "getting to understanding" is teacher feedback (Kershner, 1996; Weinstein, 1983). Flutter and Rudduck (2004, p. 10) conclude that "supportive assessment procedures can make a difference to pupils' engagement with learning." A review of the research on feedback to students reveals a number of effectiveness criteria domains, such as closeness in time to work completion, specificity, "sensitivity to the needs of . . . learners" (Flutter & Rudduck, 2004, p. 10), accuracy, frequency, detail, personalization, and usability (Stanton-Salazar, 1997; Thompson, 2004). We know that feedback that underscores learning and support rather than accountability is desirable—that is, input about things that are changeable and controllable (Pintrich, 2003). Students tell us that they prefer "honest criticism and constructive feedback that offer[s] guidance rather than empty praise and encouragement" (Peterson & Irving, 2008, p. 240). Getting students in the feedback loop by assessing their own efforts is preferable, as is the use of feedback that "does not undermine intrinsic motivation" (Wigfield, Eccles, & Rodriguez, 1998, p. 96).

The third element of "getting to understanding" is the provision of academic care (Murphy & Torre, 2014; Murphy, 2016), or "pedagogies of care" (Johnson, 2009, p. 100), a state that leads to enhanced student motivation, engagement, and learning (Feldlaufer, Midgley, & Eccles, 1988; Howard, 2002). When academic care is felt, students describe their teachers as people who create a supporting classroom (Lehr et al., 2004). Critical here for students is the sense that they have meaningful relationships with their teachers that they are not simply cogs in the learning machine (Davis, 2003). They describe caring teachers as helpful, as making time to provide assistance (Mergendoller & Packer, 1985). They see them as active listeners, as guides who understand "that making time to talk with pupils about learning can reap tremendous rewards" (Flutter & Rudduck, 2004, p. 8). Studies underscore the nonadversarial behavior of teachers who care (Murdock, Anderman, & Hodge, 2000), as well as their willingness to stay with them even when it is inconvenient (Wilson & Corbett, 2001), a kind of "hangwithitness." These studies also characterize care in terms of teachers pushing students to do their best work and staying with them to ensure success (Fredricks, Blumenfeld, & Paris, 2004; Sanders & Harvey, 2002). Young people, in turn, see the importance of teachers working hard in the caring equation (Felner, Seitsinger, Brand, Burns, & Bolton, 2007; Roeser, Eccles, & Sameroff, 2000), as well as teachers taking an interest in them (Johnston & Nicholls, 1995). When pedagogical care is present, "students perceive their teachers as someone who respects their interpretations, provides opportunities for personal expression, and in general 'honor[s] their voices'" (Davis, 2003, p. 220).

Turning the research lens on students, youngsters define academic care as being seen and known on a personal level (Lewis, 2008; McLaughlin, 1994; Shannon & Bylsma, 2002), of being acknowledged (Powell, Farrar, & Cohen, 1985; Wehlage, Rutter, Smith, Lesko, & Fernandez, 1989). They describe the feeling of being allowed to be vulnerable (Rudduck & Flutter, 2004). "Students applauded teachers who did more than just pass along content to them. They especially appreciated teachers who made the effort to understand and believe in them" (Wilson & Corbett, 2001, p. 86). Being valued, believed in, respected, and taken seriously as individuals are core ingredients in the idea of academic care (Arnot et al., 2004; Chaplain, 1996a; Phelan et al., 1992). "Teachers who fail to acknowledge the knowledge, beliefs, and skills students bring to activities and interactions and the ways in which students resist conceptual change limit their ability to connect with their students" (Davis, 2003, p. 20).

Finally, and related to the developing narrative, we turn to the fourth factor of "getting to understanding," providing support (Bru et al., 2002; Nieto, 1994), not giving up on students (Patterson, Beltyukova, Berman, & Francis, 2007). Although we have seen support threaded through the analysis to this point, for purposes of clarity and reinforcement we extract it for special analysis here as well. The critical insight here has been penned well by Wilson and Corbett (2001, p. 64)—"the particular strategies used were less important than the underlying belief they symbolized: that every child had to have the in-school support necessary for learning to occur." "The most important resource the teacher provided was the assurance that if the student invested, learning would take place" (Muller, Katz, & Dance, 1999, p. 319). We also reemphasize the keystone place that support enjoys in nourishing student engagement (Boekaerts, 1993; Midgley, Feldlaufer, & Eccles, 1989): "When teachers provide appropriate learning support, students are more likely to succeed instead of becoming frustrated and withdrawing" (Bru et al., 2002, p. 290). "Both the students' attitudes about favorite teachers and their advice to teachers reveal that students invest in teachers who care enough to do whatever is necessary to facilitate learning" (Muller et al., 1999, p. 316), both for individuals and for communities of learners (Howard, 2001).

We can capture the essence of pedagogical support in two buckets: push and help. On one front, push is about conveying the seriousness of school work to youngsters (Cooper et al., 2005; Fine et al., 2007). It is about challenging youngsters and demanding that each of them bring her or his "*A* game" to the work (Bru et al., 2002; Lipman, 1995); it is about motivation and encouragement (Flutter & Rudduck, 2004; Rodríguez, 2008). "We interpreted students to be saying that these effective teachers adhere to a 'no excuses' policy. That is, there were no acceptable reasons why every student eventually could not complete his or her work, and there were no acceptable reasons why a teacher would 'give up' on a child" (Flutter & Rudduck, 2004, p. 83). In her work, Lee (1999, p. 230) concluded that "students said they wanted, and needed, teachers to 'keep on them,' to continually push them to do their work." In addressing "the push factor," Rodríguez (2008, p. 71) reached a similar conclusion: "A significant number of students spoke about the role that encouragement or being 'pushed' played in their engagement with school." And from Wilson and Corbett's 2001 work with children: "Students said they wanted to learn; they just did not act like it. It fell to the teacher to continually stay on them to do otherwise" (p. 34).

This student's preference was typical of most of the students we interviewed. With rare exceptions, they wanted a teacher who nudged them along and made sure that they worked. Students felt that few of them had the confidence, drive, perseverance, or determination to do it on their own. They wanted and expected to be motivated to learn. And that unwavering push usually had to come from their teachers (p. 70).

In short, students judge teachers as effective when those teachers "pushed them to excel" (Murdock, Anderman, & Hodge, 2000, p. 329) and when they see those demands "as coming from a place of teacher concern about students themselves" (Patterson et al., 2007, p. 136).

Scholars also talk about the importance in students "getting to understanding" narrative of teachers providing assistance to turn push into success (Hayes, Ryan, & Zseller, 1994; Kershner, 1996; Miron & Lauria, 1998), a ferocious willingness to help struggling students. "What I am saying is if teachers took that extra time and really tried to pull you in, some things could be different. That's all I'm saying" (student as cited in Sanon, Boxer, & Opotow, 2001, p. 77):

> Her message suggested that if a student did not understand the subject matter, then she assumed the problem was not caused by a deficit in the student; she merely needed to find an additional way of conveying the information to the student. (Thompson, 2004, pp. 60–61)

Students see this academic care as an avenue "to cope with academic stressors" (Wenz-Gross & Siperstein, 1998, p. 97). They equate it with proficiency (Wilson & Corbett, 2001). They are generally responsive and grateful for it as well (Howard, 2001; Wallace, 1996a).

Chapter 4

5

Constructed Learning

I n Chapter 4, we centered the spotlight on engaged teaching. Here we illuminate the work that unfolds in classrooms. We acknowledge that distinction between these two broad categories is somewhat artificial, but nevertheless necessary for analysis. Inside the category of constructed learning, we find seven core concepts, work that is intellectually challenging, cooperative, empowering, meaningful, authentic, student-centered, and mastery-oriented.

INTELLECTUALLY CHALLENGING WORK

The first pillar of constructed work is challenge, what practitioners and scholars label "critical demandingness." Challenge is particularly relevant when embedded in interesting tasks, "providing kids with interesting and challenging things to do" (Rogers, 1994, p. 41). Flutter and Rudduck (2004, p. 81) talk about this pillar as follows: "Good lessons are ones which challenge you and make you think . . . and therefore help you to learn."

Analysts are quite diligent in teasing out the subconcepts that define challenge. Level of task is critical (Wallace, 1996b). While students caution against work that is too complex, or "too distant or destabilising" (Flutter & Rudduck, 2004, p. 113)—or beyond the zone of proximal development, they much more routinely underscore the fact that much of what unfolds in classrooms lacks challenge, that students are routinely bored with the work that they are assigned. Scholars also remind us that challenge "is about learning and not just performing" (Maehr & Midgley, 1996, p. 188). Challenge is also marked by a thread of risk taking, an "academic venturesomeness" (Steele, House, & Kerins, 1971, p. 30), and by higher levels of cognition. A touch of novelty is often seen in portraits of challenge as well (Flutter & Rudduck, 2004). It is characterized by "opportunities to expand knowledge and competencies" (Bandura, 1993, p. 130) and by the press we spoke about previously (Moos, 1978). Because "the principle of intellectual challenge . . . helps students to experience learning as a dynamic, engaging and empowering activity" (Rudduck & Flutter, 2004, p. 136), researchers who provide perspectives on this aspect of constructed work talk about outcomes, such as commitment to work, and a positive work ethic (Rudduck & Flutter, 2004). "Tasks that are perceived by students as relevant and appropriately challenging are associated with increased intrinsic interest" (Davis, 2003, p. 226) and motivation (Bandura, 1993). "Optimal challenge" is, in turn, linked to "optimal engagement" (Connell & Wellborn, 1991, p. 70).

COOPERATIVE WORK

Students consistently report that they value collaborative work (Lodge, 2005; Nolen & Nicholls, 1993), "more group work" (Lee, 1999, p. 238): "They particularly enjoy working with their peers" (Poplin & Weeres, 1994, p. 32). They express "an overall preference for small-group discussions over whole-group discussions" (Alvermann et al., 1996, p. 254), "contexts for learning that facilitate collaboration among peers" (McIntyre, Pedder, & Rudduck, 2005, p. 154). Students also "report that they work better and learn more in groups" (Thomson & Gunter, 2006, p. 849), that creating "social contexts amenable to collaborative learning are helpful to learning" (McIntyre et al., 2005, p. 149). Fortunately, this felt need and preference by students fits with what the research tells us about meaningful work and learning (Shade, Kelly, & Oberg, 1997), that is "a social process" (Flutter & Rudduck, 2004, p. 11), one that "emphasizes communality" (Smerdon, 2002, p. 289) and "stimulates social connections and collective identity" (p. 289). Thus, according to Cabello and Terrell (1994, p. 20), "lesson excerpts and interviews show that exemplary teachers as a whole strongly emphasize teaching students how to work collaboratively."

Researchers also reveal information to leaders about the forms of and ingredients in collaborative work. On the form or strategy front, we learn of a variety of ways for students to work collectively (Mergendoller & Packer, 1985) and of a variety of "collaborative techniques" (Flutter & Rudduck, 2004, p. 33). Cooperative learning stands out (Wilson & Corbett, 2001). "Pupil-to-pupil support schemes" (Flutter & Rudduck, 2004, p. 123) fit here as well, as does "heterogeneous grouping that resembles a family" (Shade et al., 1997, p. 89), such as peer mentoring (Cabello & Terrell, 1994). On the DNA or principle front, we find that "students share the responsibilities not only of their own learning, but also for promoting others' learning" (Davis, 2003, p. 227). Cooperative work includes "the establishment of democratic principles and the promotion of interdependence" (Howard, 2001, p. 146). It includes "peer-led small group discussions" (Alvermann et al., 1996, p. 154) and "depends heavily on the establishment of a discourse community . . . , an atmosphere where students feel their ideas are taken seriously" (Ellwood, 1993, p. 74). The DNA of collaborative work features what Brewster and Fager (2000, p. 15) refer to as "reciprocal relationships," learning opportunities "where each student's knowledge is needed by others in the group to complete an assignment" (p. 15). The focus is on "collectivity rather than individualism" (Shade et al., 1997, p. 55). "Group discussions [that] foster material respect and understanding among members" (Alvermann et al., 1996, p. 264) are important. So too are values such as "the importance of contributing to the discussion, listening to others, being tolerant, and staying on topic" (p. 264). Within this social dynamic, qualities needed to be a productive working partner are important as well.

> Being prepared to listen was seen as important, caring about school work, being able to explain things, being funny and tolerant—and being ready to help when you are having difficulties. (Rudduck & Flutter, 2004, p. 97)

> They noted group members' responsibilities toward each other such as initiating talk, getting others involved through questioning, and keeping order. Demonstrating responsibility for their own behavior included actions such as offering pertinent points about a topic, sharing personal beliefs, and working to fulfill the academic task. (Alvermann et al., 1996, p. 257)

Opportunities for self-management are also key to good collaborative work.

As was the case with intellectual challenge, positive consequences are yoked to collaborative work. We discover from both researchers and practitioners who study schooling that cooperative work is a valuable experience (Flutter & Rudduck, 2004). It often improves social relations (Johnson, 2009; McLaughlin, 1994). It leads to "improved liking of classmates" (Wilson, Karimpour, & Rodkin, 2011, p. 97). It strengthens "interethnic relations" (Zanger, 1991, p. 29) in racially and culturally diverse classrooms. Cooperative student effort is a catalyst that helps nurture the growth of core dynamics such as active learning, meaning, and ownership (Kershner, 1996; Wigfield, Eccles, & Rodriguez, 1998). For individuals, "caring attitudes" (Wilson et al., 2011, p. 90) among students are enriched as well (Anderman, 2003; Wilson & Corbett, 2001).

Collaborative work is reported to strengthen aspects "in the process of learning" (Wigfield et al., 1998, p. 100) as well. There is also considerable agreement that "grouping students to engage in sustained collaborative tasks is associated with boosts in students' self-esteem" (Wilson et al., 2011,

p. 92). Cooperative work has also been connected to enhanced student responsibility (Ellwood, 1993) and increases in motivation (Kershner, 1996; Nolen & Nicholls, 1993), expectations for success (Wigfield et al., 1998), and self-confidence (Bragg, 2007; Flutter & Rudduck, 2004). Finally, the chain of evidence reveals that collaborative work ends with stronger learning outcomes. These are discussed, not surprisingly, in terms of academic performance (Thompson, 2004; Wilson et al., 2011)—"positive, work-oriented groups and pairs strengthen achievement" (Rudduck & Flutter, 2004, p. 96). The evidence chain also reveals that cooperative work leads to "new forms of wisdom" (Lincoln, 1995, p. 89) and "understanding" (Alvermann et al., 1996, p. 253). A surprising but important finding is that while academic gains are visible across all students, those placed at peril by race, class, and ethnicity are more advantaged by cooperative work than are mainstream students (Irvine, 1990; Seiler & Elmesky, 2007; Slavin & Oickle, 1981).

EMPOWERING WORK

As with most of the aspects of this chapter on constructed learning, there is a fairly large gap between what happens in schools and what researchers tell us should be unfolding. That is, empowering work is the exception not the rule for most students in schools (Rudduck & Flutter, 2004). We also have abundant evidence that "those who arguably most need to control learning appear to experience the least control over their learning, that [is] lower-achieving working class pupils are least likely to feel that they have control over their learning" (Arnot, McIntyre, Pedder, & Reay, 2004, p. 72). And where children have little influence over their learning, they are often disengaged (Wallace, 1996a). All of this returns us to our starting point: students generally express a desire for "greater independence and autonomy in their classroom learning" (McIntyre et al., 2005, p. 154), "increased control over their learning" (Arnot et al., 2004, p. 87).

Empowerment in the literature is expressed in a variety of overlapping, but somewhat differently nuanced terms. In places, for example, the discussion centers on degrees of autonomy (Brewster & Fager, 2000). When autonomy surfaces, it is often employed as a modifier to such ideas as "thinking" (McIntyre et al., 2005, p. 155) and "self-expression" (Mergendoller & Packer, 1985, p. 591). Empowering work is often defined by the presence of student voice. Here at the most general level we see encouraging students "to be vocal about the things they feel [they] need to be vocal about" (Garcia, Kilgore, Rodriguez, & Thomas, 1995, p. 141). It is about general respect for students' viewpoints (Johnston & Nicholls, 1995). More specifically, it means input in "the learning process" (Roeser, Eccles, & Sameroff, 2000, p. 466) and greater influence on classroom topics (Lee, 1999), about "involving pupils in making decisions about teaching activities" (Flutter & Rudduck, 2004, p. 11), "suitable discussion topics"

(Alvermann et al., 1996, p. 264), and the use of time (Flutter & Rudduck, 2004). The test, of course, is "the establishment of an atmosphere where students feel that their ideas [are] taken seriously" (Ellwood, 1993, p. 74). More tangibly still, voice is about "creating opportunities and encouraging student-centered questioning" (Commeyras, 1995, p. 101) and "opportunities for self-evaluation" of class activities (Flutter & Rudduck, 2004, p. 113).

Empowering work is also about the closely related topic of choice, what Poplin and Weeres (1994, p. 32) refer to as "self-chosen situations," and control over learning (Roeser et al., 2000). One aspect of choice refers to "control over working conditions" (Smerdon, 2002, p. 289). And one piece of this storyline focuses on open as opposed to more constrained or closed activities (Wigfield et al., 1998). Choice and control are associated with the concepts of student ownership and identity (Rudduck & Flutter, 2004), independence (Burke & Grosvenor, 2003; Steele et al., 1971), self-determination (Oldfather, West, White, & Wilmarth, 1999), agency (Arnot et al., 2004), peer leadership (Alvermann et al., 1996), student authority (Johnston & Nicholls, 1995), and self-management (Mergendoller & Packer, 1985). All in turn are dependent on the "authority structure of the school or class" (Epstein, 1981b, p. 109). Finally, empowering work is defined by individual accountability for the results of choice and autonomy (Shade et al., 1997). Agency and ownership mean "that students must begin to take responsibility for their own intellectual performance" (Rudduck & Flutter, 2004, p. 85), what Kershner (1996, p. 68) refers to as "a strong sense of personal responsibility for working and learning in school" as well as their own behavior (Dillon, 1989).

MEANINGFUL WORK

Given the development of the narrative to this stage, we should not be surprised to learn that youngsters in schools find much of what they do without meaning. This is troublesome because in this situation, engagement is limited (Crosnoe, 2011; Eckert, 1989; Weis, 1990). Or in alternative form, "it only makes sense that the more interesting an assignment is, the more likely students are to immerse themselves in the task and stick with it through completion" (Mergendoller & Packer, 1985, p. 593).

On the topic of absence of meaning, students often describe work as tedious (Mergendoller & Packer, 1985), as little more than busywork (Miron & Lauria, 1998), and as boring to the point of painfulness (Larkin, 1979; Sanon, Baxter, & Opotow, 2001). From two studies, Thompson (2004, p. 94) informs us that "students complain about a boring curriculum, a boring style of instructional delivery, and low standards . . . busy work that was designed merely to keep students occupied." In a study conducted half a century ago, 59 percent of students told investigators that more than half of their classes were boring. The most common classroom activities, "listening to teachers explain things [and] doing worksheets" are found to create the most disinterest (Spires, Lee, Turner, & Johnson, 2008, p. 505). Indeed, Flutter and Rudduck (2004, p. 110) document that in children's comments "there are constant references to boredom when students felt that lessons are not presented in imaginative ways and when learning activities are limited to a repetitious format of worksheets and textbooks." A student in the study by Mergendoller and Packer (1985, p. 590) describes this boredom quite nicely:

> He would just talk straight. And that gets boring if the teacher just talks like a machine or a robot or something. It bores you to death and you're sitting there drifting off into another land or something. (Student A13)

And Nieto (1994, p. 405) tells us that students in his study "had more to say about pedagogy than about anything else, and they were especially critical of the lack of imagination that led to boring classes."

One element of the poor news here is that the organizational system of schooling and the framework for learning in education have been forged in ways that make boring work the norm in schools (Larkin, 1979; Poplin & Weeres, 1994; Sarason, 1990): "the routines of traditional schooling and particularly the language of reward and punishment indicated a belief that the child will only learn under . . . duress" (Burke & Grosvenor, 2003, p. 68). The second piece of bad news is the abundant evidence that students resist boring activities, work taken under duress, and "busy work" (Miron & Lauria, 1998, p. 207), especially "busy work [seen] as a means of controlling student behavior" (p. 206): "When you are in class and you lose concentration, you are tempted to just leave. That's the boredom thing again. If students are not actively engaged they lose concentration" (Sanon et al., 2001, p. 75). The third piece of bad news is that student withdrawal is a proven recipe for poor learning (Bruggencate, Luyten, Scheerens, & Sleegers, 2012; Feldman & Matjasko, 2005). Or, in reverse form, the critical point is that "features of activities that individuals do in school can increase their personal interest in the activities" (Wigfield et al., 1998, p. 78), engagement with work, and social and academic learning (Allensworth & Easton, 2005; Rodríguez, 2008). On the other hand, students derive meaning and enjoyment in "those classes where teachers incorporate fun and interesting materials, presentation styles, and activities" (Lee, 1999, p. 233), when teachers "engage them in learning rather than relegating them to passive tasks that engender boredom" (pp. 233–34). Research also helps tease out what meaningful work looks and feels like to young persons. Meaningful work is about "experience[ing] school as living rather than more preparation for future living" (Johnston & Nicholls, 1995, p. 97). It is about "interesting and challenging things to do" (Rogers, 1994, p. 41), about getting interesting tasks to undertake or the possibility to make existing work interesting (Hayes, Ryan, & Zseller, 1994; Nolen & Nicholls, 1993):

> To summarize, students expressed preferences for topics that they experienced as likeable, interesting, and debatable. Most students valued topics that were naturally interesting; some held the teacher responsible for arousing interest in dull topics. (Alvermann et al., 1996, p. 260)

> If the topic is not interesting, Tyrone and Nicke [two students] note, then it is the teacher's responsibility to make it sound exciting. In Tyrone's words, 'Stress it more, you know. I mean . . . you gotta project it to the students more. Make them want to understand it.' (Alvermann et al., 1996, p. 260)

> I [a student] think you have to be creative to be a teacher; you have to make it interesting. You can't just go in and say, 'Yeah, I'm going to teach the kids just that; I'm gonna teach them right out of the book and that's the way it is, and don't ask questions.' Because I know there were plenty of classes where I lost complete interest. But those were all because the teachers just said, 'Open the books to this page.' They never made up problems out of their head. Everything came out of the book. You didn't ask questions. If you asked them questions, then the answer was 'in the book.' And if you asked the question and the answer wasn't in the book, then you shouldn't have asked that question. (Nieto, 1994, p. 405)

Part of this is about avoiding covering too familiar ground (Arnot et al., 2004). And remember that about 30 percent of teacher time is spent teaching children what they already know (Hattie, 2009).

Meaningfulness is "a curriculum driven by curiosity, adventure and collective endeavour" (Burke & Grosvenor, 2003, p. 70). It is about gearing lessons to meet "the interests and needs of students" (Dillon, 1989, p. 250), including, as we discuss later, their cultural backgrounds. Also, as we emphasize throughout the book, interest for students means "undertak[ing] valued challenges with the guidance and support of trusted adults" (Mitra & Gross, 2009, p. 529) and peers. It is, at least to some extent, about "focus[ing] on what students want to talk about" (Moos, 1979, p. 150) and a willingness of teachers to delve into interesting topics (Flutter & Rudduck, 2004). It is about a little novelty, variety, and different modalities (Thompson, 2004; Wallace, 1996b). It is about inviting and creative and imaginative work (Mergendoller & Packer, 1985)—about constructed learning (Burke & Grosvenor, 2003; Wilson & Corbett, 2001).

Chapter 5

Perhaps the most common, and in some ways powerful, center of meaningfulness is that work is fun (Spires et al., 2008; Zanger, 1993) and that time passed uncharted (Csikszentmihalyi & Larson, 1986). A critical "attribute the students described about their teachers was their ability to make learning a fun and exciting process" (Howard, 2001, p. 144). And they tell us:

> I think the only thing that I want teachers to know on behalf of the students and myself is that if they want to be here, we do. If they make the class fun and interesting, maybe we will be more fun to teach. I know that this statement doesn't go for all teachers or students, but we do want to learn. We don't want lectures all day and take notes. We want you to make learning fun and interesting. (Lee, 1999, p. 242)

> I think that the key to success and learning is interest, support, and most importantly enjoyment. (Burke & Grosvenor, 2003, p. 130)

> If it is more exciting it helps you to give it more of a try, like give it a real go. (Flutter & Rudduck, 2004, p. 87)

These youngsters express an overwhelming penchant for enjoyable activities, for excitement, and for fun (Arnot et al., 2004; Poplin & Weeres, 1994). They tell researchers "that making lessons 'fun' was not only important for pupils, but it was also important that teachers should enjoy what they were doing" (Flutter & Rudduck, 2004, p. 61).

Research also provide insights into what we think of as the principles and conditions of meaningful work, matters that are mixed with, but that carry us beyond, issues of excitement, interest, and fun. Youngsters describe meaningful work as integrated and as coherent (Burke & Grosvenor, 2003). They are not clamoring for easy activities (Arnot et al., 2004). They see reaching understanding at the heart of meaningfulness (Dillon, 1989; Sanon et al., 2001), what Arnot and team (2004, p. 14) describe as "clear learning purpose," and what Flutter and Rudduck (2004) refer to as purposeful work. As Kershner (1996, p. 18) tells us from his study, "pupils' critical understanding of education was demonstrated in the way they were able to make a distinction between school activities that were unpleasant, but necessary or worthwhile, and those that seem to them to have little educational value." But at the same time, students are unwilling to decouple understanding from usefulness (Anderman, 2003; Taylor-Dunlop & Norton, 1997). Meaningfulness is defined as "thoughtful engagement" (Arnot et al., 2004, p. 13) and seen as the chance to examine serious issues (Poplin & Weeres, 1994) with which students can become personally identified (Wallace, 1996b).

Researchers have also uncovered the types of activities that are likely to carry the title of meaningful work as well. We examine this line of analysis below when we explore student perspectives on authentic and active work. Here we provide a few notes to help us make that transition. We have already shown students preferences for multiple approaches to learning and a variety of activities. "Manipulative and 'hands-on-activities'" (Thompson, 2004, p. 617) are described as strategies that permit meaningful work to flourish, and "interactive strategies" (Shade et al., 1997, p. 92) pull students into direct involvement (Sanon et al., 2001). Physical movement seems to be an enhancing factor, "aspects of learning which engage the body as well as the mind" (Arnot et al., 2004, p. 64). This seems to be especially important for kinesthetic learners (Thompson, 2004). Multisensory learning in general scores high with students (Shade et al., 1997). Projects and practical assignments, that is, "tangible 'end product[s]'" (Flutter & Rudduck, 2004, p. 110), open doors to meaningfulness (Lee, 1999; Riley & Docking, 2004), especially ones that have life outside the immediate moment of the classroom (Burke & Grosvenor, 2003). "The positive feelings pupils have about 'practicals' was widespread. Pupils talked enthusiastically not just about doing things for themselves, but also about teacher demonstrations of 'what happens if . . . '" (Wallace, 1996b, p. 57).

There is a palpable sense in the literature that what they see routinely unfolding in schools is not "real life" (Spires et al., 2008). Students report meaning when schools draw nourishment from beyond the walls of the school (Shade et al., 1997; Wilson & Corbett, 2011). Students speak favorably of "having more opportunity to learn outside of the school boundaries, to see, touch, smell and feel real artifacts or nature" (Burke & Grosvenor, 2003, p. 69), to get away from "the dead air of the classroom and hurried intellectual abstractions" (p. 69). "Thematic and interdisciplinary units" (Anderman, Maehr, & Midgley, 1999, p. 142) often carry the meaning gene as do entertaining episodes of learning (Howard, 2001). Sharing "events, issues, and people in their lives" (Howard, 2002, p. 421) in the community of peers can also enrich the seedbed from which meaning takes root, what Johnston and Nicholls (1995, p. 96) describe as the relevance of personal knowledge. Choice often trumps imposition in nurturing meaning (Johnson, 2009). Finally, students routinely acknowledge the power of "technology-related work" to make school activities meaningful (Spires et al., 2008, p. 507).

AUTHENTIC WORK

The fifth dimension of constructed learning is captured well by the concept of authenticity, an idea that we separate into three parts for analysis: linkages to students as cognitive actors, linkages to the lives of students as culturally defined persons, and linkages of learning to real life. We examine how these ideas unfold in the world of schools. We begin with an important reminder, that authentic work is connected to the social and academic success of young persons: "when school experiences 'fit' students' needs, successful development is enhanced and when they do not, problems ensue" (Roeser et al., 2000, p. 463). The essential ground here is that "pupils do not enter classrooms stripped of . . . their own life-historical circumstances" (Wallace, 1996b, p. 60). They are who they are as learners, as members of society, and as actors in the world they inhabit.

Authenticity means on one front an alignment with who students are as cognitive actors, "for relevancy in their intimate relationships with knowledge" (Burke & Grosvenor, 2003, p. 60). Shade and team (1997, p. 18) remind us "that students approach each learning task with his or her own particular history of development and learning—with their own point of view about ideas, the world, and learning tasks." We learn here that a key responsibility is connecting learning "to students' prior knowledge" (Thompson, 2004, p. 591). McIntyre and colleagues (2005, p. 153) refer to this as "contextualizing the learning in appropriate ways, [that is] learning tasks that connect new ideas with things that were familiar," or O'Loughlin calls it "learning grounded in students' autobiographical stories of their life experiences" (1995, p. 111). Thus "teachers need to be open to the interests and prior knowledge of their students so they can craft lessons that touch meaningful life events and experiences" (Roeser et al., 2000, p. 466), "put students' questions at the center of classroom discourse" (Commeyras, 1995, p. 105), and create opportunities "for students to draw upon their narrative structures to make sense of material for themselves on their own terms" (O'Loughlin, 1995, p. 109).

> Pupils told us that work became more appropriately contextualised if there were evident connections between the task at hand and their current knowledge and understanding. The connections that pupils seemed to find helpful were sometimes achieved through their teacher's introduction of materials, objects and images that were already familiar to them. (Arnot et al., 2004, p. 14)

Authenticity means "build[ing] on earlier learning, not only in terms of content, but also in terms of ways of working" (Rudduck & Flutter, 2004, p. 40). Students find in schools that "information gained through their lives is often split off or subordinated as irrelevant" (Fine, 1986, p. 402). On the other hand, exemplary teachers "frequently give students the opportunity to relate personal experiences to the content at hand" (Cabello & Terrell, 1994, p. 20), to create "personal relevance" (Kershner, 1996, p. 71).

> Pupils seemed to be telling their teachers in concrete ways and with clear examples how the authenticity of their learning experiences

could be enhanced by bringing tasks into closer and more striking alignment with the mental and social worlds that they inhabit both inside and outside the classrooms. (McIntyre et al., 2005, p. 154)

Authenticity also has a good deal to do with what students describe as real-world relevance (McIntyre et al., 2005). One thick thread here holds together the importance of the "here and now" as opposed to some undetermined time (Kershner, 1996, p. 72), what Spires and team (2008, p. 510) refer to as "real world anchors" as opposed to children's work. An additional piece of the narrative here underscores "the kinds of knowledge that are required for real life in the world outside the school gates" (Flutter & Rudduck, 2004, p. 115). Also found here is schoolwork that "provide[s] opportunities to explore the community and have experiences that broaden their understanding of the broader community" (Shade et al., 1997, p. 89), the idea that "the school would be much more integrated into the wider community" (Burke & Grosvenor, 2003, p. 63). That is, "contextualising learning appropriately involve[s] designing and using tasks that authentically resonate with pupils' wider concerns, experiences and aspirations . . . outside the school gate and beyond their learning careers at school" (Arnot et al., 2004, p. 15). On this last point, we learn relevance for students has to do with topics "important for their future lives" (Flutter & Rudduck, 2004, p. 118). "Specifically, students would like school experiences to be more directly related to careers that they might have in the future" (Spires, 2008, p. 509). The chance to address "difficult, contentious, or conflicting issues" (Nieto, 1994, p. 400) in the larger world that confronts students, i.e., "the difficulties facing the community and society" (Shade et al., 1997, p. 89). Embedded in this piece of the authenticity storyline are the ideas that "the work must have some value beyond the workplace" (Smerdon, 2002, p. 289) and that students must nurture a sense of responsibility for their work (Shade et al., 1997).

Finally, we learn from students that authentic work is viewed playing out in certain ways in their classrooms. There is emphasis, for example, on blended or integrated subject matter and knowledge that is not divorced from application (Burke & Grosvenor, 2003). There is acknowledgment and use of students' primary language (Shade et al., 1997). There is also attention to "selecting materials that closely match students' interests" (Dillon, 1989, p. 243), to "personal relevance" (Wigfield et al., 1998, p. 77)—in "pursuing a curriculum that is relevant and that connects to young lives" (Smyth, 2006, p. 282) and to interrupting "cultural discontinuity" in the classroom (Zanger, 1991, p. 7). Learning here "flows from exciting, rich, significant experiences" (Bragg, 2007, p. 676).

Most students desire more interesting and relevant choices in the content and process of instruction. They enjoy classes where assignments require them to think about issues for themselves, involve critical issues embedded with values and controversy, and allow them to talk with peers. They particularly enjoy and learn from experiential activities. . . . Descriptions of the most boring, least relevant school activities suggest that the more standardized the curriculum, text and assignment, the more disengaged the students. (Poplin & Weeres, 1994, p. 32)

Relevance here has as much to do with the pedagogy as with the "tasks teachers present and the topics or subject matter they assign" (Alvermann et al., 1996, p. 253) and includes attention to the work orientations of different groups of students (First & Carrera, 1988). The takeaway message runs as follows: in effective classrooms "teachers make relevant connections and consider subject matter through the eyes of learners" (McLaughlin, 1994, p. 10).

Insights into what children value and care about help us structure the classroom worlds in which children are most apt to learn. They suggest that we pay attention to what children value as learners and consider children's voices if we are to genuinely support children's learning. (Dahl, 1995, p. 129)

STUDENT-CENTERED WORK

Laced throughout the analysis in this chapter is the following maxim: engaging work is student focused and student built. That is, creating work that is more meaningful and authentic "require[s] the use of strategies that are more interactive [and] student-centered" (Shade et al., 1997, p. 129), strategies that are prized by students and that are effective in promoting learning.

Students at all achievement levels told us that they prefer classrooms where they can take an active part in their own learning, classrooms where they can work interactively with their teachers to construct knowledge and understanding. We found these active student roles to be particularly important to the engagement and academic success of non-traditional students, who generally failed to thrive in teacher-dominated classrooms. (McLaughlin, 1994, p. 10)

For purposes of analysis we separate student-centered work into two lines of discussion, the elements of constructive work and the characteristics of active, participatory work. The status quo in schools leaves a good deal to be desired in both areas. O'Loughlin (1995, p. 109) captures this reality quite accurately, reporting that since many "teachers are usually preoccupied with 'covering' the curriculum, there is little opportunity in school for students to draw upon their own narrative structures to make sense of the material for themselves on their own terms." Commeyras (1995, p. 102) adds confirmation here documenting that "discussions that revolve around student-generated questions do not typically occur in most classrooms in the United States. . . . In classroom discourse, students rarely use questioning to seek knowledge, explanations, or understanding." The norms in schools are "teacher-in-control" and "student-as-passive learner" (Dillon, 1989, p. 254). And we would do well to remember that "according to student descriptions of the most boring and least relevant schoolwork, they include activities which stick closely to standardized materials and traditional transmission teaching methods" (Poplin & Weeres, 1994, p. 15).

The elements of constructed work are less complex than often argued. We begin with the material outlined earlier in our analysis on engaged work. We add the idea of students "working under their own initiative . . . with the teacher acting as a guide and source of support" (Flutter & Rudduck, 2004, p. 36). Student-centered work entails "emphasis on ownership of ideas and personal construction of knowledge" (O'Loughlin, 1995, p. 108). It underscores an "abandonment" of the nearly exclusive focus on "teacher-centered instructional methods" (Lee, 1999, p. 238) and movement toward a more balanced portfolio of teacher-directed and student-focused learning activities, a movement away from "instructional models in which the flow of information is unidirectional" (Harter, Waters, & Whitesell, 1997, p. 170) and a movement toward "self-regulated learning" (Maehr & Midgley, 1996, p. 31), and a "psychology of inquiry" (Commeyras, 1995, p. 102)—"a dialectical process in which teachers seek students' questions and fashion their teaching in response to students' interests and queries" (p. 102). Attention is devoted to the "notion that we need to connect students' experience with the concepts and organizing principles of the academic disciplines" (Ellwood, 1993, p. 68). In student-centered work, "both the teacher and students share the responsibility for teaching, learning, and interacting, including defining what constitutes a motivating curriculum" (Davis, 2003, p. 220). Constructivism "privileges students' natural questions, and the questions become the center of teaching and learning experiences" (Commeyras, 1995, p. 105). As should be clear at this stage of our analysis, student-centered work suggests "major changes in the traditional patterns of schooling . . . a major teaching function [here] is to guide students in a well-informed exploration of areas meaningful to them" (Noddings, 1988, p. 221). There is a commitment to the "mutuality" of work: "Teachers have an obligation to support, anticipate, evaluate, and encourage worthwhile activities, and students have a right to pursue projects mutually constructed and approved" (p. 221). This is what Cook-Sather (2006, p. 354) refers to as a "more reciprocal, mutually

Chapter 5

informing teaching and learning dynamic," which means, of course, that students have a more "significant role in the teaching-learning process" (Shade et al., 1997, p. 90) or more powerfully "the 'somethings' the student say become the stuff of the curriculum" (Johnston & Nicholls, 1995, p. 94). "Students construct their own vision of the concepts, ideas, and events" (Shade et al, 1997, p. 129), a construction process facilitated by their teachers (Alvermann et al., 1996).

> Did the instructor make changes during the class that were responsive to learning needs expressed by students? If addressing this question, and providing evidence of change based on its answers, were not only legitimate but required, the structures that currently support the exclusion of student perspectives from conversations about educational policy and practice would be changed. This move in education would be in keeping with the recognition among other service professionals that they have failed to attend sufficiently to the experiences and perspectives of those they aim to serve and revision of their professional practices to include clients' perspectives to rectify this failure. (Cook-Sather, 2002, p. 11)

The second strand of student-centered work attends to the active, interactive, and participatory nature of student engagement. The core messages are as follows: "it is important to engage students actively in the learning process rather than expect them passively to receive information" (Shade et al., 1997, p. 115); that is, "most critical is the active involvement of pupils" (McIntyre et al., 2005, p. 153). Students need to be "knowledgeable participants in the life of classrooms" (Arnot et al., 2004, p. 20). "Good lessons are about participation and engagement" (Rudduck & Flutter, 204, p. 79); "good lessons include activity" (p. 80).

Analysts routinely describe schools as "student 'talk-deprived'" places (Alvermann et al., 1996, p. 264), places lacking in interaction and participatory work. They often characterize classrooms as oppressive venues of teacher talk and student boredom (Arnot et al., 2004; Wallace, 1996b). Researchers, in turn, document that teachers' perceptions of institutional pressures, such as "institutionally sanctioned curriculum, subvert their attempts to engage students in genuine acts of learning" (Zamel, 1990, p. 96) and encourage them to define students in passive and subordinate roles (Bragg, 2007).

> Students go along with their teachers' requests, pay attention, and do not challenge the teachers' authority. It is through this apparent passivity that they, in fact, are able to take control of their future (obtaining passing grades and ultimately graduating). (Miron & Lauria, 1998, p. 197)

> Classes were dominated by the teachers, leaving students in the role of spectators most of the time. (Hamilton, 1983, p. 319)

These same young people are, on the other hand, often direct and vocal in their request for greater student action and participation in schools (Rudduck & Flutter, 2004; Sanon et al., 2001), "for more active learning" (Chaplain, 1996a, p. 108). "For these students, education isn't just about learning math, social studies, or science; it is about being active partners in learning—contributing their ideas, being listened to, making choices in their studies" (Cook-Sather & Shultz, 2001, p. 5). It is about "participation in the teaching/learning process" (Poplin & Weeres, 1994 p. 32) and "taking more responsibility for themselves" (Arnot et al., 2004, p. 16).

> Pupils seemed to be calling for classroom learning to be driven by a different kind of dynamic: one that gave less prominence to the textbook or worksheets and the skills of reading and discursive note-taking and greater prominence to their own active involvement and decision-making. (Arnot et al., 2004, p. 13)

A particularly important dimension of active learning is what Boomer (cited in Oldfather et al., 1999, p. 293) labels the "elsewhereness" of knowledge. Turning knowledge into firsthand activity is an important epistemological shift that can have significant impact students' views of themselves.

"Giving pupils opportunity to participate more actively in the learning process is important" (Flutter & Rudduck, 2004, p. 11). "Interactive teaching for understanding" (McIntyre et al., 2005, p. 153) and "activity structures" (Hamilton, 1983, p. 326) pull youngsters into the learning work (Epstein, 1981a; Sanon et al., 2001); it is "almost synonymous with being engaged" (Rudduck & Flutter, 2004, p. 79). In addition to being greatly appreciated by students, it fosters a "sense of agency and ownership" (McIntyre et al., 2005, p. 149). It can also "lead to classroom teaching of enhanced quality" (Arnot et al., 2004, p. 41) and "have a positive impact on pupils' attainment" (Flutter & Rudduck, 2004, p. 40): "Indeed students of teachers who spend more time scaffolding student responses, encouraging risk taking, and transferring control to students make greater gains in reading compared to students of teachers who spend less time using these interactive strategies and more time evaluating students" (McMahon & Wernsman, 2009, p. 281).

The research illustrates "action and participation" in classrooms, some of which we discussed in earlier sections. When we turn to students for answers here, they often talk of "extensive use of problem solving and discovery methods in classroom work" (Shade et al., 1997, p. 94). They also highlight "attempts to generate knowledge that is both valuable and might form a basis for action" (Atweh & Burton, 1995, p. 562). The importance of discussions is underscored as well (Alvermann et al., 1996; Oldfather et al., 1999), especially discussions featuring the sharing of one's own ideas.

> Students' perceptions in this study support some long-held beliefs about the benefits of discussion. Our findings indicate that discussion allows students to become engaged with ideas, to construct meaning, to take responsibility for their own learning, and to negotiate complex cognitive and social relationships. (Arnot et al., 2004, p. 264)

Dillon (1989, pp. 244–245), in turn, lists

> several actions that promote students' active, meaningful learning. These include allowing students to use their natural language during lesson interactions and transforming his [the teacher] language to that of his students, anticipating possible difficulties students may have with assignments and adapting lessons to meet the needs of students, and bridging gaps between background knowledge students have and new concepts and materials they are to learn.

Scholars document that working "in groups or pairs . . . finding things out from sources outside the classroom or designing solutions to problems that matter" (Rudduck & Flutter, 2004, p. 79) fuel active learning. So also can "involvement in curriculum development" (McLean-Donaldson, 1994, p. 28) and engagement "in self-assessment or peer assessment strategies" (Flutter & Rudduck, 2004, p. 11), particularly evaluation that conveys "knowing by demonstration" (Arnot et al., 2004, p. 18). Finally, we learn that physical activity can promote interactive learning (Flutter & Rudduck, 2004) as can "an increased use of hands-on and experimental learning opportunities, more classroom discussion that models and discusses reasoning, the problem-solving approach, and more frequent use of cooperative groups and peer support systems" (Shade et al., 1997, p. 93).

TASK-ORIENTED WORK

The seventh and final dimension of constructed learning is what researchers describe as "task orientation." The essential matter is the difference between task-centered and ability-oriented learning platforms, or the importance of "mastery expectations" (Sagor, 1996, p. 32). Analysts portray "a task-oriented classroom environment as one in which personal improvement, effort, and progress are emphasized as both the purpose of academic tasks and the measure of success" (Anderman, 2003, p. 7).

Relatedly, researchers refer to the difference between mastery and performance goals, goals that "significantly modify the students' approach to learning" (Maehr & Fyans, 1989, p. 243).

> Mastery goals orient the student toward learning and understanding, developing new skills, and a focus on self-improvement using self-referenced standards. In contrast, performance goals represent a concern with demonstrating ability, obtaining recognition of high ability, protecting self-work, and a focus on comparative standards relative to other students and attempting to best or surpass others. (Pintrich, 2003, p. 676)

> When students are oriented to task goals they are mainly concerned with learning for the sake of learning, and striving to master tasks, to improve, and to develop intellectually. Such students are interested in problem solving, novel tasks, and challenging situations. Task-focused students are likely to attribute their success to effort. In contrast, when students are oriented to performance goals, they are mainly concerned with demonstrating their ability or concealing a lack of ability. (Anderman et al., 1999, p. 132)

An essential point here is that in a task-oriented classroom students come to "judge their capabilities more in terms of personal improvement than by comparison against the achievement of others" (Bandura, 1993, p. 120). In creating items around these two goal dimensions, Anderman and team (1999, p. 136)

> include items assessing the use of interesting and challenging materials, concern with involving all students in decisions and in discussions, and making work meaningful to students. Our scale assessing a performance goal structure includes items assessing an emphasis on relative ability, the importance of correct answers, and moving through the work regardless of the level of understanding.

Or, as Wigfield and colleagues (1998, p. 79) tell us,

> with ego-involved (or performance) goals, children try to outperform others, and they are more likely to engage in tasks they know they can do. Task-involved (or mastery-oriented) children choose challenging tasks and are more concerned with their own progress than with outperforming others.

In addition to goal structure and learning framework, analysts capture the importance of task-oriented work in terms of engagement, differentiating between engendered and instrumental work.

Chapter 5

> The first kind of engagement, engendered by school work which offers interest, novelty, challenge and significant personal control over the process, is qualitatively different from instrumental covering of syllabuses and rote learning for examinations. (Bandura, 1993, p. 125)

Important conclusions emerge from analysts in this area. Findings confirm that task orientation in the domain of goals and classroom actions is not the norm in schools. The reality is "competitive individualism" (Wallace, 1996b, p. 63), a norm that steadily increases in saliency as children age (Feldlaufer, Midgley, & Eccles, 1988). Researchers also report that ability and performance frameworks exact real costs on students. They reveal that competitive frames "promote an ego goal orientation in students" and show that "such practices can contribute to the declines in students' academic competence beliefs, interest, and intrinsic motivation" (Wigfield et al., 1998, p. 97). "Emphasis on social comparison in classrooms decreases task or intrinsic involvement" (Nolen & Nicholls, 1993, p. 415) and has the "detrimental effect of lowering self-image and reducing efforts" (Chaplain, 1996b, p. 124). When "control over grades" trumps "control over learning," work becomes highly instrumental, and we know "that work done for instrumental reasons alone achieves little more than relief when the end is finally reached" (Wallace, 1996b, p. 62). Youngsters "become oriented toward avoiding failure . . . and eventually will become less achievement oriented" (Moos, 1979, p. 199).

> School emphasis on ability goals makes it virtually inevitable that a large group of children will develop all too many misgivings regarding their competence to learn. In particular, children who come to school with little preparation and with no continuing support will begin to view themselves not only as different, but also dumb and, worse, of lesser value. The rewards in the ability-oriented school lie in doing better than others regardless of the opportunities or resources you have been granted. It is a race with the participants starting at different points on the track and with those behind having little or no chance to catch up. So it does little good to hug or praise when the whole environment is sending a message that winners—not learners—count. (Maehr & Midgley, 1996, pp. 44–45)

Maehr and Midgley (1996) and other scholars also document how performance architecture leads naturally to ability grouping in schools, a practice that presents many hazards. "In particular, it most often serves to reinforce the idea that school is concerned more with establishing ability hierarchies than fostering the personal and intellectual development of all students" (Maehr & Midgley, 1996, p. 121). Analysts also shed light on the connections between ability goals and assessment in schools. Pupils come "to see assessment as a measurement of their ability rather than attainment and they seem to feel that grades and marks effectively define their potential" (Flutter & Rudduck, 2004, p. 99).

Finally, investigators have unearthed an assortment of benefits that accompany the task-oriented work. Although not deeply explored, there is a sense that task-oriented work is linked to enhanced fairness and equity in schools (McMahon & Wernsman, 2009), that the broad notion of justice is enhanced as the deeply entrenched norms discussed above that "reinforce inequality" (Roeser et al., 2000, p. 463) are eliminated. We also know that mastery focus accents gains rather than uncovering deficiencies. In turn, "accenting the gains achieved enhances perceived self-efficacy, aspirations, efficient analytic thinking, self-satisfaction, and performance accomplishments" (Bandura, 1993, p. 125). "Perceived goals of the classroom significantly modify the students' approach to learning. Thus when mastery goals are more salient than performance goals, students are likely to be more inclined toward academic challenge and learning for its own sake" (Maehr & Fyans, 1989, p. 243). Not surprisingly, "the task-focused instructional practice leads to improved student motivation" (Anderman et al., 1999, p. 134). We see evidence of "more adaptive psychological and behavioral adjustment" (McMahon & Wernsman, 2009, p. 268) when task-oriented goals and classroom environments are ascendant. Bandura (1993, p. 125) also finds that learning environments that construe ability as an acquirable skill, deemphasize competitive social comparison, and highlight self-comparison of progress and personal accomplishments are well suited for building a sense of efficacy that promotes academic achievement.

Wigfield and team (1998, p. 94) also conclude that "in mastery-oriented classrooms, everyone who performs adequately can experience success. As a result, youngsters in mastery-oriented rooms are more likely to focus on self-improvement than social comparison, to perceive themselves as able, and to have high expectations for success." In turn, Anderman (2003, p. 7) shows that

> middle school students' reported perceptions that their teachers emphasize a task goal orientation have been shown to predict more positive school-related affect. It seems likely that this type of learning environment might also predict higher levels of school belonging for students. That is, students who perceive their teachers as promoting personal improvement and mastery of content

Chapter 5

might be more likely to maintain a sense of acceptance and validity in their school.

Thus, task-focused work "underscores personal capabilities" (Bandura, 1993, p. 125), "personal competence" (Sagor, 1996, p. 39), "and commitment to life-long learning" (Maehr & Midgley, 1996, p. 91) as well as enhancing "sense of community" (Anderman, 2003, p. 20).

6

Curriculum and Assessment

In the last two chapters, we examined what is known about productive schooling by highlighting the norms of engaged teaching and constructed learning. We continue that work here by focusing the lens on the curricular and assessment dimensions of schooling, recognizing that how leaders manage these domains represents a critical aspect of how principals impact teaching and learning.

CURRICULUM

Before we move too deeply into curriculum, it is advisable to surface some reminders and cautions. In this chapter, we will be talking about curriculum somewhat independently of the context in which it is nested. However, leaders need to remember that context is always important and that curriculum is tightly bound to the "structure, policies, and processes that are used to distribute learning opportunities in schools" (Cooper, 1996, p. 197). Leaders must remind themselves that curriculum unfolds in specific cultures, cultures that can reinforce or damage the messages conveyed in the curriculum. Here we will also be examining each subdimension of curriculum by itself. However, in real schools, leaders hold in mind that these subdimensions are overlapping patterns in a larger tapestry. It is also true that this tapestry is itself a piece of a larger picture of the core technology of a school, sharing space and interacting with instruction and assessment. The three subdimensions of curriculum to which district and school leaders need to attend—rigor and opportunity to learn, authenticity and cultural relevance, and program coherence—are discussed in order below.

Rigor and Opportunity to Learn

Curriculum is the "what" of the instructional program, the content to which students are exposed. At a core level, it is useful to describe curriculum in terms of quality or rigor and quantity or content coverage (Carbonaro & Gamoran, 2002; Hallinan & Kubitschek, 1999). On the topic of quality, the spotlight is focused on the breadth and depth of content standards (Bryk, Sebring, Allensworth, Luppescu, & Easton, 2010; Conchas, 2001), concepts that are established by curricular frameworks and the scope and sequence of courses (Wilson & Corbett, 1999). In addition to inspecting the power of individual courses, it is also helpful to define quality in terms of the rigor of the sequences of courses available to students (Oakes & Guiton, 1995).

Building on the work of Brophy, Leithwood and colleagues (Leithwood, Louis, Anderson, & Wahlstrom, 2004, p. 62) outline the elements of a robust curriculum.

This is a curriculum in which the instructional strategies, learning activities and assessment practices are clearly aligned and aimed at accomplishing the full array of knowledge, skills, attitudes and dispositions valued by society. The content of such a curriculum is organized in relation to a set of powerful ideas. Skills are taught with a view to their application in particular settings and for particular purposes. In addition, these skills include general learning and study skills, as well as skills specific to subject domains.

In a quality curriculum, "what is taught is worth knowing in the first place and is treated in sufficient depth to engage students' interests and offer them a challenge" (Cotton, 2000, p. 10). The touchstones are meaningfulness and challenge, what Louis and Marks (1998, p. 537) refer to as "intellectually serious work" and Carbonaro and Gamoran (2002, p. 819) label "intellectually challenging content." As we will see below, some patterns of coursework have considerably less rigor than others. We will also see that this "distribution of less" is charged with the dynamics of class, race, and ethnicity (Murphy & Hallinger, 1989).

On the quantity side of the curriculum ledger, the essential issue is content coverage or opportunity to learn (Murphy & Hallinger, 1989). That is, quantity is determined by the overall amount of work students complete in individual courses and across their programs (i.e., sequence of courses) (Carbonaro & Gamoran, 2002). Quantity opportunities are defined not only by "credit accumulation" (Allensworth & Easton, 2005, p. 16), but by a press to do more intellectually challenging work (Shouse, 1996; Murphy, Weil, Hallinger, & Mitman, 1982). Opportunity to learn also has a good deal to do with the pacing of content over individual classes and over time across schooling (Bryk et al., 2010; Goldenberg, 2004).

A combined narrative about curriculum quality and quantity is visible most clearly in analyses of curriculum differentiation, commonly known as ability grouping and tracking.

The first thing leaders need to remember about tracking is that it is a direct proxy for opportunity to learn. On this point, we know, "Tracking functions as a major source of unequal opportunities to learn" (Mickelson & Heath, 1999, p. 569).

The second acknowledgment to be made about tracking is that "track placements are strongly correlated with students' race and social class" (Mickelson & Heath, 1999, p. 567). The "assignment process . . . favors whites over blacks of equal ability" (Thompson & O'Quinn, 2001, p. 13) and affluent children over poor children of similar abilities (Miller, 1995). On this front, we know that these assignments have deep historical roots, beginning in the early twentieth century with the inculcation of the social efficiency philosophy into education (Murphy, Beck, Crawford, & Hodges, 2001). Under this banner, schools became places in which youngsters were tapped and then educated to fill slots in the larger economy, a process decoupled from merit and laced with both classism and racism (Kliebard, 1995; Krug, 1964). Thus, "from the early beginnings of 'tracked' educational programs to contemporary schools, white and more affluent students have had opportunities and access to an education that differs markedly from the education provided for students of color and poverty" (Shannon & Bylsma, 2002, p. 29). Alternatively, "students of low-socioeconomic status are more likely to be placed in academic tracks less conducive to achievement" (Roscigno, 1998, p. 1035). Because of tracking, "serious inequalities in access to knowledge continue to exist in the nation's schools among students from different social classes and racial groups" (Miller, 1995, p. 233).

The third point to be made about tracking/ability grouping is that it is highly consequential (Lee & Burkam, 2003; Oakes, 1985). We concentrate our attention here on the link between tracking and learning outcomes. However, it is important to acknowledge that tracking is associated with other outcomes as well. For example, research informs us that track placements "affect students' self-concepts" (Irvine, 1990, p. 15) and self-esteem (Alexander & McDill, 1976; Land & Legters, 2002) as well as exposure to "friendship networks" (Lucas & Gamoran, 2002, p. 175) in general, and to motivated (or unmotivated) peers in particular (Berends, Lucas, Sullivan, & Briggs, 2005; Cotton, 2000).

Track assignments also shape an especially key variable in the student success story—"aspirations for the future" (Lucas & Gamoran, 2002, p. 175). There is considerable evidence that track membership has marked consequences for the development of academic orientations and for aspirations for continued education, and particularly post-high school education plans (Alexander, Cook, & McDill, 1978; Oakes, 1985). Alexander and Cook (1982) and Heyns (1974) suggest that schools exercise their primary influence over pupil socioeconomic attainment through their role in helping students establish orientations toward educational goals. As Heyns (1974, p. 1445) notes, "it is possible that schools play a more decisive role in the stratification system through encouraging and implementing aspirations than through altering patterns of achievement." Work on the reproduction of cultural inequalities in American education through differential teaching of both the form and the "hidden curriculum" at different track levels and at schools with students of varying biosocial backgrounds lends support to this position. Since they cluster students of color, track placements and ability grouping have also been implicated in the resegregation of education, this time within schools, by race and class (Irvine, 1990; Rumberger & Palardy, 2005), what Mickelson and Heath (1999) call "second-generation segregation within schools" (p. 577). As such, it is held, "tracking policies and practices serve as the major vehicle to institutionalize and perpetuate racial divisions" (Cooper, 2000, p. 620) among school-age youth and adults (Land & Legters, 2002).

Turning to student learning outcomes, research confirms that sorting students into curricular tracks is associated with high school graduation (Camara & Schmidt, 1999; Lee & Burkam, 2003) and degree completion in college (Singham, 2003): "The academic rigor of the courses taken in middle school and high school not only affects students' current achievement, but also is the single most important predictor of college success" (Kober, 2001, p. 27). Studies also reveal the linkage between track assignment and measures of academic achievement (Alexander et al., 1978; Gamoran, 2000; Goodlad, 1984; Oakes, 1985; Roscigno, 1998; Strutchens & Silver, 2000; Tate, 1997; Weinstein, 1976). Here we find that students in the lower-level track with the less rigorous courses perform worse than their peers on standardized tests. Overall then, "research shows that academic achievement is closely related to the rigor of the curriculum" (Barton, 2003, p. 8), that the rigor of the curriculum is tightly aligned to track placement (Miller, 1995; Murphy, Hallinger, & Lotto, 1986), and that "ability grouping, on average, has a negative effect on students on the lower tail of the distribution" (Roscigno, 1998, p. 1039).

Authenticity and Relevance

Authenticity in the domain of curriculum refers to the ability to match learning context to the ways in which students learn most effectively. It refers to curriculum that moves from abstract concepts to include tangible work. It carries meaning for students to learning activities. That is, authentic work is grounded not only in the standards, but also in the values, goals, and interests of students (Noguera, 1996; Roney, Coleman, & Schlichting, 2007). Relevance is a core concept here, embedding learning in "contexts in which students are interested and involve topics about which they are curious" (Roney et al., 2007, p. 290). In short, curriculum is seen through the eyes of students as well as the eyes of the disciplines

(Cook-Sather, 2006; Flutter & Rudduck, 2004; Rudduck, Chaplain, & Wallace, 1996). Considerable attention is devoted to "valid educational content" (Newmann, 1992, p. 206). Authentic work also has value and meaning beyond the instructional context (Newmann, 1992, p. 206). It includes "linking academic instruction to examples in students' everyday experiences" (Christle, Jolivette, & Nelson, 2005, p. 86). It features real life problems (Johnson & Asera, 1999); problems often emerging from young people themselves (Eggert, Thompson, Herting, & Nicholas, 1995; Farrell, 1990); a "broad curriculum base" (Day, 2005, p. 576); "active and inquiry-based learning" (Desimone et al., 2002, p. 87); project-based learning (Shear et al., 2008); and co-construction of products, including support from peers as well as teachers (Farrell, 1990).

Culturally relevant curriculum extends the notion of congruence to the backgrounds of children (Gault & Murphy, 1987), especially children (and families) that have been marginalized in the traditional curriculums in schools (Antrop-González & De Jesús, 2006; Shannon & Bylsma, 2002). More specifically, in many schools "there often is a mismatch between curriculum and students' values" (Mukuria, 2002, p. 434). The curriculum often "devalues the home and experience" (Eckert, 1989, p. 10) of those from non-mainstream backgrounds (Quiroz, 2001). In short, in a culturally relevant curriculum there is greater sensitivity to the assorted cultures at the school (Datnow, Borman, Stringfield, Overman, & Castellano, 2003; Scanlan & Lopez, 2012) and in the community and nation (Burns, Keyes, & Kusimo, 2005). This means, more concretely, that "the formal and informal curricula reflect the cultural values and political realities of the communities and provide students with educational and social experiences closely aligned with community and cultural resources" (Antrop-González & De Jesús, 2006, p. 410).

Analysts who focus on culturally relevant curriculum have distilled a number of its defining elements. Such curriculum "bridges students' home lives with their school lives" (Scanlan & Lopez, 2012). There is direct attention to "crossing racial and ethnic borders [and] integrating cultural, linguistic, and historical connections in the curriculum" (Galletta & Ayala, 2008, p. 1971). Culturally relevant curriculum "challenges the notion that assimilation is a neutral process" (Antrop-González & De Jesús, 2006, pp. 412–413). There is a conscious link of academic content with the cultural and ethnic lives of students (Blair, 2002; Scanlan & Lopez, 2012), especially the use of relevant materials (Antrop-González, 2006; Galletta & Ayala, 2008). Underlying this perspective is an embedded belief that "students bring something of value to contribute to the curriculum" (Ancess, 2003, p. 99) as well as "a commitment to provide students with important historical knowledge grounded in their identities" (Antrop-González & De Jesús, 2006, p. 417). Schools marked by cultural relevance assume an additive approach to schooling (Antrop-González, 2006; Steele, 1997).

Chapter 6

While there is little research to date collected on the outcomes of culturally relevant curriculum, there is strong theoretical evidence that students are advantaged when cultural relevance becomes a reality in schools (Jordan & Cooper, 2003; Leithwood, Jantzi, & Steinbach, 1999). On the question of intermediate outcomes, logic holds that curricularly relevant standards and materials will enhance student integration into the school, social capital, self-esteem, and motivation (Antrop-González, 2006; Scanlan & Lopez, 2012). These enhancements lead to heightened student engagement (Ancess, 2003), which in turn is associated theoretically and empirically with strengthened academic skills and better achievement scores (Murphy & Torre, 2014).

Program Coherence

The third domain of curriculum to which leaders need to attend is coherence and alignment (Wellisch, MacQueen, Carriere, & Duck, 1978) or what we have called "tightly coupled curriculum" (Murphy, Weil, Hallinger, & Mitman, 1985, p. 367). We preface this work with some important reminders. To begin with, we see that curriculum coherence is nested in the larger concept of overall "organizational integration" (Youngs & King, 2002, p. 646). This operational coherence addresses the extent to which the various systems and domains of the school are integrated and are all pulling in the same direction (Balfanz, Herzog, & MacIver, 2007; Stringfield & Reynolds, 2012). One way to describe this has been provided by Mitchell and Sackney (2006, p. 422), who talk about "the degree of order within and consistency across various directions and instructional movements in a school." On this point, Robinson (2007, p. 13) notes the "importance of overall guidance through a common set of principles and key ideas." Another strategy for district and school leaders is to focus on the cohesion among systems and areas of work, such as personnel management, instructional program, school operations, support activities, student services, and so forth. Here we see a school that "operates more as an organizing whole and less as a loose collection of disparate systems" (Murphy, 1992b, p. 98). Bryk and team (2010, p. 63) put the direction and systems strategies together in the concept of "strategic orientation." Strategic orientation creates a theory of action for how and why actions work and provides a center of gravity for the various systems so they all hold together (Murphy, Hallinger, & Mesa, 1985; Murphy, 1992b). In so doing, each of the domains and systems takes on life beyond itself. Each ends up touching one or more of the other domains (Spillane, Diamond, Walker, Halverson, & Jita, 2001b).

As we move to understand the concept of organizational integration, we see a theme ribboned throughout this volume. That is, school and district leaders play the central role in bringing alignment, coherence, and integration to life in schools (Murphy, 1990a; Robinson, Lloyd, &

Rowe, 2008). Where cohesion is found, the fingerprints of principals are universally visible (Marzano, Waters, & McNulty, 2005). The principal, in particular, is the critical gluing agent, the person who gets things to cohere or permits them to operate in isolated fashion (Anderson, Moore, & Sun, 2009; Newmann, Smith, Allensworth, & Bryk, 2001). We would also be wise to remember that organizational coherence is not the norm in schools. "Problems of continuity" (Newmann, King, & Youngs, 2000, p. 289) are inherent. Most people work hard to operate their own piece of the overall operation (e.g., a fifth-grade classroom, a library). "Everyone [is] kind of in their own world doing their own thing" (Eilers & Camacho, 2007, p. 624). The weaving of threads of connection is generally only a small part of that work. In addition, new ideas, programs, and reforms are often grafted onto rather than integrated into schools (Murphy, 2013). Adoption proceeds absent coordination (Newmann et al., 2001). Even on the occasions when they do migrate into the school, linkages to existing operations, programs, and people are often an afterthought: overload, fragmentation, and isolation are often dominant conditions.

We turn the lens now directly onto the topic of curriculum coherence. There are a number of ways to link content together, various methods for leaders to engage program integration and alignment. An important strategy has to do with creating alignment between the curriculum in special programs (e.g., special education, English language learners) and the curriculum in the regular program. A second is the coordination of the curriculum with district and state standards and objectives (Johnson & Asera, 1999; Murphy et al., 1985). A third has to do with the classes where the curriculum unfolds: (a) the integration of curriculum standards in a course (Newmann et al., 2000); (b) the same subject across classes (e.g., writing across the curriculum) (Bryk et al., 2010); (c) integration among classes in a discipline (i.e., sequenced program of study) (Burch & Spillane, 2003); (d) among subjects (e.g., science and history); and (e) the alignment with higher education courses (Kleiner & Lewis, 2005). A fourth lens on curriculum coherence is to see through the experiences that occur for each student, whether they experience "academic drift and curricular debris" (Murphy, Hull, & Walker, 1987, p. 351) or cohesive programs of study (Oakes & Guiton, 1995). Of special importance here is how well new material links to students' prior learning (Huberman, Parrish, Hannan, Arellanes, & Shambaugh, 2011). All of these aspects of curricular coherence find space in the idea of "curriculum mapping" (Eilers & Camacho, 2007, p. 614), "the subject matter that students are exposed to as they move across grades" (Bryk et al., 2010, p. 74).

There are also principles of operation and systems of support that influence curriculum alignment for better or worse. One is the linkage between school vision and goals and curricular content (Kruse, Seashore Louis, & Bryk, 1995; Spillane, Halverson, & Diamond, 2001a). As Leithwood and Montgomery (1982, p. 324) reported at the start of the effective schools era,

Chapter 6

the difference between ineffective and effective school leaders on coordination of the curriculum was "the relatively precise focus of the effective principal on curriculum goals as the basis for integration rather than the more ambiguous diffuse goals of the typical principal on curriculum work being done in the school." Because "curriculum alignment is a social activity as well as a technical act" (Bryk et al., 2010, p. 117), the principle of collaborative teacher work in a reciprocal manner comes into play in the curriculum alignment narrative. Or, alternatively, curriculum alignment work is most productive in the context of professional learning communities. So also, we see supportive policies around how time is allocated and protected in the curriculum coherence storyline (Eilers & Camacho, 2007; Firestone & Wilson, 1985). Relatedly, longer time commitments and consistent policy environments support program alignment (Desimone, 2002; Newmann et al., 2001). Finally, policies and guidelines that link resources and the curriculum help build alignment (Halverson, Grigg, Prichett, & Thomas, 2007), especially professional development (Newmann et al., 2000).

ASSESSMENT

Assessment is the third point on the instructional program triangle, in combination with pedagogy and curriculum. While we address the technical dimension of assessment below, we are concerned primarily with exploring the overarching narrative of a climate or culture of inquiry (Eilers & Camacho, 2007; Halverson et al., 2007), "a school environment conducive to data-based decision making" (Ingram, Seashore Louis, & Schroeder, 2004, p. 1260). Supovitz and Klein (2003, p. 2) refer to this conception of assessment as a "culture of systematic inquiry into the relationship between the instructional practices of teachers and the learning of their students." And Wohlstetter, Datnow, and Park (2008) remind us that this culture is about the development of widely shared norms and expectations about how data are employed.

Before we move into the main narrative here, we begin with our conclusions. To start, the research on effective schools and districts identifies well-crafted assessment as an explanatory variable in the success storyline (Kerr, Marsh, Ikemoto, Darilek, & Barney, 2006; Lachat & Smith, 2005). That is, we find that widespread and thoughtful use of data on student learning is essential in school improvement work (Collins & Valentine, 2010) and in enhancing the outcomes of that work, especially of student academic achievement.

Concomitantly, over the last forty years, researchers have consistently found that leaders are central figures in the growth of a culture of inquiry in schools. They are often the "driving force behind strong data use" (Supovitz & Klein, 2003, p. 36). They are key in setting goals for the use of

Chapter 6

assessment information (Levin & Datnow, 2012), helping establish a "press for using evidence" (Cosner, 2011, p. 291). They are assessment champions. Leaders play a critical role in establishing an atmosphere of trust and collaboration that is a requirement of productive assessment systems. They provide support for teachers in collecting, analyzing, and using data, for turning numbers into action.

In the balance of our analysis of assessment, we take on five leadership responsibilities. We begin with a discussion of the cultural and structural barriers that make meaningful assessment difficult to inculcate in many schools. In the second section, we examine the "frames" for building great assessment systems. We then turn to the essential elements and principles of productive assessment systems. In the fourth section, we analyze enabling supports. We conclude by unpacking the benefits of data-informed activities in schools.

Barriers

Cultural Discontinuities

The message that one derives from the research is that the current culture in schools is not conducive to data-driven assessment. That is, "the concept of data-based decision making . . . is unrealistic" (Ingram et al., 2004, p. 1283) in many schools and for large numbers of teachers. At a deep level, many educators do not view assessment as a "legitimate improvement strategy" (Young, 2006, p. 522). Ingram and team (2004, p. 1273) "surmise that being dismissive of externally generated achievement data is a cultural [marker] that teachers learn." What this conveys is that the technical aspects of assessment are insufficient. In the average school, the use of data is formulaic, episodic, and superficial (Blanc et al., 2010; Ingram et al., 2004). As a result, "most teachers do not rely on data to examine the effectiveness of teaching. Changing this requires not only changes in behavior, but also in deeply held values" (Ingram et al., 2004, p. 1281).

In schools today, we know that teachers have considerable mistrust of data and the use of data in schools. Consequently, they rarely embrace and often reject assessment information (Wayman & Stringfield, 2006). Teachers tend to see data quite differently than do analysts in the larger policy community. It is normal for them to question both the accuracy and validity of assessment systems as well as the resulting data (Kerr et al., 2006; Timperley, 2009). They often view assessment data as "inaccurate or not relevant to teacher concerns" (Lachat & Smith, 2005, p. 344). Teachers also see that at times data interfere with classroom work—that it is in competition with instruction (Blase & Blase, 2004; Kerr et al., 2006). They often note that much of the data that assessment systems provide simply duplicates what they know already. Likewise, teachers often discern conflict between assessment and the curriculum. Assessments that count are sometimes viewed as forcing curricular compaction, necessitating the use of less robust curriculum (Datnow, Park, & Kennedy, 2008; Desimone, 2002). On other occasions, teachers find that the demands of curricular coverage make using data a moot point (Kerr et al., 2006).

Also ingrained in the teaching (and leadership) ranks is the belief that the real goal of much of the data machinery in place is not for the improvement of instruction, but for either compliance, accountability, or political ends (Ingram et al., 2004; Young, 2006), ends which teachers view as not benefitting classroom instruction (Blanc et al., 2010; Young, 2006). Here we often find not only a lack of trust, but a sense of threat as well (Firestone & Martinez, 2007; Kerr et al., 2006). Teachers often see the data as a basis for others crafting professional judgments rather than as a foundation for constructive work (Blanc et al., 2010; Halverson et al., 2007); that is, as a vehicle to assign blame (Ingram et al., 2004).

Equally, if not more troubling, is the sense among some educators that "traditional assessments do not include or reflect what they perceive as valued and important outcomes . . . such as higher order thinking skills" (Desimone, 2002, p. 445). Thus, as Ingram and his colleagues (2004, pp. 1281–1282) have noted, "teachers, even when they accept their state's testing and accountability system as necessary don't view the test data as sufficient." There is also at times a noticeable tension between modes of traditional assessment and professional judgment (Ingram et al., 2004). Also discernible is an undercurrent that many of the topics and measures on which teachers and leaders desire information rest outside the realm of academic performance regardless of how it is assessed (Cosner, 2011; Ingram et al., 2004).

Inadequate Support

There is considerable agreement that school people often lack the supports required to collect, analyze, and employ data either individually or in communities of practice. That is, they are not prepared to address the obstacles they confront (Ingram et al., 2004). Lack of time is the most troubling condition uncovered in the research. As noted above under cultural discontinuities, teachers often see assessment systems as stealing classroom time and interfering with their work with children. The absence of leadership is a common lament as well (Levin & Datnow, 2012); criticisms molded in terms of formal school leaders who are not data literate as well as unskilled teacher leadership in professional communities. Lack of collective leadership is especially detrimental to sustainability (Wayman & Stringfield, 2006). Inadequate and unwieldy data systems are often seen, especially on the technology side (Datnow et al., 2008; Supovitz, 2002), promoting what Blanc and colleagues (2010, p. 216) describe as a lack of "capacity for open discussion."

Compounding the obstacles of time and leadership is the reappearing conclusion that teachers and school leaders often lack the knowledge needed to handle well-crafted assessment systems (Kerr et al., 2006; Wayman & Stringfield, 2006). Or as Brunner and colleagues (2005, p. 4) conclude, "researchers are hard pressed to find substantial numbers of educators who have adequate training and knowledge and are prepared to make appropriate use of data and transform it into useable information and practice." Ingram and associates (2004, p. 1280) conclude that while teachers are not data phobic and even when the culture is positive, "they don't have recent experience in working with data to improve specific classroom practices." Limited preparation, inadequate mentoring by principals, and lack of capacity at the district are each underscored in this storyline (Blanc et al., 2010; Lachat & Smith, 2005).

Data systems routinely present obstacles for schools. Teachers believe that they are often inundated with data, receive data in unsophisticated forms, and lack strategies to process information (Ingram et al., 2004; Kerr et al., 2006). There are many places, teachers remind us, where timelines in receiving assessment data are less than desirable (Datnow et al., 2008). A consistent complaint is that data are not adequately aligned to the curriculum unfolding in classrooms; a return to our earlier point about teachers questioning the meaningfulness of external assessments.

Frames for Assessment

In this section, we begin our discussion of planning or agenda-setting assessment (Young, 2006) with some notes about the deep essentials of the work and then describe the reciprocal cycle of assessment. We then delve deeply into the steps of that recursive, overlapping cycle. Our first observation is that all stages of the system need to unfold for assessment to work well (Blanc et al., 2010; Datnow et al., 2008). Great collection and weak analysis will not work well. Neither will excellent analysis and poor use of data. A second note informs us that planning for data-based activity is essential, it makes the assessment process efficient and effective (Kerr et al., 2006). Third, as Young (2006) reveals, working on the technical and rational aspects of assessment alone is insufficient to garner important gains. Without simultaneous attention to values and norms around assessment, meaning and relevance are too easily left out of the equation, a recipe for producing formulaic work (Blanc et al., 2010; Collins & Valentine, 2010). Fourth, it is generally helpful to begin with the end in mind and then work backward (Supovitz, 2002). Lastly, the issues of guiding principles and supports will have considerable influence in determining how effective we are in crafting productive assessment systems.

We move now to the discussion of the four stages in the cyclical process or "cybernetic cycle" (Scheerens, 1997, p. 276) of assessment to which school leaders need to attend: determining the goals or purposes of assessment and identifying the data buckets of importance; collecting and managing data; analyzing and sensemaking; and using data.

Chapter 6

While the information from assessment "can be a powerful ally in stimulating positive change and improvement" (Lachat & Smith, 2005, p. 333) and without data there is blindness in school improvement work (Blase & Blase, 2000; Datnow et al., 2008), the starting position for us is that "unless . . . agreement can be reached among stakeholders on fundamental goals, there will be little agreement on what constitutes meaningful data" (Ingram et al., 2004, p. 1273). Goals precede collection and analysis and are in turn informed by assessment data (Brunner et al., 2005; Wohlstetter et al., 2008). Absent this perspective, data can "inadvertently compromise the overarching purpose of data-driven practice" (Datnow et al., 2008, p. 8).

At the macrolevel, data can be placed in the service of learning and/or holding students and education responsible for outcomes (Riester, Pursch, & Skria, 2002). On the learning front, analysts have shown us that data can be employed for an assortment of purposes, almost all of which are linked to strengthening the instructional program (Blanc et al., 2010; Supovitz, 2002). Researchers illuminate three overlapping sets of learning purposes.

> Student achievement data can be used for various purposes, including evaluating progress toward state and district standards, monitoring student performance and improvement, determining where assessments converge and diverge, and judging the efficacy of local curriculum and instructional practices. (Wohlstetter et al., 2008, p. 240)

> We have identified seven major ways in which teachers and administrators in our sample explained how they used student performance data for instructional or organizational improvement. First and foremost, they used student performance data to inform instruction. Second, they used data specifically to identify low-performing students and inform assistance plans for these students. Third, they used data to plan professional development. Fourth, they used data to set targets and goals. Fifth, they used data to celebrate both faculty and student accomplishments. Sixth, they used data as a visual means of reinforcing school priorities and focus. Seventh, data were used as supporting evidence in conversations with parents about students. (Supovitz, 2002, pp. 13, 15)

> Studies have documented a multitude of purposes where schools have successfully applied data-based inquiry. Most commonly, data are used for tasks such as setting annual and intermediate goals as part of the school improvement process. Data may also be used to visually depict goals and visions, motivate students and staff, and celebrate achievement and improvement. Schools use data for instructional decisions, such as identifying standards, refining course offerings, identifying low-performing students,

Chapter 6

and monitoring student progress. School structure, policy, and resource use may be informed by data. Schools have also used data for decisions related to personnel, such as evaluating team performance and determining and refining topics for professional development. (Kerr et al., 2006, p. 498)

Embedded in these three summaries is affirmation of the central theme that goals drive data collection and that data collection, in turn, shapes goals. We also see confirmation of the two core assessment pathways to build schools as academic places: strengthening the quality of the instructional program and enhancing student academic performance (Kerr et al., 2006; Riester et al., 2002). In each of these pathways, particular emphasis is placed on identifying and addressing student weaknesses in relation to standards (Cosner, 2011; Gray et al., 1999; Rumberger, 2011). Researchers report that this ongoing and meaningful use of performance information fosters (1) a "culture of inquiry" in schools (Datnow et al., 2008, p. 10), a culture defined by teacher ownership of data (Blanc et al., 2010; Levin & Datnow, 2012) and (2) collaborative decisions on the allocation of resources (Blanc et al., 2010; Brunner et al., 2005).

According to analysts who study assessment, the second leg in the inquiry process is data collection or data acquisition (Halverson et al., 2007; McDougall, Sanders, & Goldenberg, 2007), to which we would add managing the data (Lachat & Smith, 2005). Key ingredients here include collection in the service of purpose and goals; the use of multiple sources of information; and ongoing, regular collection activities (Cotton, 2003; Supovitz & Klein, 2003). Digital technology is especially helpful at this stage both with the collection and managing data work (Brunner et al., 2005). Collecting, managing, and storing data carries us to the questions regarding which data will be collected and how (e.g., survey, tests, observations) (Cotton, 2003). Research here reminds us that data need to be well organized and easily accessible if gathering efforts are to bear fruit (Blanc et al., 2010). The important issue of displaying data merits noting here as well (Blanc et al., 2010).

Keeping in mind that there is considerable overlap among the steps or stages of the cyclical assessment process, we turn now to data analysis. Our work convinces us that the essential issue here is "sensemaking," the process employed to develop understanding of what data tell us (Blanc et al., 2010; Halverson et al., 2007). A key point to hold in mind here is that data often do not provide answers. They point in certain directions, raise questions, and help open possibilities (Allensworth & Easton, 2005; Kerr et al., 2006). The interpretation of the data holds high ground, and that work is predicated on what educators know. Data can also be complex and messy, leading to the emergence of alternative explanations and avenues of action (Supovitz & Klein, 2003). The defining process in the transformation is interrogation, e.g., disaggregation, reflection, and discourse (Murphy, 2010; Young, 2006), paying special attention to the different messages that the data convey (Supovitz & Klein, 2003).

Making sense of data is the prelude to the next phase of the assessment cycle, constructive use of data or "taking action based on what [was] learned" (Supovitz & Klein, 2003, p. 33). This includes the "willingness to change instructional practice in the face of new information" (Halverson et al., 2007, p. 17). Data use exposes the recursive nature of the assessment cycle. It depends on the previous phase, data analysis. That is, "the type of data collected determine the type of decisions that are made" (Lachat & Smith, 2005, p. 335). It is employed in the service of the first phase of the cycle: goals and purposes. It leads directly back to phase two of the cycle as well, i.e., the collection of data, at this point around the success of actions taken to improve the school. And the cycle is set in consistent motion.

Elements and Principles

Research underscores the essential elements and principles of productive systems. While these ingredients are blended in schools and districts, we pull them apart for analysis. We discuss them under the following descriptors: actionable, coherent, and professionally anchored.

Actionable assessment systems, as noted above, are purpose and goal driven. Actionable means also that assessment programs are understandable (i.e., user friendly) (Datnow et al., 2008; Kerr et al., 2006) and that the information produced is valid, relevant, and useful (Datnow et al., 2008). Actionable systems offer guidance and concrete data (Hayes, Christie, Mills, & Lingard, 2004; Wayman & Stringfield, 2006). There is efficiency in access to data (Wayman & Stringfield, 2006). Teachers view the data as necessary (Levin & Datnow, 2012). It allows them to see "how they [can] address emerging issues in their classrooms" (Halverson et al., 2007, p. 41). It pushes the spotlight onto instruction. In the words of Wayman and Stringfield (2006, p. 569), actionable systems "help teachers use data rather than being used by data." Data are accessible, but not intrusive (Friedkin & Slater, 1994). Information is made available in a timely manner (Kerr et al., 2006; Lachat & Smith, 2005) to "enable teachers to quickly analyze data for instructional decision making" (Datnow et al., 2008, p. 32). Actionable systems provide comparable data (Blanc et al., 2010); there is a focus on authentic measures of demonstrating learning (Bryk et al., 2010); and they promote the unpacking and disaggregation of data (Lachat & Smith, 2005; Murphy, 2010).

Analysts routinely describe a second element of productive assessment systems, coherence, as well as the principles that help define the element. Cohesiveness covers a good deal of space in the assessment narrative and overlaps with the other two essential elements, actionability and professional "ingrainment." One principle of integration is the continuous nature of assessments (Huberman et al., 2011; Kerr et al., 2006). So too is the reliance on a comprehensive platform of both internal and external forms of data collection (Ingram et al., 2004) and the systems collection of data (Ingram et al., 2004).

Coherent assessment features multiple and varied types of data to provide insights into quality instruction and student learning (Lachat & Smith, 2005; Leithwood, 2008).

A core principle here is that there is "breadth and depth to data-related functions" (Young, 2006, p. 544). That is, coherence arises in part from multiple and overlapping functions. Mayrowetz and Weinstein (1999, p. 423) capture this aspect of coherence when they report that "redundancy" is a critical dimension of productive assessment systems. Another principle highlights the linkage between assessment and the larger task of school improvement (Hallinger & Murphy, 1985). Because data-driven decision making is not something that can be brought to life in isolation (Datnow et al., 2008), in cohesive assessment systems these two domains are intricately linked (Lachat & Smith, 2005). We also find in a coherent world that adult learning and assessment are deeply intertwined (Murphy et al., 1983; Murphy, Elliott, Goldring, & Porter, 2007). Coherence here also means that there is planful alignment between assessments and the other domains of the instructional program, that is, curriculum and instruction (Hallinger & Murphy, 1986; Wohlstetter et al., 2008).

This final element carries us into the domain of culture, what we refer to as a professionally ingrained assessment system (Datnow et al., 2008; Young, 2006). Cosner (2011, p. 794) characterizes this as "an inquiry-oriented schoolwide culture," a climate in which "using data to guide instruction become[s] a habit of mind for teachers" (Cooper, Ponder, Merritt, & Matthews, 2005, p. 12). There is a culture of collective development of and use of assessment systems and the resulting data (Young, 2006; Wohlstetter et al., 2008). Here we find teachers that talk more "of collaboration that [is] academic and professional" (Wayman & Stringfield, 2006, p. 565). In professionally anchored assessment systems, "teachers are provided with opportunities to work collaboratively in building their capacity to use data" (Lachat & Smith, 2005, p. 236). "Norms of interaction" (Young, 2006, p. 540) and deprivatization (Louis, Marks, & Kruse, 1996; Murphy & Torre, 2014) hold high ground where professional grounded assessment cultures flourish. Collaborative work and learning norms are underscored (Halverson et al., 2007; Murphy, 2015a). The reflective sensemaking we explored earlier is a sense of ownership of results from data collection and analysis (Levin & Datnow, 2012), teachers coming together to see that the data are their data (Lachat & Smith, 2005). The front side of this ownership is commitment and sense of responsibility for student learning (Johnson & Asera, 1999; Murphy, 2016), a collective and "overwhelming consensus about the importance of using data to improve teacher performance and student achievement" (Datnow et al., 2008, p. 5). The backend is mutual accountability (Murphy & Torre, 2014, Wohlstetter et al., 2008), "a community that holds its members accountable for learning" (Young, 2006, p. 538).

Enabling Supports

Supports are the final piece in the assessment system. Support includes leadership, resources, and systems and structures, i.e., "school conditions and practices that . . . promote staff use of data" (Lachat & Smith, 2005, p. 334). We begin with the central theme of the book: leadership is a required support for productive assessment systems to take root and grow (Beck & Murphy, 1996; Hallinger & Murphy, 2013). In the best sense of the term, leaders are "instigators" (Supovitz & Klein, 2003, p. 2) and advocates and champions (Lachat & Smith, 2005). In a real sense, leadership helps the other supports to materialize (Murphy et al., 2001). The research illuminates a number of important leadership activities, all of which center on creating organizational capacity (Young, 2006).

> Leadership focused on data use or agenda setting affects teachers' impetus for using data and correspondingly loosens or tightens the connections between data-driven rhetoric and teachers' data practices. (Young, 2006, p. 532)

> Principals have been found to be pivotal in modeling effective data use and in enabling teachers to use technology. Principals are also critical in providing ongoing learning opportunities for teachers to discuss and analyze their students' data. (Levin & Datnow, 2012, p. 180)

> Four roles individually enacted by principals include (a) establishing, communicating, and reinforcing an evidence-based agenda and necessary work tasks, (b) modeling data use and maintaining an organizational routine that made public the practice of evidence-based grade-level collaboration, (c) buffering and filtering the school from the district in ways that support evidence-based grade-level collaboration, and (d) supporting and shaping shared leadership in service of evidence-based grade-level collaboration. (Cosner, 2011, p. 801)

Leaders in schools and districts with effective assessment systems are key in getting the goals of measurement in place (Blanc et al., 2010; Supovitz & Klein, 2003). They are often in a unique position to move financial and human resources to assessment work (Blanc et al., 2010), especially individual and collective capacity-building activities (Lachat & Smith, 2005; Wayman & Stringfield, 2006).

In robust assessment programs, we see considerable energy linked to the following interconnected resources: money, time, people, training, and tools. Where assessment works well, money is dedicated to developing the required pieces of the continuous data system (Brunner et al., 2005; Cosner, 2011). Funds are set aside to provide time for teachers to learn about the workings of assessment programs (Young, 2006). Ample time for collaborative work is routinely cited in the research (Ingram et al., 2004). Time to collect, analyze, and put data to use is essential (Kerr et al., 2006; Wayman & Stringfield, 2006). Particularly salient is "furnishing instructional resources linked to issues arising from data analysis" (Young, 2006, p. 540), helping teachers master more effective teaching strategies (Dannetta, 2002; Datnow et al., 2008). At a more concrete level, resources include tools and protocols to use with the data system and in turning information into more effective instruction (Kerr et al., 2006; Levin & Datnow, 2012).

Important also is time for professional development, the building of individual and collective knowledge and skills in the assessment domain (Blase & Kirby, 2009; Cosner, 2011) or the "building of strong human capacity for data-driven inquiry" (Kerr et al., 2006, p. 498). Targeted assistance or "data support personnel" (Datnow et al., 2008, p. 34) is a resource in the area of professional development often seen in the assessment research. Here, we find the provision of help in the form of data coaches and opportunities to work on data teams (Kerr et al., 2006). This work is designed to mentor "teachers in managing and using data" (Datnow et al., 2008, p. 34). This type of mentoring is sometimes extended to include the new instructional practices that derive from thoughtful use of data (Johnson & Asera, 1999; Young, 2006). Overall then, we find time being devoted to understanding the data system and to learning how to strengthen teaching and learning (Kerr et al., 2006; Young, 2006).

The final resource is the presence of a well-developed system of assessment that guides data-based inquiry (Kerr et al., 2006), what Cosner (2011, p. 793) calls "enabling organizational conditions that offer support for the substantive inquiry-oriented work embedded in evidence-based collaboration." Halverson and colleagues (2007, p. 184) refer to this support as a "data-driven instructional system" while Kerr and team (2006, p. 508) call it a "data management system." We know that these systems attend to both the "infrastructure and methods" of assessment (Datnow et al., 2008, p. 32), especially the needed structural supports (Lachat & Smith, 2005; Levin & Datnow, 2012). These structures provide frameworks for the data collection inquiry cycle (McDougall et al., 2007; Supovitz & Klein, 2003), frameworks that are essential to "establish[ing] coherent and high-level data-system capability" (Lachat & Smith, 2005, p. 336).

Benefits

Assessment systems that work to address the barriers outlined earlier and that adhere to the elements and principles noted immediately above are expected to have positive impacts on teacher and students. The theory of action and the empirical evidence that powers this assumption rely on the creation of more effective schools by strengthening teaching and learning. The end point in this theoretical and conceptual chain is that "when teachers use in-depth analysis of assessment information to assist them to modify their programme, student achievement is raised" (Robinson, 2007, p. 15). That is, "previous research suggests that data-driven decision making has the potential to increase student performance" (Wohlstetter et al., 2008, p. 239).

The intermediate point between productive assessment and student learning is more informed, more responsive, and more effective teaching. More specifically, research on teacher perceptions reveals that well-grounded assessment systems lead to a number of improved conditions. There is an increased sense of clarity about teaching, a stronger sense of focus (Stringfield & Reynolds, 2012) in general and enhanced focus on student learning and success in particular (Lachat & Smith, 2005). Professionalism grows (Wayman & Stringfield, 2006). That is, "studies indicate that effective use of data . . . enhances the ability of schools to become learning organizations" (Datnow et al., 2008, p. 10). In important ways, there is a tightening up of the looseness of instructional practice in schools (Bryk et al., 2010). Data focus attention, concentration, and action (Blanc et al., 2010). Especially important here is that teachers often get to know their students better (Supovitz & Klein, 2003). That is, a productive assessment system "allow[s] them a deeper and more rounded view of their students' learning" (Wayman & Stringfield, 2006, p. 563), more "detailed pictures of their students' strengths and weaknesses" (Johnson & Asera, 1999, pp. 146–147). This, in turn, leads to "improved identification of students' learning needs" (Kerr et al., 2006, p. 501), particularly the needs of students "who are in need of additional assistance" (Supovitz & Klein, 2003, p. 19). The use of data to identify needs is associated with more and better responses to those needs (Wayman & Stringfield, 2006). This includes increases in expectations (Gray et al., 1999) and more appropriate diversification and differentiation of instruction (Datnow et al., 2008; Johnson & Asera, 1999), including more productive use of student groups (Wayman & Stringfield, 2006). Concomitantly, highly functional data systems allow teachers to discern their effectiveness with greater clarity and validity (Supovitz & Klein, 2003).

7

Community of Care and Support for Students

As we have reported throughout the book, schools that serve children and young people well are defined by two anchoring pillars, strong academic press and supportive culture of care and support. Ancess (2000, p. 595) refers to this as "a combination of nurture and rigor or affiliation and intellectual development," and Bryk, Sebring, Allensworth, Luppescu, & Easton (2010, p. 74) characterize it as "a press toward academic achievement . . . coupled with personal support from teachers." We reviewed the evidence on this mixture and reported that focusing primarily on the academic side of the equation is insufficient (Shannon & Bylsma, 2002; Thompson & O'Quinn, 2001), especially for students placed in peril by poverty (Becker & Luthar, 2002; Rumberger, 2011). Academic press alone "does not attend sufficiently to the quality of social relations required for effective teaching and learning" (Goddard, Salloum, & Berebitsky, 2009, p. 293). That is, schools with strong press can still prove inadequate if they provide little attention to the social and relationship dimensions of education (Crosnoe, 2011; Felner, Seitsinger, Brand, Burns, & Bolton, 2007; Quint, 2006).

At the same time, we know that nearly exclusive attention to culture is problematic as well, that it is a "necessary, but not sufficient factor in promoting worthwhile forms of student achievement" (Newmann, Rutter, & Smith, 1989, p. 225). A number of landmark studies have revealed how overemphasis on culture can lead to a lowering of academic expectations (Cusick, 1983; Powell, Farrar, & Cohen, 1985; Sedlak,

Wheeler, Pullin, & Cusick, 1986). More recent analysis confirms that featuring culture at the expense of academic press is not a wise pathway for school leaders to pursue, nor a destination to which they should steer their schools (Murphy, Beck, Crawford, & Hodges, 2001; Shouse, 1996). Too great an emphasis on providing nurture and support can constrain educators from promoting serious academic engagement (Farrell, 1990). The concern is that students may "be exposed to socially therapeutic rather than intellectually demanding values and activities, and that their schools' efforts to build supportive and cohesive communities may actually help divert attention from academic goals" (Shouse, 1996, p. 52). Communal support for students, separate from focus on achievement, creates distinct complications for students (Newmann & Wehlage, 1994; Page, 1991). When teachers want "more than anything . . . [for] students to know [they] care about them" (Nystrand, 1997, p. 53), they can "kill with kindness" (Sadker & Sadker, 1994, p. 124). When this occurs, "there [does] not seem to be any subject matter other than . . . cordial relations" (Cusick, 1983, p. 53), and caring separated from challenge contributes to student disengagement (Page, 1991). We must not lose sight of the fact that community is in the service of learning (Ancess, 2003; Antrop-González & De Jesús, 2006; Shouse, 1996).

We also know that because there is a "fundamental relation between learning and social interaction" (Eckert, 1989, p. 183) that press and support work best when they are viewed as an amalgam (Murphy, 2013), or conceptualized as two strands of DNA that wrap around each other (Dinham, 2005; Kruse, Seashore Louis, & Bryk, 1995; Strahan, 2003). "Rigor and care must be braided together" (Fine, cited in Antrop-González, 2006, p. 274) to work best. There are some differences in the literature, however, about the relative importance of each strand and the order in which they load into the success equation. What is not in question is the fact that both need to be present and that the specific context will help determine issues of importance and timing (Murphy, 2013).

THE POWER OF COMMUNITY FOR STUDENTS, TEACHERS, AND PARENTS

In this section, the focus is on the cultural element in the school improvement algorithm. However, given what we just reported, academic emphasis is never far from the center stage. Yet, the spotlight is consciously centered on culture. According to Sweetland and Hoy (2000, p. 705), culture is a "concept used to capture the basic and enduring quality of organizational life." It encompasses the values and norms that define a school (Dumay, 2009; Franklin & Streeter, 1995; Rossmiller, 1992). It is "those facets of organization that reflect underlying assumptions guiding decisions, behavior, and beliefs within organizations" (Scribner, Cockrell, Cockrell, & Valentine, 1999, p. 155). It can be thought of as the personality of the school (Hoy, Hannum, & Tschannen-Moran, 1998). In this volume, we use culture, climate, and environment synonymously.

We describe school culture in terms of community, a construct that is defined in a variety of overlapping ways (Beck & Foster, 1999). Battistich, Solomon, Kim, Watson, and Schaps (1995, p. 628) use community to capture "the psychological aspects of social settings that satisfy group members' needs for belonging and meaning." It consists of ingredients, such as membership, integration, and influence (Baker, Terry, Bridger, & Winsor, 1997; Osterman, 2000). As we have illustrated throughout earlier chapters, community stands in juxtaposition to institutionalism and hierarchy as an organizational frame of reference (Beck & Foster, 1999; McLaughlin & Talbert, 2001; Murphy, 1991; Scribner et al., 1999; Sergiovanni, 1994).

> Communally organized schools are marked by three *core components:* (1) a set of shared and commonly understood organizational values and beliefs about institutional purpose, what students should learn, how adults and students should behave, and students' potential as learners and citizens; (2) a common agenda of activities that defines school membership, fosters meaningful social interaction among members, and links them to school traditions; and (3) the distinctive pattern of social relations embodying an ethic of caring visible in both collegial and student-teacher relationships. (Shouse, 1996, p. 51)

In later chapters, we attend to "communities of professionalism" for teachers and "communities of engagement for parents." Here the focus is on "communities of pastoral care for students." We suggest that understanding of such communities is critical for school leaders because at the heart of the educational narrative is this essential truth: "It is students themselves, in the end, not teachers, who decide what students will learn" (Hattie, 2009, p. 241) and students do not volunteer effort when they are detached from school (Crosnoe, 2011; Newmann, 1981; Weis, 1990). Creating attachments is key to the work of educators, and leaders need to learn all we can about accomplishing that goal (Murphy et al., 2001). Analysis is also critical because, as we document below, supportive community for students exercises strong influence on school improvement defined in terms of student learning (Carbonaro & Gamoran, 2002; Rodríguez, 2008; Rumberger, 2011), "it explains a large amount of the variation in school effects" (Leithwood, Jantzi, & Steinbach, 1999, p. 83). Indeed, "failure to examine school culture can easily lead to ineffective reform" (Rodríguez, 2008, p. 760).

SUPPORTIVE LEARNING COMMUNITY FOR STUDENTS: A FRAMEWORK

Backdrop

We begin by reintroducing the essential point raised above: schooling for students is profoundly voluntary. Children have to "go to school." They need to debark from the bus and go into the building. Beyond that, especially as they mature, the decision to "do schooling" is substantially their own. This means, of course, that they are key decision makers in the learning production. The major purpose of supportive learning community is to positively influence students' willingness to learn what the school believes they require to be successful in life, to cause students to embrace academic challenges, and to help them reach those ends. Two corollaries arise here. First, to a much greater extent than has been the case, schooling needs to be understood through the eyes of students, not as a goal in itself but rather because it provides the framework for a school to achieve its mission: ensuring that all children reach ambitious targets of academic success. Second, adult actions need to be shaped based on those insights from students (Murphy, 2016).

Educators here have three choices, ignore this reality, fight to change it, or use it as a platform for action. The first and second options have been the tools of choice for education historically. This is hardly surprising given the institutional nature of schooling and the managerial logic of school leadership (Callahan, 1962; Cuban, 1988). The problem is, however, that these choices have not been especially effective (Boyer, 1983; Crosnoe, 2011; Cuban, 1988; Eckert, 1989; Farrell, 1990; Goodlad, 1984; Newmann, 1981; Patterson, Beltyukova, Berman, & Francis, 2007; Sizer, 1984; Weis, 1990), especially for students placed at risk by society and schooling (Alexander, Entwisle, & Horsey, 1997; Chavis, Ward, Elwell, & Barret, 1997; Murphy & Tobin, 2011a). Supportive learning community for students moves us to option three, weaving the wisdom, needs, concerns, interests, and worries of students deeply into the "doing of schooling" without sacrificing academic press. Or more globally, it requires school leaders to acknowledge that achieving valued outcomes for students "involves, as a first step, recognizing that school culture is the setting in which [students] are being educated" (Crosnoe, 2011, p. 40). For example, we know that social concerns form the caldron of interest for students in schools (Crosnoe, 2011; Newmann, Wehlage, & Lamburn, 1992). We also understand that to reach working-class youngsters, leaders need to address social connections beyond the schoolhouse (Eckert, 1989; Farrell, 1990). The charge for school people is to learn how to work these and related realities productively in the service of helping students master essential academic goals.

In terms of background knowledge, it is also important to underscore a deep line of empirical findings in the research. Specifically, the school communities in which many young persons find themselves, especially older students and youngsters in peril (Adams, 2010; Baker et al., 1997; Quint, 2006), do not exert the positive influence and support necessary for them to commit to "do schooling" (Balfanz, Herzog, & MacIver, 2007; Croninger & Lee, 2001; Newmann et al., 1992). While this is not the place to examine this line of analysis in detail, we need to point out that student disengagement, often passive, sometimes active, is common in schools (Conchas, 2001; Patterson et al., 2007; Quint, 2006). This is hardly surprising given that one of the pillars of institutions and bureaucracy is impersonality (Murphy, 1991). As Ancess (2003, p. 83) reminds us, because of this "schools are conventionally organized as though relationships are not only unimportant and irrelevant, but an obstacle to efficient operation."

Model

Analysts have uncovered a good deal of knowledge about what supportive communities of care and support for students look like and how they function. Building from that work, we provide our model of personalized community in Figure 7.1. We see there that supportive learning community is defined by essential norms (e.g., care). These norms combine to produce intermediate outcomes like student learning dispositions which, in turn, lead to academic engagement. All of this powers student learning.

The model employs a two-stroke engine, one working to overcome liabilities and the other to build up assets. To begin with then, communities of pastoral care "foster productive learning by removing developmentally hazardous conditions" (Felner et al., 2007, p. 210). They suppress factors

Figure 7.1   Communities of Pastoral Care for Students

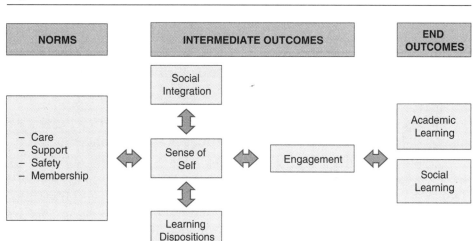

that undermine hopes for success, such as the formation of dysfunctional and oppositional peer cultures. Personalization damps down aspects of schooling that push students away from engaging the work of "doing school" well. A supportive learning community provides a "protective power" (Garmezy, 1991, p. 427) while attacking social problems that place students in peril (Christle, Jolivette, & Nelson, 2005; Crosnoe, 2011). It helps create a "social environment that neutralizes or buffers home stresses" (Alexander & Entwisle, 1996, p. 77) and community problems and individual characteristics that foster social marginalization and academic disengagement (Demaray & Malecki, 2002b; Garmezy, 1991).

Concomitantly, supportive learning environments create assets, social and human capital, to draw youngsters into the hard work that is required to be successful in school (Ancess, 2003; Goddard, 2003; Supovitz, 2002, 2008). They transform schools into places "where the social and pastoral environment nurture[s] a desire to learn in students" (Blair, 2002, p. 184). Assets, such as care and warmth, are stockpiled to assist in helping students reach ambitious learning targets (Demaray & Malecki, 2002b; Quint, 2006; Roth & Brooks-Gunn, 2003).

Cautions and Reminders

Before we unpack the model of student personalization in Figure 7.1, we reintroduce some reminders, central themes that appear throughout these chapters that have special importance for student culture. We begin with the hallmark finding that leadership is the essential catalyst to ensure that a positive school culture takes root and flourishes (Barnett & McCormick, 2004; Bruggencate, Luyten, Scheerens, & Sleegers, 2012; Mukuria, 2002): "Critical to the creation of maintenance of school culture are the leadership practices of the school principal" (Barnett, McCormick, & Conners, 2001, p. 25; see also Brookover et al., 1978; Brookover, Beady, Flood, Schweitzer, & Wisenbaker, 1979; Cosner, 2011; Dinham, 2005; Hallinger & Murphy, 1985; Heck & Hallinger, 2010; Supovitz, Sirinides, & May, 2010; Wahlstrom & Louis, 2008). Indeed, a principal's influence on the learning culture of the school may be his or her most powerful tool to influence student achievement (Blase & Kirby, 2009; Louis, Dretzke, & Wahlstrom, 2010), especially in middle and high schools (Sebastian & Allensworth, 2012).

We also need to reinforce the structural law that surfaced in earlier chapters. That is, structural changes do not predict organizational outcomes. The key is the powerful medicine that structures are supposed to carry. As has been seen more often than not, structures arrive without the medicine. Schools are left with the empty containers. This cautionary tale is especially relevant in the domain of communities of pastoral care for students because much of the reform here is structural in design, e.g., advisory periods, academies, small schools, and so forth (Iatarola, Schwartz,

Stiefel, & Chellman, 2008; Patterson et al., 2007; Smerdon, Borman, & Hannaway, 2009). There is a robust if misguided sense in many schools, and by many school leaders, that these interventions by themselves will power up desired improvements in culture along with the accompanying organizational outcomes. School administrators need to be vigilant about being seduced by the logic of structure.

It is instructive to recall another of our laws of school improvement here: context always matters. "Effective practice is inevitably highly contextualized" (Battistich, Solomon, Watson, & Schaps, 1997, p. 150), and "where students attend school matters" (Crosnoe, 2011, p. 56). Context holds an especially important role in the supportive student learning play (Fredricks, Blumenfeld, & Paris, 2004; Guest & Schneider, 2003). We know, for example, that demographic factors have a robust influence on student culture (Farrell, 1990; Feldman & Matjasko, 2005; Newmann et al., 1989). Family conditions (e.g., family size, age of mother) influence school culture, sometimes for the better, sometimes for the worse (Eckert, 1989; Ensminger & Slusarcick, 1992; Rumberger, 2011). So too do neighborhood conditions (e.g., availability of social services) (Gonzalez & Padilla, 1997; Murphy, 2010). Cutting across all of these, of course, are the thick cords of socioeconomic status (SES) (e.g., occupation, income) (Eckert, 1989, Guest & Schneider, 2003) and race (Balfanz et al., 2007; Bloomberg, Ganey, Alba, Quintero, & Alvarez-Alcantara, 2003; Jordan & Cooper, 2003). The unmistakable conclusion here is "that sense of community for students is negatively correlated with school poverty" (Battistich et al., 1997, p. 142), membership in racial and ethnic minority groups (Adams, 2010; Lee & Burkham, 2003), and marginalized status in society (Crosnoe, 2011).

We know that there is a varying relationship between school level and the importance of a personalized culture (Demaray & Malecki, 2002a). Community becomes especially significant in the early to mid-teen years and less so at the tail end of high school (Crosnoe, 2011; Goodenow, 1993; Ma, 2003). School has a strong effect on supportive learning culture, independent of family SES (Rumberger, 2011). School size has been linked to personalization as well (Bryk et al., 2010; Fredricks et al., 2004; Lee & Burkham, 2003), with small size creating opportunities for communal norms to take root, especially in schools with large percentages of students in peril (Lee & Burkham, 2003; Hattie, 2009). A more supportive community is especially important for students who have limited access to social capital outside of school (Croninger & Lee, 2001; Goddard, 2003; Murphy, 2010), for students from low-income homes (Battistich et al., 1995, 1997), and for students who are socially and academically at risk (Battistich et al., 1997; Croninger & Lee, 2001; Darling-Hammond, Ancess, & Ort, 2002). Pastoral care "shows its strongest positive relations with student measures in the highest poverty schools" (Battistich et al., 1997, p. 144).

Chapter 7

NORMS OF COMMUNITIES OF PASTORAL CARE FOR STUDENTS

The DNA of pastoral care for students, "a philosophy of caring and personalization" (Ackerman & Maslin-Ostrowski, 2002, p. 79), is contained in the norms listed on the left-hand side of the model in Figure 7.1. These elements are most powerful when they are in play at both the classroom and school levels and in both individual and group relationships. Consistent with our two-stroke engine, efforts here are designed both to deinstitutionalize the school climate and to add community assets to the culture. Four macrolevel norms are featured in the model: care, support, safety, and membership. Before we examine these values, however, we highlight the theme that forms the heart and soul of pastoral care.

Teacher-Student Relationships

We know that positive relationships are essential to all forms of community in schools, for students, teachers, and parents (Ancess, 2003). As Bryk and colleagues (2010), Rumberger (2011), and Baker et al. (1997) remind us, these relationships are a hallmark ingredient in school improvement work, the "most powerful driving force of schools" (Ancess, 2003, p. 127). This is the case because "schools are fundamentally social institutions that depend daily on the quality of interpersonal relations with which they are imbued" (Goddard et al., 2009, p. 293).

More specifically, analysts help us see that "student-teacher relationships matter for the development of children" (Adams, 2010, p. 258), that positive linkages between students and teachers are foundational for creating personalized communities for students (Ancess, 2003; Newmann, 1992; Roth & Brooks-Gunn, 2003). These relationships are heavily responsible for establishing the educational value of classrooms. They make academic press a possibility for many students (Darling-Hammond et al., 2002; Rodriguez, 2008). Because many students "learn only from teachers promoting healthy personal relationships" (Opdenakker, Maulana, & Brock, 2012, p. 99), "the power of positive teacher-student relationships is critical for learning to occur" (Hattie, 2009, p. 118) and for students to experience academic success (Darling-Hammond et al. 2002; Goddard, 2003; Goodenow, 1993). These relationships have "far-reaching significance in terms of the various trajectories that children follow throughout their schooling experience" (Birch & Ladd, 1997). Positive connections create the social capital needed for effective work to unfold in classrooms (Adams & Forsyth, 2009; Ancess, 2003; Croninger & Lee, 2001). They provide the engine and the drivetrain to power the norms in personalized communities (Epstein & McPartland, 1976; Farrell, 1990; Patterson et al., 2007).

These positive relationships are of singular benefit for students from low-income homes and in schools with high concentrations of students in peril (Battistich et al., 1995; Marks, 2000; Murphy, 2010). When these relationships do not exist, students are placed in a compromised position relative to learning (Rodriguez, 2008). Or as Croninger and Lee (201, p. 569) assert, "an absence of positive social relationships and contacts with teachers denies students resources that help them develop positively." Deteriorating and negative relationships are even worse (Fredricks et al., 2004). They are "destructive to student outcomes and development" (Opdenakker et al., 2012, p. 95). In short, "relationships mediate student performance" (Ancess, 2003, p. 82; Baker et al., 1997; Crosnoe, 2011; Goodenow, 1993). We examine these relationships between teachers and students below in our analysis of the four norms of community for students.

Norm of Care

We know that students arrive at school ready to learn. They naturally engage in the work of schooling. As they progress, many youngsters divert from the pathway of active engagement. They pull away from school. Some of these students become passively engaged. They attend school, collect Carnegie units, stay quietly at the back of the room of academic pursuits, do not work especially hard, and do not receive a quality education. These are the withdrawn and anonymous. Other youngsters exercise a more aggressive form of disengagement. They move in opposition to school values and expectations. These are the resistant and the alienated. Some from each of these two groups, the passive and actively disengaged, simply withdraw from the game altogether, dropping out of school. The number of students who follow each of these pathways varies by school level and critical context variables, such as socioeconomic status and minority status (Crosnoe, 2011; Eckert, 1989; Farrell, 1990), and of course the quality of student community.

We know that the actions of schools have a good deal to do with the engagement choices of students. Particularly salient here, as we reported above, are the relationships between teachers and students. Good schools keep students actively engaged by demonstrating an ethic of care and robust systems of academic and social support. Because some students in all schools are free to disengage and many students in some schools are free to do so, schools are filled with a good number of unconnected youngsters. Care and the other norms of communities of pastoral care for students close the door to disengagement and failure.

In Chapter 9, we explore norms from the perspective of teacher professional communities. Here we simply note that these professional norms are also woven into the relational tapestry between teachers and students (Murphy, 2016). Included here are values, such as commitment and

Figure 7.2   Levels of Engagement and Disengagement in Schools

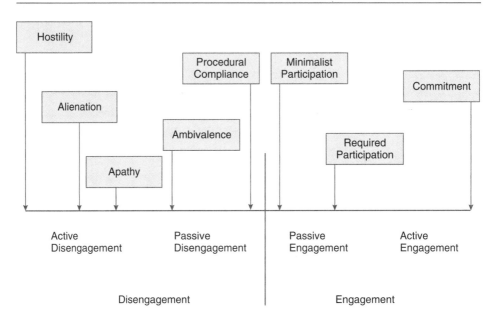

dedication (Newmann, 1992; Phillips, 2003), sense of efficacy (Leithwood et al., 1999; Silins & Mulford, 2010), persistence (Ancess, 2003), acceptance of responsibility for student success (Wilson & Corbett, 1999), and effort (Louis, 2007).

Caring has been studied by scholars in a variety of disciplines and professions (Smylie, Murphy, & Louis, in press). Here the spotlight is on caring relationships between teachers culled from studies of schools that are effective in ensuring that all pupils reach ambitious targets of performance.

Although it is much too infrequently discussed as such, students routinely remind us that a cardinal element of the norm of care is *teachers who work to the best of their ability,* who consistently bring their *"A"* games to the classroom—who challenge students to do their best work (Felner et al., 2007; Marks, 2000; Sanders & Harvey, 2002). Scholars also document what an instructional *"A"* game looks like. It includes working hard to make classes meaningful and to show that meaningfulness to youngsters. It means teachers not simply going through the motions, doing their jobs, but rather demonstrating palpable interest in whether students learn or not (Fredricks et al., 2004; Newmann et al., 1992; Wilson & Corbett, 1999). Teachers who work to peak performance acknowledge the difficulties of teaching, especially teaching students who are struggling, but they embrace those challenges not offering excuses and justifications (Roney, Coleman, & Schlichting, 2007). They, according to Shouse (1996, p. 66), "appreciate the rugged demands of learning." They are firm and orchestrate structured classrooms (Ancess, 2003; Wilson & Corbett, 1999). These teachers are painstaking in their efforts to ensure that all students are brought along and successfully complete learning journeys, not jettisoned on the trip (Ancess, 2003; Wilson & Corbett, 1999). According to students, teachers accomplish this by establishing clear goals, maps, and benchmarks of success and by providing close monitoring, abundant feedback, and targeted encouragement and help (DeRidder, 1991; Wilson & Corbett, 1999). They work hard to connect with students, not simply to present information (Wilson & Corbett, 1999).

Teachers bring their best to the classroom day in and day out, that is, they demonstrate care and emphasize what Newmann (1981) calls authentic work. They employ varied approaches to learning and emphasize active and creative work while ensuring that students clearly understand what they need to do, how they need to meet the challenges, and why (Fredricks et al., 2004; Wilson & Corbett, 1999). "A" game teachers make learning relevant to their young charges (Conchas, 2001; Newmann, 1981). They focus on intrinsically interesting activities (Fredricks et al., 2004; Newmann, 1992) and "tasks that are considered meaningful, valuable, significant, and worthy of one's efforts" (Newmann et al., 1992, p. 23). They also underscore collaborative activities for students and flexible use of time (Fredricks et al., 2004; Newmann et al., 1992). Teachers who routinely strive for personal excellence in the classroom put learning in perspective for youngsters and work hard to align and integrate goals, activities, and structures for learning (Battistich et al., 1995; Marks, 2000). Caring teachers demonstrate considerable imagination, live beyond the textbook, and unearth multiple pathways to accomplish work and show success (Wilson & Corbett, 1999).

Another hallmark element of caring relations in schools is the willingness of adults to reveal *themselves to children* as persons, not solely as organizational functionaries (Adams & Forsyth, 2009; Antrop-González, 2006; Newmann et al., 1992). They do this by opening aspects of their nonprofessional lives to their pupils, especially incidents that are relevant to the decisions and struggles that confront youngsters (Rodriguez, 2008). "The self that teachers offer is a student self rather than a career self" (Farrell, 1990, p. 25). According to Adams (2010), part of this opening process is the willingness of teachers to allow themselves to be vulnerable in front of their students. This stance "humanizes the teacher as a person" (Rodriguez, 2008, p. 765) and helps establish a frame of authenticity for student-teacher connections (Raywid, 1995). It also permits students to feel safe in sharing their "hopes, dreams, problems, and disappointments" (Reitzug & Patterson, 1998, p. 167).

Although as overlooked as teachers giving students their best, care is also fundamentally about standards and about *challenging students* to meet and exceed robust expectations (Alexander & Entwisle, 1996; Johnson & Asera, 1999; Roth & Brooks-Gunn, 2003). There is abundant evidence on this point: "Teachers who push students prove to be an important dimension to the personalized student-adult relationship" (Rodriguez, 2008, p. 772). Perhaps the essential point here is the integration of push and press with other elements of care discussed above (Murphy, 2013), a practice labeled as "hard caring" by Antrop-González and De Jesús, 2006, p. 413 and "rugged care" by Shouse (1996, p. 48). There is an especially valuable line of research that confirms that many students, especially students in peril, will not benefit unless the elements of care and the other norms of personalization are blended (Becker & Luthar, 2002; Roth & Brooks-Gunn, 2003). When this cocktail of push and support is in place, students are able to see challenge "as coming from a place of teacher concern about the students themselves" (Patterson et al., 2007, p. 136). Challenge also means providing students with as much responsibility as they can handle (Joselowsky, 2007) and upholding a commitment to help them succeed (Wilson & Corbett, 1999). Obstacles are acknowledged, but they are not accepted as explanations for lack of performance (Rodriguez, 2008; Shouse, 1996).

Challenge for students in a caring environment is laced with clear and high expectations (Newmann, 1981; Rodriguez 2008; Wilson & Corbett, 1999). The school asks more of students. There is strong academic and social press (Ancess, 2003; Johnson & Asera, 1999). They place higher order cognitive demands on students, moving beyond basic skills to higher order thinking (Battistich et al., 1995; Marks, 2000). Educators expect students "to be active interpreters of knowledge rather than docile recipients" (Newmann, 1992, p. 185). In schools where care is engrained in the culture, teachers provide more challenging assignments and tasks (Fredricks et al., 2004), "more complex and cognitively challenging class work" (Marks, 2000, p. 157) and greater depth of understanding (Newmann, 1981). They expect students to take intellectual risks and reward them for doing so (Cooper, 1996).

In strong communities, care is more than providing high expectations and challenge, that is, academic and social press. Effective schools take away the possibility of passive involvement. Students cannot check out or drift through class (Ancess, 2003; Huberman, Parrish, Hannan, Arellanes, & Shambaugh, 2011). They are pulled into the game. No spectators are allowed. Neither are students allowed to easily accept failure. "Teachers not only believe that students [can] complete their work, they do everything possible to make that happen" (Wilson & Corbett, 1997, p. 77). In caring environments "teachers make it harder to fail than succeed" (Ancess, 2000, p. 74). They "stay on students" to complete their work (Wilson & Corbett, 1999, p. 80), requiring them to bring their "*A*" games to the classroom. Teachers are there to help students succeed, not simply to teach subject matter. They push and pull students to the goal line (Ancess, 2003; Darling-Hammond et al., 2002; Oakes & Guiton, 1995) and acknowledge and celebrate successes along the way. Classes are rich with extra help and teacher-guided second chances (Wilson & Corbett, 1999). They are particularly adept at addressing "patterns of behaviors and performances that are unproductive and problematic" (Ancess, 2003, p. 76) for student development (Cooper, 1996).

Earlier, we argued that high-functioning communities for students close down opportunities for students to select pathways of disengagement and disaffiliation. Here we suggest that they also preclude the selection of failure in the face of rigorous expectations and standards (Ancess, 2000; Huberman et al., 2011; Shear et al., 2008). Efforts here pivot on the positive perspective of assets-based analysis we outlined above and the concomitant to the elimination of deficit-based thinking (Antrop-González & De Jesús, 2006; Hattie, 2009). Possibilities hold the high ground: "Youth are resources to be developed, not problems to be fixed" (Bloomberg et al., 2003, p. 50). All of this "hard care" is layered over significant opportunities for students to be successful (Antrop-González, 2006; Strahan, 2003).

A fourth dimension of caring is *knowing students well*, a quality Ancess (2003, p. 65) refers to as "intimacy" and a condition that Bryk and colleagues (2010, p. 58) establish as "essential to the effective design of classroom lessons that advance academic learning for all." In a caring environment, educators make efforts to learn about the youngsters (Antrop-González, 2006). They commit the time necessary for this understanding to form and grow (Ancess, 2000). Principals and teachers know what is unfolding in the lives of their students, "socially and at home. They know their students as learners in the class and in the classes of their colleagues" (Ancess, 2000, pp. 65–66). They are cognizant of the social and cultural worlds in which their pupils live (Antrop-González & De Jesús, 2006; McLaughlin, 1994;

Table 7.1   Aspects of the Norm of Caring in Student Community

Working to the best of their ability
Challenging students
Sharing one's self as a person
Knowing students well
Valuing students
Demonstrating interest and investment
Accessing
Seeing through the eyes of students
Establishing trustworthiness
Respecting students
Treating students fairly
Providing recognition

Rodriguez, 2008). Teachers employ this knowledge to help students learn and to pursue their personal goals (Bryk, Lee, & Holland, 1993).

In personalized communities, caring is defined also by *students being valued* (Battistich et al., 1995; Conchas, 2001; Scheurich, 1998). According to Reitzug and Patterson (1998), this translates into teacher efforts to connect with students on a personal level rather than on a categorical basis (McLaughlin & Talbert, 2001). More specifically, it means that each student is accepted as a person, someone who has value as an individual and as a member of communities in the school (Ancess, 2003; Conchas, 2001; Rodriguez, 2008), someone "worthy of mentorship and guidance" (Antrop-González, 2006, p. 288). In caring communities, being valued is conveyed through teachers being "person centered" (Hattie, 2009, p. 119). Valued status is communicated to youngsters when educators express concern for what is happening in the world of the student and when they invest time and energy in developing and maintaining personal linkages to students (Farrell, 1990; Hattie, 2009; Wilson & Corbett, 1999). Included here is a not-so-subtle switch from seeing students as problems to seeing them as "willing and capable human beings" (Reitzug & Patterson, 1998, p. 168) who need help to address challenges in their lives. In these valued relationships there is a tendency to avoid blaming youngsters when things do not go well (Patterson et al., 2007).

In a related vein, caring is demonstrated when teachers and leaders *take interest in and invest in their students* (Galletta & Ayala, 2008; Croninger & Lee, 2001; Wilson & Corbett, 1999). This includes devoting considerable personal and professional capital into one's work with children (McDougall, Saunders, & Goldenberg, 2007; Strahan, 2003) and the development and honoring of reciprocal obligations (Antrop-González & De Jesús, 2006). It includes being accessible to students on both academic and personal fronts (Goddard, 2003; Hattie, 2009; Noguera, 1996), "in their education and their lives" (Patterson et al., 2007, p. 128). Investment tells students that they are acknowledged for who they are as persons and for their potential (Ma, 2003; Steele, 1992). At the deepest level, it includes a ferocious unwillingness to permit students to founder or fail (Farrell, 1990). Students see "teachers as truly interested and invested in enabling [them] to succeed" (Wilson & Corbett, 1999, p. 73). They feel that adults are willing to provide personal attention (Cooper, Ponder, Merritt, & Matthews, 2005; Cotton, 2000; Rodriguez, 2008).

Caring means that educators are *accessible to students* (Darling-Hammond et al., 2002; Newmann et al., 1992). A dimension of accessibility is willingness to help, an ingredient that cuts across the norms of care and support (Rutter, Maughan, Mortimore, & Ouston, 1979). Another aspect is making time available to students, of building closeness (Birch & Ladd, 1997) in the context of warm relationships (Opdenakker et al., 2012, Strahan, 2003). Invitational threads are also woven into the fabric of accessibility (Ancess, 2003). So too are efforts to pull students into active participation. That is, accessibility means not exiting in the face of student resistance or oppositionality and not permitting youngsters to exit either (Newmann, 1981). The literature refers to this as maintaining beliefs in students through hardships and refusing to give up on students (Ancess, 2003). More aggressively, it is appropriate to think about accessibility in terms of advocacy for youngsters (Ancess, 2003). In strong, personalized communities, educators stand up for students to ensure that conditions for success are forthcoming (Rodriguez, 2008). Students feel that their teachers are looking out for them. They are not left to pursue success on their own or only with the help of peers (Roney et al., 2007): "Teachers can be counted on to be accessible, accepting, and helpful" (Ancess, 2003, p. 68).

Another theme in the chronicle on the norm of care in personalized communities is constructed around the ability and willingness of principals and teachers to *see things through the eyes of students* (Farrell, 1990; Murphy, 2016), in popular parlance to know where students are coming from (Rodriguez, 2008). It includes a willingness to see and understand the developmental needs of students (Ancess, 2003) and to "embrace students' priorities" (p. 8). It means taking the world of students seriously (Csikszentmihalyi & Larson, 1984), remembering that things that are important to students are important regardless of whether they are important to teachers or not (Murphy, 2013). More importantly, it entails efforts to adapt schooling to the needs of students, not requiring students to constantly remold themselves to fit the school (Bulkley & Hicks, 2005; Day, 2005; Quint, 2006). This in turn requires seeing children as whole and in a positive light, not as defiant and damaged (Becker & Luthar, 2002). Viewing from the perspective of students requires an active responsiveness to youngsters. It means that when the norm of care is present, educators listen to students (Adams & Forsyth, 2009; Antrop-González, 2006), and that students believe that they are heard (Reitzug & Patterson, 1998; Rodriguez, 2008).

As we described above, trust is the foundation for relationships (Adams & Forsyth, 2009). Thus we should not be surprised to learn that an important piece of the caring storyline is educators *assessing youngsters as trustworthy* (Battistich et al., 1997) and students reciprocating (Adams, 2010; Antrop-González & De Jesús, 2006). The rule here is universal: no trust, no relationship (Bryk et al., 2010; Newmann, 1981). As with other dimensions of care, we find asset-based as opposed to deficit-based assessments in our analysis of trustworthiness (Ancess, 2003). Educators need to earn the mantle of trustworthiness from pupils. This they do by being open, reliable, honest, benevolent, and competent in the eyes of students (Adams & Forsyth, 2009).

Treating youngsters with respect is a tenth dimension in the web of care (Ancess, 2003; Antrop-González & De Jesús, 2006; Hattie, 2009). Central points here are that educators must give respect to receive it in return

(Rodriguez, 2008) and "that for many students respect precedes engagement" (p. 767). One half of the storyline here is the avoidance of actions that demean or belittle youngsters (Antrop-González, 2006; Murphy, 2010). The other half of the narrative is the use of positive actions that demonstrate the fact that students are held in high regard (Raywid, 1995; Rodriguez, 2008). Treating students as young adults is important here (Ancess, 2003), with a sense of dignity (Leithwood et al., 1999). So too is the provision of opportunities for participation and voice. Actions that affirm students' cultural, racial, and ethnic backgrounds show respect (González & Padilla, 1997; Noguera, 1996; Scanlan & Lopez, 2012). So too do behaviors that honor the assets students bring to the classroom more generally (Hattie, 2009).

Students possess a refined sense of equity. For that reason, care is often defined in terms of fairness, especially the perceived *fairness* of educators in their treatment of students (Ma, 2003; Patterson et al., 2007; Wilson & Corbett, 1999). Reliability and consistency are key elements of fairness for students (Adams, 2010; Adams & Forsyth, 2009).

Finally, recognizing the link between the learning environment and motivation (Opdenakker et al., 2012), care includes students experiencing success and opportunities to receive *recognition* for that success (Csikszentmihalyi & Larson, 1984; Foster & St. Hilaire, 2003; Sather, 1999). That is, schools create a "culture of success" for students (Rodriguez, 2008, p. 776) and opportunities for acknowledgement. Newmann and his colleagues (1992, p. 22) underscore this element of care when they report that "if the school is to nurture a sense of membership, its most important task is to ensure students experience success in the development of competence."

Norm of Support

A second critical norm in communities of pastoral care for students is support (Battistich et al., 1995; Conchas, 2001; Goodenow, 1993). As is the case with care, it operates on two fronts. On one hand, support buffers students from events that can damage them and their success in school (Bloomberg et al., 2003; Demaray & Malecki, 2002a). Or as Jackson and Warren (2000, p. 1452) so nicely capture the idea, "social support is a possible immunity to the effects of life events." On the other hand, support unleashes a host of positive actions in the service of students. Researchers help us see that this norm of support is most critical as youngsters mature (i.e., with adolescents), with children who lack a dense web of support outside of school, and for students placed at risk by society (Croninger & Lee, 2001; Murphy & Tobin, 2011a; Roth, Brooks-Gunn, Murray, & Foster, 1998). Support can best be thought of as the extension of help by educators coupled with students' understanding that they can count on that assistance (Ancess, 2003; Antrop-González & De Jesús, 2006; Louis & Marks, 1998). It is personalized relationships with teachers that make help-seeking and the provision of assistance part of the culture (Demaray & Malecki,

2002a; Rodriguez, 2008). The starting point here is teachers "understanding that their supportive role appears to play a significant part in students' attitudes about teachers and their school experience in general" (Demaray & Malecki, 2002b, p. 314).

Support is tightly linked to the norm of care. Indeed the two share a good deal of conceptual and applied space (Roth & Brooks-Gunn, 2003). Perhaps the best way to think about the two norms is to observe that much of the ability of schools to create support is a function of caring connections between teachers and students (Rodriguez, 2008). Getting to know students and creating personal relationships are important in their own right. The maximum gain occurs, however, when teachers use these caring linkages to support the academic and social development of their students (Ancess, 2003; Croninger & Lee, 2001).

The research allows us to distill overlapping types of support in personalized student communities of pastoral care. In particular, analysts highlight the importance of emotional support (Crosnoe, 2011; Demaray & Malecki, 2002a), social support (Goddard et al., 2009; Jackson & Warren, 2000), and academic support (Ancess, 2003; Antrop-González & De Jesús, 2006).

As with each of the norms, support can be defined by its essential elements, six in total. It is useful to think of these ingredients as overlapping and intertwined strands in the web of support. The first is the *provision of assistance* in the face of student help-seeking or intuited need for such help (Adams & Forsyth, 2009; Croninger & Lee, 2001). Informal and formal counseling is often noted in the research here (Raywid, 1995). Navigational assistance is also discussed (Quint, 2006). So too is the provision of assistance with school work (Antrop-González, 2006; Croninger & Lee, 2001). Assistance in helping youngsters master transitions in life is underscored as an especially powerful (and needed) form of aid (Jackson & Warren, 2000; Maguin & Loeber, 1996; Rodriguez, 2008).

Support includes *encouragement* as well (Balfanz et al., 2007). Mastering school is difficult work for many students and "to invest time and energy in the present young people need to believe that there is a viable future" (Joselowsky, 2007, p. 272). Teachers are in a unique position to help

Table 7.2   Aspects of the Norm of Support in Student Community

Provision of assistance
Encouragement
Availability of safety nets
Monitor
Mentor
Advocate

students see the potential for success, what Crosnoe (2011, p. 186) calls a "future orientation," when such possibilities are unclear for students (Rodriguez, 2008). Educators can open these doors through encouragement (Newmann, 1992; Roth et al., 1998), especially around the importance of investments in academic work (Hoy et al., 1998).

Providing safety nets is a third essential aspect of student support (Cooper et al., 2005). The core idea here is to prevent students from falling through the cracks, to "go missing" and be unnoticed (Allensworth & Easton, 2005). These protections provide another backstop against disengagement and failure. Good schools build these nets and legitimize and encourage the use of the interventions found therein (Ancess, 2000). In these schools, educators help students, they do not blame them for requiring assistance (Patterson et al., 2007).

Support also encompasses *monitoring* how well students are doing in school, socially, emotionally, and academically (Antrop-González & De Jesús, 2006; Gray et al., 1999; Quint, 2006), a type of "proactive troubleshooting" (Raywid, 1995, p. 53). It includes *mentoring young persons* toward success, a dimension that is especially powerful for students at risk of failure (Woloszyk, 1996).

Finally, *advocating for students* is a well-illuminated strand in the web of support (Murphy, Elliott, Goldring, & Porter, 2007; Rumberger, 2011). Here, support is defined as "personally negotiating" (O'Connor, 1997, p. 616) to ensure that students garner all the aid they require to be successful, both from the school and the larger community (Ancess, 2003; Cooper et al., 2005; Patterson, 2007). Collectively, support can be thought of as "responsibility for shepherding the student" (Balfanz et al., 2007, p. 232).

Before we close our discussion of the norms of care and support, it is helpful to highlight some of the concepts that make supportive and caring relationships work. The lynchpin is student access. Without contact, it is impossible to make caring and supportive relationships come to life (Reitzug & Patterson, 1998; Rodriguez, 2008). For care and support to power up attachment and subsequent student commitment and engagement, and to enhance academic and social learning, the quality and depth of interactions between students and teachers needs to increase. The time dimension here, a direct measure of students' judgments of teacher commitment (Ancess, 2003), can be addressed in a variety of ways. School expectations for student participation in teacher-facilitated academic and social activities are important. So too are educators' intentional communications of accessibility (Ancess, 2003). Increasing the ratio of adults to students can create time for relationships to take root and develop (Noguera, 1996). Enhancing proximity between teachers and students is helpful (Opdenakker et al., 2012). Ancess (2003, p. 27) describes this as "creating regular and spontaneous opportunities for frequent contact."

Both quality and depth of care and support can be increased through an emphasis on "extended rather than limited, role relationships" (Newmann,

1981, p. 554) (e.g., as classroom teacher, advisor, and co-curricular program sponsor). Engagement in a range of activities rather than a single function is preferable (Ancess, 2003; Newmann, 1981). Social and academic domains both can be used to enrich student-teacher relationships (Fredricks et al., 2004), and multiple dimensions within each domain provide the hooks for linkages. A focus on "guidance and friendship inside and outside the classroom" (Antrop-González, 2006, p. 289) is helpful. Before-school, during-school, and after-school times can be turned into avenues that foster relationships in the service of personalized communities for students. Both one-on-one connections (e.g., an advisor-advisee relationship) and linkages formed in groups (e.g., a coach) can be the basis of providing care and support (Demaray & Malecki, 2002a; Woloszyk, 1996). A focus on both formal and informal interactions opens the door to the formation of teacher-student attachments that promote student engagement and success (Ancess, 2003; Joselowsky, 2007). Finally, training for teachers about the importance and content of caring and supportive norms, i.e., how to establish personalized communities for students, is essential (Roth, Brooks-Gunn, Murray, & Foster, 1998).

So overall the keystone issues here are a strong understanding of the interlaced strands of care and support and a blueprint that provides time for access to materialize and attachments to form. Once these pieces of the improvement narrative are well understood, there is a plethora of activities from which to forge a coherent package to deepen care and support for students in specific contexts. The cardinal rule for leaders is to begin with the norms and the subcomponents, not specific initiatives. When strategies follow norms, student community is deepened. When strategies are expected to power norm development, more often than not community remains largely unaffected (Murphy, 1991, 2013).

Norm of Safety

Communities of pastoral care for students are defined by a norm of safety (Christle et al., 2005), which in effective schools research is often referred to as the correlate of a safe and orderly learning environment (Cotton, 2003; Hallinger & Murphy, 1985; Robinson et al., 2008). We learn from studies across a variety of areas of interest (e.g., child development, school reform) that security needs are of major importance for youngsters (Dinham, 2005; Joselowsky, 2007) and that meeting those needs is essential for their healthy development, academically, socially, and emotionally (Baker et al., 1997; Christle et al., 2005; Rumberger & Palardy, 2005).

As was the case with the norms of care and support, positively charged and negatively charged analyses are intertwined throughout the research narrative on safety (Felner et al., 2007). The latter storyline attends to efforts to banish, or at least minimize, unsafe and damaging elements in the school culture (e.g., criminal capital, crumbling infrastructure)

Chapter 7

(Allensworth & Easton, 2005). The positive chronicle underscores actions schools undertake to promote warmth and protection (e.g., creating authentic relationships between teachers and students) (Felner et al., 2007). Collectively, these efforts create spaces in which it is safe and enjoyable for students to engage with the business of schooling and develop as persons (Antrop-González & De Jesús, 2006; Creemers & Reezigt, 1996; Robinson, 2007). Schools become sanctuaries for students (Ackerman & Maslin-Ostrowski, 2002; Ancess, 2003). We also discover from an assortment of investigators that the norm of safety is often conspicuous by its absence in schools, especially schools serving high concentrations of students placed at risk for failure (Mendez, Knoff, & Ferron, 2002; Mukuria, 2002).

A few touchstones require resurfacing before we unpack the norm of safety. To begin with, we know that leaders plays a hallmark role in the formation of a safe, protective, warm, and orderly learning environment (Rutter et al., 1979; Valentine & Prater, 2011; Wynne, 1980). We understand that safety works well when it shares space with the norms of care and support (Clark, Lotto, & Astuto, 1984; Russell, Mazzarelli, White, & Maurer, 1985), when these three norms are seen as overlapping strands of the student community rope. Also, it is important to remember that relationships with teachers and peers are a major vehicle for carrying the norm of safety in schools (Ma & Klinger, 2000). Impersonality, a core element of institutionalism and hierarchy, is toxic to the formation of a protective and warm learning environment, especially for students listed on the disadvantaged side of the opportunity ledger (Quint, 2006; Scanlan & Lopez, 2012). We point out again that context (e.g., student age, school SES) is important in examining the norm of safety (Maguin & Loeber, 1996; Mendez et al., 2002). The essence of the storyline with safety, as with the other norms, is to keep underlying values on center stage. Strategies, policies, structures, activities, and so forth can work, but only when they carry essential values. Finally, while "classroom management" is an important beam in the safe and orderly learning construct, we do not focus on it here. Rather, the spotlight is on schoolwide climate.

Later in this chapter, we review the evidence on the impact of safety on the academic and social learning of students. Here we simply provide an advance organizer on the linkage. We confirm that lack of safety undermines the academic function of the school (Finn & Rock, 1997; Freiberg, Huzinec, & Templeton, 2009; Wilson & Corbett, 1999). Many traditional school safety moves are also harmful to learning (Christle et al., 2005; Nichols, Ludwin, & Iadicola, 1999). On the flip side, relationship-anchored improvements in the safety of the school environment enhance academic performance (Maguin & Loeber, 1996; Smerdon & Borman, 2009).

The safety norm can be unpacked into seven overlapping and integrated elements. To begin with, safety is built on foundations of *personalization*, not a scaffolding of hierarchy. While expectations are clear, firm, and consistently enforced, actions center on students as persons not simply as occupants of the institution of school (Robinson, 2007). Inculcating the norm of safety, or what Bryk and colleagues (2010, p. 8) call norms of "civil conduct," occurs by using "soft power" (Adams, 2010, p. 265) and by engaging in "gentle schooling" (Reitzug & Patterson, 1998, p. 179). Rules, regulations, and system responses are about more than simply effective control (Wilson & Corbett, 1999). They encompass community and personalization properties, such as identification and engagement (Adams, 2010; Baker et al., 1997; Bryk et al., 2010). Warmth is a hallmark ingredient in the personalization element of safety (Mendez et al., 2002). Positive expectations dominate the environmental climate (Roth & Brooks-Gunn, 2003). A protective culture is formed in large part through respectful relationships between educators and children (Baker et al., 1997; Mendez et al., 2002; Robinson, 2007). Students are seen "as resources to be developed rather than as problems to be managed" (Roth et al., 1998, p. 427). Attention is directed to learning the values of the community not simply learning to comply with rules (Freiberg et al., 2009). The rules in play "are based upon principles and virtues (kindness, fairness) and are connected to respect for the community" (Baker et al., 1997, p. 592).

Care is infused into the development and operation of personalization (Antrop-González & De Jesús, 2006; Reitzug & Patterson, 1998). Support for adherence to community ideas is more important than consequences for inappropriate behavior. Appropriate behavior is defined in light of the full range of students' social and emotional needs (Antrop-González, 2006; Mendez et al., 2002). Nourishing internal control is important (Baker et al., 1997). Students are viewed holistically, not only as violators of regulations.

Developmentally appropriate work (Mendez et al., 2002) and individualization (Cheney, Blum, & Walker, 2004) are visible in the personalization element of safety. So too is an emphasis on helping students learn to assume responsibility for their behavior (Ancess, 2003; Csikszentmihalyi & Larson, 1984; Johnson & Asera, 1999). Schools characterized by a norm of safety are adept at providing youngsters with three types of protective armor, personal, interpersonal, and group (Crosnoe, 2011).

Table 7.3   Aspects of the Norm of Safety in Student Community

Personalization (noninstitutional) focus
Preventative focus
Systematic focus
Positive (nonpunitive) focus
Academic engagement
Shared development and ownership
Appealing physical space

As we touched on above, a safe environment is one in which the focus is on the *prevention* of unwanted behavior rather than on the punishment of inappropriate behavior (Freiberg et al., 2009; Mendez et al., 2002). Early identification and treatment lie at the heart of the prevention element. That is, early screening for potential and actual discipline problems and early intervention are highlighted in preventive climates (Cheney et al., 2004; Ensminger & Slusarick, 1992), especially efforts to damp down individual risk factors associated with disorder (St. Pierre, Mark, Kaltreider, & Aikin, 1997). So too is early involvement of parents before problems begin to spin out of control (Mendez et al., 2002).

Prevention strategies that work well are identified in the research on safety. Generally speaking, integrating safety with the other norms of student community—care, support, and membership—receives high marks. Shaping peer cultures to support rather than contradict the values and ideals of community provides a strong platform to prevent disorder and unsafe conditions (Rutter et al., 1979). Working to understand and address causes of problems that interfere with the development of a safe climate is particularly helpful (Antrop-González & De Jesús, 2006; Balfanz et al., 2007; Nichols et al., 1999). Keeping longer-term objectives in mind rather than only addressing immediate problems is important as well (Mendez et al., 2002). Involving parents is a wise policy (Mendez et al., 2002). Training in the area of social skills for students is a good preventative strategy (Catalano, Loeber, & McKinney, 1999; St. Pierre et al., 1997). Collaborative development of positively framed expectations for conduct with clear expectations for behavior is essential here (Fredricks et al., 2004). So too is a reliance on positive rather than negative reinforcement (Cotton, 2003; Rutter et al., 1979). Seeking external assistance for help in working on problems, real and potential, can be productive in preventing problems from mushrooming and damaging the climate of safety in a school (Cheney et al., 2004).

What should be clear from the above discussion is that while most of the time we see safety through the prisms of the institution and implementation, warm and protective schools are primarily concerned about the well-being of students and maintain a focus on prevention. Plans to bring the norm of safety to life are comprehensive and *systematic* (Mukuria, 2002). They are schoolwide in design (Cheney et al., 2004). They attend to safety at the macrolevel of values and the microlevel of expectations in an integrated and coherent manner (Cotton, 2003; Fredricks et al., 2004; Rutter et al., 1979), allowing little room for confusion to emerge (Mukuria, 2002; Quint, 2006; Robinson et al., 2008). Systematic focus extends to development of plans as well. They are often the product of a good deal of input and collaboration (Baker et al., 1997; Mendez et al., 2002). Comprehensiveness also means that a safe and orderly learning environment is defined by consistency and coordination across teachers in the school and between teachers and administrators (Balfanz et al., 2007; Greene & Lee, 2006;

Quint, 2006). Everyone in the school uses the same playbook when working with students. Systematic plans promote the use of varied methods to forge and maintain safety and warmth (Mendez et al., 2002). Finally, because "fair treatment is critical to organizational bonding" (Newmann et al., 1992, p. 21) and because fairness is an intermittent property in many schools (Bloomberg et al., 2003; Nichols et al., 1999), schools with a protective aura are attentive to equity in a crosscutting and comprehensive manner. Fairness is deeply woven into plans and codes of action found in schools defined by the norm of safety (Mendez et al., 2002; Newmann et al., 1992; Scheurich, 1998).

Scholarship affirms that reliance on negative and exclusionary practices to create safety is often dysfunctional for the school and harmful to students (Christle et al., 2005; Mendez et al., 2002; Nichols et al., 1999). An emphasis on punitive actions, especially ones unanchored to understanding, support, and personal and social development, has been found to be uniformly ineffective in the struggle to forge the norm of safety (Antrop-González & De Jesús, 2006; Catalano et al., 1999; Nichols et al., 1999). On the other hand, *positive,* asset-based approaches to bringing safety to life are much more likely to be productive. Especially relevant here is an emphasis on positive consequences (Crosnoe, 2011) and positive feedback to students (Mendez et al., 2002; Rutter et al., 1979).

Safety is also intricately linked to the instructional program in the school (Cheney et al., 2004; Garmezy, 1991; Murphy, Weil, & McGreal, 1986). The major lesson from the research is that both the presence and the absence of the norm of safety can be traced directly to the *quality of the instructional program.* That is, safety is as much a product of "meaningful academic work" (Baker et al., 1997, p. 592) as it is community-building efforts. Instruction and curriculum that foster academic engagement and promote student success go a long way to creating a warm and protective climate (Catalano et al., 1999; Cheney et al., 2004; Garmezy, 1991). Good schools rely more on quality programs than control strategies in their quest for creating productive student communities (Weil & Murphy, 1982).

Research on student communities in general and the norm of safety in particular suggests a strong role for collaborative work in the formation of the architecture undergirding a climate of safety and order (Blase & Kirby, 2009; Cotton, 2003; Murphy, Weil, Hallinger, & Mitman, 1985). There is *shared development and ownership* (Murphy, 2006). Plans are "achieved consensually" (Alexander & Entwisle, 1996, p. 80). Involvement begins with teachers; it extends to parents. Here, involvement in the development of codes and with the implementation of efforts to ensure safety both seem important (Cheney et al., 2004; Mendez et al., 2002). Students are a part of the action here as well (Baker et al., 1997; Mukuria, 2002). It is also essential that the fingerprints of the principal and the school leadership team are visible on the values and goals that buttress a protective environment and the implementation actions that help define the norm of safety

(Cheney et al., 2004; Gray et al., 1999; Wynne, 1980). A "unified stand is critical" (Mukuria, 2002, p. 441). Collectively, shared ownership for student community and the norm of safety emerges (Hallinger, Murphy, & Hausman, 1992; Patterson et al., 2007). There is a thick strand of analysis in the literature that collective professional development for faculty is especially helpful in anchoring a shared stance on safety (Christle et al., 2005; Mendez et al., 2002).

Safety can also be traced to the *physical condition of the school*, to its well-being and appearance (Gray et al., 1999). For, as Joselowsky (2007, p. 272) astutely notes, community for young people "often begins with the physical space." Safe and orderly communities are characterized by an absence of evidence of vandalism, degenerative facilities, and crumbling infrastructure (Christle et al., 2005; Dinham, 2005; Edmonds, 1978). The institutional patina of the building is lightened (Christle et al., 2005). On the positive side of the physical space narrative, safe schools are defined by cleanliness and an appealing appearance (Johnson & Asera, 1999; Wilson & Corbett, 1999). They are welcoming spaces with a positive ambience (Christle et al., 2005; Joselowsky, 2007). People care about and attend to the image of the school (Dinham, Cairney, Craigie, & Wilson, 1995; Gray et al., 1999). In safe schools, adults provide "pleasant working conditions" for their youngsters (Rutter et al., 1979, p. 195).

Norm of Membership

We see here again the essential crosscutting theme of relationships between educators and students at the center of membership work. We also uncover a critical role for peers with the membership norm. As with the norms of care, support, and safety, we feature two lines of analysis on the work undertaken to foster membership for students. One attends to the removal of the negatives associated with developing belonging (e.g., working to overcome oppositional peer culture). The other is the construction of positive rungs on the membership ladder (e.g., developing opportunities for students to assume responsibility). Again, we reemphasize the fact that there is considerable overlap among and integration of the four norms of student community. This storyline of overlap and integration also applies to the three elements of the norm of membership.

The central law of school improvement that context matters is brightly illuminated here as well (Feldman & Matjasko, 2005; Guest & Schneider, 2003). Individual-level characteristics and school, family, peer, and neighborhood contexts each exert force on whether youngsters become members of a school or not (Feldman & Matjasko, 2005; Voelkl, 1997). "The school and community in which participation takes place matters" (Guest & Schneider, 2003, p. 91) a good deal in whether students are bystanders or active citizens in the school (Freiberg et al., 2009) and whether the desired outcomes of membership materialize or not (Guest & Schneider, 2003).

Table 7.4   Aspects of the Norm of Membership in Student Community

Ownership
Involvement
Accomplishment

Finally, and consistent with our examination of the other norms, authentic membership seems to be especially important and productive for students at risk of failure (Felner et al., 2007; Murphy, 2010; Murphy &Tobin, 2014). Indeed, "belonging could be *the* single most crucial factor in the motivation and engagement of certain categories of at-risk students" (Goodenow, 1993, p. 39). We examine the form and texture of membership through an analysis of its three defining elements: ownership, involvement, and accomplishment.

Ownership is often defined in terms of student empowerment (Joselowsky, 2007; Silins & Mulford, 2010). As Roth and Brooks-Gunn (2003, p. 175) discovered, ownership is marked by "an empowering atmosphere [that] encourages youth to engage in useful roles [and] practice self-determination." Students become "stakeholders" in the school (Joselowsky, 2007). One aspect of the ownership subtheme of membership is student agency (Joselowsky, 2007), commitment to improvement and opportunities to influence actions at the school coupled with the belief that efforts will lead to positive effects (Jackson, 2000; Reitzug & Patterson, 1998). Student voice is also a component of ownership. Students are allowed and encouraged to express themselves and their ideas (Battistich et al., 1997). Their voices are not silenced or devalued (Patterson et al., 2007; Rodriguez, 2008). Rather, they "have voice in school affairs" (Newmann, 1981, p. 553). More importantly, student views are heard (McLaughlin & Talbert, 2001; Patterson et al., 2007) and honored (Ancess, 2003). Teachers and school administrators are "physically and emotionally present in social exchanges with students" (Adams & Forsyth, 2009, p. 268). Students' perspectives are received (Reitzug & Patterson, 1998).

Ownership entails influence on the part of the owners, students in this case (Battistich et al., 1997). Schools that build powerful communities for students "maximize opportunities for students to contribute to school policy and management" (Newmann, 1981, p. 552) through both formal and informal mechanisms, assuring that students' points of view are taken into account in classroom and school decision making (Ancess, 2003; Newmann, 1981) and in the "conception, execution, and evaluation of work" (Newmann et al., 1992, p. 25) and school-based activities. Ownership includes "bringing the learner in as a full and active participant in enhancing and shaping their own learning" (Felner et al., 2007, p. 210), making youngsters "constructors of both their learning environment and learning experience" (Joselowsky, 2007, p. 265). Students with influence are "active agents in the creation of school success" (Conchas, 2001, p. 501). They own the school and their work (Ancess, 2003; Newmann et al., 1992). They are partners and producers not simply categories or recipients (Joselowsky, 2007), tourists (Freiberg et al., 2009), or consumers (Eckert, 1989). They "take ownership of their own learning" (Levin & Datnow, 2012, p. 190).

Relatedly, ownership implies common purpose, one that "builds a sense of membership that enhances engagement in work" (Newmann et al., 1992, p. 21). It entails the opportunity to engage in meaningful and challenging activities (Roth & Brooks-Gunn, 2003)—in "authentic academic work" (Marks, 2000, p. 158)—and influence over the ways in which students engage with those activities (Newmann, 1981, 1992).

Schools in the 19th and 20th centuries were heavily defined by hierarchy, bureaucracy, and institutionalism (Murphy, 1991, 1999). The result was that the school (adults) had all the control and students were, to a varying extent, invisible (Weis, 1990). Schools were characterized by what Laffey (1982, p. 64) refers to as "externality," an environment in "which students feel that they are pawns to external forces." Students in these schools were often locked in a dysfunctional battle to gain some control (Crosnoe, 2011; Csikszentmihalyi & Larson, 1984; Patterson et al., 2001). In contrast, and clearly ribboned in the discussion above, the norm of membership includes autonomy, control, and choice for those who have an ownership stake in the school. Schools that promote student autonomy and responsibility enhance engagement and learning (González & Padilla, 1997; Hattie, 2009; Rutter et al., 1979). Overly controlling environments, on the other hand, "diminish interest, preference for challenge, and persistence—all aspects of engagement" (Fredricks et al., 2004, p. 78). This two-sided rule holds at both the classroom and school levels (Battistich et al., 1997). "Community [is] inversely associated with an emphasis on the teacher as sole authority in the classroom" (Battistich et al., 1997, p. 143) whereas having students take responsibility for their learning promotes ownership (Garmezy, 1991; Joselowsky, 2007). In schools with strong student communities, youngsters are provided choice and responsibility to accomplish important work (Joselowsky, 2007; Roth et al., 1998; Rutter et al., 1979), both in terms of their own learning and development (Gurr, Drysdale, & Mulford, 2005) and the improvement of the school (Joselowsky, 2007). Opportunities for students to lead are an especially important aspect of responsibility (Jackson, 2000; Roth & Brooks-Gunn, 2003; Sather, 1999).

Ownership includes the concepts of space and place. Students in meaningful communities have their own space, and they see school as a place for them (Eckert, 1989; McLaughlin & Talbert, 2001; Weis, 1990). Such tangibleness helps students "develop a sense that they [are] an integral part of the school collective" (Cooper et al., 2005, p. 9) and instill feelings of inclusiveness (Eckert, 1989; Newmann, 1992).

Involvement is a second critical element that helps define membership, one that as noted above shares considerable space with ownership.

It features opportunities provided by the school for youngsters to engage their "talents, skills, and interests" (Crosnoe, 2011, p. 238) in meaningful and challenging work (Newmann, 1981, 1992) and in school activities (Marsh & Kleitman, 2002; Silins & Mulford, 2010). The critical issue here according to Joselowsky (2007, p. 273) is that schools "cease treating youth engagement as an add-on to improved learning outcomes, but as central to student and school success." That is, "youth engagement must be conceptualized as a guiding principle of organizational operations" (p. 270). Indeed, Ma (2003, p. 347) argues "that students' participation in school activities may be the key to their sense of belonging in school."

Schools with well-formed student communities provide a host of "participatory opportunities" (Cooper et al., 2005, p. 17) centered on chances for youngsters to contribute to the school and take positions of responsibility (Johnson & Asera, 1999; Rutter et al., 1979). Given the cardinal place of student-adult connections in fostering community, it will surprise no one to learn that opportunities to develop meaningful relationships with teachers are critical to getting students involved in schools. So too are creating chances for youngsters to participate in class and school-wide decisions (Ancess, 2003; Battistich et al., 1995; Epstein, 1996) and school governance (Baker et al., 1997; Woloszyk, 1996). Opportunities for leadership (Harris, 2009; MacBeath, 2009; Sather, 1999) and community service are often found in schools that are characterized by high levels of student involvement, both within the school (Ancess, 2003; Raywid, 1995) and in the extended community (Antrop-González & De Jesús, 2006; Bloomberg et al., 2003; Eckert, 1989).

Although participation in academic work is the keystone strand of involvement, a good deal of the literature also rightfully examines involvement in school activities, especially co-curricular or extracurricular programs. Schools that score well on involvement specifically and personalized community in general offer a significant range of such experiences (Leithwood, Louis, Anderson, & Wahlstrom, 2004). These schools are defined by inclusionary practices (Eckert, 1989), pulling large percentages of youngsters into extracurricular activities. Involvement here, as we discuss in detail in the last section of the chapter, is linked to improved academic and social learning (Finn & Rock, 1997; Hattie, 2008; Rumberger, 2011).

Studies on extracurricular activities provide considerable guidance to leaders for planning, developing, and putting these experiences into play for students. Many of those guidelines are threaded throughout the analysis above (e.g., providing students with input about activities to be offered). The core question here was provided by Marsh and Kleitman (2002, p. 465): "How should students spend their time for maximum academic, psychological, and social benefits to support future accomplishments?"

We know from the research that structured activities are better than unstructured ones for promoting positive outcomes (Catalano et al., 1999; Feldman & Matjasko, 2005; Hattie, 2009). Structured and organized activities trump leisure activities as well (Marsh & Kleitman, 2002). Experiences that lead to tangible outcomes are preferable (Roth et al., 1998). "Effective programs engage young people in a variety of ways so that they are not just physically present, but intellectually immersed, socially connected, and emotionally centered" (Joselowsky, 2007, p. 260). Activities that nurture collaboration and cooperation and those that engender teamwork among students (Conchas, 2001) are generally preferable to those featuring competition (Cooper, 1996). Guest and Schneider (2003) also report that activities that foster identity and positive recognition are linked to valued outcomes. They also help us see that identity interacts with social context. That is, "activity-based identities are given meaning by school community value systems" (p. 90).

Experiences that lead to success for students from active engagement are desirable (Feldman & Matjasko, 2005). So also are programs in which peers from one's social network participate (Feldman & Matjasko, 2005) and ones where there is a strong match with the interests of the students (Eggert, Thompson, Herting, & Nicholas, 1995). Staff characteristics matter (Roth et al., 1998). Activities shepherded by strong and supportive leaders are more productive than those that are run by adults who are less committed to the programs (Roth et al., 1998). We know that getting parents on board can be an important asset in encouraging and maintaining involvement (González & Padilla, 1997; Rumberger, 2011). Continuity of program participation is important. This includes the length of participation and the regularity of engagement (Feldman & Matjasko, 2005; Roth et al., 1998). A combination of activities from different domains (e.g., academic clubs, sports teams) is often preferable to a single concentration (Joselowsky, 2007; Roth et al., 1998). Except at the extreme end of the continuum, deeper participation, with active engagement, leads to the realization of valued ends (Feldman & Matjasko, 2005; Marsh & Kleitman, 2002). Experiences that cover "more of the contexts in which adolescents live" (Roth et al., 1998, p. 438) are desirable. "Multiple opportunities for multiple forms of access and interaction across various members of the school community" (Ancess, 2000, p. 605) provides the operational structure here.

Researchers also help us see that to be most beneficial, activities that promote involvement should be aligned with and integrated into the school culture and core school operations (Joselowsky, 2007; Marsh & Kleitman, 1992). "More comprehensive and sustained programs" (Roth et al., 1998, p. 440) lead to more positive outcomes. Within the context of the findings above, research allows us to say a few things about the types of activities that are most productive in fostering membership and community. Both academic and sports programs have been shown to produce positive outcomes (Guest & Schneider, 2003; Marsh & Kleitman, 2002), although, not surprisingly, academic activities have larger impacts on achievement (Hattie, 2009). School-related activities consistently lead to more favorable outcomes than out-of-school experiences (Marsh & Kleitman, 2002).

Finally, analysts confirm that *accomplishment* is a keystone element in the norm of authentic membership (Baker et al., 1997; Crosnoe, 2011; Farrell, 1990). Two aspects of success are important. The first is a feeling of personal accomplishment (Baker et al., 1997; Dinham, 2005; Johnson & Asera, 1999). The second is the belief that one's efforts are worthwhile, that they make a meaningful contribution to the school community (Battistich et al., 1995; Csikszentmihalyi & Larson, 1984). Schools facilitate reaching both goals by centering on student competencies rather than student problems (Roth et al., 1998). Indeed, research confirms that competency building is an essential ingredient in student community (Battistich et al., 1995; Dinham, 2005; Roth et al., 1998).

Educators exert considerable influence on students' sense of competency and success in the school by creating a plethora of ways to recognize, honor, celebrate, and reward active engagement and achievements (Battistich et al., 1995; Jackson & Warren, 2000; Wynne, 1980) across academic, behavioral, and community fronts (Blase & Kirby, 2009; Cotton, 2000). Recognition from others whose opinions matter is implicated in strengthening students' commitment, engagement, and learning.

Student-Student Relationships

To this point in the chapter, the focus has been on adult-student relationships, especially teacher-student relationships, and how these personal connections can foster the growth of powerful norms that mark highly productive student communities. Concomitantly, it is essential to acknowledge that peer relationships are equally critical in the narrative of press and support for the formation of these norms, and ultimately student social and academic learning. That is, "peers exert a powerful influence on adolescents. They influence students' social and academic behaviors, attitudes toward school, and access to resources (social capital) that may benefit their education" (Rumberger, 2011, p. 175). Indeed, although remarkably understated and generally insufficiently acknowledged, they, not teachers, define the informal aspects of schooling (Crosnoe, 2011; Smerdon et al., 2009) in which the formal aspects grow or atrophy (Eckert, 1989; Farrell, 1990). Major lines of research converge on this conclusion: "Few things matter more [than] peer relations on how young people turn out" (Crosnoe, 2011, p. 206). That is "the social structure of the student cohort dominates virtually all aspects of life in the institution, choices in all domains are restricted not so clearly by adult judgment as by peer social boundaries" (Eckert, 1989, p. 12).

Analysts show us how life changes for young persons as they advance into their teens. More and more time is spent with peers (Csikszentmihalyi & Larson, 1984; Farrell, 1990; Goodenow, 1993). In turn, "teacher influence and proximity decreases over time" (Opdenakker et al., 2012, p. 113). The centrality of parents in the lives of youngsters is reduced as well (Eckert, 1989; Lee & Burkham, 2003) As adolescents "redirect psychic energy away from members of one's family [and teachers] to one's peers" (Csikszentmihalyi & Larson, 1984, p. 130), they increasingly begin to see themselves through their peers, that is "peers serve as a looking glass for teenagers trying to figure out who they are and where they fit in the world" (Crosnoe, 2011, p. 56). It is to peers that they begin to turn for the majority of their feedback (Hattie, 2009), for validation (Smerdon et al., 2009), and for sense of identity (Eckert, 1989). It is friends rather than adults to whom they often turn for information, guidance, and emotional support (Csikszentmihalyi & Larson, 1984). For many youngsters, "the peer group is the major source of morals and values" (Farrell, 1990, p. 4) and often "the most important resource for resilience" (Crosnoe, 2011, p. 177).

Given the reality that the academic domain of the school has a limited pull on students (Newmann et al., 1992), that schooling for adolescents "is often far more about navigating a social terrain that may or may not place value on education and academic achievement" (Crosnoe, 2011, p. 9), we should not be surprised to learn that peer relationships have significant potential to enhance or undercut the formal domain of schooling (Eckert, 1989; Newmann et al., 1992). The narrative here is similar to the one we discussed about engagement and disengagement based on Figure 7.2. More specifically, a very sturdy line of research confirms that peer culture (the informal domain of education) can reinforce the academic values of the school or it can pull youngsters to different, often noncompatible (e.g., we do not kill ourselves here) or oppositional (e.g., the degradation of academic work and relationships with teachers values) and subsequent behaviors (e.g., blowing off classes) (Goddard & Goff, 1999; Maguin & Loeber, 1996; St. Pierre et al., 1997). Crosnoe (2011, p. 76) refers to this latter option as "antiacademic and antiadult attitudes and orientations," and Farrell (1990, p. 143) talks about "deviant universes." This impressive line of research is clear in its assessment that if "counterproductive norms are operating among students, any academic reform task becomes exceedingly difficult" (Smerdon et al., 2009, p. 210) and academic achievement is significantly compromised (Eckert, 1989; Opdenakker et al., 2012). Students in this scenario end up rejecting the authority of the school, privileging the norms of the peer community, and "pursu[ing] their primate activities on the fringes of the official activity" (Eckert, 1989, p. 88). We also know that the tendency to move in the direction of oppositional culture is more evident for students placed at risk by society and its schools (Dishion, Poulin, & Barraston, 2001; Farrell, 1990; Murphy, 2010).

On the other hand, in scenario number one above, peer culture can turn out to be a distinctly valuable resource for youngsters and their schools. If a student community that brings young people into alignment with the academic success values is nourished and grown, good things accrue to students in terms of social and academic outcomes. Below, we discuss what the research reveals about creating a positive peer culture. Here we simply reinforce the cardinal message: "Changes in peer context are critically important to individual student outcomes" (Felner et al., 2007, p. 15). To create productive communities for students, educators need to work to ensure that the various peer cultures reinforce rather than undermine the values the school holds for youngsters. Dishion and colleagues (2001, p. 90) make this point quite explicitly when they assert "that adults' role in structuring, managing, and attending to children's peer contexts is perhaps the most critical for promoting health and reducing risks." That is, it is not sufficient to work on individual principal- and teacher-student relationships. Teachers and administrators also need to actively shape student-student relationships in the service of nurturing positive communities for students.

Research in this area reveals tangible pathways for educators to create isomorphism between the formal and informal dimensions of schooling, or what Feldman and Matjasko (2005, p. 197) call the "integration of school and peer contexts." Many of these can be distilled from the elements of the four core norms of personalized community examined above. For example, developing opportunities for collaborative work; providing students with voice in classroom and school decision; establishing multiple ways for students to lead their colleagues; and carving out place, space, and autonomy for youngsters all assist in the formation of positive peer cultures (Battistich et al., 1997; Conchas, 2001; Hoy et al., 1998). Pursuing multiple avenues to bring and hold essential values front and center is a wise strategy (Bryk et al., 2010; Goddard, 2003), especially values about social interactions (Eckert, 1989). Inviting and encouraging youngsters to participate in school-sponsored activities, that is, shaping friendships is good policy as well, both in regular and extracurricular programs (Crosnoe, 2011; Newmann, 1981). So too is providing training in how to use peer support networks (Eckert, 1989). Special attention to peer relationships when assigning youngsters to academic interventions can be helpful here (Demaray & Malecki, 2002a). Conscious attention by teachers and administrators to issues of race can do much to help build productive student-student relationships. The research also highlights the power of honoring different cultures and ethnicities and deliberately mixing youngsters by class and race (Conchas, 2001; Murphy, 2010), helping break down formal and informal patterns that foster prejudices and social inequalities (Conchas, 2001; Crosnoe, 2011). Considerable attention to teacher and principal relationships when students move across levels and grades can pay dividends to the bank of school community. The operant rule is that inclusiveness is almost always a good idea (Antrop-González, 2006; Galletta & Ayala, 2008; Scanlan & Lopez, 2012).

INSTITUTIONAL AFFILIATION AND IDENTITY

In this section, we turn to the initial outcomes that accrue when schools create communities of pastoral care for students, environments defined by personalized relationships and marked by care, support, safety, and membership. We examine three intermediate results, social integration, psychological well-being, and learning dispositions, collectively often described in terms of human and social capital (Feldman & Matjasko, 2005). As we see in Figure 7.1, these factors are critical to the development of strong engagement with and in school which, in turn, is essential to student academic and social learning. We address these last two links of our model in the final sections of the chapter.

Before we lay out the narrative on institutional and social integration, we want to spotlight an essential point that appears in various places throughout this volume. Specifically, we find that the effects of pastoral care are especially powerful for students placed at risk by society for failure in schools (Battistich et al., 1995; Feldman & Matjasko, 2005; Marsh & Kleitman, 2002)—socioeconomically disadvantaged students, youth of color, second-language children, students historically underserved by schools, and youngsters in schools with high concentrations of students from low-income families. We also want to remind the reader of the reciprocal, interrelated nature of the variables in our model. Overlap among the elements, what we call shared spaces, is the norm.

Social Integration

We know from the research that both academic proficiency and positive school culture promote integration (Catalano et al., 1999; Croninger & Lee, 2001; Ma, 2003). Our focus here is on the second element in the integration equation, culture. Studies regularly report that a culture defined by norms of care, support, safety, and membership helps attach or bond young people to school (Battistich et al., 1997; Crosnoe, 2011; Voelkl, 1997). These bonds, in turn, lead to a cascade of other important effects (e.g., enhanced self-esteem, greater motivation), all of which presage engagement and learning (see Figure 7.1).

Pastoral care leads first to student identification with the school, what Eckert (1989) labels as a merging of the personal and institutional. Scholars describe this state in a variety of ways: membership (Eckert, 1989; González & Padilla, 1997), belonging (Battistich et al., 1995; Fredricks et al., 2004), integration (Scanlan & Lopez, 2012), affiliation (Newmann, 1981; O'Connor, 1997), attachment (Alexander et al., 1997; Conchas, 2001), inclusion (Ma, 2003; Voelkl, 1997), connection (Feldman & Matjasko, 2005; Roth & Brooks-Gunn, 2003), fitting in (Crosnoe, 2011), and acceptance (Goodenow, 1993). Underlying these various markers for identification is a sense of being part of the school, of being valued by the institution and by peers, of "feeling oneself to be an important part of the life and activity of the class" (Goodenow, 1993, p. 25) and school—"of feel[ing] personally accepted, respected, included, and supported in the school" (Ma, 2003, p. 340). It is about affinity (Conchas, 2001).

Muted pastoral care, on the other hand, is an invitation to weak student identification with and/or possible disaffiliation with the school, "an absence of highly developed feelings of valuing and belonging" (Voelkl, 1997, p. 296). Students in such schools are often portrayed as "just passing through" (Eckert, 1989, p. 65). Rather than being bonded to the school, they are independent actors, ones who often feel a sense of disconnection and alienation toward teachers and peers (Antrop-González, 2006; Newmann, 1981). They display what Farrell (1990, p. 112) calls "absenting behavior," a "culture that is dominated by the private as opposed to the institutional" (Eckert, 1989, p. 172). Separation and exclusion are elements of disidentification. So also are estrangement, detachment, and isolation (Newmann 1981)—"emotional and physical withdrawal" (Voelkl, 1997, p. 294).

Identification (or disidentification) impacts commitment to the school and a sense of obligation to those at the school (Gamoran, 1996). Positive identification helps build a sense of legitimacy around the school and a valuing of the institution (Fredricks et al., 2004; Goodenow, 1993). According to Voelkl (1997, p. 296), the idea of valuing schooling

> include[s] the recognition of the value of the school as both a social institution and a tool for facilitating personal advancement. That is, the youngster regards school as a central institution in society and feels that what is learned in class is important in its own right and that school is instrumental in obtaining his or her personal life objectives . . . the belief that schoolwork is both interesting and important.

Valuing also leads to a "commitment to and identification with the goals of the institution" (Eckert, 1989, p. 103); its values and purposes (Ancess, 2003; Baker et al., 1997; Marsh & Kleitman, 1992); its norms and practices (Battistich et al., 1995, 1997; Voelkl, 1997); "the means it prescribes for members to pursue goals" (Newmann et al., 1992, p. 20), that is, its structures, policies, and practices (Hallinan & Kubitschek, 1999); and its sanctioned outcomes (Marsh & Kleitman, 2002, Voelkl, 1997). In schools with strong pastoral care "students become invested in the operations of the classroom" (Freiberg et al., 2009) and school (Marsh & Kleitman, 2002).

Psychological Well-Being

Researchers also document strong linkages between a community of care and belonging and the psychological health of students (Feldman & Matjasko, 2005; Ma, 2003) and conclude that the relationship is reciprocal in nature (Ma, 2003). These scholars remind us that the work here is two-pronged, the creation of pathways to positive psychosocial character-istics (e.g., self-concept) and the development of fortifications to protect against negative life events that could undermine mental health (Jackson & Warren, 2000).

We know that the major quest for youngsters is for personal identity (Csikszentmihalyi & Larson, 1984; Farrell, 1990), what Crosnoe (2011) calls identity work and Feldman and Matjasko (2005) talk about as learning to understand oneself. Analysts also document that identity and self-esteem are tightly yoked. Each student's self-concept is forged in good measure through the sense of community he or she feels at school, by the relationships forged with teachers and peers (Battistich et al., 1997; Guest & Schneider, 2003; Marsh & Kleitman, 2002). That is, students "come to an understanding of their own social worth by seeing how they are treated by others" (Crosnoe, 2011, p. 139). Supportive communities help nourish the formation of healthy self-concept and stronger self-esteem (Demaray & Malecki, 2002a; Pounder, 1999), thus positively shaping the nature of students' developmental pathways (Feldman & Matjowski, 2005) and consequently, prosocial attitudes and actions (Battistich et al., 1997; Rothman & Cosden, 1995). Nonsupportive communities for students, on the other hand, can lead to reduced self-esteem, nonproductive devel-opmental pathways, and counterproductive attitudes and behaviors (Crosnoe, 2011). These behaviors and attitudes, in turn, are related to engagement and school success (Finn & Rock, 1997; Mulford & Silins, 2003; Rumberger, 2011)—for better or worse.

Communities of belonging and support are associated with student sense of expectancy and self-efficacy (Battistich et al., 1995; Goodenow, 1993; Scanlan & Lopez, 2012), concepts that are "among the most robust predictors of academic achievement" (Scanlan & Lopez, 2012, p. 607). Personalized student community also promotes a sense of control and autonomy (Ancess, 2003; Goodenow, 1993). Caring environments "ignite agency" (Rodriguez, 2008, p. 774) as well (Felner et al., 2007; Fredricks et al., 2004), providing students with what Csikszentmihalyi and Larson (1984) depict as internalized standards of performance. Communities of pastoral care strengthen students' internal locus of control (Marsh & Kleitman, 1992). That is, as Osterman (2000) in her seminal review reminds us,

> autonomy develops most effectively in situations where children and teenagers feel a sense of relatedness and closeness rather than disaffiliation from significant adults. Autonomy is not about isola-tion and private space but, instead, refers to the individual's sense of agency or self-determination in a social context. (p. 329)

Related dynamics of a healthy self also grow in positive student com-munities. We know, for example, that self-confidence is often augmented in schools characterized by authentic membership and support (Croninger

& Lee, 2001; Farrell, 1990; Goodenow, 1993). Caring and support are also welded tightly to feelings of competence (Laffey, 1982; Osterman, 2000; Silins & Mulford, 2010) and resilience (González & Padilla, 1997; Crosnoe, 2011).

Dispositions Toward Learning

A thick line of research has established that pastoral care influences students' orientation toward school and learning and promotes the development of positive educational values and attitudes (Battistich et al., 1995; Sweetland & Hoy, 2000; Osterman, 2000) and subsequent achievement-related behaviors (Adams & Forsyth, 2009; Goodenow, 1993). Students in safe and caring environments are more likely than their peers in communities of low pastoral care to find value in school (Adams & Forsyth, 2009) and have "a positive orientation toward school" (Osterman, 2000, p. 331). These youngsters often have a greater interest in school and like school and classes more than students in communities assessed as low in support and belonging (Birch & Ladd, 1997; González & Padilla, 1997; Osterman, 2000). They identify with their schools more and invest more in their learning (Ancess, 2003; Marsh & Kleitman, 2002). Community also exerts a strong shaping force on "prosocial attitudes, beliefs, and behaviors, including concern and respect for peers and teachers, conflict resolution, acceptance of out groups, [and] intrinsic prosocial motivation and behavior" (Osterman, 2000, p. 334). The obverse of the research themed storyline above is true as well. Weak communities in which students have impersonal connections with teachers and perceive a lack of pastoral care produce negative orientations toward school (Osterman, 2000). They nurture values and attitudes that often lead to counterproductive coping strategies (Crosnoe, 2011; Eckert, 1989; Farrell, 1990), ones that undercut meaningful engagement and social and academic learning (Demaray & Malecki, 2002b; Hattie, 2009; Ma, 2003).

Motivation is the most examined learning disposition in the literature on student community. Here scholars routinely find that pastoral care is highly associated with student motivation to work and to succeed in school (Barnett & McCormick, 2004; Bryk et al., 2010; Opdenakker et al., 2012). According to Battistich and associates (1995, 1997), personalized community motivates students to adopt and honor school classroom norms and values and enhances the desire to acquire competence. Motivation is important, in turn, because it impacts engagement and social and cognitive outcomes (Battistich et al., 1995; Hattie, 2009; Opdenakker et al., 2012).

Studies have also shown that sense of support and belonging forged in relationships with administrators, teachers, and peers is correlated with student commitment to the school and the work they do there (Ancess, 2003; Baker et al., 1997; Battistich et al., 1995). Self-confidence is impacted by pastoral care (Ancess, 2000; Wilson & Corbett, 1999). With high pastoral care, students become more invested in their academic achievement

(Ancess, 2000); demonstrate a greater appetite for learning (Felner et al., 2007; Munoz, Ross, & McDonald, 2007), that is, a "greater interest in challenging instructional activities" (Johnson & Asera, 1999, p. 100); and exhibit more "academically oriented forms of agency" (Conchas, 2001, p. 501). Community grows the important disposition of future orientation (O'Connor, 1997). In particular, educational aspirations are shaped by pastoral care (Laffey, 1982; Marsh & Kleitman, 2002).

Community nourishes possibility and hope (Eckert, 1989; Farrell, 1990; Rodriguez, 2008). Students ensconced in a strong climate of safety and care are likely to develop a robust sense of industry and a robust work ethic, a commitment to and feeling of accomplishment in undertaking schoolwork, and a commitment to learn the adaptive skills (Demaray & Malecki, 2002b) and to master "the habits of work necessary for school success" (Ancess, 2003, p. 21). In particular, students in such school environments demonstrate greater self-directedness (Birch & Ladd, 1997; Farrell, 1990) and exercise more leadership (Demaray & Malecki, 2002b). They are willing to take risks in the service of learning (Goodenow, 1993), exercise meaningful "pursuit in the demands and struggle for quality performance" (Ancess, 2003, p. 41), and assume responsibility for their work (Ancess, 2003; Birch & Ladd, 1997; Silins & Mulford, 2010). Students in positively anchored cultures learn to take and display pride in their efforts and their accomplishments (Marsh & Kleitman, 2002).

ENGAGEMENT AND LEARNING

When we examine the model of community of pastoral care for students, we see that everything examined to this point is designed to impact the variable most proximal to learning, student engagement. As Conchas (2001, p. 480) succinctly captures this essential reality, "institutional mechanisms mediate school engagement," that is, "changing students' experiences within schools can enhance engagement" (Newmann et al., 1992, p. 17). More specifically, we note that powerful relations, robust norms, and social integration and self-development promote active engagement while the absence of these cultural ingredients leads to disaffiliation and disengagement. We also learn, and explore in the next section, that there is a moderate to strong link between engagement and student academic success, one that has the power to trump aptitude (Laffey, 1982).

Engagement

Effective schools are defined by high levels of student engagement. In these schools, teachers work to make the option of disengagement difficult to impossible for youngsters (Ancess, 2003). To strengthen schools, it is essential, therefore, that increasing student engagement is relocated to the center stage of the school improvement production (Datnow, Park, & Kennedy, 2008; Hattie, 2009; Joselowsky, 2007; Newmann, 1981) and that we work to deepen our understanding of this pivotal construct (Fredricks et al., 2004; Marks, 2000). We turn to that work shortly. However, we revisit recurring reminders before we do so. It is essential to remember that both academic press and pastoral care are central pathways toward active student engagement, pathways that regularly intertwine. Our focus in this chapter is on the second avenue, creating communities of pastoral care. Our discussion of academic press is limited to the points where the two pathways cross and/or travel together. As is the case with the other pieces of the model, context matters with engagement. There are, for example, nuances associated with level of schooling, at risk status, gender, and so forth (Fredricks et al., 2004; Galletta & Ayala, 2008; Laffey, 1982). Also, while we do not continuously highlight the fact in our unpacking of engagement, leadership is an essential catalyst in fostering this deep commitment. Our goal is to enrich the toolbox in ways for school administrators to accomplish that work.

Definition

As with a good number of the elements in our model, engagement is not directly observable. It needs to be inferred from observations, observations informed by knowledge and influenced by judgments (Newmann et al., 1992; Rumberger, 2011). It has a manipulable or malleable quality absent from many of the context variables that surround and interact with the model (e.g., gender). However, as Fredricks and associates (2004) explain in their keystone review, like other elements of the model (e.g., self-concept) engagement is a theoretically and conceptually messy construct.

Research provides different lenses to think through the idea of student engagement in school, all of which illuminate the multidimensional nature of the construct (Balfanz et al., 2007; Fredricks et al., 2004; Marks, 2000). One of the most important is place of action: inside classrooms, outside the classroom, but inside the school, and outside regular school activity (i.e., extracurricular experiences) (Finn & Rock, 1997; Rumberger, 2011). Another approach is to define engagement by its intensity and/or duration (Fredricks et al., 2004). Finn and Rock (1997) explore levels of engagement, with level one signifying compliance and level two representing active initiative taking, what Alexander and team (1997) designate as procedural versus psychological engagement and others label procedural versus substantive commitment. All emphasize the fact that active engagement is required if youngsters are to reap the benefits of schooling (Fredricks et al., 2004). At other times, engagement and disengagement are defined in terms of its components—which are generally coupled to level—such as participation, investment, and commitment (Fredricks et al., 2004). It is best, perhaps, to think of engagement as both ways of acting and states of mind (Alexander et al., 1997), often described in the literature as behavioral and emotional engagement, with the former dimension picking up involvement and the latter incorporating the affective responses of youngsters to schooling.

Fredricks and associates (2004) provide us with the richest conceptual map of engagement, one that is scaffolded on three core pillars: cognitive engagement, emotional engagement, and behavioral engagement. Cognitive engagement attends to issues of self-regulation. The focus here is on metacognition and cognitive strategy use and investment in learning. It "includes flexibility in problem solving, preference for hard work, and positive coping in the face of failure" (p. 64). Emotional engagement according to these scholars is often cast in terms of student identification with school, including an assortment of "emotions related to the school, schoolwork, and the people at the school" (p. 66). Finally, for Fredricks and colleagues and other scholars of student engagement (Alexander et al., 1997; Balfanz et al., 2007; Voelkl, 1997), behavioral engagement includes general and specific actions, including work-related and conduct actions, such as putting forth effort, attending, participating, paying attention, and demonstrating persistence. More specifically, they define behavioral engagement in three ways.

> The first definition entails positive conduct, such as following the rules and adhering to classroom norms, as well as the absence of disruptive behaviors, such as skipping school and getting in trouble. The second definition concerns involvement in learning and academic tasks and includes behaviors, such as effort, persistence, concentration, attention, asking questions, and contributing to class discussion. A third definition involves participation in school-related activities, such as athletics or school governance. (Fredericks et al., 2004, p. 61)

A Model of Engagement

Earlier, we introduced pathways of engagement and disengagement in schooling (see Figure 7.2). Here we delve more fully into disaffiliation and disengagement, what we hold to be the most critical problem in education today, in general and even more so for subordinate minorities (Fredricks et al., 2004; Steele, 1992, 1997) and students from low income (Murphy, 2010) and working class homes (Eckert, 1989; Farrell, 1990; Weis, 1990)—students who are least likely to fit the existing model of schooling and most likely to have cultural norms and values that are at odds with the prevailing expectations and norms of schooling (O'Connor, 1997; Voelkl, 1997).

We start with the fact that engagement and disengagement are two sides of a continuum (Newmann et al., 1992). The job of the school is to get and keep students at the farthest right-hand side of that continuum, full and meaningful engagement in the classroom and the school, "arranging conditions so that people expend energy in ways that enhance engagement with work" (Newmann, 1981, p. 548). As suggested above, the roots of disengagement (or engagement) in schools can be traced to conditions in the larger world of childhood and adolescence, to the alignment between this larger world and the focus and methods of schooling, and to actions specific to schools. At times, schools cause disengagement. More often than not, however, they fail to ameliorate or exacerbate nascent disaffiliation (Baker et al., 1997), either by ignoring the realities of the larger world in which youngsters operate, or ineptly (often thoughtlessly) attempting to force students to fit into prevailing school models (e.g., demonstrating unawareness of or rejecting cultural norms and values of working-class and minority cultures) (Crosnoe, 2011; Murphy, 2010; O'Connor, 1997). We also build on Laffey's (1982) sage advice and employ multiple indicators to measure engagement. In terms of an advance organizer, we note that the model in Figure 7.2 is designed to provide a comprehensive profile of commitment and effort featuring indicators across the various categories we discussed above (e.g., places, types, components).

The model is heuristic. It shows "levels" of engagement on a continuum, from active disengagement to active engagement. The categories represent overlapping bands on that continuum. On the positive side of the line, we refer to the lowest level of engagement as "minimalist participation." At this point, students are investing very little in schooling, "doing just enough." Minimal effort, involvement, and psychological investment are evident (Eckert, 1989; Newmann et al., 1992; Weis, 1990). This is a marginal form of engagement, overlapping with "procedural compliance" on the disengagement side of the line. They share the gene of passivity, with students "doing what they are told, but not consciously doing anything at all" (Weis, 1990, p. 32). The middle point on the engagement side of the continuum is best thought of as "required participation," where more than minimum is invested by students. Students exert sufficient energy to meet classroom and school expectations. Students appear to be "on-task" here. There is involvement, but little psychological investment. The high point on the engagement continuum is "commitment." At this level, we see active involvement and meaningful investment in learning on the part of students. Active involvement

> involves psychological investment in learning, comprehending, or mastering knowledge, skills, and crafts, not simply a commitment to complete assigned tasks or to acquire symbols of high performance, such as grades or social approval. (Newmann et al., 1992, p. 12)

Five levels define disengagement, "the emotional and physical withdrawal of students from school" (Voelkl, 1997, p. 294), rungs on the ladder of disaffiliation representing degrees of "students' feeling of not belonging in school and not valuing school and school-related behaviors" (p. 294). We examine them from passive to active withdrawal. We see first "procedural compliance" which we argue is the modal point of student engagement with schooling today, a reality that is both troubling and sobering for those in the schooling business (Newmann et al., 1992; Voelkl, 1997; Weis, 1990). As we revealed above, it shares space with minimalist participation. Students here work to "get by" (Weis, 1990). They are not especially interested in the goals of the school (Csikszentmihalyi & Larson, 1984) and demonstrate very little interest in their education (Crosnoe, 2011; Weis, 1990). They have mastered the art of appearances, however. They have learned how to get along by going along. By and large, they "do not engage in overt or calculated rejection of school" (Weis, 1990, p. 18) or its values and norms. They participate in the form, but not the substance of education (Eckert, 1989; Farrell, 1990). Here, as Weis (1990, pp. 32–33) documents, engagement "plays itself out largely in student participation in the maintenance of the appearance of order and a willingness to hand something in in order to pass courses." There is adherence to school routines and little more than perfunctory effort (Ancess, 2003; Newmann et al., 1992). "Students just sit in class and do what they are told" (Weis, 1990, p. 30).

On the next two rungs down the ladder of disengagement, we see "ambivalence" and "apathy." They overlap and share a few defining elements with procedural compliance as well. They key difference between them and their lethargic cousin is that some active resistance to schooling, to its goals, values, norms, procedures, and ways of operating, begins to appear. Going along to get along is supplemented at times by even less positive and more negative energy, push back on school routines and structures, although more implicit and less subversive than we find further down the continuum (Crosnoe, 2011; Farrell, 1990).

"Alienation" represents a still more robust form of disengagement. It includes withdrawal of personal agency and withdrawal from accepted forms of community in school (Ancess, 2003), a deepening estrangement (Newmann, 1981). The resistance gene is enriched and becomes increasingly explicit (Eckert, 1989). School goals and values are not simply rejected, but often trampled on. The most vigorous form of disengagement is "hostility." Getting by and going along to get along are rejected as personally demeaning actions. Counterproductive (from the schools' perspective) values formed on "ways of being" at school are on display (Crosnoe, 2011; Eckert, 1989). Controlled battles with teachers are engaged, and sometimes sought out. Maladjustment becomes a viable protective faction in the short term (Jackson & Warren, 2000). "Delinquent" subcultures often materialize based on this hostility to school (Eckert, 1989).

Community and Engagement

Investigatory work that maps backward from student success is quite informative at this point of the narrative. It demonstrates that engagement does indeed occupy a keystone position in the framework of student learning. That is, it establishes the validity of the right hand side of the model in Figure 7.1. This scientific analysis confirms the validity of the left hand side of the model as well. That is, a positive culture for young-sters is shown to be a central catalyst in fostering student engagement, especially for students from lower SES families (Felner et al., 2007; Ma & Klinger, 2000; Rumberger, 2011). Research helps us see that each of the earlier pieces of the model in Figure 7.1 (e.g., safety) enhances student con-nections to school and that collectively they provide a powerful platform for active engagement (Marks, 2000). Communities of pastoral care for students make weak engagement and disengagement difficult options for youngsters to select (Ancess, 2003).

To begin, we learn that the quality of student relationships with teachers is "significantly associated with students' active engagement in schools" (Goodenow, 1993, p. 23): "School culture that prioritizes relation-ships can significantly mediate academic engagement" (Rodriguez, 2008, p. 768). Scholars also illustrate a parallel connection between peers and student engagement (Fredricks et al., 2004). Peers push and pull friends toward commitment to school goals, values, and norms, investment and effort that helps foster communities of care and membership, communities that ratchet up student engagement in school (Fredricks et al., 2004).

Turning to the norms of personalized culture that unfold in the con-text of student-teacher and student-student relationships, researchers confirm a strong, positive linkage between care and engagement (Baker et al., 1997; Ma, 2003; Quint, 2006). They also substantiate an associa-tion between students' perceptions of teacher support and active invest-ment and involvement in the classroom, in school, and in extracurricular activities (Battistich et al., 1995; Conchas, 2001; Goodenow, 1993); with all three types of engagement reviewed by Fredricks and colleagues (2004)—cognitive, emotional, and behavioral; and in both the academic and social support categories (Balfanz et al., 2007; Demaray & Malecki, 2002a). There is evidence of a viable connection between the norm of safety and order and a variety of indices of student engagement as well (Bryk et al., 2010). In schools characterized by a lack of order, disengagement flourishes (Bryk et al., 2010). Finally, an abundance of research draws empirical links between membership (belonging) and student engagement (Fredricks et al., 2004), as reflected in investment, effort, and commitment (Goodenow, 1993; Ma, 2003; Osterman, 2000).

A nearly identical theme is evident in the research narrative on the intermediate outcomes displayed in Figure 7.1. Each of the three mediat-ing variables here can enrich or diminish student effort and identification with the school. Social integration has a vibrant association with student engagement (González & Padilla, 1997; Newmann, 1992; Voelkl, 1997). We reported above that pastoral care enhances self-concept. Here we add that self-concept, as reflected in measures of competence (Fredricks et al., 2004), "student appraisals of personal skillfulness" (Laffey, 1982, p. 62), and agency (Fredricks et al., 2004; Rodriguez, 2008), is powerfully linked with student engagement. Finally, studies substantiate that the enhancement of learning dispositions, such as motivation (Goodenow, 1993; Hattie, 2009; Opdenakker et al., 2012), orientation toward school (Bruggencate et al., 2012; Crosnoe, 2011; Marks, 2000), and persistence (Voelkl, 1997) deepen student engagement.

Learning

Getting Started

The research is consistent and firm in demonstrating a relationship between communities for students and their success in school (Battistich et al., 1997; Demaray & Malecki, 2002a, b; Rodriguez, 2008), especially in terms of academic and social learning (Allensworth & Easton, 2005; Goodenow, 1993; Rodriguez, 2008). That is, "different school cultures can indeed distinguish consequences for student outcomes" (Witziers, Bosker, & Kruger, 2003, p. 416). At times, these connections are drawn for single elements of the model in Figure 7.1 (e.g., the norm of safety, learning dispositions) (Croninger & Lee, 2001; Lee & Burkham, 2003; Newmann et al., 1989) and in other cases for clusters of the elements (Gamoran, 1996) consistent with the core notion of community, "exchanges of social resources enhance the effectiveness not only of individual actions, but also collective actions" (Lee & Burkham, 2003, p. 362). There are also spillover effects here to professional communities for teachers and communities of engagement for parents.

In some of the research of interest here, the engagement piece of our model is implicit, it remains unhighlighted in the story of student community and learning outcomes. Other studies do, however, throw a bright spotlight on student commitment and effort with engagement operating as the summative catalyst to power final valued outcomes. Fredricks and team (2004, p. 61) make this point explicitly when they conclude "that engagement, once established, builds on itself, thereby contributing to increased improvements in more distal outcomes of interest." Analyses in these studies uncover strong associations, for better or worse, between engagement and academic and social-emotional student development (Bruggencate et al., 2012; Feldman & Matjasko, 2005; Finn & Rock, 1997; Marks, 2000). As highlighted in other sections of this chapter, there is also a good quantity of solid scientific evidence that pastoral care and engagement are of particular significance for students in peril, that is, for children from low-income households, for youngsters from subordinated minority groups, and for students on the wrong side of the achievement gap (Croninger & Lee, 2001; Felner et al., 2007; Rumberger, 2011).

Before we explore the specific outcomes that are influenced by engagement, it is beneficial to revisit a few key points and introduce the importance of variability in connections between engagement and learning. On the first issue, it is important to once again remind our-selves that it is both academic and social support and press interlinked that carry us to the goal of strong learning outcomes. We also resur-face the importance of reciprocity and interactiveness throughout the model. Here that means that while strengthened, student engagement produces better student outcomes; better outcomes, in turn, enhance engagement—and the earlier variables in the model as well (e.g., the norm of membership, sense of self).

It is also important to reacknowledge that our understanding of engage-ment is composed of multiple concepts or components, components that can have different effects on various outcomes. And components them-selves are often composed of multiple elements. For example, as discussed above, engagement can occur in three places, classrooms, the school extend-ing beyond the classroom, and extracurricular venues. Extracurricular activities, in turn, include diverse offerings, such as sports, academic and nonacademic clubs, student government activities, and so forth. Effects on academic and social outcomes are not the same for each type of activ-ity. Some of these activities are more valuable for one type of outcome, i.e., social learning, rather than academic learning or vice versa. Within each outcome there can also be variation. For example, on the matter of academic achievement, engagement in sports may produce stronger results in literacy than mathematics (Leitner, 1994) while the opposite may hold for active participation in school governance. We note also that engagement effects on outcomes are not linear (Marsh & Kleitman, 2002). There is often an optimal amount of participation, a sweet spot if you will. A surfeit of engagement will often produce deteriorating effects.

Finally, it is necessary to direct attention to the meaning of outcome effects. Such effects are almost always registered in terms of enhance-ments of the outcomes under scrutiny (e.g., better student attendance, higher graduation rates). Our understanding is broader. Positive effects also include breaking downward spirals of achievement and socioemo-tional states. As Felner and team (2007, p. 215) discovered, this "preventive effect" is essential in the chronicle of communities of pastoral care for students.

Socioemotional and Academic Outcomes

The primary function of schooling is to create positive possibilities for students, an outcome that is often not met, especially in schools with large numbers of students from minority, low-income, and working-class homes (Eckert, 1989; McLaughlin & Talbert, 2001; Weis, 1990). The most important avenue schools have to achieve this goal is to help students reach ambitious targets of social and academic learning. This, of course, is the essential rationale for fostering and nurturing communities of pastoral care for students.

Social Learning On the socioemotional dimension, pastoral care is associated with both personal and social adjustment (Ancess, 2003). Included here are outcomes, such as prosocial values and reasoning (Baker et al., 1997; Battistich et al., 1997), emotional well-being (e.g., mental health and psychological adjustment) (Feldman & Matjasko, 2005; Felner et al., 2007), satisfaction with school (Baker et al., 1997), and effective social skills (Demaray & Malecki, 2002a).

When attending to social-emotional outcomes, scholars focus heavily on what Guest and Schneider (2003, p. 89) and Birch and Ladd (1997, p. 78) respectively call "social adjustment" and "school adjustment." This concept can be partitioned into three sub-areas. The first is the well-documented power of a cooperative culture to reduce behavioral risks, risks often linked to limited sense of community membership, or what Crosnoe (2011, p. 128) refers to as "not fitting in socially." Particularly salient here, according to Crosnoe (2011, p. 103), is the link between positive culture and the prevention of "coping responses that are self-protective in the short term, but are problematic, even disastrous, in the long term," that is, counterproductive coping strategies, such as depression and withdrawal.

A second, and related, function is the ability of community to "constrain and prevent delinquent behavior" (Maguin & Loeber, 1996), to damp down misbehavior (Felner et al., 2007; Osterman, 2000; Rumberger, 2011). For example, in her comprehensive review of student community, Osterman (2000) reports that pastoral care is negatively correlated with student use of illegal drugs and delinquency. Similar conclusions on behavioral problems have been documented by others as well (Bloomberg et al., 2003; Catalano et al., 1999; Goddard & Goff, 1999), including Demaray and Malecki (2002a, p. 235), whose "results provide strong evidence to suggest that there is a negative relationship between the amount of social support students perceive and the amount of problem behavior in which they are engaging." Research affirms also that damping down misbehavior extends to attendance issues such as skipping classes and truancy (Felner et al., 2007; Fredricks et al., 2004; Quint, 2006).

The third aspect of social and school adjustment addresses the ways by which positive student community nurtures the development and growth of social skills. Marsh and Kleitman (2002) highlight effects on character and social adeptness. Feldman and Matjasko (2005, p. 191) note that pastoral care leads to stronger community engagement later in life.

Academic Outcomes Two overlapping academic outcomes are linked to communities for students in the research, best captured under the broad heading of "positive academic behaviors" (Croninger & Lee, 2001, p. 565). The first is attainment. The second is achievement.

Attainment One set of data here is collected in the two-sided ledger of dropping out and graduation. Investigators report vibrant linkages between pastoral care in general and these two indices of effectiveness. It is widely documented that anemic amounts of community, defined by relationships, norms, institutional affiliation, and engagement, are highly associated with students not finishing high school (Balfanz et al., 2007; Farrell, 1990; Ma, 2003)—college as well (Braxton, Hirschy, & McClendon, 2011).

Conversely, through the chain of action presented in Figure 7.1 the presence of supportive communities promotes graduation (Alexander et al., 1997; Balfanz et al., 2007; Croninger & Lee, 2001). Relationships are linked to school completion, reducing the likelihood of leaving school early by nearly half (Croninger & Lee, 2011). The community norms and intermediate outcomes in Figure 7.1 are also implicated in the narrative of school completion (Croninger & Lee, 2001; Fredricks et al., 2004; Lee & Burkham, 2003; Osterman, 2000; Patterson et al., 2007; Rumberger, 2011). So too is the critical bridging variable of student engagement, with "dropping out consistently linked to disengagement" (Balfanz et al., 207, p. 225) and "engagement leading to higher retention rates" (Bruggencate et al., 2012, p. 703). We close with the recognition that the three aspects of school and social adjustment—reducing behavioral risks, constraining misbehavior, and developing social skills, are deeply intertwined (Balfanz et al., 2007). They are also tightly linked to the indicators of achievement we explore below.

A sibling of high school graduation is "academic progress," how effective students are in earning the academic credits they need to be successful, including promotion between grades, what Crosnoe (2011, p. 106) refers to as "the accumulation of valued academic credentials." We find here again that there are quite meaningful associations between communities of pastoral care (i.e., relationships, norms, institutional affiliation, engagement) and academic progress (Balfanz et al., 2007; Patterson et al., 2007). According to Crosnoe (2011), the long-term effects of interfering with progress starting in the early grades is of special concern.

A third measure of attainment addresses college enrollment. As with the other two indicators of attainment, academic progress and high school graduation, communities rich in positive relationships of care and support open doors to college. Students with less productive relationships with their teachers and peers and those who are marginalized and/or disengaged in high school are less likely to enroll in institutions of higher education.

Academic Achievement Not surprisingly, although there are some cautions in the literature about tunnel vision (Csikszentmihalyi & Larson, 1984), most of the findings on outcomes of communities for students are in the domain of academic achievement. While the storyline here is not completely cloudless (see Battistich et al., 1995; Bryk et al., 2010; and Quint, 2006 for some cautionary notes), the cumulative weight of the evidence leads to the conclusion that there are robust connections between the early pieces of the model in Figure 7.1 and academic achievement (Hoy et al., 1998; Roney et al., 2007) and, not surprisingly given the discussion above, that there is an even stronger bond between the final two pieces of the model, engagement and achievement.

Focusing in on relationships, a good deal of research connects "familial-type environments" (Antrop-González, 2006, p. 289) and academic success (Conchas, 2001; Sebastian & Allensworth, 2012; Sweeney, 1982). Theorists have posited and researchers have documented that strong relationships help, indirectly, students learn more than when those relationships are absent, or worse, negative (Ancess, 2003; Hattie, 2009; Leithwood, Patten, & Jantzi, 2010). Closeness matters for student learning (Birch & Ladd, 1997). Relationships "constitute a form of social capital that is of value in children's academic success" (Goddard, 2003, p. 59). In a parallel manner, analysts also confirm that there are vibrant indirect linkages between the norms that define student-teacher and student-peer relationships and academic success. Care (Adams & Forsyth, 2009; Antrop-González, 2006; Ma, 2003), support (Balfanz et al., 1997; Conchas, 2001), safety (Newmann et al., 1989; Robinson et al., 2008; Wilson & Corbett, 1999), and membership (Crosnoe, 2011; Ma, 2003; Voelkl, 1997) are each implicated in this finding. The same conclusion holds for the intermediate outcomes, each of which—social integration (Marsh & Kleitman, 2002), self-concept (Hallinan & Kubitschek, 1999; Rothman & Cosden, 1995), and learning dispositions (Hattie, 2009)—is associated with academic success.

Turning to the last link in the model, we uncover a familiar theme. The benefits of education require activities that "elicit and maintain involvement" (Laffey, 1982, p. 62). When this occurs, scholars uniformly demonstrate "a positive correlation" between engagement and "achievement-related outcomes" (Fredricks et al., 2004, p. 70). This finding holds for all types of children (Feldman & Matjasko, 2005; Osterman, 2000; Voelkl, 1997); or as Marks (2000, p. 155) says, "Across diverse populations." Of course, the obverse is true as well, "lack of engagement adversely effects student achievement" (Marks, 2000, p. 155). Returning to the positive side of the ledger, we find evidence that engagement that fuels achievement may induce "a positive self-confirming cycle supportive of continued engagement" (Balfanz et al., 2007, p. 230) and aspirations for further achievement (Guest & Schneider, 2003; Marsh & Kleitman, 2002). We also uncover confirmatory evidence that these positive gains in academic performance stretch across a variety of assessments, for example, grades, scores on standardized test, and measures of deeper understanding (Crosnoe, 2011; Fredricks et al., 2004; Voelkl, 1997).

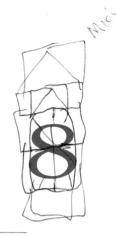

Instructional Capacity of School Personnel

Here our attention is devoted to leader support focused on building human capacity in schools. This human capital is composed of the knowledge and skills possessed by teachers, what Bryk and team (2010, p. 108) refer to as "teachers' capacity to articulate engaging instructional pedagogy," and Drago-Severson (2004) defines as the bundle of cognitive, interpersonal, and intrapersonal skills needed to function effectively.

There is a considerable paradox associated with efforts to enhance teacher capacity in schools. On the one hand, human capital is routinely described as perhaps the key element in the health of organizations (Tichy & Cardwell, 2004) and professions (Garet, Porter, Desimone, Birman, & Yoon, 2001). Commitments of learning are essential, a precondition to individual and organizational growth (Porter, Garet, Desimone, & Birman, 2003; Scribner, Cockrell, Cockrell, & Valentine, 1999). Or as Blanc et al. (2010, p. 222) remind us, "investments in human capital cannot be bypassed": "organizational improvement requires substantive and ongoing opportunities to learn" (Goldenberg, 2004, p. v).

In educational organizations, the same narrative is evident: (1) "Schools can do no better than the teachers who work in them" (Guskey, 2003, p. 16); (2) "school improvement and the improvement of teaching and student learning depend fundamentally on the development of teachers' knowledge [and] abilities" (Smylie, Conley, & Marks, 2002, p. 171); and (3) "improvement in the stock of teacher quality provides an important channel through which principals can raise the quality of education" (Branch, Hanushek, & Rivkin,

2012, p. 30). This conclusion holds for district and school change (Felner, Seitsinger, Brand, Burns, & Bolton, 2007; Heller & Firestone, 1995) and systematic reform efforts (Blanc et al., 2010; Garet et al., 2001) as well: "One cannot assume that schools can transform themselves into productive and successful places of learning without first addressing the learning that must occur among teachers" (Morrissey, 2000, p. 24) to enhance instruction. There is an axiom in schools: "If educators want to improve instruction then the skills of teachers must be upgraded" (Cooley & Shen, 2003, p. 18). And what holds for schools in general is of special importance for leaders in schools and districts serving children placed at risk (Lomotey, 1989; Murphy, 2010).

In short, it is widely held that talent development is "the best bet for teaching practice" (Supovitz & Turner, 2000, p. 964), a conclusion confirmed in some of the best qualitative (Blase & Blase, 1999) and quantitative (Hattie, 2009) research and scholarly reviews (Cotton, 2003). Later in this section we examine ways that leaders broker capacity development and the accumulation of human capital. Here we simply provide an advance organizer, confirming that "the most successful principals exhibit strong commitments to the professional development of the teaching staff" (Ross, Sterbinsky, & McDonald, 2003, pp. 18–19) and reinforcing the conclusion that "promoting teachers' professional development is the most influential instructional leadership behavior at both the elementary and high school levels" (Blase & Blase, 2004, p. 12).

On the other hand, although generally "touted as the ticket to reform" (Wilson & Berne, 1999, p. 185) professional development has enjoyed a checkered history in education (Hawley & Valli, 1999). Insufficient attention has been devoted to this critical domain of schooling. Traditional mechanisms are routinely found to be wanting, both at specific times in the life of schools and across the careers of teachers (Newmann, King, & Youngs, 2000; Palincsar, Magnusson, Marano, Ford, & Brown, 1998). "Schools generally do not have a coherent, coordinated approach to professional development" (Desimone, Porter, Garet, Yoon, & Birman, 2002, p. 105). They maintain a casual attitude that promotes dysfunctional norms such as isolation and privacy (Murphy, 2005a). Much of the professional learning that has occurred has been "fragmented, intellectual superficial" and has failed "to take into account what we know about how teachers learn" (Borko, 2004, p. 3). Overall the assessment is that "existing models of professional development are not adequate to achieve ambitious learning goals" (Supovitz & Turner, 2000, p. 964). We should not be surprised to discover a strategy with tremendous upside has not had the impact it could.

Over the last few decades, researchers and developers have helped us better grasp the construct of human development by forging frameworks to discuss the research. Owen (2003) and others employ dimensions such as form, duration, content, collective participation, active learning, and coherence. Garet and colleagues (2001) portray five aspects of professional development under the two major headers of core features and structural features. Borko (2004, p. 4), in turn, identifies the following as key components of professional development:

- The professional development program
- The teachers, who are the learners in the system
- The facilitator, who guides teachers as they construct new knowledge and practices
- The content in which the professional development occurs

In this chapter, we build from these assorted frameworks using three domains to capture the essentials of high quality professional development to which leaders need to attend: systems principles of learning, principles of adult learning, and principles of organizational learning. We also spend considerable time examining specific, effective actions of leaders in this arena.

PRINCIPLES OF HUMAN DEVELOPMENT

Systems Principles of Learning

On the systems front, research exposes a set of characteristics of effective professional development around the domain of time. To begin with, the central importance of time for learning to occur is consistently cited in the research (Firestone & Martinez, 2009; Goldenberg, 2004). We discern positive findings about subdimensions of time there as well. The importance of depth of learning experiences is visible across the literature (Barnes, Camburn, Sanders, & Sebastian, 2010; Penuel, Fishman, Yamaguchi, & Gallagher, 2007). For example, in their study, Supovitz and Turner (2000, p. 975) found that dramatic results from professional development "emerged when the experiences were deep and more sustained. Both teaching practices and classroom cultures were affected most deeply after intensive and sustained staff development activities." Embedded here also is the time dimension of sustained work (Darling-Hammond & McLaughlin, 1995; Youngs & King, 2002). That is, "professional development is likely to be of higher quality if it is both sustained over time and involves a substantial number of hours" (Garet et al., 2001, p. 933). The research also exposes other related time dimensions that are important in the professional development algorithm, such as the span or the time period over which learning unfolds and the extensiveness of learning opportunities (Freiberg, Huzinec, & Templeton, 2009; Hawley & Valli, 1999). Follow-up time is critical (Blumenfeld, Fishman, Krajcik, Marx, & Soloway, 2000) as is time during the school day for learning activities (Phillips, 2003).

Chapter 8

In short, quality professional development is a long-term endeavor (Goldenberg, 2004; McDougall, Saunders, & Goldenberg, 2007). The logic here is captured by Penuel and associates (2007, p. 929): "Professional development that is of longer duration and time span is more likely to contain the kinds of learning opportunities necessary for teachers to integrate new knowledge into practice."

Researchers provide some specificity to these dimensions of time in their analyses. Joyce and Showers (cited in Freiberg et al., 2009, p. 75), for example, found that teachers require one year at a minimum to master a new curriculum. Supovitz and Turner (2000, p. 973) concluded that teachers in their study required eighty hours of professional development before they began "using inquiry-based teaching practices significantly more frequently . . . than the average teacher." And significant change in the classroom culture occurred only after one hundred and sixty hours of professional development.

Systems learning also provides insights about the coherence aspect of professional development. We know, for example, that capacity building is most productive when it is school based (Owen, 2003; Penuel et al., 2007). That is, it is "well matched to the school's needs" (Desimone et al., 2002, p. 449), "integral to school operations" (Hawley & Valli, 1999, 140), attends to learning within the school (Hayes, Christie, Mills, & Lingard, 2004), and provides "useful" knowledge to teachers (Hawley & Valli, 1999). We learn also that professional development is most productive when it "reflect[s] best demonstrable practice and [is] research based" (Hawley & Valli, 1999, p. 137) and when the spotlight is on student learning goals and outcomes (Newmann et al., 2000; Youngs & King, 2002), when it is "rooted in the knowledge base for teaching" (Wilson & Berne, 1999, p. 175). Likewise, effective capacity building is related to coherence between activities and the mission and goals of the school (Garet et al., 2001; Leithwood, Jantzi, & Steinbach, 1999), state and district standards (Garet et al., 2001), the individual goals (Owen, 2003) and needs (Newmann et al., 2000) of teachers. Researchers confirm that "activities that are connected to teachers' other professional development experiences and other reform efforts are more likely to produce enhanced knowledge and skills" (Garet et al., 2001, p. 933). In a similar vein, "a professional development activity is more likely to be effective in improving teachers' knowledge and skills if it forms a coherent part of a wider set of opportunities for teacher learning and development" (Garet et al., 2001, p. 927), that is, it "is integrated with a comprehensive change process that deals with the full range of impediments to and facilitators of student learning" (Hawley & Valli, 1999, p. 138).

More specifically, system learning reveals the importance of coherence of professional development with students' needs (Hawley & Valli, 1999) and "to what schools expect students to know and be able to do" (p. 134). Coherence also addresses linkages to the results of teaching on children (Robinson, 2007) and to the processes by which children learn (Garet et al., 2001), including focus on specific youngsters (McLaughlin & Talbert, 2001; Supovitz & Turner, 2000). Gravity here fuses professional development to "specific and concrete instrumental tasks" (McDougall et al., 2007, p. 85). On this issue, we know that professional development that "is integrated into the daily life of school is more likely to produce enhanced knowledge and skills" (Garet et al., 2001, p. 935). Palincsar and team (1998, p. 9) refer to this as "activity at the workbench," "practical ideas [that can be] incorporated directly into teaching" (Owen, 2003, p. 120), that is, "interactive with teaching practices" (Penuel et al., 2007, p. 929). We also know that focus on content is an essential element of quality professional development (Garet et al., 2001). Research helps us see that "an explicit focus on subject matter" (Borko, 2004, p. 5) rather than on more general instructional practices defines effective professional development (Desimone, 2002). Indeed, Porter and associates (2003, p. 32) conclude that "generic professional development that focuses on teaching techniques without a content focus does not appear to be effective." We return to the consequences of productive professional development. Here we simply note that coherence has been linked to teacher knowledge (Garet et al., 2001; Penuel et al., 2007), teacher change (Porter et al., 2003), curriculum implementation, and academic gains for students (Bryk et al., 2010).

Adult Learning Principles

We know that talent development has both individual and collective (community) dimensions (Borko, 2004). That is, "change in classroom teaching is a problem of individual learning as well as organizational learning" (Garet et al., 2001, p. 922). In this section, we concentrate on the former, examining the principles of adult learning uncovered in studies of professional development that lead to important positive outcomes for teachers and children. In the following section, we redirect the spotlight to learning communities, principles that have important consequences for individuals and groups. As we will see, there is a unifying overlap between the individual and collective aspects of teacher learning, with principles of adult learning also playing out in community-based professional development (Stigler & Hiebert, 1999).

In the broadest sense, talent development "recognizes teachers as professionals and adult learners" (Wilson & Berne, 1999, p. 175). It is informed by and applies theories and principles of adult development (Blase & Blase, 2004; Drago-Severson, 2004). It is also "grounded in a common set of professional development standards" (Supovitz & Turner, 2000, p. 965). It begins with this reality: "One cannot assume that schools can transform themselves into productive and successful places of learning for students without first addressing the learning that must occur among teachers" (Morrissey, 2000, p. 24).

We learn also that impactful professional development fosters a sense of ownership for learning (Robinson, 2007). It is not the responsibility of others, but an integral, self-regulated activity (Hawley & Valli, 1999). Learning depends less on control than on "teachers' personal and professional commitment to improve" (Blumenfeld et al., 2000, p. 156). Professional development scaffolded on adult learning principles underscores active learning and engaged learning opportunities (Desimone et al., 2002; Garet et al., 2001). According to Wilson and Berne (1999, p. 194), this means "that teacher learning ought not to be bound and delivered but rather activated." "From this perspective, effective professional development programs would aim for more than transmitting knowledge, but would also teach problem-solving knowledge in the work context" (Barnes et al., 2010, pp. 244–245). It is more hands-on work than what is normal in the profession (Penuel et al., 2007). Learning has a robust generative dimension. It is constructed (Franke, Carpenter, Lei, & Fennema, 2001; Desimone et al., 2002).

Effective professional development is characterized by authenticity (Supovitz & Turner, 2000). Work is meaningful and relevant (Blase & Blase, 2004; Leithwood, Anderson, Mascall, & Strauss, 2011), not simply abstract (Desimone et al., 2002). It is practice-based, that is, "situated in classroom practice" (Wilson & Berne, 1999, p. 176) and is "an integral part of the occupation and career of teaching" (Little, 1982, p. 334) in current time (Darling-Hammond & McLaughlin, 1995). Learning is about "actively wrestl[ing] with actual problems embedded in work" (Barnes et al., 2010, p. 244).

Human development actions that are successful are practice anchored and job embedded; that is, they are context sensitive. "Context specificity" (Hiebert & Pearson, 1999, p. 13) contains a number of key ideas, but primarily it means "building from analysis of [one's] own setting" (p. 13). Sensitivity to context implies that "teachers learn in the classrooms and schools in which they teach" (Stigler & Hiebert, 1999, p. 135). They "learn how to teach more effectively while teaching" (Lyons & Pinnell, 1999, p. 205) rather than in traditional out-of-class and school activities. Growth is "connected to and derived from teachers' work with children" (Askew & Gaffney, 1999, p. 87), and effectiveness comes to be defined in terms of "what works with the children [one is] teaching" (Duffy-Hester, 1999, p. 489; see also Pinnell, Lyons, DeFord, Bryk, & Seltzer, 1994). The center of gravity is real challenges in the classroom (Au & Asam, 1996), that is, "resolving instructional problems" (Manning, 1995, p. 656). "All theory building is then checked against practice" (Askew & Gaffney, 1999, p. 85) and "application is direct and obvious" (Stigler & Hiebert, 1999, p. 165).

Impactful professional development "offer[s] a healthy mixture of both support and challenge" (Drago-Severson, 2004, p. 33). Development based on the principles of adult learning challenges teachers' current understandings (Robinson, 2007), creates productive disequilibrium (Hawley & Valli, 1999), unfreezes current knowledge (Wilson & Berne, 1999), "creat[es] opportunities for analysis and reflection" (Bryk et al., 2010, p. 55), and challenges problematic assumptions (Robinson, 2007). Challenge "push[es] the edges of a person's thinking and/or feeling so as to expose the person to new ways of thinking" (Drago-Severson, 2004, p. 33).

The above ideas underscore that there is a sense of localness about effective professional development (Anderson, Hiebert, Scott, & Wilkinson, 1985; Owen, 2003). We discern the importance of application and reflection (Barnes et al., 2010). Adult learning-based professional development is heavily inquiry based (Franke et al., 2001; Penuel et al., 2007). "Quality professional development immerse[s] participants in inquiry, questioning, and experimentation. [It] models inquiry forms of teaching" (Supovitz & Turner, 2000, p. 964). Just-in-time and ongoing feedback and reflection are distinctly visible (Owen, 2003; Garet et al., 2001). Professional development anchored in adult learning perspectives highlights the involvement of teachers in learning (Burch & Spillane, 2003; Rutter, 1983), including teacher input into the form, content, and activities of learning opportunities (Hawley & Valli, 1999; Patty, Maschoff, & Ranson, 1996). There is a fluidness and messiness to impactful professional development that belies the idea of tightly boxed learning (Hawley & Valli, 1999; Wilson & Berne, 1999). Because application of learning is critical, considerable attention is devoted to use of learning insights. Attention is also given to context, with particular emphasis on where teachers are in their professional careers (Drago-Severson, 2004). High quality professional development is deeply embedded in the tapestry of the school, "learning is considered part of the work" (Hawley & Valli, 1999, p. 140). "Teachers are engaged in professional learning every day, all day long" (Owen, 2003, p. 103).

Community Learning Principles

A robust line of research confirms that much of the professional development in high-performing schools also has a collective focus; what Newmann and associates (2001) refer to as a schoolwide focus, Bryk and team (2010) call a supportive professional work culture, and Desimone and colleagues (2002) and Penuel and team (2007) describe as collective participation. That is

> collective participation of groups of teachers from the same school, subject, or grade is related both to coherence and active learning opportunities, which in turn are related to improvements in teacher knowledge and skill and changes in classroom practice. (Garet et al., 2001, p. 936)

The spine of community-based learning principles is collegial action or communal arrangements (Askew & Gaffney, 1999). We also know that excellent schools "model a learning community in the way teachers engage with new learning to achieve common goals" (Bryk et al., 2010, p. 99). In short, community learning principles provide an invaluable framework for professional knowledge and growth (Barnes et al., 2010; Garet et al., 2001), school improvement (Bryk et al., 2010), teacher instruction, and student learning (McLaughlin & Talbert, 2001). "Without collaborative problem solving, individual change may be possible, but school change is not" (Hawley & Valli, 1999, p. 141). Collaborative professional development works in straightforward ways. According to Penuel, Riel, Krause, and Frank (2009) and Mulford and Silins (2003), such efforts nurture the development of trust, enhance the acceptance of reform solutions, augment resources, motivate teachers, and provide clarity to change initiatives. Each, in turn, deepens the capacity for learning.

Cautions

There are some important cautions to surface here, however. First, learning community is not a panacea (Bryk et al, 2010; Supovitz & Christman, 2003). "There is nothing particularly virtuous about collaboration per se. Individuals can collaborate to block change or inhibit progress just as easily as they can enhance the process" (Guskey, 2003, p. 12).

Thus, one of the most critical concerns is a misguided faith in the ability of structure and policy to power change (Murphy, 1991). Specifically, by ignoring the tendency for reforms to materialize sans engine and drive train we often end up with a change in name only (McLaughlin & Talbert, 2001). In this case, that would be a group of teachers bound together by time, but without the trust, vision, resources, and responsibility to transform into a community (Penuel et al., 2009; Youngs, 2007).

While we often describe this in terms of the creation of an "empty shell," a second "in name only" problem needs to be surfaced. We refer to the formation of inauthentic, artificial, or pseudo community (Grossman, Wineburg, & Woolworth, 2001; Vescio, Ross, & Adams, 2008). Pseudo community may actually be more harmful than the empty structure because it has the potential to actively solidify nonproductive patterns of interactions among teachers (Hoy et al., 1998), for example, burying conflicts and problems and silencing joint exchange (Grossman et al., 2001).

Second, teacher learning communities are defined by universal ideas (e.g., collective responsibility). But this does not mean that getting those principles and norms into play is the same in all situations (Supovitz, 2008; Vescio et al., 2008). As Craig (2009, p. 615) reminds us, community work "fuses[s] or collide[s] with the mixture of what is already going on." The cost of overlooking context in the area of learning communities is especially high (Walker & Slear, 2011). We know that "teachers bring their own contexts with them" to the community (Penuel et al., 2007, p. 931). We also know subject matter is important in the community-building process (Burch & Spillane, 2003; McLaughlin & Talbert, 2001). That is, subject matter norms will mediate how teachers think about and respond to community-building initiatives. The obvious corollary is that the department context matters for practice communities (Siskin, 1994; Stoll, Bolam, McMahon, Wallace, & Thomas, 2006). History matters as well (Kochanek, 2005), as does the existing stock of relational trust (Bryk et al., 2010). Level of schooling is important (McLaughlin & Talbert, 2001; Moller & Eggen, 2005). District context and school size exert influence over community development (Dannetta, 2002; Louis, 2007). Personal characteristics such as gender, race, and years of experience also shape the formation of professional communities (Grissom & Keiser, 2011; Visscher & Witziers, 2004).

Third, there is the possibility that a practice community will misfire, producing negative results (Curry, 2008; Grossman et al., 2001). For example, researchers have documented how learning communities can operate: (1) "to perpetuate stereotypes, prejudice, and staid or destructive practices" (Printy, 2008, p. 188); (2) to reinforce exclusion, insularity, and marginalization; (3) to herald the status quo and staunch innovation (McLaughlin & Talbert, 2001; Smylie & Hart, 1999); (4) to nurture dysfunctional relationships (Stoll et al., 2006); and (5) to privilege management goals at the expense of professional objectives (Hayes et al., 2004).

One emerging concern is that communities will become vehicles to engage work unrelated to mission, in much the same way that guidance counselors have been transformed into quasi-administrators at times. That is, teachers in communities will work on everything but instructional practice (Supovitz, 2002), a type of administrative usurpation and organizational goal displacement (Firestone & Martinez, 2007; Penuel et al., 2010). Another growing worry is that these professional communities will simply bury teachers under the weight of added responsibilities (Murphy, 2005a; Webb, 2005). More bothersome is some evidence that the downsides of open dialogue and constructive critical conversations can be unleashed in professional communities; that is, "community can have ambivalent as well as positive tendencies" (King, 2001, p. 247). Tensions and anxieties are often toxic byproducts of learning communities (Mullen & Hutinger, 2008).

It is also appropriate here to remind ourselves that once in place, communities are often fragile (Palincsar et al., 1998; Printy, 2008). Regression to old patterns of behavior and norms is not unusual (Goldstein, 2004). Thus, cautions about stalling out merit scrutiny as well (Greene & Lee, 2006; Levine & Marcus, 2007).

Collaboration as the Center Pillar

As introduced above, communities of practice are defined by the norm of collaboration (Blase & Blase, 2000; Ross et al., 2003). Ermeling (2010, p. 386) defines collaboration as a "joint productive activity where participants assist each other to solve a common problem or produce a common product." Because it is more tangible than other elements of community and often provides the backdrop on which the elements come to life, it occupies disproportionate space in the community of practice narrative. For collaboration to be productive, shifts in how teachers think about, talk about, and go about their work are required (Drago-Severson, 2004; Levine & Marcus, 2010). It rests on the understanding that what teachers do outside their classrooms is as important as what unfolds inside those settings (McLaughlin & Talbert, 2001; Stoll et al., 2006) and that collective work done well can accelerate their learning and the achievement of their students (Heck & Hallinger, 2009; Supovitz, 2002).

An assortment of researchers have crafted robust frameworks to expose the aspects of collaboration. For example, for McLaughlin and Talbert (2001, p. 41) "teachers are mutually engaged in teaching; they jointly develop their practice; and they share a repertoire of resources and history." For Printy (2008, p. 199), the following are all important pieces of collaborative effort: "the range of activities available for participation, the quality of members' participation as legitimate or peripheral, the rules for social interaction of members, and the joint understanding of the work that brings individuals together." More generally, Wenger (1998, 2000) describes collaboration as an algorithm of events, commitments, membership, and tasks. From our analysis, we assert that the power of professional communities of practice can be measured by how well the sub-elements of engagement—purpose, structure, focus, and nature—adhere to known quality criteria. More concretely, we find that effective collaboration is mutual, purpose-driven work. It is learning centered and instructionally focused. It is driven by the tenets of evidence-based inquiry. And it is directed to improved teacher practice and student achievement via teacher learning (Murphy & Torre, 2014).

Purpose Effective collaboration is defined by clear purpose, "persistently working toward detectable improvements" (Ermeling, 2010, p. 378). The work itself is the avenue to improvement, not the outcome (Ermeling, 2010). Effectiveness plays out in the application of a teacher's learning practice (Cochran-Smith & Lytle, 1999). What Wenger (1998, 2000) refers to as the "purpose of shared enterprise" (1998, p. 45) pivots on clear measures of outcomes benchmarked against expectations (Louis, 2007) or common goals (Johnson & Asera, 1999) and compelling direction (Fullan, 2002).

Mutuality provides the structure or frame of collaboration, the process of joint work (Johnson & Asera, 1999; Supovitz, 2010). It is grounded on the understanding that relationships are the heart and soul of community (Bryk et al., 2010; Gronn, 2009). One of the fathers of communities of practice, Wenger, talks about "mutual engagement" (2000, p. 229) and "shared enterprise" (1998, p. 45). Colleagues in education refer to mutuality as group practice, changing a roster of individuals into a collaboration of "relational cultures" (Drago-Severson, 2004, p. 40), "joint enterprise" (Young, 2006, p. 538), and "joint identity" (Grossman et al., 2001, p. 1005) featuring a "culture of collaboration" (Southworth, 2002, p. 88), "collective engagement" (Visscher & Witziers, 2004, p. 786), and a "process of participation" (Horn, 2005, p. 211). Mutuality according to Printy (2008) requires that members be advantaged by access to the resources of the group and that they add to that capacity (Heller & Firestone, 1995; McLaughlin & Talbert, 2001). It is about "enabling a rich fabric of connectivity" (Wenger, 2000, p. 232). It is about making shared engagement, peer support, mutual assistance, and joint enterprise a generalized condition in schools (Goldenberg, 2004; Kruse, Seashore Louis, & Bryk, 1995), about working and learning together (Olivier & Hipp, 2006; Stein & Coburn, 2008). It is about active engagement in "meaningful discussion, planning, and practice" (Garet et al., 2001, p. 925). Mutuality is essential because it "provides a point of convergence for teachers' inquiry—the joint enterprise for community of practice" (McLaughlin & Talbert, 2001, p. 122). It underscores needed job-centered learning (Drago-Severson, 2004; Olivier & Hipp, 2006) and fosters capacity development (Clark, Dyson, Millward, & Robson, 1999). Shared enterprise features what Louis and Marks (1998, p. 538) refer to as "the quality of relationships among group work members." Collegial support and general norms of teamwork and joint engagement are paramount under conditions of mutuality (Grossman et al., 2001; Phillips, 2003). Without mutuality, purpose of engagement cannot be fulfilled (Levine & Marcus, 2010).

Mutuality and its family members, participation, engagement, and joint activity, are dependent, of course, on opportunities to work together, on "enabling structure and supportive organizational context" (Fullan, 2002, p. 15) or "knowledge space" (Hattie, 2009, p. 264). These opportunities are often conspicuous by their absence in schools and require the strong hand of leadership broadly defined. Of course, this means that there needs to be something on which time to plan, work, and learn together makes sense (Johnson & Asera, 1999), "some intersection of interest, some activity" (Wenger, 2000, p. 232), what Ermeling (2010, p. 386) refers to as "common ground to talk." Without this, there can be no authentic joint exchange (Beck & Foster, 1999; Hawley & Valli, 1999).

Structure Creating structure for productive joint enterprise requires attending to an array of issues. Most importantly, there is the need to establish the domain of collaboration (Wenger & Snyder, 2000). We know also that thought must be devoted to what Wenger (2000) refers to as the types of activities that will ground the collaborative. Important here is ensuring that both formal and informal mechanisms are engaged (Ancess, 2003; Olivier & Hipp, 2006)—and in a coordinated and synchronized manner (Drago-Severson, 2004). The size of groups is important and the question of how much to align with existing organizational arrangements (e.g., departments, grade levels, teaching teams) needs consideration (Wenger, 1998, 2000). Thus the topic of boundaries is important, including how these demarcations are managed (Penuel et al., 2010; Wenger, 2000). So too is the fluidity and stability of collaborative work teams (Curry, 2008; McLaughlin & Talbert, 2001), what Wenger (2000) describes as rhythms of the work. Amount of time to work and the regularity of exchanges merit consideration. So too does the life span of a work group (Leithwood et al., 1999; McLaughlin & Talbert, 2001). The topic of how teachers become members of collaborative teams also must be addressed. Contrary to normal practice in education, self-selection receives high grades in the general literature as a mechanism of selection (Wenger, 1998). Also important is how much of one's professional identity is committed to and defined by collaborative work (Wenger, 2000). Finally, research informs us that how work is structured and the tools employed to guide the work make valuable contributions to how well joint enterprise is conducted (Levine & Marcus, 2010; Saunders, Goldenberg, & Gallimore, 2009). The concreteness of the work and the collaborative organizational form employed are quite relevant as well (Vescio et al., 2008).

The research carries us one level deeper in thinking about collaboration, to the criteria for judging the authenticity of joint work. Issues here include the presence or absence of reciprocal influence (Kruse et al., 1995), density of ties (Wenger, 2000), and mutual dependence (Beck & Foster, 1999; Young, 2006). Measures of the amount of the teaching-learning process (i.e., the work of classrooms) that is made open for inspection helps determine authenticity (Grossman et al., 2001; Horn, 2005); that is, how much of the work becomes "public" (Printy, 2008; Young, 2006). The depth of sharing can reveal a good deal about the validity of collaboration (Harris, 2009; Young, 2006). The "fingerprint" test for joint construction work is useful here. How many members of the collaborative actively contributed to the work? How many were mere spectators? Authenticity can also be determined in part by the robustness of the leadership displayed by members in the collaborative (Murphy, 2005a). The extent to which teachers change their practice is a key criterion (Printy, 2008; Visscher & Witziers, 2004). We revisit many of these issues below when we examine specific responsibilities of principals in collaborative community work.

Focus Structure is an essential dimension of all support and of community in particular. But as Ancess (2003, p. 4) cautions, "achievement of community requires more than the space for developing commodity." More specifically, "what collaboration is designed to focus on will have significant implications for what teachers can and can't learn from work with colleagues" (Levine & Marcus, 2010, pp. 392–393). For example, researchers report that simply addressing logistical issues and nonlearning conditions does not translate into robust collaboration and community nor result in intermediate or summative outcomes.

On the positive side of the storyboard, analysts have uncovered productive foci for collaborative work. To begin with, it is clear that the center of gravity should be the classroom (Gray et al., 1999; Hayes et al., 2004) and on challenges of work there. Educational concerns trump nonacademic issues (Murphy, Beck, Crawford, & Hodges, 2001). Attention flows to the core technology (Mulford & Silins, 2003; Useem, Christman, Gold, & Simon, 1997). That is, interactions should be anchored in issues of learning and teaching (Supovitz, Sirinides, & May, 2010; Useem et al., 1997), and be deep and ongoing.

Not surprisingly given the above comments, there is near universal agreement that the focus of collaborative engagement should be on students (Ancess, 2003; Ermeling, 2010). Both for teachers to mature into a productive community and to power up learning, students need to be at the center of collaborative work (Goldenberg, 2004; Grossman et al., 2001). Becoming more specific, these analysts find that the focus should be on student academics (Olivier & Hipp, 2006; Saunders et al., 2009): "A collective focus on student learning is central to professional community" (Louis & Marks, 1998, p. 539), especially analyses of student learning needs, problems, and progress (Halverson, Grigg, Prichett, & Thomas, 2007; Vescio et al., 2008). There is a "shared understanding of teaching and learning" (Bryk et al., 2010, p. 133) and shared language (Hawley & Valli, 1999).

Backward mapping from student learning, the focus of this collective engagement is instructional practice embedded in specific curricular domains (Curry, 2008; Young, 2006), collaboration to strengthen the school's instructional program (Huberman, Parrish, Hannan, Arellanes, & Shambaugh, 2011; Supovitz & Poglinco, 2001) and the pedagogical skills of each teacher (Gurr, Drysdale, & Mulford, 2006; McLaughlin & Talbert, 2001). Vescio and colleagues (2008, p. 85) succinctly summarize the research on this issue as follows: "Findings reinforce the importance of persistently pursuing an instructional focus as teachers engage in their work in learning communities." As discussed above, "problems of practice" focus is privileged in highly productive collaborative work (Levine & Marcus, 2010; McLaughlin & Talbert, 2001). The spotlight is on specific, observable, malleable practices that are described with transparency, clarity, and concreteness (Little, 1982; Mitchell & Sackney, 2006), a "collaborative examination of day-to-day practice" (Vescio et al., 2008, p. 81). Finally, as we explain more fully below, a particular type of shared instructional practice is routinely discussed in the research on teacher communities in general and collaboration particularly: evidence-based analysis (Blanc et al., 2010; Cosner, 2011), a condition that Visscher and Witziers (2004, p. 798) refer to as the "sine qua non for the development of professional communities."

Nature So far we have examined three of the four core ingredients of collaboration (purpose, structure, and focus). We now turn to the final aspect of shared enterprise, the ways in which productive communities operate. To maintain consistency with colleagues who have researched this domain, we describe the method of engagement as reflective practice (Blase & Blase, 2004). According to Stoll and her team (2006, pp. 222–227),

> *reflective professional inquiry* includes: "reflective dialogue" conversations about serious educational issues or problems involving the application of new knowledge in a sustained manner; "deprivatization of practice," frequent examining of teachers' practice, through mutual observation and case analysis, joint planning and curriculum development; seeking new knowledge; tacit knowledge constantly converted into shared knowledge through interaction; and applying new ideas and information to problem solving and solutions addressing pupils' needs.

We parcel the research on "method of engagement" into two overlapping concepts: inquiry and evidence-based practice.

On the first topic, in dissecting collaboration scholars consistently highlight professional practice informed by individual and group reflection (Grossman et al., 2001; Louis, Dretzke, & Wahlstrom, 2010). Indeed, inquiry is generally presented as a hallmark "method" or "stance" that defines shared enterprise in communities of practice (Grossman et al., 2001; Visscher & Witziers, 2004). The concept travels under a variety of different names in the literature—reflective inquiry, reflective discussions, group inquiry, sustained inquiry, inquiry-oriented practice, reflective practice, collegial inquiry, and so forth. It means, according to Drago-Severson (2004, p. 18), "reflecting on one's assumptions, convictions, and values as part of the learning process," the investigation and critical assessment of practice, research, and logic (King, 2001). That is, it is a "stance" which honors the interrogation of knowledge, skills, and dispositions around instructional practice (Levine & Marcus, 2007). Its purpose is to forge joint understanding of and shared practices in the service of student learning (Kruse et al., 1995; Mitchell & Sackney, 2006). Productive inquiry in professional communities of practice is analytic, dynamic, continuous, and constructivist in nature (Horn, 2005; Little, 1982).

Reflective inquiry has as much to do with dialogue, or what Horn (2005, p. 229) calls "conversational involvement," as it does with patterns of thinking (Stoll et al., 2006; York-Barr & Duke, 2004). Indeed, it is reasonable to add conversation to the methods of engagement label, what Wilson and Berne (1999, p. 200) nicely capture with the term "narrative of inquiry." Grossman and her colleagues (2001, p. 1001) maintain that teacher communities create an "invitational conversational climate," a reflective-based constructed dialogue, what Cochran-Smith and Lytle (1999, p. 280) nail with the idea of "teacher learning through talk." It is in these continuous professional conversations that reflections become visible for inspection (Curry, 2008), venues in which feedback can be provided and debated (Kruse et al., 1995).

Two aspects of dialogue in the service of building collaboration are routinely highlighted in the research on professional culture. The public nature of conversations is consistently seen as essential (Horn, 2010; Young, 2006), what Levine and Marcus (2010) describe as detailed and open representations. This public stance centered on student work is especially productive (Goldenberg, 2004). A good deal of recognition is also awarded to the openness of collaborative exchange (Garet et al., 2001), an idea that Horn (2010, p. 255) beautifully captures as "a willingness to reveal and work at the limits of one's knowledge." Dialogue is not merely an act of civility. Difficult conversations unfold in collaborative work (Drago-Severson, 2004; Huberman et al., 2011). Critique is expected (Grossman et al., 2001; Silins & Mulford, 2004). "Questioning and challenging colleagues" (Horn, 2010, p. 234) is normal. Concerns and doubts are to be aired, "difference, debate, and disagreement are viewed as the foundations" (Stoll et al., 2006, p. 227) of reflective inquiry. In addition, there is solid evidence that formalizing collaborative conversations in education can be helpful (Beachum & Dentith, 2004; Levine & Marcus, 2010). There is a strong sense that "protocol-guided conversations" (Curry, 2008, p. 742) enhance the public and critical aspects of collaborative dialogue (Curry, 2008; Horn, 2005).

Collegial dialogue is half of the method or stance on engagement. The other half, based on the findings of Levine and Marcus (2010) and Penuel and colleagues (Penuel, Frank, & Krause, 2006, p. 527) that "the effectiveness of collaboration depends on what kinds of interactions take place," is evidence based (Fullan & Ballew, 2002; Grossman et al., 2001). This means that not only is there critical, collegial exchange, but the conversations are anchored in knowledge and data, especially support for ideas and more importantly evidence of impact on one's students (Ermeling, 2010; Hattie, 2009).

In highly productive collaboratives, considerable attention is devoted to the "visible and explicit cause-effect connections between instructional decisions and student outcomes" (Ermeling, 2010, p. 379). "Analysis and interpretation of some form of student learning data" (Cosner, 2011, p. 789) is the grist for collaborative dialogue (Visscher & Witziers, 2004). As was the case for inquiry, researchers find that tools such as protocols and artifacts to guide evidence-based collaboration can assist greatly in the work (Horn, 2005).

TYPES OF PROFESSIONAL DEVELOPMENT

As we have documented above, building capacity of existing staff is about bringing to life systems learning principles, adult learning principles, and community learning principles, almost always in an integrated manner. In this section, we spotlight the ways in which capacity building takes form.

At the macrolevel, reviewers discuss both "linking teachers to external assistance and creating internal conditions that support teacher development" (Youngs & King, 2002, p. 656). They also routinely emphasize both the formal and informal modes of learning (Johnson & Asera, 1999; Leithwood & Jantzi, 2006). A two-dimensional perspective that divides professional development into those focused on individual teachers and those attending to collaborative work is also well established in the research (Bulkley & Hicks, 2005; McLaughlin & Talbert, 2001). Ross and team (2003, p. 23), also highlighting the macrolevel, divide professional development into these two aspects: "encouraging teachers to attend training sessions and enabling teachers to meet during school and provide support to each other." Similarly, Saunders and associates (2009, p. 1029) divide professional development into "two engagements, learning teams and conventional professional development." In their seminal study, Porter and colleagues (2003) discuss both traditional activities (e.g., workshops) and reform activities (e.g., action research teams). Drago-Severson (2004, p. 23) distinguishes

> between transformational learning—learning that helps adults to develop capacities to better manage the complexities of work and life—and informational learning—increases in knowledge and skills that are also important and can support changes in adults' attitudes and possibly their competencies.

Ancess (2000) deepens this framework by categorizing learning experiences into those where teachers generate or construct new knowledge and those where they reproduce knowledge.

Hawley and Valli (1999) provide a framework that features five "models" of professional development, including the individually guided model; the training model; the observor assessment model; the development/improvement process model; and the teacher researcher model. Drago-Severson (2004) posits a six-part architecture: training; observation/coaching/assessment; improvement process; inquiry, collaborative action research; self-directed; and mentoring.

Blase and Blase's (1999, 361) investigation linking leadership and professional development produced six professional development strategies:

> (a) emphasizing the study of teaching and learning; (b) supporting collaboration efforts among educators; (c) developing coaching relationships among educators; (d) encouraging and supporting redesign of programs; (e) applying the principles of adult learning, growth, and development to all phases of staff

development; and (f) implementing action research to inform instructional decision making.

Also focusing on leaders directly, Drago-Severson (2004, p. 17) found that

> principals employ four mutually reinforcing initiatives that support adult growth and development; they form the four pillars on which the weight of this new learning-oriented model rests. They are (1) teaming/partnering with colleagues within and outside of the school, (2) providing teachers with leadership roles, (3) engaging in collegial inquiry, and (4) mentoring.

Cochran-Smith and Lytle (1999) provide an especially insightful and helpful set of "conceptions" in the area of teacher learning featuring "knowledge of practice." The Cochran-Smith and Lytle (1999) framework is especially useful because it addresses the key elements of what, how, and why teachers learn. These scholars unpack three conceptions of teacher learning. The first is "knowledge-for-practice." Here the focus is on the external generation of knowledge that teachers then employ to improve teaching. The second is "knowledge-in-practice." Here we see that "the most essential knowledge is practical knowledge," knowledge "embedded in practice and in teachers' reflections on practice" (p. 250). The third conception is knowledge of practice. Here the assumption is

> that the knowledge teachers need to teach well emanates from systematic inquiries about teaching, learners and learning, [and] subject matter and curriculum. The knowledge is constructed collectively. (p. 274)

At the microlevel, analysts catalogue the types of experiences in which, and with which, teachers participate. The list is long and covers important activities such as professional development workshops; university-offered classes; mentoring relationships; opportunities to work with colleagues; action research projects; dissemination of written materials such as articles and protocols; opportunities to observe and to be observed by colleagues at one's school; visits to other sites; coaching; guided professional readings; and opportunities to lead in one's school or district (Cotton, 2003; Owen, 2003).

Below we turn our attention more explicitly to the role of leaders in making the architecture and forms of teacher learning productive. Before we do so, however, we highlight four contextual notes. First, as Hattie (2009) has documented, not all forms of professional development are equal in their impact on teacher knowledge and instructional practice.

The four types of instruction found to be most effective on teacher knowledge and behavior were: observation of actual classroom methods; microteaching; video-audio feedback; and practice. Lowest effects were from discussion, lectures, games/simulations, and guided field trips. Coaching, modeling, and production of printed or instructional materials also had lower effects. (p. 120)

Second, not all teachers benefit equally from professional learning opportunities. For example, Hill, Rowan, and Ball (2005, p. 400)

> suggest that those who may benefit most are teachers in the lowest third of the distribution of knowledge and that efforts to recruit teachers into professional development and preservice coursework might focus most heavily on those with weak subject matter knowledge for teaching.

Third, learning "type" is a holding container that does not make the topic of quality obvious. Other aspects of professional development need to be added to the narrative as well (Anderson, Moore, & Sun, 2009). To improve professional development, it is more important to focus on the duration, collective participation, and the core features (i.e., content, active learning, and coherence) than type (Garet et al., 2001, p. 936). Fourth, we need to remember that regardless of type, professional development works best when it is in the service of goals and school reforms (Hawley & Valli, 1999) and when it is part of a coherent and integrated system of school improvement (Bryk et al., 2010; Newmann et al., 2000). Two of the most significant studies of the last twenty years make these points quite explicitly:

> High-quality professional development in the context of a supportive professional community and where teachers were oriented toward improvement appears powerfully related to gains in academic productivity. (Bryk et al., 2010, p. 113)

> This suggests that compared to teachers whose professional development is not coherent, teachers who experience professional development that is coherent—that is, connected to their other professional development experiences, aligned with standards and assessments, and fosters professional communication—are more likely to change their practice. This positive effect for teachers whose professional development is coherent is true even compared to teachers who have gained the same underlying knowledge and skills as a result of their professional development experiences. (Garet et al., 2001, p. 934)

EXPLICIT NOTES ON THE ROLE OF LEADERS IN PROFESSIONAL DEVELOPMENT

In an earlier section, we described three dimensions of professional development—system learning principles, adult learning principles, and community learning principles. We expand on that work in this section by making explicit what leaders in effective schools do to promote teacher learning. We begin with general insights about leaders and then examine what researchers tell us about the activities of leaders in the area of communities of professional practice.

The General Role

Three points ground our analysis. First, promoting teacher learning is one of the most, if not the most, powerful leverage points in the portfolio leaders have to promote school improvement and increase student learning (Askew, Fountas, Lyons, Pinnell, & Schmidt, 2000; Rowe, 1995). In a major review, for example, Cotton (2003, p. 71) discovered that

> Principals of high-achieving schools offer more, and more varied, professional development activities than those in lower achieving schools. They are creative in securing the resources—financial, human, time, materials, and facilities—the school needs to improve.

In a second major review, Robinson (2007, pp. 15–16) concludes that the large impact here offers "empirical support for calls to school leaders to be actively involved with their teachers as the 'leading learners' of their schools." And Newmann and team (2000, p. 283) find a "powerful positive association between comprehensive professional development and the extent to which the principal exerts leadership."

Second, the salience of leaders in this domain is heightened by the fact that the critical elements of learning are almost impossible to bring forth "in the absence of leadership initiative" (Leithwood et al., 1999, p. 150), that is, "building professional capacity requires principal support" (Heck & Hallinger, n.d., p. 31). Teachers cannot pull this off on their own. Third, we reintroduce the caveat that leadership can also flummox the domain of teacher learning. Leadership can be "counterproductive if it is done without reference to the evidence about the particular qualities and processes of teacher professional development that produce effects on the students of participating teachers" (Robinson et al., 2008, p. 669).

One aspect of the good news here is that there are a variety of ways that leaders can bolster and enhance teacher learning and development. Major frameworks (some of which include actions in the area of professional community that we address below) have been provided by Drago-Severson (2004, p. 17), who describes four pillars or "mutually reinforcing initiatives that support adult growth and development." They include (1) teaching/ partnering with colleagues within and outside of the school, (2) providing teachers with leadership roles, (3) engaging in collegial inquiry, and (4) mentoring. Blase and Blase (2000, p. 135) describe six strategies leaders in their studies employed to promote teacher learning:

1. Emphasizing the study of teaching and learning

2. Supporting collaboration efforts among educators

3. Developing coaching relationships among educators

4. Encouraging and supporting redesign of programs

5. Applying the principles of adult learning, growth, and development to all phases of staff development

6. Implementing action research to inform instructional decision making

Youngs and King (2002, p. 665) suggest, in turn,

that effective principals can sustain high levels of capacity by establishing trust, creating structures that promote teacher learning, and either (a) connecting their faculties to external expertise or (b) helping teachers generate reforms internally.

And Leithwood and associates (1999, p. 161) in their extensive review point out that leadership contributes to teacher learning and growth when school administrators

- ensure that adequate financial, time, personnel, materials, and other resources necessary to support teacher development activities are available;
- provide opportunities for teachers to develop a shared view of the school's overall mission and more specific goals to which they are strongly committed;
- help teachers assess their own needs for growth and gain access to sources of assistance inside or outside the school;
- foster the development of a collaborative school culture within which opportunities exist for authentic participation in decision making about school-improvement efforts and meaningful interaction with colleagues about collective purposes and how to achieve them;

- build feelings of self-efficacy by recognizing teachers' accomplishments and by providing support to help reduce anxiety about tackling new initiatives; and
- share or distribute the responsibility for teacher development broadly throughout the school—for example, to teachers' colleagues, to teachers themselves, to external people who may be assisting in the school-improvement effort, and to the school-improvement initiative in which teachers are engaged.

While many school administrators "are involved only in the mechanical arrangements" of professional development (Leithwood & Montgomery, 1982, p. 327), leaders in high-performing districts and schools understand the value of teacher learning and honor that value in their work (Dinham, 2005; Youngs & King, 2002); they demonstrate deep personal involvement in the learning of adults. Or as Useem and colleagues (1997, p. 68) remind us, "the impact of professional development initiatives on a school [is] conditional to a large extent by the degree to which principals themselves become part of a collegial effort." Leaders in high performing schools expend more time on the professional development of teachers than do typical principals who "allocate very little of their time to activities aimed at improving teachers' teaching skills" (Heck, 1992, p. 30). They make "support for adult learning a demonstrated personal priority" (Drago-Severson, 2004, p. 4). Equally important, because one cannot lead what she or he does not know, effective leaders build commitment to and involvement in professional development on a deep understanding of instruction, curriculum, and assessment (Coldren & Spillane, 2007; Nelson & Sassi, 2005).

Leaders in high performing schools and districts are also strong catalysts for teacher learning (Bryk et al., 2010). They are out and about the school encouraging teachers in their efforts to grow. They encourage teachers to "open their doors" to colleagues inside and outside the school (Eilers & Camacho, 2007) and encourage and support them to become resources for their colleagues as well—what Anderson and team (2009, p. 123) call "residential experts." They provide a good deal of sensemaking to the work in and around teacher learning (Murphy, 2015a). These leaders are powerful facilitators as well. They "understand professional development can be a difficult journey that requires courage, risk taking, and even some failure along the way" (Blase & Blase, 1999, p. 18). Because of this, they are active in building bridges to learners, facilitating teachers' learning of content knowledge (Supovitz & Poglinco, 2001). And they incentivize and acknowledge teachers for their learning activities (Spillane, Halverson, & Diamond, 2001a) and "remove penalties for making mistakes as part of efforts toward professional improvement" (Leithwood et al., 1999, p. 76). As we reported in the area of support in general, a good deal of the leader's efforts here is centered around time and structural and material assistance (Owen, 2003).

Effective leaders make active investments in the professional learning of teachers in their districts and schools (Hiebert & Pearson, 1999). These leaders "provide the monetary or the other types of resources required to support teacher development activities" (Leithwood et al., 1999, p. 161). "They earmark resources for the professional development" (Cotton, 2000, p. 14) of teachers. They release staff to pursue learning opportunities that will benefit their children (Bryk et al., 2010; Dinham, 2005). They secure substitutes to cover release time for learning (Heller & Firestone, 1995; Timperley, 2009) so that teachers can "observe other teachers' classrooms and work with outside staff developers" (Bryk et al., 2010, p. 214). As necessary, high-performing leaders "help teachers gain access to sources of assistance inside or outside the school "(Bryk et al., 2010, p. 161).

The research informs us that more effective principals demonstrate a "hands on" or personal touch on professional development (Manning, 1995; Samuels, 1981). They spend more time than the average principal interacting informally around issues of learning for teachers (Burch & Spillane, 2003). They are also "more likely to be described by their teachers as participating in informal staff discussion of teaching and teaching problems" (Robinson et al., 2008, p. 663). They exercise a more consultative stance with their teachers (Youngs & King, 2002). Analysts also routinely report that effective leaders model what they expect their teacher colleagues to do (Dinham, 2005; Leithwood et al., 1999). They lead with action, not simply exhortation. They personally demonstrate the values and principles of quality professional development, especially the habit of "modeling continual learning in [their] own practice" (Mulford & Silins, 2003, p. 179). Nelson and Sassi (2005, p. 174) capture this beautifully when they tell us that these leaders "open themselves up to be learners as well as leaders." We also know that "modeling the importance of learning while leading is one way that principals build a healthy school climate" (Drago-Severson, 2004, p. 50).

Effective leaders promote learning "by widening the compass of leadership potential" (MacBeath, 2009, p. 49) in their schools and helping teachers assume leadership roles (Spillane, Halverson, & Diamond, 2001a). Leaders in effective schools tend to be active participants with teachers in learning opportunities (Cotton, 2003; Robinson, 2007), "participat[ing] more consistently in meetings and teachers professional development sessions than principals at comparison schools" (McDougall et al., 2007, p. 70). They are also more active in presenting to their staffs in groups and working one-on-one with teachers in their classrooms (O'Donnell & White, 2005; Sweeney, 1982). They become "fellows in communities of learners and activists for professional learning" (Mullen & Hutinger, 2008, p. 280). Such personal involvement seems to enhance the value of professional development activities by communicating something important to teachers (Blase & Blase, 2004; Datnow & Castellano, 2001).

The Role of Leaders in Professional Development
via Learning Communities

Although we possess less knowledge than we might desire, we have accumulated some understandings about leaders and learning communities over the last twenty-five years, some of which stretch across the more general findings just examined. We know, for example, that there is a set of key domains in which preemptive prevention, removal of existing barriers, and/or the construction of an infrastructure to support professional communities occur. We also understand now that leaders have a hallmark position in this work, a conclusion found in nearly every study of teacher communities of practice (Cosner, 2011; Halverson et al., 2007; Louis et al., 2010; Mitchell & Sackney, 2006; Stoll et al., 2006). We are aware that there are important differences in the shape and texture of leadership in schools with robust communities and those with weak communities (Youngs & King, 2002): "principals can construct their role to either support or inhibit the strength and quality of teacher community" (McLaughlin & Talbert, 2001, p. 101). More and more we are discovering that it is the principal who acts as the catalyst to bring other important supports to life (Bryk et al., 2010; Murphy, 2013). Without effective leadership, resources, time, and structures have almost no hope of emerging to support collaborative work (Cosner, 2009; Hayes et al., 2004). We also know that administrative leadership and professional community are interdependent, having an iterative relationship (McLaughlin & Talbert, 2001). Perhaps most important, there is a growing knowledge base which suggests that of all the ways that leaders have at their disposal to influence teacher learning, developing and supporting collaborative communities of professional practice may be the most powerful (Supovitz, Sirinides, & May, 2010).

It is important to acknowledge that for many leaders growing community necessitates a difficult transformation of their own understanding of leadership and their own leadership roles (Goldstein, 2004; Murphy, 2005a). "The implications for school principals are considerable" (Crowther, Kaagan, Ferguson, & Hann, 2002, p. 64), and this repositioning presents a real challenge for principals (Brown & Sheppard, 1999). Communities of practice are in some essential ways "at odds with the dominant conceptions of the principalship that have been in place in most educational systems for decades" (Crowther et al., 2002, p. 6). Thus just as teachers are being asked to step outside traditional perspectives of their roles (Mayrowetz, Murphy, Seashore-Louis, & Smylie, 2009), so also must leaders think in new ways about their roles (Harrison & Lembeck, 1996; Murphy, 2005a). Fostering the development of communities (Blegen & Kennedy, 2000) of practice necessitates a new knowledge and skill base and a new set of performances that are not often found in the education of school administrators (Childs-Bowen, Moller, & Scrivner, 2000; Murphy, 2005a). New metaphors for leadership emerge as well (Beck & Murphy,

1992; Sergiovanni, 1991a, b)—metaphors that reflect the role of school leader not in terms of their fit in the organizational structure but in terms of membership in a community of learners (Klecker & Loadman, 1998; Scribner et al., 1999).

The point to be underscored here is that for many leaders a personal transformation in leadership must accompany the quest to rebuild schooling to cultivate communities of practice. Absent this change, it is difficult to imagine that principals will develop a sense of security. Likewise, cultivating teacher community in a hierarchical and bureaucratic organizational seedbed is problematic at best (Murphy, 1991, 2013). New conceptions of organizations provide the foundations for developing the skills to foster norms of community (Murphy, 2002). This is challenging work, but leaders who do not begin here are not likely to be effective in making teacher inquiry a reality in schools.

Frameworks of Support

Over the years, analysts have cobbled together various frameworks to capture the array of factors and conditions that leaders can use to support the development of teacher communities. Stoll and colleagues (2006, p. 23) employ four categories: focusing on learning processes; making the best of human and social resources; managing structural resources; and interacting with and drawing on external agents. Mullen and Hutinger (2008, p. 280) also describe four sets of leader actions: manage resources, provide support and direction, exert appropriate pressure to achieve goals, and mediate group dynamics. Printy (2008, p. 211) discusses three leader functions: communicate vision, support teachers, and buffer teachers from outside influences. McLaughlin and Talbert (2001, p. 98) offer this list of related actions:

> For better or worse, principals set conditions for teacher community by the ways in which they manage school resources, relate to teachers and students, support or inhibit social interactions and leadership in the faculty, respond to the broader policy context, and bring resources into the school.

In their work, Supovitz and Poglinco (2001, p. 7) uncovered five strategies that leaders employ in their efforts to create professional communities of practice:

> First, these instructional leaders carefully developed a safe environment within which their teachers could take the risks associated with change. Second, they emphasized open channels of communication and strong collaboration amongst their faculty for the purpose of expanding the networks of engagement around issues of instructional improvement. Third, they cultivated informal and

formal leaders in their schools to both allow themselves time for instructional attention and to broaden the base for change in the school. Fourth, [they] employed powerful and symbolic actions and events to dramatize and reinforce their message. Finally, they developed strong systems for accountability even as they expanded teachers' flexibility to further develop their instructional practices.

A slightly different architecture is provided by Printy (2008, p. 199) who sees community building occurring through three roles:

> As agenda setters, leaders select policy messages to communicate to teachers and establish specific expectations or goals for teachers' work. As knowledge brokers, leaders focus teachers' attention on instructional matters, create the conditions for productive teacher conversations, scaffold teachers' learning as appropriate, and facilitate the translation and alignment of meanings across communities. As learning motivators, leaders nurture positive relationships, establish urgency for new approaches and hold teachers accountable for results, in essence tightening the connections between policy and practice.

Saunders and team (2009, p. 1028) highlight the centrality of time, administrative support, and structures, issues examined throughout this volume. This is consistent with our claim that the traditional "functions" of leaders can be engaged to nurture collaborative work (e.g., coordinating, monitoring). More parsimonious leadership frames have been provided by Kruse and associates (1995, p. 34): structural conditions and characteristics of human resources; by Hurd (cited in Morrissey, 2000, p. 6): structural conditions and collegial relationships; and by McDougall and colleagues (2007, p. 54): settings and processes. Taking a slightly different approach, Scribner and team (1999) describe administrative, moral, and political support from leaders employed in the service of creating communities of practice.

Starting with the groundwork presented above, we explore what the research confirms about the specific leader acts that foster professional communities. Before we do so, however, we need to reinforce some core ideas. First, the goal of leadership is not the development of learning communities. The objective is the creation of human and social capital that enhances the quality of instruction in the service of student learning. The wager here is that such communities provide a robust pathway to reach these more distal ends. Second, the focus is not primarily on beefing up each element of communities of practice individually. The best strategy is to deploy supports that forge an integrated scaffolding.

Finally, there are two activities that receive very limited treatment in the educational literature, but rise to the level of considerable importance in the research on organizations more broadly defined (Wenger & Snyder,

2000). To begin with, an essential responsibility of the leader is to identify people with the commitment, energy, and skills to do good work and bring them together, recognizing that these forged communities often do not follow existing organizational structures (e.g., grade level). Also important is the need for leaders to identify existing informal associations of people with shared interests (e.g., worries about a spike in the number of homeless children in the school) and support them functioning as collaborative communities. A key insight from these two lessons is that community is not isomorphic with the organizational chart.

Activity Domains

As is the case throughout the book, we carefully and deliberately build on the work of colleagues to arrive at our framework of leader supports for teacher communities. Concomitantly, we add new pillars to the structure and contextualize and add nuance to the collective body of evidence. We examine the following supports: creating structures and time, supporting learning, and managing the work—all of which are integrated with earlier analyses.

Creating Structures and Time We know a good deal about organizational structures in general and in the area of school improvement more specifically. As we reported earlier, structures shape what unfolds in districts and schools, partially determining what is and what is not possible. As the flip side of culture (Leithwood, Day, Sammons, Harris, & Hopkins, 2006; Leithwood, Jantzi, & McElheron-Hopkins, 2006), structures allow norms to flourish, or wither (Brooks, Milburn, Rotheram-Borus, & Witkin, 2004; Kruse et al., 1995). Our focus at this point in the analysis is on the positive side of the narrative, that is, how well-resourced and thoughtfully developed forums in districts and schools can help collaborative communities grow. The door through which we enter the analysis is "collaboration," the element of shared work that provides a seedbed for the growth of relationships, shared trust, and mutual responsibility (Bryk et al., 2010). In short, we review what is known about creating the supportive collaborative frame we detailed above.

A recurring theme throughout our work is that structural change does not predict organizational performance, student learning in the case of schools (Murphy, 1991, 2013). We are also cognizant that simply giving teachers a platform to talk will not ensure the development of valued professional norms and human and social capital (Levine & Marcus, 2007; Newmann et al., 2001). So while we acknowledge the essentiality of time and space to undertake collaborative work, we define structure in terms that underscore what is required for leaders to power community. At the core then, structure is about "interactive settings" (Cosner, 2009, p. 255) and "interaction patterns" (p. 273). It is about opportunities for forging relationships, for creating patterns of networks, and for promoting professional exchange through new channels of communication (May & Supovitz, 2011; Stoll et al., 2006). In short, it is about fostering professional collaboration (Ancess, 2003; Cosner, 2009).

Research helps us discern some ways principals work "structurally" to create and nurture teacher communities. On the issue of forums, first there is unanimous agreement that schools must take advantage of existing space and time configurations, to repurpose them (Cosner, 2009; Stein & Coburn, 2008). For example, community-building work is conspicuous by its absence from most faculty meetings. Principals can repurpose these, and many other meetings can be redesigned to deepen collaboration. At the same time, as we detail below, there is general agreement that new forums will need to be created as well (Ermeling, 2010). Third, a variety of community-building structures are needed, not simply reliance on professional learning community (PLC) meetings (Leithwood et al., 2006; McLaughlin & Talbert, 2001).

Analysts also advance the idea that both formal and informal opportunities for building community need to be realized, with an eye open especially for the informal opportunities that often lay fallow (Cosner, 2009; McLaughlin & Talbert, 2001). As we discussed above, joining together teachers who in informal ways already demonstrate working connections, beliefs, and relationships can be an important piece of a principal's community building plan (Penuel et al., 2009; Useem et al., 1997). Additionally, Raywid (1995) reminds us of the importance of nurturing the relationships among individual teachers in the service of community development.

Lastly, it appears that creating structures that promote both horizontal and vertical networks and exchanges is wise (Johnson & Asera, 1999). Here scholars point to collaborative structures that stimulate cross-grade and cross-departmental linkages, what Cosner (2009, pp. 268–269) calls "new interaction patterns." Also emphasized here are forums that allow teachers from different collective teams to collaborate (Kruse et al., 1995; Stein & Coburn, 2008), by "structuring communities with overlapping boundaries and multimembership" (Printy, 2008, p. 217).

The handmaiden to structure is time (Harris, 2003; York-Barr & Duke, 2004). Without time, the development of collaborative forums becomes nearly impossible (Darling-Hammond & McLaughlin, 1995; Eilers & Camacho, 2007). Alternatively, teacher community researchers reveal that in schools community flourishes when leaders make time available for collaborative work and professional learning (Huberman et al., 2011; Youngs, 2007). A similar conclusion is evident in studies of effective schools in general (Blase & Blase, 2004; Drago-Severson, 2004).

Researchers have also teased out clues about how leaders can employ space and time in the service of community development. One approach to enhance interactions is to bring members of current or proposed collaboratives into close physical proximity (Bulkley & Hicks, 2005; Supovitz, 2008). According to these investigators, proximity can assist in overcoming dysfunctional norms, such as privatization and egalitarianism (Gray et al., 1999; Kruse et al., 1995). A second suggestion is to take maximum advantage of formal teacher leadership positions in schools (e.g., data coach), to have them organize and lead forums in which small groups of teachers can interact (Cosner, 2009; Murphy, 2005a). Relatedly, collaboration can be nurtured by infusing integrated leadership throughout the school (Leithwood et al., 2006; Silins & Mulford, 2004). Lastly, leaders moving to deepen collaborative communities of professional practice can create what Saunders and team (2009, p. 1011) call "predictable, consistent settings;" what Blase and Blase (2004, p. 68) refer to as "teacher collaborative structures;" and what Ermeling (2010, p. 387) describes as "dedicated and protected times where teachers meet on a regular basis to get important work done." As posited above, these can be new arrangements or repurposed existing settings. Whatever the designs, these predictable, patterned forums are the most efficacious method school administrators have of enhancing community development among teachers (Pounder, 1999).

Our review also uncovers information on specific forums leaders can put in play to foster stronger collaboration (Penuel et al., 2009). Repurposed staff and departmental meetings find a home here (Mitchell & Castle, 2005; Spillane et al., 2001b). So too do reconfigured school schedules to allow for late start or early dismissal on selected days (Cosner, 2009; King, 2001). Creating blocks of time for teachers to observe in the classrooms of peers is a special category of collaboration (Blase & Blase, 2004; Harris, 2003). Ad hoc groups, such as book study teams, inquiry groups, and action research teams, are found in some community-anchored schools (Cosner, 2009; Newmann et al., 2001). So too are structures and time for teachers to collaborate around school governance and planning (Leithwood et al., 2006a; McLaughlin & Talbert, 2001). Induction and mentoring programs can provide forums to stimulate collaboration and learning (Kruse et al., 1985; Youngs, 2007). So also does the use of team teaching arrangements (Johnson & Asera, 1999). The strategy most often employed by leaders is the creation of a master schedule that establishes common planning time for groups of teachers, usually by grade level, subject area, or teaching team (Cosner, 2009).

Finally, a crosscutting analysis of the research on teacher communities exposes some of the essential touchstones of these collaborative forums. We learn that these gatherings for work and learning should (1) occur frequently, for a reasonable block of time, and across the full year (Felner et al., 2007; Raywid, 1995); (2) be intensive (Hiebert & Pearson, 1999; Murphy, 2005a); (3) focus on student learning and instructional matters (Johnson & Asera, 1999); (4) maximize interdependency (Cosner, 2009; Kruse et al., 1995); and (5) feature specific tasks that structure time usage (Center for Teaching Quality, 2007; Penuel et al., 2009). We also know that resources like protocols are often associated with productive use of collaborative time.

Supporting Learning   Time and working structures are important and necessary. But they are insufficient to power communities of practice (Ancess, 2003; Ermeling, 2010). As we have noted above, teacher communities produce valued outcomes by fostering the development of professional norms and promoting teacher learning. Leaving this to happen by chance is not a wise idea. What is required is what we call "learning to learn," the development of the knowledge and the mastery of skills that make teacher growth a reality, what Supovitz (2002, p. 1618) refers to as "continuous capacity building." We examine the work of the principal in activating the "learning" in the "learning to learn" paradigm for learning communities below.

For most teachers, working with students is a nearly all-consuming activity. Consequently, they have spent very little time working with other adults. Not surprisingly, therefore, having principals work with teachers to develop "managerial skills in dealing with people" (Ainscow & Southworth, 1996, p. 234) is an essential component of professional development designed to help teachers work effectively in learning communities (Adams, 2010; Borko, 2004). Or, as Little (1987) captures it, "the specific skills and perspectives of working with a colleague are critical" (p. 512) for teacher communities to develop. The centrality of building relationships cannot be overstated in the work of practice communities (Cosner, 2009); neither can the development of relationship-building capabilities (Lynch & Strodl, 1991); neither can the role of the principal in making this happen.

Scholars have isolated an assortment of interpersonal capacities that principals can help nurture to promote productive working relationships among teachers (Brooks et al., 2004). They conclude that professional development should assist teachers in developing proficiencies around a number of interpersonal issues (Crow & Pounder, 2000). For example, Katzenmeyer and Moller (2001) conclude that development should begin with personal knowledge. Professional development in this area builds from the assumption that focusing "on increasing their own self-awareness, identify formation, and interpretive capacity" (Zimpher, 1988, p. 57) is critical. It is this understanding that permits teachers to (1) recognize the values, behaviors, philosophies, and professional concerns that underlie their personal performance and (2) understand their colleagues, especially those whose experiences and viewpoints do not mirror their own (Katzenmeyer & Moller, 2001).

A bushel of competencies that lubricate effective working relations are often mentioned as candidates for inclusion in professional development for teacher groups. For example, analysts assert that "skills that will make teachers sensitive to seeing others' points of view" (Katzenmeyer & Moller, 2001, p. 67) and "sensitive to others' needs" (LeBlanc & Shelton, 1997, p. 38) are important. Also, because teachers often "report that they became more influential through using good listening techniques with peers" (Katzenmeyer & Moller, 2001, p. 93), helping teachers increase proficiency in the area of listening skills is important. In a similar view, because friction that sometimes surfaces in group interactions is greatly influenced by the form of those exchanges, communities are advantaged when teachers possess well-developed facilitation skills (Zimpher, 1988). In its broadest form, facilitation means "knowing how to help a group take primary responsibility for solving its problems and mitigat[ing] factors that hinder the group's ability to be effective" (Killion, 1996, p. 72). More specifically, it includes the ability to establish trust and rapport and to navigate through problems (Kilcher, 1992). Likewise, there is agreement that leaders need to arrange opportunities for teachers to develop consulting skills (Manthei, 1992) and proficiency in conferencing with colleagues (Zimpher, 1988) if they are to be effective in inquiry communities. The "principles and skills of advising" (Little, 1985, p. 34) are also key pieces in the portfolio of tools that help establish a productive context for collaborative work. So too are influencing skills (Hart, 1995; Katzenmeyer & Moller, 2001).

In addition to the social lubrication skills just outlined, analysts assert that leaders should arrange professional development activities that address a variety of skills for attacking joint work endeavors and provide a set of group process skills (Kilcher, 1992) for understanding and managing the "group dynamics" that accompany collaborative work (Murphy, 2005a). Perhaps most important here is the broad array of communication skills needed to interact with colleagues (LeBlanc & Shelton, 1997). Indeed, it is almost an article of faith in the literature in this area that inquiry communities "benefit from ongoing learning and practice in effective communication" (Killion, 1996, p. 72). Problem-solving and decision-making skills are also seen as quite important. As Killion (1996) reports, "knowing various decision-making methods, selecting the most appropriate method for a particular situation, and having a repertoire of strategies for helping others reach a decision with the chosen methods are [also] critical skills" (p. 74). Finally, leaders can help teachers benefit from community by ensuring that they master conflict management (Hart, 1995) and conflict resolution skills (Fay, 1992). "Teacher[s] who not only understand the factors that lead to conflict, but also have a range of strategies for managing and resolving it will be more successful" (Killion, 1996, p. 73) in communities of practice.

Managing for Collaboration The general message is that leaders have two roles in the domain of managing collaboration. First, they need to get professional communities up and running. Second, they need to hold at bay the natural entropy associated with collaborative work. They must help keep communities viable and vibrant. They also need to master the craft of layering in multiple, integrated supports (Murphy & Torre, 2014).

Leaders need to be diligent in setting expectations for communities of practice. A clear vision for inquiry communities must be crafted along with a tangible set of expectations (Murphy, 2005a). Also because prospects for community will be heavily influenced by school practices, values, and expectations, principals need to bolster community by crafting "enabling policies" (Lieberman & Miller, 1999, p. 28). Bishop, Tinley, and Berman (1997, p. 78) outline the case as follows:

> Since policies usually guide the course of action of an organization, and their statements include objectives that guide the actions of a substantial portion of the total organization, teachers will believe that they are empowered when they feel that their actions are undergirded and protected by such formalized policy statements.

Little (1987) concurs, arguing that "at its strongest—most durable, most rigorously connected to problems of student learning, most commanding of teachers' energies, talents, and loyalties—cooperative work is a matter of school policy" (p. 512) and that "high levels of joint action are more likely to persist" (p. 508) when a supportive policy structure is in place.

As we documented earlier, throughout the research on implementation, change, and school improvement, the importance of adequate resources is a recurring theme. Nowhere is this finding more accurate than in the area of teacher communities (Mitchell & Sackney, 2006; Mullen & Hutinger, 2008). Resources, in addition to time, in the professional community research include materials, such as "teachers' guides, activity sheets, and commercially prepared videos" (Burch & Spillane, 2003, p. 530). Protocols that direct collaborative work into productive channels is a type of material often underscored in studies of effective teacher communities (Cosner, 2011; Saunders et al., 2009). These designed activities help generate shared language, maintain focus, teach group process skills, and reinforce professional norms, while damping down dysfunctional behavior and project derailment often observed in work teams (Cosner, 2011; Young, 2006).

For teacher communities to function effectively, school administrators need to become active and central figures in communication systems, using both formal and informal procedures (Brooks et al., 2004; Walker & Slear, 2011). When this happens understanding is deepened and questions and misconceptions are addressed before they can become toxic (Cosner, 2011; Kochanek, 2005).

Other "managing communities" responsibilities for school leaders can be teased out of the research as well. Not surprisingly given its importance in the general literature, the principal has a central role in ensuring that explicit understandings of the rationale for, workings of, and outcomes needed from teacher communities are established (Printy, 2008; Quint, 2006). Analysts also affirm that leaders in schools with well-functioning teacher communities are adept at buffering teachers from external

Chapter 8

pressures that can hinder progress (King, 2001; Rossmiller, 1992). They filter demands that are not aligned with community work (Cosner, 2011; Robinson, 2007) and reshape others so that they do fit (Printy, 2008).

The necessity for leaders to be engaged in ongoing monitoring of the activities and outcomes of collaborative work is routinely discussed in the research as well (Quint, 2006; Stoll et al., 2006). Participation in community meetings, review of group documents, and comparative benchmarking are often featured in the monitoring portfolio (Heller & Firestone, 1995; Mullen & Hutinger, 2008). Monitoring which keeps "leaders in touch with teacher's ongoing thinking and development" (Levine & Marcus, 2007, p. 134) leads directly to another responsibility: that of providing feedback to collaborative work teams. A school culture that honors shared engagement (Harrison & Lembeck, 1996) is yet another indispensable element in the managing collaboration portfolio. So, too, is a system of incentives and rewards that motivates teachers to privilege mutually (Murphy, 2005a). Currently, the picture that emerges from the literature is one in which there are few external incentives for community work. In fact, there are numerous disincentives to change to collaborative work at the heart of teacher communities (Little, 1988). In many schools, there is limited recognition for the work and there are few rewards for additional effort (Crowther et al., 2002). In too many places, "the only rewards for teacher leadership are added responsibilities" (Moller & Katzenmeyer, 1996, p. 14).

In districts and schools, two types of recognition are employed by leaders to energize community building. First, since the actions of persons of status and influence (Hart, 1994) carry considerable weight they consciously work this domain. Administrators, union leaders, and well-respected veteran teachers merit notice (Hart, 1994; Silins & Mulford, 2004). Second, school leaders ensure that the peer acceptance and recognition that is important to teachers, the absence of which can negatively affect the growth of teacher community in a school (LeBlanc & Shelton, 1997; Mulford & Silins, 2003), is forthcoming.

While "rewarding teachers who are willing to move beyond their classrooms to lead is a complicated issue" (Moller & Katzenmeyer, 1996, p. 13), in the end leaders "must provide incentives and rewards for teachers who take the lead in tackling tasks and solving problems" (Boles & Troen, 1996, p. 60): leaders need to identify ways to acknowledge teachers in ways teachers value (Harrison & Lembeck, 1996). Moller and Katzenmeyer (1996, pp. 13–14) uncovered three ways in which principals were able to provide support and incentives for teacher work in communities of practice:

> First, the principals provided access to information and resources and gave their personal time. Second, they honored teacher leaders' request for professional development and sometimes initiated opportunities for them to attend conferences or represent the school at important meetings. Finally, they gave them the gift of

time, covering classes for them, providing substitute teachers, or assigning support personnel to assist them.

Responsibility for showcasing and providing recognition for quality work rests squarely with the principal (Drago-Severson, 2004; Mulford & Silins, 2003).

CONSEQUENCES

Throughout this chapter, we have introduced caveats into the analysis. As we turn now to the impact of professional development, we add to that list of cautions, focusing here on the firmness of knowledge around the consequences of teacher learning. We commence with the fact that the literature on the effects of professional development routinely features theoretical expectations about outcomes: for example, what, given a supposed chain of logic, should happen. Second, measures of effects are often based on the perceptions of the people in whom change is expected. Direct observation of change is much less visible in the research. Third, the line of reasoning that creates "a chain of evidence that links student learning [backward] to teaching learning, professional development, and policy is remarkably challenging" (Penuel et al., 2007, p. 953). As a result, there is considerably more evidence in the beginning links of the chain (e.g., change in teacher knowledge) than at the end of the chain (e.g., student learning) (Hattie, 2009). Finally, studies that are able to follow the full length of the logic chain from professional development experiences to student learning note more robust effects for earlier than later links (Hattie, 2009).

With these caveats in hand, there are still valuable insights about consequences ribboned throughout the research. We learn from scholars employing varied lenses that quality professional development can have a strong and positive influence on teacher knowledge (Hattie, 2009; Penuel et al., 2007). Well-crafted and enacted professional learning also impact teacher attitudes. For example, researchers document impacts on teacher motivation; self-esteem; commitment to school, fellow teachers, and one's students; and individual and collective efficacy (Blase & Blase, 2000; Dannetta, 2002; Garet et al., 2001; Hawley & Valli, 2001; Leithwood et al., 2011). Keeping in mind the caveat about measuring impacts, we also know that quality professional development promotes changes in teachers' practice in classrooms (Desimone et al., 2002; Hamilton et al., 2003). It also ramps up "innovation/creativity, variety in teaching and risk taking" (Blase & Blase, 2000, p. 136).

Moving to the impact of professional development on schools, there is evidence that quality learning helps leaders along the same chain of logic as for teachers, that is, knowledge, attitudes, and practice (Burch & Spillane, 2003; Robinson, 2007). In reciprocal fashion, it often strengthens professional community (McLaughlin & Talbert, 2001). Professional development has been linked to improved school capacity (Bryk et al., 2010; Newmann et al., 2000), increases in academic press (Leithwood et al., 2011) and increased teacher retention (Youngs, 2007). Finally, quality professional development impacts students. We learn that effective professional development that includes productive feedback has a moderate influence on student learning (Borko, 2004; Bryk et al., 2010; Caldwell, 1998; Hattie, 2009; Hawley & Villi, 1999).

Chapter 8

9

Professional Community for Teachers and Staff

At the heart of this volume is the assertion that great schools build powerful educational programs and learning cultures, and that principals play an essential role in the construction processes. In the last chapter, we focused on culture for students, culture reflected in communities of support. In this part of the book, we address professional culture, culture reflected in collaborative communities of professional practice. In the balance of this introductory section, we discuss the "seedbed" from which professional culture is growing as well as what some of the flowers look like when they have emerged. We provide definitions and list well-known frameworks of the components of professional learning communities. The bulk of the chapter is then devoted to presenting and unpacking a model of community of professionalism for teachers that school leaders need to operationalize. We integrate a discussion of the logic of how community works with the essential ingredients of the model.

ROOTS OF PROFESSIONAL LEARNING CULTURE

Absent shifts in how we think about learning and the organization of schooling, the seeds of community would never grow. You will remember that at the technical core level there has been a discernible shift from teaching to learning. Also, behaviorally anchored understandings of learning and transmission models of teaching are being replaced, or at least joined, by social learning and constructed models of instruction. We also examined how the organizational scaffolding of schooling is being rebuilt using different materials. Management slabs taken from the bureaucratic quarry are being replaced with stone taken from the quarry of community (Beck & Foster, 1999; Sergiovanni, 1994; Scribner, Cockrell, Cockrell, & Valentine, 1999).

Four bodies of work have given substance and shape to the concept of professional communities of practice in education. All are anchored on social understandings of learning and community-grounded perspectives of organization. One is the emergence of the importance of "social capital," an idea generally attributed to James Coleman (see Penuel, Riel, Krause, & Frank, 2009; Spillane, Hallett, & Diamond, 2003). A second is the theory of "learning organizations" first formally fleshed out by Senge in 1990 (see Mitchell & Sackney, 2006; Vescio, Ross, & Adams, 2008). A third is the expanding body of knowledge on the importance of "teams" in highly effective organizations (Pounder, 1999). The last is the development of the concept of "communities of practice," a framework forged by Lave and Wenger in the 1990s (Wenger, 1998; 2000).

DEFINITIONS AND MODELS

Definitions

There are a variety of definitions of professional community in play in the educational research and development worlds (Saunders, Goldenberg, & Gallimore, 2009). While there is no universal definition (Morrissey, 2000), there is, fortunately, a great deal of overlap in the various perspectives (Stoll, Bolam, McMahon, Wallace, & Thomas, 2006). We highlight three representative definitions below.

> A joint effort to generate new knowledge of practice and the mutual support of each other's professional growth. (McLaughlin & Talbert, 2001, p. 75)

> A group of people sharing and critically interrogating their practice in an ongoing reflective, collaborative, inclusive, learning-oriented, growth-promoting way. (Stoll et al., 2006, p. 223)

> A professional community, therefore, is one where teachers participate in decision making, have a shared sense of purpose, engage in collaborative work and accept joint responsibility for the outcomes of their work. (Harris, 2003, p. 321)

Numerous terms are used in the research and development branches of the educational family to capture the idea of shared work toward a common vision (DuFour & Eaker, 1992), almost all of which do justice to core ideas such as a focus on the human aspect of schooling (Curry, 2008); "common enterprise" (Levine & Marcus, 2007, p. 122), and shared responsibility (Curry, 2008)—community of teachers (Grossman, Wineburg, & Woolworth, 2001); teacher learning community (McLaughlin & Talbert, 2001); inquiry communities (Cochran-Smith & Lytle, 1999); discussion networks (Bidwell & Yasumoto, 1999); communities of practice (Penuel et al., 2009); communities of knowing (Craig, 2009); community of instructional practice (Spillane, Halverson, & Diamond, 2001a); professional learning communities (DuFour & Eaker, 1998); communities of commitment (Ancess, 2003); professional communities (Curry, 2008); communities of continuous inquiry and improvement (Stoll et al., 2006); and so forth.

These collectives take a variety of forms in schools. The full school may become a "macro-professional community" (Curry, 2008, p. 737). Schools may also have "micro-professional communities" (p. 737), such as critical friends groups, department and grade-level groups, action research teams, study groups, inquiry groups, learning teams, and so on (Ermeling, 2010; Mullen & Hutinger, 2008). They can extend beyond the school as well (Spillane et al., 2003). We know that these communities can be naturally occurring (see Wenger, 1998) or designed by leaders in the organization (Printy, 2008). They can form, or be created, around curricular content, problems, functions, unit of work, to name a few (Saunders et al., 2009). Individuals can and often are members of multiple communities of practice (Palincsar, Magnusson, Marano, Ford, & Brown, 1998; Wenger, 2000). It is important to remember through all this description that professional community "is not a thing, it is a way of operating" (Morrissey, 2000, p. 23).

Based on the extensive work completed in this area over the last two decades, we have forged a model to explain how professional culture comes to life in communities of practice. Our model is contained in Figure 9.1. On the "what" side, a professional learning culture is characterized by six core elements. It is these ingredients that define professional learning culture and produce the social control and social capital needed to promote teacher learning and foster the growth of professional norms (Bidwell & Yasumoto. 1999; Spillane et al., 2001a).

On the "how" side, we see that a community of practice works by adding capital to the school. One dimension of this capital is knowledge. Thus professional community promotes learning and intellectual capital (e.g., deeper content knowledge, enriched pedagogical skills). The other dimension is professional cultural capital. A community of practice deepens professional norms and accompanying attitudes (e.g., commitment). Note also that the capital accumulating in both of these areas is of two types, that accruing to individuals (i.e., human capital) and that accruing to the group (i.e., social capital). Both are important. However, it is the emphasis on social capital development that distinguishes practice communities from many other reforms.

Increased capital, in turn, leads to changes in the ways teachers conduct their work with students. Practice is improved in two core fields of

Figure 9.1   Communities of Professional Practice for Teachers

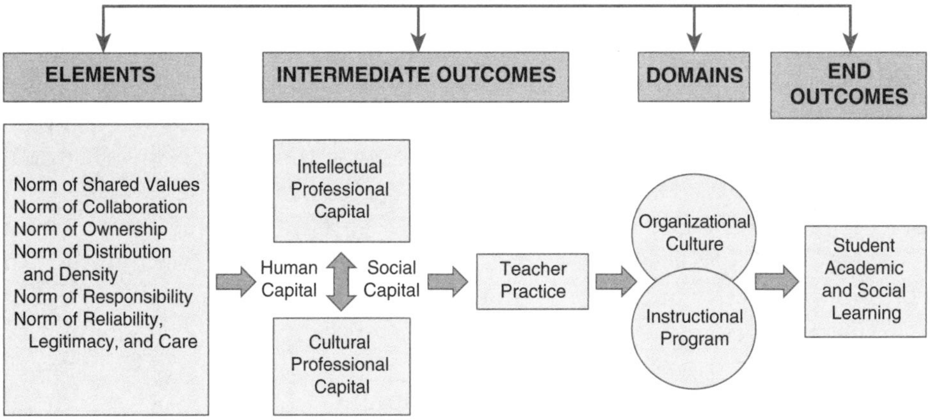

action, classroom climate and instruction. More effective instruction and an enhanced climate lead to better learning outcomes for students.

In the balance of the chapter, we explore the model in Figure 9.1 in considerable detail. Before we do so, however, it is important to draw the attention of school leaders to the interrelated, reciprocal nature of the framework. For example, while professional norms influence teacher practice and student outcomes, they also influence the essential elements of community (King, 2001; Olivier & Hipp, 2006; Tschannen-Moran & Barr, 2004). In short, energy flows in both directions in the model across the columns, left to right and right to left (Bryk, Sebring, Allensworth, Luppescu, & Easton, 2010; Levine & Marcus, 2007; MacBeath, 2009), what Goddard, Hoy, and Hoy (2000, p. 483) call "reciprocal causality" and Heck and Hallinger (2009, p. 681) refer to as "mutually reinforcing constructs." We note that energy flows among concepts within each column as well. For example, in the "elements" column shared accountability shapes shared values and collaborative work. Energy flows up and down the model as well as in both directions across the framework. Communities of practice are, to use the language of Strahan (2003, p. 130), "spirals of reform activities."

> Teachers work collaboratively to identify priorities for school improvement and initiate conversations about instruction. As they do so, they target areas for instructional improvement and coordinate their efforts to implement shared instructional strategies. These coordinated efforts enhance student achievement and strengthen the professional learning community. Consequently, the school provides more social support for learning; school culture grows more collaborative; and teachers develop strong collective efficacy. (p. 130)

It is also important for leaders to understand that professional community provides an integrative framework. It is not so much a reform as it is a caldron for the infusing and mixing of professional norms and for pushing change efforts into the collaborative work of teachers (Huberman, Parrish, Hannan, Arellanes, & Shambaugh, 2011; Stoll et al., 2006)—"a verb rather than a noun" (Grossman et al., 2001, p. 1012). Finally, a number of analysts report that well-functioning professional communities have fusion-like properties. Once set in motion, they have a self-generating dynamic, what Newmann, Rutter, & Smith (1989, p. 224) refer to as an "interactive, progressive cycle" and Tichy and Cardwell (2004, p. 7) call a "virtuous teaching cycle." The father of communities of practice makes this point explicitly when he reports that

> the strength of communities of practice is self-perpetuating. As they generate knowledge, they reinforce and renew themselves. That's why communities of practice give you not only the golden eggs, but also the goose that lays them. (Wenger & Snyder, 2000, p. 143)

Shared Vision

At the broadest level, vision is about moral purpose and possibilities (Auerbach, 2007; Barnett, McCormick, & Conners, 2001; Day, 2005), concepts forged from values and beliefs that define the instructional program and shape school climate in ways that enhance student learning (Creemers & Reezigt, 1996; Dinham, 2005; Siu, 2008). Mission is the bedrock of school improvement writ large (DuFour & Eaker, 1992; Fullan, 1982, 1993, 2002) and professional communities specifically (Kruse, Seashore Louis, & Bryk, 1995; Louis, Dretzke, & Wahlstrom, 2010). Schools do not progress well without it (Borman, 2005; Leithwood, 2005; Riester, Pursch, & Skria, 2002). Indeed, "without a shared vision . . . the various trajectories of learning that occur may have little synergy or coherence and thus may not have a powerful positive impact on teaching and learning" (Levine & Marcus, 2007, p. 134). Below, we examine three levels of vision: mission, goals, and expectations.

Mission

Researchers have harvested important clues about how mission serves school improvement. Mission influences the instructional program and the learning climate, which in turn shape the behaviors of teachers and students (Murphy, 2000). As Mitchell and Sackney (2006) found, because schools are loosely coupled systems (see Cohen, March, & Olsen, 1972; Meyer & Rowan, 1975, Weick, 1976) they lack clear goals. In such situations, there is a natural tendency for effort to splinter and for community to lay fallow, effects only exacerbated by the frenetic nature of schooling. Mission begins to tighten systems by establishing the boundaries in which "schooling" occurs (Murphy, Weil, Hallinger, & Mitman, 1983). Mission coheres begins (Louis & Miles, 1990, 1991; Morrissey, 2000) and ends

(Hallinger & Heck, 1998; Louis et al., 2010) around shared values and beliefs (Levine & Marcus, 2010; Silins & Mulford, 2004).

It is important to note that not all school missions harness equal amounts of energy (Barnett & McCormick, 2004; Mitchell & Sackney, 2006; Scheurich, 1998). From our analysis, we distill eight core ideas that anchor the strong missions that help define professional culture, those that consistently direct the school into productive channels of collaborative work. To begin with, the mission needs to convey *a sense of hope*, to open the door of possibility (Brookover, Beady, Flood, Schweitzer, & Wisenbaker, 1979; Murphy, 1996; Olivier & Hipp, 2006). As Leithwood and colleagues (Leithwood, Jantzi, & Steinbach, 1999; Yu, Leithwood, & Jantzi, 2002) instruct us, missions should be inspirational. They need to convey a palpable sense that through collective engagement conditions (e.g., low levels of success, disaffiliation) are malleable and that improvement is possible, even likely (Oakes & Guiton, 1995; McLaughlin & Talbert, 2001; Scheurich, 1998).

In addition, mission in teacher communities should address *commitment to success* (Bryk et al., 2010; Louis & Miles, 1991; Timperley, 2009) and to the work that such commitment entails (Blair, 2002; Olivier & Hipp, 2006; Riehl & Sipple, 1996). This encompasses the understanding that second best is insufficient (Dinham, 2005; Raywid, 1995; Southworth, 2002) and the conviction that the school can and will improve (Bryk et al., 2010; Riester et al., 2002; Strahan, 2003). In a related vein, mission should reflect the belief that all students will be successful (Eilers & Camacho, 2007; Gurr, Drysdale, & Mulford, 2005; Lezotte, Hathaway, Miller, Passalacque, & Brookover, 1980). That is, no one is permitted to fail. The embedded understanding is that schooling is the game changer for students (Bryk et al., 2010; Cotton, 2003; Raywid, 1995), a conviction and moral imperative about success (Dinham, 2005; Edmonds, 1979; Raywid, 1995).

Relatedly, mission should reflect *asset-based thinking* about students and the larger community (Auerbach, 2007, 2009). As Edmonds (1979) and Brookover and colleagues (1977, 1978, 1979) reported at the beginning of

Table 9.1 Core Elements of Mission in Effective Schools

Sense of hope
Norm of commitment
Asset-based thinking
Student focus
Academic anchoring
Outcome focus
Norm of continuous improvement
Norm of collective responsibility

the modern era of school improvement (see also Purkey & Smith, 1983), this third core idea pushes back against the deficit-based thinking often found in struggling or failing schools and schools with large numbers of students placed at risk (Murphy, 2010; Rutter, Maughan, Mortimore, & Ouston, 1979; Scanlan & Lopez, 2012). It is anchored on the belief that all students are capable of learning, that the school does not underestimate the abilities and efficacy of children (DuFour & Eaker, 1992; Goldenberg, 2004; Lezotte et al., 1980). Assets-based thinking means not accommodating instruction to preconceived assumptions of limitations, but rather conducting schools in ways that change students' abilities and interests (Murphy, 1989; Oakes & Guiton, 1995). Optimism rather than pessimism holds the high ground (Edmonds, 1979; Theoharis, 2007). Problems and failure are not attributed to children and their families (McDougall, Saunders, & Goldenberg, 2007; Murphy, 1992b; Theoharis, 2007). Deficiencies are not assumed (Blair, 2002). Negative attitudes are conspicuous by their absence (Cooper, 1996). Constraints are recognized, but they are challenged as impediments to success (Gurr et al., 2005; Leithwood et al., 1999; Murphy, 2013). Schools push back on resistance to norms of success proactively not reactively (Cotton, 2003; Crum & Sherman, 2008; Murphy, 1996).

Student focus is the fourth core element in mission. Student-centered values hold the high ground in schools with strong cultures of professionalism (McLaughlin & Talbert, 2001). The spotlight is on children and youth (Eilers & Camacho, 2007), what is in the best interests of students (Gurr et al., 2005; Johnson & Asera, 1999). Concretely, that means developing professional culture that features ideology (Blair, 2002; Caldwell, 1998; May & Supovitz, 2006) in context of the specific youngsters in the school (Leithwood et al., 1999).

Fifth, a mission in a school with strong professional community is *academically anchored* (Hoy, Hannum, & Tschannen-Moran, 1998; May & Supovitz, 2011; Venezky & Winfield, 1979). Mission highlights student learning (Blase & Blase, 2004; Orr, Berg, Shore, & Meier, 2003) and academic success (Dinham, 2005; Hallinger, Bickman, & Davis, 1996). An academically anchored mission focuses the community on the instructional program (Cotton, 2000; Murphy, Beck, Crawford, & Hodges, 2001; Supovitz, Sirinides, & May, 2010). Teaching and learning hold center stage, and better instruction is job one (Collins & Valentine, 2010; Gurr, Drysdale, & Mulford, 2006).

Learning-community schools have *outcome-focused* missions (Supovitz & Poglinco, 2001). These outcomes feature measures of student learning in general (Leithwood, 2005) and provide markers of student achievement in particular (Hallinger & Heck, 1998; Timperley, 2009; Waters, Marzano, & McNulty, 2003). Missions in schools with robust teacher communities highlight the idea of *continuous improvement* (Ancess, 2003; Crum & Sherman, 2008; Jackson, 2000). Norms of complacency are challenged. Risk taking is promoted and there is an appetite for change (Blair, 2002;

Foster & St. Hilaire, 2003; Louis & Miles, 1991). Finally, when strong professional culture is in place, mission carries the seeds of *collective responsibility* (Edmonds, 1979; Huberman et al., 2011). A culture of accountability emerges (Barker, 2001; May & Supovitz, 2006) replacing traditions of externalizing responsibility (Bryk et al., 2010; Spillane, Diamond, Walker, Halverson, & Jita, 2001b; May & Supovitz, 2006). Success is a collective endeavor of the community (McLaughlin & Talbert, 2001).

Goals

Our analysis suggests the goals for teacher professional communities should be defined by critical markers. The most essential of these is a focus on the academic domain in general and on student learning in particular (Barnes, Camburn, Sanders, & Sebastian, 2010. Robinson, Lloyd, and Rowe (2008) remind us that goals are most productive when they are specific, not generic. Supovitz and Poglinco (2001, pp. 3–4) make this point as well, concluding that while generic goals can be a starting point, the "exponential value comes from a marriage of intensive organizational focus on instructional improvement with a clear vision of instructional quality." Barnett and McCormick (2004) call this a "task focus," and Strahan (2003) refers to it as a specific "stance about learning." Goldenberg (2004) weighs in, arguing that the critical issue is establishing a clear notion of what the school is attempting to accomplish and that it is explicit. Thus "academic focus" and "learning stance" are essential (Blase & Kirby, 2009; Brewer, 1993; Robinson et al., 2008). They positively impact student achievement (Barnes et al., 2010; McDougall et al., 2007; Silins & Mulford, 2004). Robinson (2007) drives these points home when she asserts that academic goal focus needs to become an explicit dimension of school culture writ large and professional communities of practice in particular.

Implicitly and explicitly other cardinal elements can be discerned in analyses of academic learning focus. We discover, for example, that goals are best when the spotlight is on students (Leithwood et al., 1999; Rutherford, 1985; Wimpelberg, 1986), when there is a children-first perspective and when student achievement is the central theme (Clark, Lotto, & McCarthy, 1980; Robinson et al., 2008; Wynne, 1980). Researchers also inform us that the goals that are found in well-functioning professional communities are challenging, but achievable (Cotton, 2003; Leithwood & Jantzi, 2005) and apply to all students (Louis & Miles, 1991; Murphy, 1990a). Goals that work well are meaningful to the community (Dinham, 2005; Leithwood & Jantzi, 2000b; Murphy et al., 2001). Meaningfulness includes knowledge of, internalization of, and group ownership of goals (Blanc, Christman, Liu, Mitchell, Travers, & Bulkley, 2010; Goldenberg, 2004; Supovitz & Poglinco, 2001).

Almost every study of school improvement has concluded that goals need to be clear and concrete (Blase & Kirby, 2009; Goldenberg, 2004; Ogden & Germinario, 1995), not abstract or subject to interpretation

(Brewer, 1993; Gray et al., 1999; Robinson, 2007). They should provide "stakes in the ground" indicating the destination for the learning community and the way to travel (Murphy, Elliott, Goldring, & Porter, 2007). Parsimony and simplicity are desirable (Lomotey, 1989; Newmann, Smith, Allensworth, & Bryk, 2001). Scholars also report that goal clarity in productive professional communities directs the allocation and development of human and financial resources (Gray et al., 1999; Huberman et al., 2011; Wilson & Corcoran, 1988). Recent studies of teaching communities have also identified the importance of tailoring goals to the specific needs of students in a given school (Ancess, 2000; Wohlstetter, Datnow, & Park, 2008). Short-term goals that move the school to larger ends are desirable (Cotton, 2003) as they permit staff to experience reinforcing, short-term wins (Bryk et al., 2010; Johnson & Asera, 1999). It is important, however, that these short-term wins derive from and support the more encompassing mission of the school (Leithwood & Montgomery, 1982; Robinson et al., 2008).

Analyses across time also reveal important insights for leaders about the ways in which goals are forged in schools with robust professional cultures. One critical discovery is the importance of a process that fosters ownership of goals (Leithwood, Day, Sammons, Harris, & Hopkins, 2006). What is particularly important is the creation of ownership of the work to reach goals and responsibility for the results of those efforts, a recurring theme in our analysis of a culture of professionalism (Leithwood, Day et al., 2006; Murphy, 1992). Wide participation of community stakeholders and reliance on hard data to arrive at decisions should also define goal development (Datnow, Park, & Kennedy, 2008; Murphy, Hallinger, & Mesa, 1985).

We close this part of our analysis with a note on what that research tells us about how goals function to improve student learning in schools characterized by a culture of professionalism. At a fundamental level, goals adhering to the description above provide tangible meaning to the school mission (Bryman, 2004; Leithwood, Louis, Anderson, & Wahlstrom, 2004; Supovitz & Poglinco, 2001). In so doing, they solidify community action around shared values and purpose (Leithwood & Jantzi, 2000b; Robinson, 2007). As such, they help people see more clearly. They keep a professional community from becoming distracted by separating the really important work from the balance of activity (Goldenberg, 2004; McDougall et al., 2007). Effort becomes more focused and more productive (Louis & Miles, 1991). Goals also serve as a powerful mechanism for organizational cohesion (Goldring & Pasternack, 1994; Robinson, 2007), helping teachers collectively to coordinate action (Bryk et al., 2010; McDougall et al., 2007; Robinson et al., 2008).

Strong goals can be powerful motivators for staff (Datnow et al., 2008; Geijsel, Sleegers, Leithwood, & Jantzi, 2003; Leithwood et al., 2006), encouraging educators to reach for higher standards (Ancess, 2000; Barnett & McCormick, 2004). Goals have been shown to have an energizing effect

(Leithwood et al., 1999; Newmann, 1992). They also have the potential to strengthen professionalism by helping dismantle the wall between teaching and school administration (Lomotey, 1989; Murphy, 2005a). Shared work, in turn, can strengthen commitment and responsibility (Hallinger & Heck, 1998; Youngs & King, 2002).

Expectations

Expectations are the third layer of school vision. They make even more concrete the understandings of performance for professional teacher communities (Day, 2005; Mulford & Silins, 2003). They create a platform to bring goals to life (Goldenberg, 2004). They are both a measure of (Brookover et al., 1979) and a method to develop academic press in the school (Edmonds & Frederiksen, 1978; Goldenberg, 1996).

Over the last thirty-five years, researchers have shown that high expectations widely shared have important organizational consequences (Miller, 1995; Magnuson & Duncan, 2006; Shannon & Bylsma, 2002). Most importantly, they differentiate between more and less effective schools, with higher academic expectations linked to better outcomes, outcomes defined in terms of student learning (Bryk et al., 2010; Christle, Jolivette, & Nelson, 2005; Rutter et al., 1979). They work in part by helping to shape school culture in general and professional norms and organizational learning in particular (Brookover et al., 1978; Hallinger & Heck, 1998; Leithwood, Jantzi, & Steinbach, 1999). Expectations have their largest impact on children on the wrong side of the achievement gap, especially children from low-income families (Hughes, 2003; Meehan, Cowley, Schumacher, Hauser, & Croom, 2003; Murphy, 2010).

Expectations help professional communities define understandings of quality in concrete terms (Leithwood & Jantzi, 2000a). According to Leithwood and colleagues (1999, p. 69), who have examined this issue in considerable depth

> expectations of this sort help teachers see the challenging nature of the goals being pursued in their school. They may also sharpen teachers' perceptions of the gap between what the school aspires to and what is presently being accomplished. Done well, expressions of high expectations also result in perceptions among teachers that what is being expected is also feasible.

High expectations convey in tangible fashion the hard work and improvement required by a community of teachers to create a school where all youngsters reach ambitious targets of performance (Barnett & McCormick, 2004). They can energize community to keep student improvement in the spotlight (Leithwood et al., 1999; Leithwood, Day et al., 2006; McLaughlin & Talbert, 2001). At the heart of the success equation here are consistency and repetition of expectations (Blase & Kirby, 2009; Kochanek,

2005) that mediate the work of professional communities of learning (Hallinan, 2001; Hughes, 2003).

Collaboration

We continue our analysis of what Horn (2005, p. 230) refers to as the "conceptual infrastructure" of teacher community by turning the spotlight on collaboration. Ermeling (2010, p. 386) defines collaboration as a "joint productive activity where participants assist each other to solve a common problem or produce a common product." Because it is more tangible than other elements of community (e.g., vision, trust) and often provides the backdrop on which the elements come to life, it occupies disproportionate space in the community of practice narrative. For collaboration to be productive, shifts in how teachers think about, talk about, and go about their work are required (Cotton, 2003; Drago-Severson, 2004; Levine & Marcus, 2010). It rests on the understanding that what teachers do outside their classrooms is as important as what unfolds inside those settings (McLaughlin & Talbert, 2001; Stoll et al., 2006) and that collective work done well can accelerate their learning and the achievement of their students (Heck & Hallinger, 2009; Supovitz, 2002).

An assortment of researchers have crafted robust frameworks to expose the dimension of collaboration. For example, for McLaughlin and Talbert (2001, p. 41) "teachers are mutually engaged in teaching; they jointly develop their practice; and they share a repertoire of resources and history." For Printy (2008, p. 199), the following are all important pieces of collaborative effort: "the range of activities available for participation, the quality of members' participation as legitimate or peripheral, the rules for social interaction of members, and the joint understanding of the work that brings individuals together." More generally, Wenger (1998, 2000) describes collaboration as an algorithm of events, commitments, membership, and tasks. From our analysis, we assert that the power of professional communities of practice can be measured by how well the sub-elements of engagement—purpose, structure, focus, and nature—adhere to known quality criteria. More concretely, we find that effective collaboration is mutual, purpose-driven work. It is learning-centered and instructionally focused. It is driven by the tenets of evidence-based inquiry. And it is directed to improved teacher practice and student achievement via teacher learning.

Purpose of Engagement: Improvement

Effective collaboration is defined by clear purpose, "persistently working toward detectable improvements" (Ermeling, 2010, p. 378). The work itself is the avenue to improvement, not the outcome (Ermeling, 2010). Effectiveness plays out in the application of a teacher's learning practice (Cochran-Smith & Lytle, 1999). What Wenger (1998, 2000) refers to as the "purpose of shared enterprise" (1998, p. 45) pivots on clear measures of outcomes benchmarked against expectations (Louis, 2007) or common goals (Johnson & Asera, 1999) and compelling direction (Fullan, 2002).

Structure and Organization of Engagement: Mutuality

Mutuality provides the structure or frame of collaboration, the process of joint work (Johnson & Asera, 1999; Supovitz, 2010). It is grounded on the understanding that relationships are the heart and soul of community (Bryk et al., 2010; Gronn, 2009; Sergiovanni, 1994). One of the fathers of communities of practice, Wenger, talks about "mutual engagement" (2000, p. 229) and "shared enterprise" (1998, p. 45). Colleagues in education refer to mutuality as group practice, changing a roster of individuals into a collaboration of "relational cultures" (Drago-Severson, 2004, p. 40), "joint enterprise" (Young, 2006, p. 538), and "joint identity" (Grossman et al., 2001, p. 1005) featuring a "culture of collaboration" (Southworth, 2002, p. 88), "collective engagement" (Visscher & Witziers, 2004, p. 786), and a "process of participation" (Horn, 2005, p. 211).

Mutuality, according to Printy (2008), requires that members be advantaged by access to the resources of the group and that they add to that capacity (Heller & Firestone, 1995; McLaughlin & Talbert, 2001). It is about "enabling a rich fabric of connectivity" (Wenger, 2000, p. 232). It is about making shared engagement, peer support, mutual assistance, and joint enterprise a generalized condition in schools (Goldenberg, 2004; Kruse et al., 1995; Newmann, King, & Youngs, 2000), about working and learning together (Olivier & Hipp, 2006; Stein & Coburn, 2008). Mutuality is essential because it "provides a point of convergence for teachers' inquiry—the joint enterprise for community of practice" (McLaughlin & Talbert, 2001, p. 122). It underscores needed job-centered learning (Drago-Severson, 2004; Olivier & Hipp, 2006) and, as shown in the model in Figure 9.1, fosters capacity development (Clark, Dyson, Millward, & Robson, 1999). Shared enterprise features what Louis and Marks (1998, p. 538) refer to as "the quality of relationships among group work members." Collegial support and general norms of teamwork and joint engagement are paramount under conditions of mutuality (Grossman et al., 2001; Phillips, 2003). Without mutuality, purpose of engagement cannot be fulfilled (Levine & Marcus, 2010).

Mutuality and its family members, participation, engagement, and joint activity, are dependent, of course, on opportunities to work together, on "enabling structure and supportive organizational context" (Fullan, 2002, p. 15) or "knowledge space" (Hattie, 2009, p. 264). These opportunities are often conspicuous by their absence in schools and require the strong hand of leadership broadly defined. Of course, this means that there needs to be something on which time to plan, work, and learn together makes sense (Johnson & Asera, 1999; Wenger, 2000), "some intersection of interest, some activity" (Wenger, 2000, p. 232), what

Ermeling (2010, p. 386) refers to as "common ground to talk." Without this, there can be no authentic joint exchange (Beck & Foster, 1999).

Creating structure for productive joint enterprise requires attending to an array of issues. Most importantly, there is the need to establish the *domain* of collaboration (Wenger & Snyder, 2000). We know also that thought must be devoted to what Wenger (2000) refers to as the *types of activities* that will ground the collaborative. Important here is ensuring that both formal and informal mechanisms are engaged (Ancess, 2003; Fullan & Ballew, 2002; Olivier & Hipp, 2006)—and in a coordinated and synchronized manner (Drago-Severson, 2004). The *size* of groups is important and the question of how much to align with existing organizational arrangements (e.g., departments, grade levels, teaching teams) needs resolution (Wenger, 1998, 2000). Thus the topic of *boundaries* is important, including how these demarcations are managed (Penuel et al., 2010; Wenger, 2000). So too is the fluidity and *stability* of collaborative work teams (Curry, 2008; McLaughlin & Talbert, 2001), what Wenger (2000) describes as rhythms of the work. *Amount of time* to work and the *regularity of exchanges* merit consideration. So too does the *life span* of a work group (Leithwood et al., 1999; McLaughlin & Talbert, 2001). The topic of how teachers become members of collaborative teams also must be addressed. Contrary to normal practice in education, self-selection receives high grades in the general literature as a *mechanism of selection* (Wenger, 1998). Also important is how much of one's *professional identity* is committed to and defined by collaborative work (Wenger, 2000). Finally, the research informs us that *how work is structured* and the *tools employed* to guide the work make valuable contributions to how well joint enterprise is conducted (Curry, 2008; Levine & Marcus, 2010; Saunders et al., 2009). The *concreteness of the work* and the *collaborative organizational form employed* (e.g., book clubs, joint lesson planning) are quite relevant as well (Vescio et al., 2008). We delve deeply into these topics in the following chapter.

The research helps leaders see one level deeper in thinking about collaboration, to the criteria for judging the authenticity of joint work. Issues here include the presence or absence of reciprocal influence (Kruse et al., 1995), density of ties (Wenger, 2000) and mutual dependence (Beck & Foster, 1999; Young, 2006). Measures of the amount of the teaching-learning process (i.e., the work of classrooms) that is made open for inspection helps determine authenticity (Grossman et al., 2001; Horn, 2005); that is, how much of the work becomes "public" (Printy, 2008; Young, 2006). The depth of sharing can reveal a good deal about the validity of collaboration (Harris, 2009; Wenger, 2000; Young, 2006). The "fingerprint" test for joint construction work is useful here. How many members of the collaborative actively contributed to the work? How many are mere spectators? Authenticity can also be determined in part by the robustness of the leadership displayed by members in the collaborative (Murphy, 2005a). The extent to which teachers change their practice is a key criterion (Printy, 2008; Visscher & Witziers, 2004).

Focus of Engagement: Student Learning

Structure is an essential dimension of community. But as Ancess (2003, p. 4) cautions, "achievement of community requires more than the space for developing commodity." More specifically, "what collaboration is designed to focus on will have significant implications for what teachers can and can't learn from work with colleagues" (Levine & Marcus, 2010, pp. 392–393). For example, researchers report that simply addressing logistical issues and nonlearning conditions does not translate into robust collaboration and community nor result in the intermediate or summative outcomes seen in Figure 9.1.

On the positive side of the storyboard, analysts have uncovered productive foci for collaborative work. To begin with, it is clear that the center of gravity should be the *classroom* (Goldenberg, 2004; Gray et al., 1999; Hayes, Christie, Mills, & Lingard, 2004) and on challenges of work there. Educational concerns trump nonacademic issues (Murphy et al., 2001; Printy, 2008). Attention flows to the core technology (Mulford & Silins, 2003; Newmann et al., 2001; Supovitz & Christman, 2003). That is, interactions should be anchored in issues of *learning and teaching* (Supovitz, Sirinides, & May, 2010; Useem, Christman, Gold, & Simon, 1997) and be deep and ongoing.

Not surprisingly given the above comments, there is near universal agreement that the focus of collaborative engagement should be on *students* (Ancess, 2003; Ermeling, 2010; McLaughlin & Talbert, 2001). Both for teachers to mature into a productive community and to power up learning, students need to be at the center of collaborative work (Goldenberg, 2004; Grossman et al., 2001; Kruse et al., 1995). Becoming more specific, these analysts find that the focus should be on student academics (Olivier & Hipp, 2006; Saunders et al., 2009): "A collective focus on *student learning* is central to professional community" (Louis & Marks, 1998, p. 539), especially analyses of student learning needs, problems, and progress (Halverson, Grigg, Prichett, & Thomas, 2007; Vescio et al., 2008; Visscher & Witziers, 2004).

Backward mapping from student learning, the focus of this collective engagement is *instructional practice* embedded in specific curricular domains (Curry, 2008; Visscher & Witziers, 2004; Young, 2006); collaboration to strengthen the school's instructional program (Bryk et al., 2010; Huberman et al., 2011; Supovitz & Poglinco, 2001); and the pedagogical skills of each teacher (Gurr et al., 2006; McLaughlin & Talbert, 2001; Young, 2006). Vescio and colleagues (2008, p. 85) succinctly summarize the research on this issue as follows: "Findings reinforce the importance of persistently pursuing an instructional focus as teachers engage in their work in learning communities." As discussed above, *"problems of practice"* focus is privileged in highly productive collaborative work (King, 2001; Levine & Marcus, 2010; McLaughlin & Talbert, 2001). The spotlight is on specific, observable, malleable practices that are described with transparency, clarity, and concreteness (Little, 1982; Mitchell & Sackney, 2006). Finally, as we explain more fully below, a particular type of shared instructional practice is routinely discussed in the research on teacher communities in general and collaboration particularly, *evidence-based analysis* (Blanc et al., 2010; Cosner, 2011; Strahan, 2003), a condition that Visscher and Witziers (2004, p. 798) refer to as the "*sine qua non* for the development of professional communities."

Method of Engagement: Reflective Inquiry

So far we have examined three of the four core ingredients of collaboration (purpose, structure, and focus), remembering that collaboration itself is one of the six essential elements of professional communities. We now turn to the final ingredient of shared enterprise, the ways in which productive communities operate. To maintain consistency with colleagues who have researched this domain, we describe the method of engagement as reflective practice. According to Stoll and her team (2006, pp. 222–227),

> *reflective professional inquiry* includes: "reflective dialogue" conversations about serious educational issues or problems involving the application of new knowledge in a sustained manner; "deprivatization of practice," frequent examining of teachers' practice, through mutual observation and case analysis, joint planning and curriculum development; seeking new knowledge; tacit knowledge constantly converted into shared knowledge through interaction; and applying new ideas and information to problem solving and solutions addressing pupils' needs.

We parcel the research on "method of engagement" into two overlapping concepts: inquiry and evidence-based practice.

On the first topic, in dissecting collaboration scholars consistently highlight professional practice informed by individual and group reflection (Grossman et al., 2001; Louis et al., 2010; Supovitz, 2002). Indeed, inquiry is generally presented as a hallmark "method" or "stance" that defines shared enterprise in communities of practice (Grossman et al., 2001; King, 2001; Visscher & Witziers, 2004). The concept travels under a variety of different names in the literature—reflective inquiry, reflective discussions, group inquiry, sustained inquiry, inquiry-oriented practice, reflective practice, collegial inquiry, and so forth. It means, according to Drago-Severson (2004, p. 18), "reflecting on one's assumptions, convictions, and values as part of the learning process," the investigation and critical assessment of practice, research and logic (King, 2001). That is, it is a "stance" which honors the interrogation of knowledge, skills, and dispositions around instructional practice (Levine & Marcus, 2007). Its purpose is to forge joint understanding of and shared practices in the service of student learning (Ermeling, 2010; Kruse et al., 1995; Mitchell & Sackney,

2006). Productive inquiry in professional communities of practice is analytic, dynamic, continuous, and constructivist in nature (Horn, 2005; King, 2001; Little, 1982).

Reflective inquiry has as much to do with dialogue, or what Horn (2005, p. 229) calls "conversational involvement," as it does with patterns of thinking (Ermeling, 2010; Stoll et al., 2006; York-Barr & Duke, 2004). Indeed, it is reasonable to add conversation to the methods of engagement label, what Wilson and Berne (1999, p. 200) nicely capture with the term "narrative of inquiry." Grossman and her colleagues (2001, p. 1001) maintain that teacher communities create an "invitational conversational climate," a reflective-based constructed dialogue, what Cochran-Smith and Lytle (1999, p. 280) nail with the idea of "teacher learning through talk." It is in these continuous professional conversations that reflections become visible for inspection (Curry, 2008), venues in which feedback can be provided and debated (Kruse et al., 1995).

Two aspects of dialogue in the service of building collaboration are routinely highlighted in the research on professional culture. The public nature of conversations is consistently seen as essential (Horn, 2010; Young, 2006), what Levine and Marcus (2010) describe as detailed and open representations. This public stance centered on student work is especially productive (Goldenberg, 2004). A good deal of recognition is also awarded to the openness of collaborative exchange, an idea that Horn (2010, p. 255) beautifully captures as "a willingness to reveal and work at the limits of one's knowledge." Dialogue is not merely an act of civility. Difficult conversations unfold in collaborative work (Drago-Severson, 2004; Huberman et al., 2011). Critique is expected (Grossman et al., 2001; Silins & Mulford, 2004; Wilson & Berne, 1999). "Questioning and challenging colleagues" (Horn, 2010, p. 234) is normal. Concerns and doubts are to be aired, "difference, debate, and disagreement are viewed as the foundations" (Stoll et al., 2006, p. 227) of reflective inquiry. In addition, there is solid evidence that formalizing collaborative conversations in education can be helpful (Beachum & Dentith, 2004; Horn, 2010; Levine & Marcus, 2010). There is a strong sense that "protocol-guided conversations" (Curry, 2008, p. 742) enhance the public and critical aspects of collaborative dialogue (Curry, 2008; Horn, 2005; Levine & Marcus, 2010).

Collegial dialogue is half of the method or stance on engagement. The other half, based on the findings of Levine and Marcus (2010) and Penuel, Frank, and Krause (2006, p. 527) that "the effectiveness of collaboration depends on what kinds of interactions take place," is evidence-based practice (Fullan & Ballew, 2002; Grossman et al., 2001; Johnson & Asera, 1999). This means that not only is there critical, collegial exchange, but the conversations are anchored in knowledge and data, especially support for ideas and more importantly evidence of impact on one's students (Ermeling, 2010; Hattie, 2009; Young, 2006).

In highly productive collaboratives, considerable attention is devoted to the "visible and explicit cause-effect connections between instructional decisions and student outcomes" (Ermeling, 2010, p. 379). "Analysis and interpretation of some form of student learning data" (Cosner, 2011, p. 789) is the grist for collaborative dialogue (Visscher & Witziers, 2004). As was the case for inquiry, researchers find that tools such as protocols and artifacts to guide evidence-based collaboration can assist greatly in the work (Horn, 2005). More concretely, Felner and his team of Seitsinger, Brand, Burns, and Bolton (2007, p. 217) list five dimensions of collaboration in which inquiry and evidence-based work are especially productive.

> (a) curriculum coordination and integration; (b) coordination of student assessments, assignments, and feedback; (c) work together in engaging parents; (d) coordinate together the development of common performance standards; and (e) work as a team to integrate their efforts with other building resources (e.g., counselors, librarians, reading/special education specialists, etc.)

OWNERSHIP AND RESPONSIBILITY

Ownership

One of the essential reasons that collaborative communities of professional practice work is because they operationalize the cardinal understanding that teachers are fundamental to school improvement. One of the most important ways they do this is by helping teachers assume ownership of their school and their labor (Levine & Marcus, 2007; Raywid, 1995; Supovitz & Poglinco, 2001). The engine that powers this sense of empowerment is best described as "shared involvement." Our analysis suggests that three broad concepts are in play in a reciprocal and integrative manner: authority, influence, and leadership. We examine the first two here and teacher leadership because it is a distinct element in our model in a separate section below.

To begin with, we know that collaborative communities of professional practice provide teachers with considerable professional *authority* (Barker, 2001; Vescio et al., 2008). This influence can be defined on the one hand by what is absent, the privileging of hierarchical and bureaucratic systems and procedures over professional knowledge (Adams, 2010; Ancess, 2003). On the other hand, professional authority is characterized by what is present, collective, knowledge-based autonomy for the work necessary to ensure that all youngsters are successful, including organizational support for ideas and decisions crafted by communities (Beachum & Dentith, 2004; Crum & Sherman, 2008; Dannetta, 2002). Riester and team (2002) deconstruct this autonomy in terms of freedom and openness.

It is important to emphasize that this is a type of group control and influence, not the isolation and privacy masquerading as autonomy in many schools (Kruse et al., 1995). It is a collective sense of agency (Gurr et al., 2006). Professional authority is also about voice, providing teachers with meaningful forums and pathways to express their professional ideas (Brooks, Milburn, Rotheram-Borus, & Witkin, 2004; Supovitz, 2002; Vescio et al., 2008).

Communities of practice also drive improvement because they create pathways to enhance teacher *influence* over important issues in the school (Bryk et al., 2010). They manufacture ownership by featuring "collaborative, cooperative, and consultative decision making" (Silins & Mulford, 2004, p. 448) and by creating abundant opportunities for that decision making to occur (Pounder, 1999). Teachers in communities of practice are empowered to act in the best interests of children (Kruse et al., 1995; Sweetland & Hoy, 2000). "Additionally, decisional power in learning communities is more collective than positional" (Adams, 2010, p. 274). Administrative leadership is more inclusive, facilitative, and person directed than managerial or institutional (Bryk et al., 2010; King, 2001; Leithwood et al., 1999).

Researchers document that empowerment can stretch across a good deal of the school landscape, including domains such as goals, organizational operations, professional learning, and classroom instruction (Newmann et al., 2000; Sweetland & Hoy, 2000). They caution that professional communities are most interested in exercising influence over decisions that impact learning and teaching and that affect the work that they do with their students (Leithwood et al., 2004; Levine & Marcus, 2010). Investigations also document that these are the areas with the highest payoff for student learning (McDougall et al., 2007).

Although it is visible in the framework that anchors this chapter, it is worth making explicit that ownership is valued because it promotes desired outcomes, both intermediate and summative. That is, ownership fuels the development of other productive professional norms, such as efficacy and persistence and adds to the school's stock of human and social capital (Blase & Kirby, 2009; Eckert, 1989). As predicated by our model, these intermediate outcomes are linked to positive academic outcomes for students (Dannetta, 2002; Heck & Marcoulides, 1996).

Responsibility

Professional communities of practice are places where teachers hold themselves collectively accountable for school, team, and student success (Ancess, 2003; King, 2001; Printy, 2008), a norm often absent in many schools (Grossman et al., 2001; Riester et al., 2002). That is, in most schools teachers "generally are neither granted authority nor held accountable for their decisions" (McLaughlin & Talbert, 2001, p. 138). In schools with a robust professional culture, however, there is a shared sense of responsibility (Penuel et al., 2010; Raywid, 1995; Youngs & King, 2006), one that has a positive influence on student learning (Pounder, 1999).

Collective responsibility at one level means being accountable for the functioning and success of the school (Desimone, 2002; Raywid, 1995; Supovitz, 2002). Included here is responsibility for working to reach school goals and accountability for the success or failure of those efforts (Ancess, 2003; Goldenberg, 2004).

At a second level, collective control refers to teachers assuming responsibility for the instructional program, for improving the quality of instruction and curriculum across the school and in their teams (Coldren & Spillane, 2007; Eilers & Camacho, 2007). It means being on point for upholding the ethos of the school (Ancess, 2003) and community work norms (Grossman et al., 2001; Kruse et al., 2005). As Grossman and team (2001, p. 957) remind us, there is also a responsibility for meaningful participation: "In community, ideas are public property, their pursuit a communal responsibility. Group members can be held accountable for contributing their individual insights to the larger group." Shared accountability holds that problems are community property (Curry, 2008). It also suggests that each person is responsible for the learning of others in the community (Riester et al., 2002; Southworth, 2002; Youngs, 2007).

At the third and deepest level, collective accountability entails holding the community responsible for the results of their work (Darling-Hammond, Ancess, & Ort, 2002) and the success of students (McDougall et al., 2007; McLaughlin & Talbert, 2001; Wilson & Berne, 1999), especially academic achievement. In communities of practice, ownership of student learning is nested in the group (Ancess, 2003; Curry, 2008; Huberman et al., 2011).

SHARED LEADERSHIP

The Backdrop

The fifth element of practice communities underscores teachers assuming greater leadership in the school, an idea like learning community itself that is captured in a variety of overlapping terms: collective, distributed, parallel, collaborative, pluralized, and so forth. As with many of its sister elements, while widely trumpeted over the last few decades shared leadership is not thickly embedded in schools (Beachum & Dentith, 2004; Sherrill, 1999; Spillane & Louis, 2002). The primary reason for this has been highlighted throughout this volume. Over the last century, with the development of an organizational architecture of institutionalism, leadership has become equated with formal authority and roles (Crowther & Olsen, 1997; Murphy, 2005a). This understanding gave rise to conceptions of leadership that were tightly bound to domains of responsibility with the assignment of leadership in classrooms to teachers and schoolwide leadership to principals (Clift, Johnson, Holland, & Veal, 1992; Crowther et al., 2002; Murphy, 2005a). The significant point here is not that teachers were unconnected to leadership, but that their leadership was rarely acknowledged outside the realm of the classroom, teachers' role-based field of authority and influence as historically defined (Harris, 2003; Hulpia, Devos, & Rosseel, 2009; Robinson, 2008).

Because the work of teachers in terms of role and authority "has been seen as being composed of interactions with students in classes" (Griffin, 1995, p. 30), the expectation has been hardwired into the structure and culture of schools "that the only job of teachers is to teach students and to consider the classroom, at best, as the legitimate extent of their influence" (Urbanski & Nickolaou, 1997, p. 244): "The formal authority of teachers in schools remains carefully circumscribed. They exert extensive control over teaching in their classrooms and departments, but their formal influence rarely extends beyond that" (Johnson, 1989, p. 105).

This preoccupation with the hierarchical organizational system with its tenets of separation of management (leadership) from labor, chain of command, and positional authority has led to the crystallization of (1) forms of schooling in which teachers are placed in traditional roles (Kowalski, 1995) and "teacher leadership is clearly not a common contemporary condition" (Barth, 1988, p. 134) and (2) a profession in which "teachers, even those who are already leaders, do not see themselves as leaders" (Hart & Baptist, 1996, p. 87). As a consequence, "there are almost no mechanisms by which teachers can emerge as leaders for the purposes of leading work on teaching, even when they have been acknowledged as exemplary classroom teachers" (Little, 1987, p. 510).

The perspective on leadership in communities of practice is distinctly different. It begins with the belief that "the false assumption that teaching is for teachers and leading is for administrators has operated to the inutility of public schools for a long time" (Suleiman & Moore, 1997, p. 6), that the sole emphasis on principals at the core of educational leadership is ill-conceived (Crowther et al., 2002) and has real costs in terms of schooling outcomes. More positively, practice communities anchor on the proposition that shared leadership is essential to school improvement (Killion, 1996; Murphy, 2005a; Whitaker, 1995), that "genuine, long-lasting school change initiatives must derive from and involve teachers" (Kelley, 1994, p. 300), and that without teachers' "full participation and leadership, any move to reform education—no matter how well-intentioned or ambitious—is doomed to failure" (Lieberman & Miller, 1999, p. xi). In short, communities of practice challenge the underlying assumptions about existing roles for teachers and school administrators. Or, as Louis and her team (2010, p. 332) capture it "increasing teachers' involvement in the difficult task of making good decisions and introducing improved practice must be at the heart of school leadership."

The scaffolding for leadership in professional communities arises in part from the stockpile of material on leadership roles, but is inclusive of more than traditional administrative roles. That is, practice communities advance beyond the view of "educational leadership as the domain of either a particular stratum of the educational system or the individuals within that stratum" (Crowther, 1997, p. 6). For communities of professional practice to function effectively, it is important that leadership be seen as an organizational property and a dynamic of the community itself, understandings that permit the concept of shared leadership to be positioned on center stage in the leadership play (Ackerman & Maslin-Ostrowski, 2002; Jackson, 2000; Katzenmeyer & Moller, 2001).

Concept and Rationale

We acknowledge at the outset that the topic of shared leadership is cloaked in some ambiguity (Firestone & Martinez, 2007; Smylie, Conley, & Marks, 2002). Part of this is attributable to the reality that it is hardly a fully-developed area (Crowther & Olsen, 1997; Murphy, 2005a; Silva, Gimbert, & Nolan, 2000). Some is due to the broad array of ideas housed under the shared leadership mantle (Murphy, 2005a). More can be traced to the fact that it is an "emergent property" (Hulpia et al., 2009, p. 1014) and takes on different coloring in varied contents (Spillane, Camburn, & Pareja, 2009; York-Barr & Duke, 2004).

To begin with, as we explained above, teacher leadership is marked by an assortment of different names—"names that mean different things in different settings and refer to a broad array of actions" (Miller, 1995, p. 5). This variety is compounded by the fact that "when educators speak or write of teacher leadership they rarely define what they mean" (O'Hair & Reitzug, 1997, p. 67). Confusion about meanings of teacher leaders abound (Katzenmeyer & Moller, 2001), and the work of teacher leaders is often ill-defined (Johnson & Hynes, 1997; Murphy, 2005a). The consequence is, of course, a significant measure of ambiguity connected with the term (Crowther et al., 2002), the use of the term "without a clear definition of what it means" (Childs-Bowen, Moller, & Scrivner, 2000, p. 28) and the near absence of "systematic conceptual definitions . . . of the variable in the [research] literature" (Smylie, 1996, p. 543). As Moller and Katzenmeyer (1996) remind us, the lack of anything approaching a "clear definition of teacher leadership also impedes its development" (p. 5) and results in roles that remain unclear.

The rationale for shared leadership is threefold. Most importantly, and consistent with the model in Figure 9.1, it is held that collective leadership facilitates the promotion of student learning by enhancing the quality of classroom practice, practice that is strengthened by enriching teacher knowledge and deepening professional capital (Robinson, 2008; Stoll et al., 2006). Second, there is a strong sense that shared conceptions of leadership more accurately reflect the reality of what occurs in schools (Bryk et al., 2010; Hulpia et al., 2009; Spillane et al., 2009). That is, leadership is indeed distributed in schools and schools need to capitalize on that reality

(Supovitz, 2008). Third, there is a nearly universal understanding that no single person or small cadre of administrators can lead today's complex schools alone (Hulpia et al., 2009; O'Donnell & White, 2005; Walker, 2009). In particular, the new world of schooling has "highlighted constraints on the principal's time, educational expertise, and moral authority for assuming sole responsibility for leading school improvement" (Heck & Hallinger, 2010, p. 137). As a consequence, as a field school administration is turning to shared models of leadership (Hulpia et al., 2009; York-Barr & Duke, 2004).

We close our discussion of the conceptual backbone of shared leadership by highlighting its essential ingredients. The calculus of influence here is expertise in and around the core technology of schooling (Anderson, Moore, & Sun, 2009; Snell & Swanson, 2000; Wilson, 1993) and "general expertise as teachers" (Firestone & Martinez, 2009, p. 79). As Timperley (2009, p. 211) so aptly records, "Expertise rather than formal position should form the basis of leadership authority and this type of leadership often resides within the larger professional community of teachers." According to Harris (2004, p. 14), "leadership means multiple sources of guidance and direction, following the contours of expertise." In addition, influence is earned, not allotted (Grossman et al., 2001). Or as Yu and associates (2002, p. 372) observe, in a context of shared leadership "power is attributed by organizational members to whomever is able to inspire their commitment and collective aspirations." Personal and professional relationships matter deeply (Firestone & Martinez, 2007; Harris, 2003; Keedy, 1999).

Shared leadership means permeable boundaries between teachers and administrators (Ancess, 2003; Timperley, 2005). Fluidity is privileged (Hayes et al., 2004; York-Barr & Duke, 2004). It is an emergent property of the professional community (Gronn, 2009; Hulpia et al., 2009; Robinson, 2008). Shared leadership is "opportunistic, flexible, responsive, and context specific" (Jackson, 2000, p. 70). As Spillane (Spillane et al., 2001a, b) has shown across his cardinal lines of work in this area, distributed leadership is task dependent, varying from activity to activity (Moller & Eggen, 2005; Smylie et al., 2002; Timperley, 2005). It is organic and informal (Brooks et al., 2004; Mulford & Silins, 2003). It is more a process than a fixed characteristic (Anderson et al., 2009; Gronn, 2009; Silins, Mulford, & Zarins, 2002). It is more about leadership than leaders (Jackson, 2000; Sykes & Elmore, 1989). It aggregates up to more than the sum of its part.

Before we turn to pathways by which shared leadership comes to life in professionally anchored schools, a few cautions are in order. Shared leadership does not represent the demise of principal nor a "threat" to school administration. Leadership is not a zero-sum game, but rather an expandable source of capital (Conley, 1991; Leithwood & Jantzi, 2005). Leadership density is good for schools (Harris, 2004; McDougall et al., 2007). The best state of affairs is "broader and deeper capacity to lead in schools" (Heck & Hallinger, 2009, p. 684).

It is also important to remember that shared leadership is ends-driven work. It is not an outcome in itself (Gurr et al., 2005; Timperley, 2005). Indeed, "there is little point in teachers exercising more influence over one another if the content of their leadership does not deliver benefits for students" (Robinson, 2008, p. 249). Simply sharing leadership is likely to be insufficient as well. More than assumptions need to be put in place. For example, we know that shared leadership is often nothing more than shared work, with very limited additional influence (Murphy, 2005a). We also know that teachers do not necessarily seek out colleagues with the greatest expertise (Timperley, 2005). Finally, a variety of scholars remind us that research on shared leadership is still relatively new (Hulpia et al., 2009; Spillane & Louis, 2002). In particular, specifics on how teachers influence colleagues in ways that enhance student success are quite limited.

Routes to Shared Leadership

Over the last twenty years, researchers, developers, and practitioners have spent considerable time thinking about ways in which shared leadership has, is, and can be operationalized. On the research front, important frameworks have been crafted by Gronn, Harris, Louis, MacBeath, Smylie, Spillane, and others. At the broadest level, scholars differentiate between leadership exercised by teachers in formal positions (e.g., department chair, math coach) and those without formal positions (e.g., a teacher stepping forward to informally mentor a new colleague) (Brooks et al., 2004; Louis et al., 2010; Silins & Mulford, 2004). They also distinguish between leadership performed on a consistent and situational basis (Supovitz et al., 2010). Harris (2004, p. 15) underscores "top down" and "bottom up" ways to collectivize leadership, with the former dependent on the principal and the latter "occurring organically and spontaneously from the activities of teachers working together." In this latter case, as MacBeath (2009, p. 50) reminds us, "leadership is taken rather than given. It is assumed rather than conferred." Robinson (2008), in turn, helps us see that shared leadership unfolds through two pathways, distribution by task and distribution by influence.

Specific models of the operationalization of shared leadership in dense professional cultures have been forged by many of the seminal figures in the area. Gronn (2009) discusses additive and holistic perspectives. Spillane and colleagues (2001a, b) examine three sharing pathways: division of labor, co-performance, and parallel performance. Harris (2004, p. 18) in turn, refers to "involving others in decision making, allocating important tasks to teachers and rotating leadership responsibilities within the school." And MacBeath's (2009, p. 44) model highlights six methods of sharing leadership: "formally, programmatically, strategically, incrementally, opportunistically, and culturally."

Building on the foundations laid by these researchers as well as our own analyses in this area (Louis, Mayrowetz, Smylie, & Murphy, 2009; Mayrowetz, Murphy, Seashore-Louis, & Smylie, 2009; Smylie, Mayrowetz, Murphy, & Louis, 2007; Murphy, 2005a; Murphy, Smylie, Mayrowetz, & Louis, 2009), we think about bringing shared leadership into life through four overlapping bands, collective leadership by teachers: (1) participating in decision making, (2) assuming formal roles in the school, (3) shepherding tasks and functions; and (4) engaging with colleagues in the work of improving instruction for a group of students (e.g., second-grade children).

The core idea here is leadership capacity or leadership density (Sergiovanni, 1991b), a concept that analysts have shown is connected to effective schools (Leithwood et al., 2006a, b; Murphy & Datnow, 2003a, b). Robinson and her colleagues (2008, p. 668) capture this idea when they report from their research "that what matters is the frequency of various instructional leadership practices rather than the extent to which they are performed by a particular leadership role." One metaphor to employ here is "energy." In the current system of schooling, the power plants are fueled by gas and coal (e.g., authority). To make the energy production system more effective, school leaders need to add new forms of fuel to the system (e.g., classroom-based expertise). New, more informal transmission lines are built as well to add overall capacity.

A second way for school administrators to think about density is through the use of a web, a web of leadership. One objective here is to weave additional threads into the web. A second is to create more connective tissues across the threads. The third goal is to thicken each thread and piece of connective tissue. In this way, a web that was sparsely defined becomes quite dense. The sources of leadership increase. There is also greater overlap in the leadership work, less siloing, and enhanced coordination (Mayrowetz & Weinstein, 1999; Murphy, 2005a). Teacher involvement in governance decision making overlaps considerably with the learning community element of "participation" and the accompanying norm of "ownership" that we described in detail earlier. So here we only reinforce that this involvement does create opportunities for teachers to exercise leadership that are unavailable in schools with weak professional cultures (Gray et al., 1999; Hayes et al., 2004; Wahlstrom & Louis, 2008). Or as Brooks and team (2004, p. 9) explain, "participation in school-level policymaking activities constitutes a partial operational definition of teacher leadership" (see also Beachum & Dentith, 2004; Blair, 2002; and Grubb & Flessa, 2006).

The second pathway to shared leadership for district and school leaders is the creation of new roles for teachers (Hatfield, Blackman, & Claypool, 1986; Murphy, 2005a; Wasley, 1991). Initiatives here are undertaken using institutional blueprints. Two overlapping designs are featured in the role-based pathway: career-based approaches and expanded leadership structures (Firestone & Martinez, 2009; Little, 1995; York-Barr & Duke, 2004).

While the concepts of differentiated staffing and *career-based models* of teacher leadership enjoy an extensive history (Christensen, 1987; Fessler & Ungaretti, 1994), they became central characters in the school reform play in the mid-1980s with the release of the Holmes Group (1986) and Carnegie Forum (1986) reports. Career approaches to teacher leadership attack "the unstaged nature of . . . teaching" (Rowley, 1988, p. 16). They create "upward movement" (McLaughlin & Yee, 1988, p. 26), "vertical progress" (Fessler & Ungaretti, 1994, p. 220), and "staged careers" (Johnson, 1989, p. 95). These strategies provide "a hierarchical, institutionally structured notion of a career" (McLaughlin & Yee, 1988, p. 26)—as opposed to the existing "horizontal" (p. 25) and "incredibly flat career structure" (Berry & Ginsberg, 1990, p. 617)—one that is "individually constructed and experienced" (McLaughlin & Yee, 1988, p. 26). Career ladders "differentiate roles for teachers as they move up a ladder of responsibility and leadership" (Fessler & Ungaretti, 1994, p. 220). For example, the Holmes Group (1986) proposed the development of a three-phase career of instructor, professional teacher, and career professional (pp. 8–9). The Association of Teacher Educators (1985, cited in Christensen, 1987) developed a model that "includes the steps of teacher, associate teacher, senior teacher, and master teacher" (p. 101).

Administrative efforts to *broaden leadership structures*, in turn, focus on connecting teachers to new or expanded roles, roles which appear as nodes on the organizational chart (Camburn, Rowan, & Taylor, 2003; Goldstein, 2004; Pounder, 1999). The focus is less on the "hierarchically arrayed positions" (Broyles, 1991, p. 3) that define career-based efforts to develop teacher leadership and more on establishing "a richer pool of professional opportunities" (p. 3) for teachers, on "enlarg[ing] teachers' roles and responsibilities beyond their regular classroom assignments" (Smylie & Denny, 1989, p. 4; Blanc et al., 2010; York-Barr & Duke, 2004). For example, Fessler and Ungaretti (1994) assert that "modest adaptations of role structures that provide opportunities for teacher leadership include the creation of such positions as team leaders, grade-level leaders, and chairs of staff development committees" (p. 220). Efforts here include reenergizing "existing legitimized leadership roles for teachers" (Conley, 1997, p. 336), such as the department head (Little, 1995), as well as bringing new leadership roles on line, such as school reform facilitators (Berends, Bodilly, & Kirby, 2003; Datnow & Castellano, 2001; Smylie et al., 2002).

A third avenue for principals to expand teacher leadership beyond the classroom is to turn over tasks and assignments to teachers (Murphy, 2005a; Robinson, 2008; Spillane et al., 2001a, b). Here, we see leadership not in terms of roles, but rather as a "set of functions to be performed" (Mayrowetz & Weinstein, 1999). These assignments can be either lead by a single teacher or shared across staff (Goldstein, 2004; Grossman et al., 2001; Timperley, 2005). Leadership here often finds expression in professional teams as teachers lead colleagues in addressing particular challenges (Caldwell, 1998; Silins & Mulford, 2004), for example, an action research team to study and provide recommendations about student personalization. These teams can be arrayed on a continuum from ad hoc (e.g., how to address the transition from a K–6 to a K–8 school) to more ongoing (e.g., the intermediate grades data analysis team) (Blase & Kirby, 2009; Harris, 2004).

Related to the third approach is a fourth pathway that energizes a small cluster of teachers to lead inquiry-based efforts to improve learning for a specific group of students. Community inquiry leadership strategies direct our "attention away from individual and role-based conceptions of leadership" (Smylie et al., 2002, p. 172). There is a shift in focus to "the importance of teaching context and organizational development of schools" (Odell, 1997, p. 121). As a consequence, "teacher leadership is not experienced in isolation, but rather is linked with development in schools" (Zimpher, 1988, p. 54). Attention is directed to the "exercise of leadership on the part of those who do not necessarily hold power or authority by virtue of their formal position" (Frost & Durrant, 2003, p. 174).

Analysts of this pathway explore how leadership functions are "carved out by multiple individuals in different roles in redundant, mutually reinforcing" (Smylie et al., 2002, p. 173) ways. They "redefine teacher leadership as a fundamental principle and function of the teaching role" (Forster, 1997, p. 86). Teacher leadership is formulated as "more than a role; it is a *stance*, a mindset, a way of being, acting, and thinking as a learner within a community of learners" (Darling-Hammond, Bullmaster, & Cobb, 1995, p. 95).

The idea of the school as a ground of inquiry (Lieberman & Miller, 1999) trumps hierarchy. Institutional and structural (McLaughlin & Yee, 1988) issues and "organizational and production metaphors" (Livingston, 1992, p. 14) are pushed into the background (Gronn, 2009; Sergiovanni, 1994). In this fourth approach to teacher leadership, "teachers assume leadership naturally as part of a more professional conception of work" (Darling-Hammond et al., 1995, p. 88): "Teacher leaders . . . emerge as a matter of course in informally structured positions along with a communitarian social system for schools" (Odell, 1997, p. 121). The calculus shifts from filling roles to "creat[ing] an interactive community of teachers collaborating for improvement and experimentation in their schools" (Boles & Troen, 1996, p. 48), to establishing work cultures (Fullan, 1994; Spillane & Louis, 2002) and "community-related approach[es] to enhancing teaching and learning" (Griffin, 1995, p. 37).

As should be clear from the analysis presented above, the scope of work for school administrators in the inquiry pathway is different than in the role-based pathways. In latter designs, we observed that the scope of work was quite focused and limited to designated teacher leaders, that it was circumscribed and possessed an exclusive quality. In the inquiry-based design, there is acknowledgement that all teachers can carry leadership responsibility (Hart & Baptist, 1996; Murphy, 2005a). Teacher leadership "becomes a more normative role for all teachers in the school" (Odell, 1997, p. 121).

Consistent with this analysis, we find that inquiry-based strategies work tends to be natural and informal (Murphy, 2005a; Odell, 1997). They are emergent and voluntary (Katzenmeyer & Moller, 2001; Lieberman, 1992; Wasley, 1991). Teachers "assume leadership naturally as part of a more professional conception of teaching work" (Darling-Hammond et al., 1995, p. 88). Work is collaborative and collective rather than individualistic and competitive (Fay, 1992; Mitchell, 1997; Spillane & Louis, 2002). Leadership is seen as an essential component of a consequence, "the 'normal' role of the teacher is expanded" (Darling-Hammond et al., 1995, p. 87). The web of relationships in schools with inquiry-anchored teacher leadership designs is richer and more complex.

Teacher Leadership Work

When we draw an analytic magnet across the scholarship on teacher leadership tasks, activities, functions, and roles, most of the work clusters into two broad related categories: helping teacher colleagues and facilitating school improvement. In the first domain, which is in many ways foundational for the second, teacher leaders work to develop and maintain positive *working relations with their peers* (Ainscow & Southworth, 1996; Murphy, 2005a). They become mechanisms for empowering colleagues (Berry & Ginsberg, 1990; Snell & Swanson, 2000), laboring diligently to actualize what Ainscow and Southworth (1996) label the "principle of participation" (p. 233), namely, "drawing together the staff" (p. 234) and "facilitat[ing] collaboration on activities and encourag[ing] information sharing" (Hatfield et al., 1986, p. 16).

Perhaps the central dynamic of providing help and support for teacher colleagues is role modeling (Doyle, 2000). These teachers lead by example (Ainscow & Southworth, 1996). They endeavor to "create and sustain a collaborative and collegial atmosphere" (Doyle, 2000, p, 16), "a trusting atmosphere where fellow teachers can try new teaching practices" (p. 15). They promote change (Harrison & Lembeck, 1996). Or more specifically, they "positively influence the willingness and capacity of other teachers to implement change in the school" (Leithwood, Steinbach, & Ryan, 1997, p. 5)—and they confront the barriers that stand in the way of change efforts (Crowther et al., 2002; Smylie et al., 2007).

While teacher leaders exercise an array of responsibilities in *facilitating school improvement,* three broad domains stand out: administrative tasks, staff development activities, and curricular and instructional functions. To begin with, over the years researchers have consistently reported that administrative tasks are a central element of teacher leadership (Leithwood et al., 1997; York-Barr & Duke, 2004). On the one hand, given the central place of administrative work in school-level leadership in general, this conclusion is neither surprising nor troubling. On the other hand, as is the case with principal leadership, when administrative responsibilities consume teacher leaders or become disconnected from "educational" leadership, either from the natural turn of events or from the manipulations of formal school leaders, this conclusion is more problematic (Murphy, 2005a; Wasley, 1991). A key dimension of the management domain of teacher leadership work, then, is providing leadership in the service of enhanced learning and teaching and improved organizational performance.

Katzenmeyer and Moller (2001) report that much teacher leadership has to do with the professional development of colleagues. Indeed, teacher leadership for school improvement comes to life when teachers assume responsibility for professional development (Firestone & Martinez, 2007; Spillane & Louis, 2002; Supovitz et al., 2000). Here, teacher leaders take on the tasks of "identify[ing] school and individual teacher growth needs, identifying available resources to assist in meeting those needs" (Fessler & Ungaretti, 1994, p. 216), "offering professional learning experiences, and evaluating the outcomes of teacher development" (Childs-Bowen et al., 2000, p. 30). They are often active in educating preservice teachers (Fessler & Ungaretti, 1994; Troen & Boles, 1994), inducting new teachers (Leithwood et al., 1997), and serving as mentors to new faculty and peer coaches to more experienced colleagues (Katzenmeyer & Moller, 2001; Murphy, 2005a). These educators also lead by (1) exercising influence over decisions about professional development and by facilitating professional learning opportunities (Katzenmeyer & Moller, 2001); (2) as noted earlier, modeling the importance of professional development through their own actions (Harrison & Lembeck, 1996; Smylie et al., 2007); and (3) engaging in informal counseling (Doyle, 2000).

Finally, teacher leaders often assume responsibilities for and perform tasks designed to strengthen the school's curricular and instructional program and learning and teaching in classrooms (Boles & Troen, 1996; Spillane & Louis, 2002; Wasley, 1991). They often provide curricular help in particular subject domains and leadership of instructional programs (Hart, 1990).

Even more so than with the other elements and norms of professional community, relational trust is difficult to corral and hold in place. It has its own space and is the catalyst for the growth and effective functioning of the other elements of teacher community (e.g., collaboration) (Cosner, 2009; Mitchell & Sackney, 2006; Scribner et al., 1999). As such, it occupies an essential place in the leadership equation to promote learning and the formation of a professional culture (Silins, Mulford, & Zarins, 2002; Useem et al., 1997). In their landmark analysis of Chicago elementary schools, Bryk and his associates (2010, p. 202) concluded that trust is "both a lubricant for organizational change and a moral resource for sustaining the hard work of school improvement," a type of "social glue" (p. 140). Without trust, "relationships and respect are compromised and mistrust exerts a corrosive influence" (MacBeath, 2005, p. 353). Efforts unravel and "meaningful organizational learning is frustrated" (Useem et al., 1997, p. 57). The doors to professional community and school improvement rarely open in its absence (Bryk et al., 2010; Firestone & Martinez, 2009; Mulford & Silins, 2003).

Numerous studies have shown that "trust plays a key role in obtaining valued future outcomes" (Goddard et al., 2009, p. 295), such as professional norms (Bryk et al., 2010; Bulkley & Hicks, 2005; Louis et al., 2010), teacher learning (Bryk et al., 2010; Goddard et al., 2009), productive work (Cosner, 2009; Useem et al., 1997), change (Bryk et al., 2010; Wahlstrom & Louis, 2008), and student achievement (Bryk et al., 2010; Goddard et al., 2008; Leithwood, 2008). Relational trust, researchers find, is an especially significant coordinating mechanism in institutions like schools that have high task complexity (Adams, 2010; Adams & Forsyth, 2009) and in organizations where nonrelational "gluing" strategies are difficult to use (Kochanek, 2005). We also know now that the connections between trust and outcomes are even more powerful in difficult times and in schools working with underserved children (Bryk et al., 2010; Goddard et al., 2009).

Trust is defined in slightly different, but clearly overlapping ways in the research literature. For example, Louis (2007, p. 27) informs us that trust can be viewed as "confidence in or reliance on the integrity, veracity, justice, friendship, or other sound principle, of another person or group." Two seminal lines of work on trust dominate the school improvement research literature. One is by Hoy and his colleagues, especially Forsyth (Adams & Forsyth, 2009), Goddard (Goddard et al., 2009), and Tschannen-Moran (Tschannen-Moran & Barr, 2004). The other is by Bryk and assorted colleagues (Bryk et al., 2010). Hoy and his associates describe five essential attributes of trust: benevolence, honesty, openness, reliability, and competence. Bryk and team anchor trust on four pillars: respect, competence, personal regard for others, and integrity. In their foundational work on communities of practice, Kruse and Louis (Kruse et al., 1995) explain trust in terms of four ingredients: integrity, concern, competence, and reliability. Looking across these hallmark analyses and research that followed, we cull four major themes from the chronicle on mutual trust: openness, competency, integrity, and caring.

All work on trust underscores the need for *openness*, without which the other themes lay fallow. Openness is defined as a willingness to disarm, to dismantle the barriers erected to protect against the potential harm from relationships. Analysts refer to this as a willingness to assume the posture of vulnerability (Adams, 2010; Dirks & Ferrin, 2002) "under the conditions of risk and interdependence" (Robinson, 2007, p. 18; Fullan & Ballew, 2002).

Integrity encompasses a number of core ideas. Consistency between words and actions is important, as is honesty (Bryk et al., 2010; Robinson, 2007). Also lodged here are transparency and authenticity (Hoy, Hannum, & Tschannen-Moran, 1998; Leithwood, 2008). Reliability is found on center stage in most reviews of integrity, what Raywid (1995, p. 59) refers to as a "sense of reciprocity." Ethics is often contained here as well, specifically the commitment and practice of working in the best interests of children and families (Beck & Murphy, 1996; Bryk et al., 2010; Louis, 2007).

Competence is the keystone to the interpersonal framework that supports and energizes trust (Wenger, 2000). Wahlstrom and Louis (2008) describe this as the ability of colleagues to do what is needed (also Rumberger, 2011). Bryk and associates (2010) concur portraying competence as the knowledge, skills, and capacity to deliver required assistance.

Before moving to the impact of professional culture, it is productive to pause for two reminders about this sixth element that helps define communities of practice. We know that trust can flow from different sources. For example, trust can be lodged in institutional policies and regulations or negotiated contracts (Kochanek, 2005). Our focus here is on a different taproot, social, interpersonal, or relational trust (Bryk et al., 2010). We also want to be clear that these deepening relationships among teachers do not gainsay the need for a strong hand for those in formal leadership positions (Bryk et al., 2010; Murphy, 2005a).

MODEL AND THEORY OF ACTION: IMPACT OF COLLABORATIVE COMMUNITIES OF PROFESSIONAL PRACTICE

The model in Figure 9.1 shows that teacher communities are designed ultimately to enhance student academic and social learning. Our framework also reveals that the connection between community and student learning is indirect, or mediated (Supovitz & Christman, 2003; Visscher & Witziers, 2004). It also reminds us of the reciprocal connections among the pieces of the narrative. That is, community powers professional learning and learning, in turn, deepens community (Osterman, 2000; Stoll et al., 2006).

The initial effect in the model is twofold, greater learning (knowledge capital) and enhanced professional norms (professional capital). Augmentation of capital results in more effective instructional practice which, in turn, leads to greater student learning. We explain this chain of linkages in detail below.

INTELLECTUAL AND PROFESSIONAL CAPITAL

Intellectual Capital

Communities of inquiry provide caldrons for the formation of "funds of knowledge" (Palincsar et al., 1998, p. 17), of human and social capital (Penuel et al., 2009; Spillane et al., 2001a, b; Wigginton, 1992) that is used to improve the education of children (Ancess, 2003). That is, communities of practice exist to promote teacher learning (Darling-Hammond et al., 1995; Grossman et al., 2001). They provide "the basic building blocks of a social learning system" (Wenger, 2000, p. 229), participation in which is a catalyst for learning (Connolly & James, 2006; Mullen & Hutinger, 2008; Wenger, 1998). Although the research here is insufficient to advance dramatic claims, it does strongly suggest that professional cultures with the norms discussed above become productive venues for teachers to learn and develop together (Franke, Carpenter, & Fennema, 2001; Grossman et al., 2001), to enhance the knowledge and skills of teachers (Harris, 2009; Smylie & Denny, 1989; Spillane & Louis, 2002). In communities of professional practice, researchers find that educators become a "profession of learners" (Silins & Mulford, 2004, p. 448) and "communities of knowledge" (Craig, 2009, p. 601), a "source of energy to push a trajectory of learning" (Levine & Marcus, 2007, p. 133). There is also a growing body of knowledge that these communities provide a more robust method of learning than the more traditional forms of professional development to which teachers are exposed (Grossman et al., 2001; McLaughlin & Talbert, 2001).

At the core of the professional community concept is the understanding that "thought, learning, and the construction of knowledge are not just influenced by social factors but are, in fact, social phenomena" (Palincsar et al., 1998, p. 6). Learning is considered in social terms (Horn, 2005; Stein & Coburn, 2008; Wenger, 1998), as a social process (Wenger, 2000). In schools "teachers learn through situated and social interactions with colleagues who possess distributed expertise and with whom they have opportunities for sustained conversations related to mutual interest" (Curry, 2008, p. 738). Learning is site based and job embedded (Ermeling, 2010; Horn, 2010), or situated (Wenger, 1998). Learning is also constructed (Mullen & Hutinger, 2008). It is work that does not feature the transmission of knowledge, but rather the "active deconstruction of knowledge through reflection and analysis, and its reconstruction through action in a particular context" (Stoll et al., 2006, p. 233).

Community-based learning fosters both individual and group learning, with a special emphasis on the creation of collective knowledge (Harris, 2009; Ingram, Seashore Louis, & Schroeder, 2004). Learning in professional communities covers a wider spectrum of developmental work as well. Most prominently, it includes the broad range of informal exchanges, "not just those that deliberately and systematically set out to improve practice" (Horn, 2005, p. 230). It emphasizes what Wenger (2000) refers to as the ongoing experience of work.

In schools with strong professional cultures, learning is also a reciprocal process (Heck & Hallinger, 2009), "the learning that results from the participation feeds back into the community and impacts subsequent participation" (Printy, 2008, p. 189). Learning in communities of inquiry is about expertise. In addition, as a social phenomenon learning is about reconstructing professional culture (Printy, 2008; Wenger, 1998), what Grossman and associates (2001, p. 954) portray as a "transformation of the social setting in which individuals work." Finally, there is evidence that the teacher learning in professional communities is more transformative and more thoroughly internalized than knowledge acquired in more traditional formats (Levine & Marcus, 2007; Wenger, 1998).

Professional Capital

Teacher communities produce professional as well as knowledge capital. They are continually adding new fibers in the professional tapestry, repairing torn threads, and enriching existing strands. Communities transform the meaning of school as a place (Goldenberg, 2004). We examine these strands of rebuilding in three overlapping clusters: (1) changes in occupational norms, (2) reinforcement to the core elements and norms of community presented above, and (3) creating powerful professional values and attitudes. Before we do so, two points need to be made explicit. First, no one has crafted nonleaky containers to capture these "fundamental shifts." Second, as we have explained throughout these chapters, action throughout the framework in Figure 9.1 is interactive and reciprocal. Energy and influence move in all directions in a cyclical pattern. For example, core elements and norms lead to teacher learning and professionalism. Each, in turn, strengthens the elements of community (e.g., shared accountability). Likewise, learning influences professional culture and culture impacts learning (Adams, 2010; Olivier & Hipp, 2006; Saunders et al., 2009).

As professional culture gains a foothold in schools, it begins to alter the long-standing ways in which teaching unfolds. We know, for example, that for over a century teaching has been primarily a private affair. With the development of community, this deeply entrenched norm of privacy is no longer dominant (Bulkley & Hicks, 2005; Louis et al., 1996; Webb, 2005). In communities, teaching practice is made "public through peer observations, review of student work and teacher curriculum, collaborative planning and problem solving, and team teaching" (Ancess, 2003, p. 12).

Schools are also defined by norms of autonomy and isolation. Teachers work alone and sink or swim accordingly (McLaughlin & Talbert, 2001).

With its emphasis on collaboration, interaction, and interdependence (Palincsar et al., 1998) professional culture undermines these well-established occupational norms, "counteract[ing] the fragmentation of work" (Newmann et al., 1989, p. 223) and "breaking down the barriers that isolate teachers" (Scribner et al., 1999, p. 136; Lieberman, Saxl, & Miles, 1988).

Professional culture with its ethic of constructive feedback and critique also assails the deeply etched organizational norm of civility in schools, where civility is defined as an unwillingness to confront problems and a penchant to withdraw in the face of conflict. Finally, we see in narratives of professional community the displacement of the norm of separation between administration and teaching, the one that holds that administrators lead and teachers teach. There is a softening of this boundary (Sykes & Elmore, 1989; Wahlstrom & Louis, 2008). Per our discussion of reciprocity above, we should not be surprised to learn that the elements of communities of learning (e.g., shared goals) not only power professionalism but are, in turn, enriched by those values, orientations, and attitudes. *Community norms* concurrently define teacher teams and are the outcomes of the work of those groups. There is considerable evidence, for example, that as communities function they create internal feedback loops that thicken the very norms that define professional community (e.g., shared accountability). We know, for example, that in the process of changing teacher culture and renorming the organization, collaborative work reinforces the vision and purpose of the school (Walker & Slear, 2011). Collective work also deepens and extends the threads of collaboration (Curry, 2008, Supovitz, 2002; Vescio et al., 2008), thus "sustaining and strengthening professional community" (Louis & Marks, 1998, p. 560) itself (Stoll et al., 2006; York-Barr & Duke, 2004). Similarly, community is defined by ownership and increases empowerment in the process of engagement (Ancess, 2003; Blase & Kirby, 2009; Drago-Severson, 2004), especially augmenting teacher buy-in. Shared accountability is also reinforced and expanded by professional communities of practice (Kruse et al., 1995; Timperley, 2009). It is both an element of and a product of learning communities (Kruse et al., 1995; Printy, 2008). Finally, there is strong empirical support for the claim that trust and caring are enriched by enhanced professional capital (Louis, 2007; McLaughlin & Talbert, 2001).

In addition to influencing occupational and community norms, learning teams foster other *professional norms*, attitudes, and values. Scholarship on this dimension covers a good bit of territory and a variety of taxonomies to capture this research have been crafted. We organize the literature on professional norms into three clusters: agency, work orientation, and identity. Collectively, concepts in these categories address teachers' professional citizenship behaviors and attitudes regarding the school as a place of work (Dirks & Ferrin, 2002), their "affective dispositions" (Leithwood, Day et al., 2006, p. 89), and "personal and organizational behavior" (Goddard et al., 2000, p. 502).

The claim that communities of practice enhance individual and collective "agency" is one of the most visible themes in the storyline on professional norms and values (Katzenmeyer & Moller, 2001; Lieberman, 1992; Smylie et al., 2002), the belief that efficacy is perhaps the key pathway by which professional culture shapes student learning (Goddard et al., 2000; Sweetland & Hoy, 2000; Tschannen-Moran & Barr, 2004). Analysts define agency in similar ways. All definitions feature the essential idea of faculty "feel[ing] competent that they can teach in ways that enhance student success" (Printy, 2008, p. 200), the individual and collective sense that they can help ensure that the school achieves its goals and that they will have a positive impact on students (Goddard et al., 2000; Murphy et al., 1982; Olivier & Hipp, 2006). Raywid (1995, p. 70) refers to this as "a strong sense of their power over the life chances of students." Efficacy includes beliefs about competence (Dannetta, 2002; Gurr et al., 2005; Harris, 2004), the ability to employ that competence in the service of students, and the garnering of satisfaction linked to those efforts (Newmann et al., 1989, Roney, Coleman, & Schlichting, 2007; Wenger & Snyder, 2000).

Communities of learning also exercise a strong pull on the "work orientation" of teachers, both individually and collectively (Bryk et al., 2010; Riehl & Sipple, 1996). This orientation is visible in a number of values and behaviors, often in a reciprocal relationship with agency (Newmann, 1989). We know, for example, that professional communities of practice can create hope and a sense of possibility, a "more optimistic and encouraging culture" (Strahan, 2003, p. 130), frames often in short supply in schools serving students placed at risk (McLaughlin & Talbert, 2001). Professional community strengthens teachers' "willingness to struggle" (Ancess, 2003, p. 11). It adds to the "reservoir of resilience" (p. 11), providing new "sources of energy and renewal" (Strahan, 2003, p. 138) and reducing feelings of failure, cynicism, and burnout (Felner et al., 2007; Louis, 2007; Newmann et al., 1989). Community produces positive assessments from teachers about their work environments (Heck & Marcoulides, 1996). Professionalism also leads to additional effort (Newmann et al., 1989; Olivier & Hipp, 2006; Scheurich, 1998), what Useem and associates (1997, p. 58) refer to as the formation of a "norm of diligent work." Dedication is an important aspect of work orientation that grows in professional communities (Kruse et al., 1995; Pounder, 1999; Riehl & Sipple, 1996). In general, teachers in communities of practice fuel commitment to the profession of teaching and to the school as a place of work (Ancess, 2003; Osterman, 2000; Somech & Bogler, 2002), an idea "typically conceptualized as a positive, affective attachment to one's work" (Dannetta, 2002, p. 145). More specifically, communities of professional practice strengthen commitment to student success (Dannetta, 2002; Darling-Hammond et al., 2002).

Motivation is also positively impacted by learning communities (Blase & Blase, 2000; Bryk et al., 2010; Felner et al., 2007), another condition that shares a relationship with agency (Goddard et al., 2000; Leithwood, 2008;

Tschannen-Moran & Barr, 2004). So too is persistence in effort (Printy, 2008; Riester et al., 2002), with teacher professional communities coming to be defined by a "culture of teacher persistence" (Ancess, 2003, p. 77). Learning communities foster work orientations that privilege risk taking, proactiveness, and innovation (Blanc et al., 2010; Franke et al., 2001; Hoy et al., 1998), a "willingness to try new things" (Robinson, 2007, p. 20).

Researchers also affirm that communities of practice increase professional capital by strengthening personal and collective "identity" for teachers, identity that, in turn, powers better instructional practice (Bryk et al., 2010; Doyle, 2000; Stone, Horejs, & Lomas, 1997). Under conditions of community, sense of belonging and buy-in are augmented (Battistich, Solomon, Watson, & Schaps, 1997; Stoll et al., 2006). As we have noted above, the norm of ownership at the heart of professional community is enriched (Cosner, 2009; Etheridge, Valesky, Horgan, Nunnery, & Smith, 1992; Smylie, 1996). Teachers are "drawn in, involvement engagement, and affiliation" (Jackson, 2000, p. 72) expand. There is an enhanced feeling of fit (Au, 2002) and integration (Blase & Kirby, 2009).

One way that learning communities build professional capital is by bolstering teacher morale (Conley, 1991; Blase & Kirby, 2009; Tschannen-Moran & Barr, 2004). Professional culture also adds to the storehouse of confidence and self-esteem (Blase & Kirby, 2009; Hattie, 2009; Roney et al., 2007). These identity changes occur because teachers feel more valued and more successful in socially and professionally dense cultures than they do working in isolation (Felner et al., 2007; Kruse et al., 1995; McLaughlin & Talbert, 2001). Finally, identity is nourished because teachers in learning communities experience greater job satisfaction than do their colleagues in nonmacroprofessional anchored work environments (Cosner, 2009; Pounder, 1999), both in the short term and in their overall careers (McLaughlin & Talbert, 2001). They enjoy their work more (Battistich et al., 1997).

TEACHING PRACTICE AND STUDENT LEARNING

As we move to the far right-hand side of the model in Figure 9.1, we see that all the capital accumulated to date is linked to the improvement of instructional practice which, in turn, powers important outcomes, especially student academic and social learning.

Teaching Practice

Knowledge capital and professional capital formation in communities impacts instructional practice (Curry, 2008; Horn, 2010; Supovitz, 2002. There is evidence that this linkage is real, positive, and reciprocal

(Bryk et al., 2010; Leithwood, Day et al., 2006; Louis et al., 2010; McDougall et al., 2007; Visscher & Witziers, 2004; Wahlstrom & Louis, 2008). Teacher practice is changed (Curry, 2008; Finnigan & Gross, 2007; Gray et al., 1999), and more productive learning opportunities are made available to students (Horn, 2005; McKeever, 2003; McLaughlin & Talbert, 2001).

While there is relative consistency and clarity to this point in the story (see Rowan & Miller, 2007 for some cautionary notes), deeper analyses provide less full-bodied descriptions. That is, while there are summative claims about improved instruction resulting from the work of teacher professional communities—stronger instructional norms, enhancements in teacher work, more effective teaching, better teachers, better pedagogy, and so forth, the specific nature of this improved teaching is not well explained. Here is what we do know. The more effective teaching linked to strong professional culture pivots on increasing academic press (Felner et al., 2007; Mulford & Silins, 2003; Sebastian & Allensworth, 2012). Stronger instruction in professional environments is nourished by deepening knowledge of students and their learning needs (Blanc et al., 2010; Hattie, 2009; Horn, 2005). It is also fostered by new approaches to addressing those needs, by a willingness to engage in new instructional designs in the face of problems (Wenger & Snyder, 2000). Finally, there is evidence that the more effective instruction in professional communities reflects the principles of authentic pedagogy and learning (Bidwell & Yasumoto, 1999; Levine & Marcus, 2010; Louis & Marks, 1998). Included here are practices such as student-focused work, constructivist activities, emphasis on higher level thinking, an achievement orientation, instruction more finely tuned to student needs, student exploration, inquiry-oriented work, and visible linkages between classroom work and the real world (Felner et al., 2007; Supovitz, 2002).

Student Learning

The most salient question confronting everyone associated with professional communities of practice—"assuming that the magnitude of the relationship with workplace outcomes is a criterion for judging the practical importance of a construct" (Dirks & Ferrin, 2002, p. 26)—is, does professional culture result in enhanced organizational outcomes (Goddard et al., 2009; Stoll et al., 2006)? More specifically, given the current climate of high standards and accountability, the viability of professional communities as a pathway to reform will be established by their ability to enhance student learning (Mitchell & Sackney, 2006; Spillane & Louis, 2002; Vescio et al., 2008).

In terms of organizational outcomes, researchers document positive linkages between teacher professional community and school improvement, school effectiveness, goal attainment, change, and organizational efficiency (Adams, 2010; Bryk et al., 2010; Eilers & Camacho, 2007; Goddard et al., 2000; Heck & Marcoulides, 1996; Leithwood et al., 2006a, b; Newmann et al., 2001; Olivier & Hipp, 2006; Silins et al., 2002). Fine-grained analyses (Bryk et al., 2010; Goddard et al., 2009) and the most scholarly reviews (Bol & Berry, 2005; Hattie, 2009; Vescio et al., 2008) confirm positive linkages between professional culture and student achievement. Consistently, this work concludes that these impacts are significant and meaningful (Bryk et al., 2010; Leithwood & Mascall, 2008; Louis et al., 2010).

Investigators have also discovered positive relationships between teacher community and other valued outcomes. They confirm linkages between professional communities and lower numbers of student suspensions, reduced dropout rates, reduced teacher turnover, and stronger connections with parents (Bulkley & Hicks, 2005; Louis, 2007; O'Donnell & White, 2005).

We close here with two additional insights. First, there is increasing evidence that the impact of professional culture is particularly strong in schools with high concentrations of students placed at risk and schools in disadvantaged areas (Bryk et al., 2010; Stoll et al., 2006). Second, achievement effects are mediated by student motivation, persistence, and engagement (Stoll et al., 2006; Useem et al., 1997). That is, improved teacher practice works by enhancing participation and effort among students (Bruggencate, Luyten, Scheerens, & Sleegers, 2012; Horn, 2005; Silins & Mulford, 2004).

10

Meaningful Engagement of Families and Community

It might seem tempting for a principal to close the door on the community surrounding his or her school and focus on what can be done to build culture within the school's walls. However, given that the majority of the variance in student achievement can be explained by factors beyond the school and that children spend about two thirds of each day outside of the school, this approach would be shortsighted and detrimental to students. If no connection between the school and the community exists, some children will create separate identities to fit each environment (Hattie, 2009). Depending on the child's cultural capital, which is largely contingent on his or her socioeconomic status and race, school and nonschool identities can be very similar or widely divergent, and aid or inhibit student achievement. For low income, minority students, the latter outcome is more likely to be the case.

Because parents are a child's first teacher (Moles, 1996) and children spend significant amounts of time with their families, teachers and school leaders depend on parents and families to get students to school, to make sure students are healthy, to help diffuse behavior problems, and to enforce good study habits (Bryk, Sebring, Allensworth, Luppescu, & Easton, 2010). Parents, on the other hand, depend on teachers and school administrators to provide them with information on their child's progress and strategies on how to best support their children academically (Eccles & Harold, 1996).

In the first part of this chapter we provide an overview for considering home–school connections. In the second half we craft an action framework to guide leaders in creating a productive culture for parents.

THE LANDSCAPE OF PARENT INVOLVEMENT

Impact

Research has shown that when parents are involved with their children's education within the home, children tend to do better academically (Leithwood, Patten, & Jantzi, 2010; Goldenberg, 2004; Feldman & Matjasko, 2005). In fact, several researchers claim that improving the home educational environment, also called the "curriculum of the home," may yield the most leverage for increasing student achievement (Goldenberg, 2004; Mulford & Silins, 2003), and for older students, can increase graduation rates (Ensminger & Slusarcick, 1992).

Epstein found positive outcomes for students who discussed academics with family members on a regular basis (1996). In a study of high achieving, black, low-income students, Finn and Rock (1997) found that parents were actively engaged in creating a supportive, encouraging home education environment. Parents who have higher expectations for their children also tend to be more involved with their child's education (Griffith, 2001; Alexander, Entwisle, & Horsey, 1997). Moreover, students internalize those high expectations and are likely to perform better in school (Hattie, 2009) and be more resilient (Finn & Rock, 1997). Indeed, the attitudes and expectations that parents have for their children regarding their schooling are more important than family structure in predicting student achievement (Hattie, 2009).

More broadly, aspects of the home environment not directly related to schooling, influence student achievement (Bierman, 1996). Some research shows that socio-psychological components of the home, measured by indicators, such as how parents use punishment, how responsive they are to children's needs, and the types of enrichment materials present at home, are closely linked to student learning (Hattie, 2009). Other research indicates additional nonacademic characteristics of the home environment that are related to student achievement, including parents establishing clear boundaries and acting as an authority, consistently enforcing rules, having numerous books, being nurturing and supportive, and respecting the intelligence of their children (Garmezy, 1991). Garmezy also finds that a home environment characterized by minimal conflict is positively associated with student learning.

Unfortunately, the home environment can also be "a toxic mix of harm and neglect with respect to enhancing learning" (Hattie, 2009, p. 33). Neglect and abuse, as well as less extreme behaviors, such as using external rewards and negative controls to influence child behavior, are negatively correlated with achievement. Also, the number of hours of television that a student watches each day, which can be regulated by parents, is negatively related to student academic outcomes, and this relationship becomes stronger as students progress through school (Hattie, 2009).

Parent's sense of efficacy in relation to their children is linked with how involved they are with their children's academic life (Eccles & Harold, 1996). Parents with a strong sense of efficacy, defined as the belief that they have the "skills and knowledge to help their children, that they can teach or assist their children, and that they can find extra resources for their children," are more likely to be involved in their child's education in the home environment (Sheldon, 2002, p. 303).

Involving parents in schools has been shown consistently to increase the academic achievement of students at all grade levels (Feldman & Matjasko, 2005) and subjects (Bryk et al., 2010; Epstein, 1996). Parent involvement in the school and the community is also related to higher rates of high school graduation and college enrollment (Goddard, 2003). An increased proportion of involved parents in a school is related not only to individual student achievement, but also to the effectiveness of the school as a whole (Auerbach, 2007).

The academic outcomes of parent involvement depend on the type and nature of the connections. In a study of teacher practices to increase parent engagement in their child's academics, Epstein (1996) found that if parents increased their involvement in reading, reading scores improved, but there was no impact on math scores. Likewise, Hattie (2009) reports that when parents are more actively engaged with their children academically, for example by tutoring their children as opposed to listening to them read, there are stronger effects on student achievement.

Principals also need to remember that parent and community involvement is associated with improved culture in the school (Bryk et al., 2010). For example, research shows that parent involvement can increase the sense of caring within a school (Sanders & Harvey, 2002). Moreover, strong relationships between parents and the school are related to increased safety and order within the school (Bryk et al., 2010). When there is alignment between the home and the school on the values and beliefs regarding the education of the child, parents are more likely to be involved, and students are more likely to have positive, trusting relationships with teachers (Adams, 2010). Students also report having more positive attitudes toward homework and being more engaged when their parents are involved in their education (Epstein, 1996).

Increased parent involvement also influences teacher perceptions (Epstein, 1996). Goldenberg relates that when he began reaching out to parents early in the year to seek their support in achieving mutually devised goals for the students, he was able to cultivate a more asset-based view of parents (2004). As teachers increase their contact with families, they may also better understand the communities of the children they teach and thus be better able to support those children (Haynes & Ben-Avie, 1996).

Historically, schools have been tasked with inculcating students with democratic values and creating engaged citizens. Some research suggests that creating school-home-community connections can help schools attain this goal (Auerbach, 2009).

Most strategies to increase home–school connections do not directly impact student achievement (Goldenberg, 2004). We also know that many of the benefits from parent involvement are indirect. For example, research shows that partnership practices are related to an increase in student attendance (Epstein, 1996; Feldman & Matjasko, 2005), which is a clear prerequisite for student academic success. Likewise, if parents are volunteering at the school or participating in school governance, this might increase their buy-in to the vision of the school and the alignment of their home practices with those expected by the school, thus increasing student success (Bierman, 1996). Finally, while research indicates that involving parents in decision making may only have limited impact on student achievement (Murphy & Beck, 1995), including parents in school government may help keep the focus of school decision making on outcomes for students (Leithwood & Jantzi, 2006).

Involving parents in the school community can also have a positive impact on the health of the family, especially in the case when the school partners with health or social service providers (Auerbach, 2009). Bryk and colleagues (2010) document that instructional productivity depends on the supports for academic, social, and health needs available through the school and in the home. Schools that serve high numbers of students living in poverty will be better able to advance students' academic learning if they support both the students' academic and health-related needs (Bryk et al., 2010).

Types of Involvement

The outcomes related to parental involvement are contingent on the specific ways that parents are involved with their child's education (Eccles & Harold, 1996). Researchers have found that parents can be involved in their child's education in a variety of ways and in different venues. The most well-known framework for understanding home school connections is Joyce Epstein's explanation of six types of parental involvement (Epstein, 1996): basic parenting, learning in the home, communication with the school, volunteering, participating in school decision making, and making connections to the community. These activities occur in home (types one through three), at the school (types four and five), and within the wider community (type six).

Others have elaborated on aspects of this basic framework. Louis, Anderson, and Wahlstrom (2004, p. 47) delve into a more nuanced explanation of "family educational culture," which encompasses two of Epstein's involvement categories: basic parenting and learning in the home. This concept delineates the type of academic supports that schools can help parents provide in the home. These include (1) modeling and teaching positive work habits; (2) providing academic guidance and assistance, academic stimulation, adequate healthcare and nutrition; (3) holding high aspirations and expectations; and (4) creating a home setting conducive to academic work. Other research has highlighted additional activities that parents undertake to create a positive "family educational culture," including tutoring their children, reading with them, taking them to cultural events, helping their children with homework, supervising the child within the home, and engaging in academic discussions (Bierman, 1996; Eccles & Harold, 1996; Sui-Chu & Willms, 1996).

Several researchers have expanded Epstein's idea of "volunteering" to include multiple forms of participation within the school (Eccles & Harold, 1996; Haynes & Ben-Avie, 1996). This more general conceptualization includes volunteering time to help in the school or classroom and participating in or supporting school events. Eccles and Harold (1996) also expand on how parents communicate with the school, distinguishing between contacting the school about their child's progress and contacting the school for suggestions on how to help their child.

Reasons for Limited Involvement

The literature on building partnerships with parents is usually premised on the notion that parents are not sufficiently involved, but typically does not detail ideal levels of involvement. What is common is research that contrasts the relative level of involvement demonstrated by parents of different races, ethnicities, and/or socioeconomic classes. This literature typically demonstrates that minority and low-income parents participate less frequently than middle- and upper-class white parents. It also details parent/family and school-related barriers that explain differences in the level and types of involvement.

Chavis, Ward, Elwell, and Barret (1997) succinctly outline the parent-related obstacles as insufficient resources, abilities or skills, and cultural capital. Alexander and his collaborators (1997) make the important addition of the barrier imposed by parent attitudes and values. On the issue of resources, parents' time for involvement with the school or with helping their children at home may be limited by work schedules and family obligations (Chavis et al., 1997; Eccles & Harold, 1996). Limited financial resources might keep parents from providing additional educational experiences at home or in the community (Goldenberg, 2004; Chin & Phillips, 2004). Obstacles engendered by poverty are exacerbated when poverty is concentrated in the community in which the school is embedded (Bryk et al., 2010; Murphy, 2010).

Limited parental skills and abilities can be manifest in several ways. Less educated parents may be less able to help their students with course work, especially as students advance to middle and high school. Parents with higher levels of education are more likely than those with lower levels of education to read to their children, as well as tutor their children at home in a manner consistent with the teaching style typical in school, making this tutoring time more advantageous (Murphy, 2010).

Cultural barriers often arise between minority and low-income parents and middle-class, predominantly white school staff. Some parents feel uncomfortable or unfamiliar with the language or methods for learning used at school and thus may be at a disadvantage when attempting to help their children at home or unwilling to participate actively at the school (Delgado-Gaitan, 1992; Hattie, 2009). For example, Goldenberg (2004) highlights how the distinct experiences of immigrant parents, who are educated in different schooling systems, present an obstacle for building home-school connections.

Parent attitudes and values toward school are shaped by their own schooling experiences (Alexander et al., 1997; Murphy, 2012). Those parents who had positive schooling experiences are more likely than those who had negative experiences to form connections with the school (Eckert, 1989). We also know that attitudes and experiences toward schooling tend to align with class status, whereby middle-class parents have often had more positive experiences in schooling than their working-class counterparts (Eccles & Harold, 1996).

School-related obstacles can be summarized as a lack of understanding on the part of school staff of the various types of parental involvement, negative and unwelcoming attitudes on the part of teachers or administrators, and limited physical and human resources within the school (Chavis et al., 1997; Auerbach, 2009).

The first two school-based obstacles are related. School staff sometimes develop negative attitudes toward parents because they do not understand or do not value how parents are involved in their child's education outside of the school setting. For example, there is a widespread belief held by teachers and school administrators that parents are not sufficiently involved (Weis, 1990) either because they do not care about their children's education or are incapable, due to personal deficiencies, of helping their children succeed academically. Epstein (1996) concluded that teachers perceive parents very differently than parents perceive themselves and are often unaware of the goals parents have for their children. Teachers and school administrators may attribute a lack of school-based parent involvement to a "culture of poverty," a theory that ascribes present time orientation and a sense of resignation to poor and marginalized individuals (Goldenberg, 2004). Educators rooted in a belief in the culture of poverty often hold that parents are "apathetic, indifferent, or hostile about schooling" (Goldenberg, 2004, p. 111).

Assumptions such as these, which reflect the belief that parents are a major part of the problem of low student achievement, can result in a school not pursuing parent involvement, either because staff expect a lack of response, or, in more extreme cases, because they believe that poor minority parents will "mess [the kids] up" (Auerbach, 2007, p. 711; Eccles & Harold, 1996). These attitudes may lead to neglect of or palpable hostility toward parents, which in turn makes parents feel unwelcome in the school (Eccles & Harold, 1996).

School leaders may not trust parents sufficiently to yield power, or find that involving parents directly may decrease their autonomy (Powell, 1991). Dornbusch (1996, p. 40) reaches the conclusion that "school officials and teachers gain from the ignorance of students and their parents" in terms of the power and autonomy that they can wield. While school staff may be adamant in their desire for parents to contribute to the home learning of their children, they may be less interested in parents being actively involved in making decisions at the classroom or school level because they find this type of engagement "risk . . . and conflict ridden" (Haynes & Ben-Avie, 1996, p. 46; Auerbach, 2007). Many leaders thus act not as a bridge between parents and the school, but rather as a buffer between school staff and what staff regard as overzealous parents (Auerbach, 2009).

School-related obstacles to parent involvement also arise due to lack of resources, which include time, financial capital, trained staff, and space. Work that demands time from principals and teachers impedes their ability to focus their energy on parents (Auerbach, 2007). In other cases principals may wish to advance policies and practices to involve parents and the community, but are constrained by district, state, or federal mandates (Auerbach, 2009).

Training for schools staff on how to effectively involve parents may also be a resource that is in short supply (Chavis et al., 1997). Greenwood and Hickman (1991) suggest that teachers need training on the importance of parent involvement, the types of parent involvement, and strategies for engaging parents. Other researchers add that teachers need additional training in understanding and engaging parents who are culturally and linguistically diverse (Gandara, Maxwell-Jolly, & Driscoll, 2005).

Lack of physical space can also be an impediment to developing strong ties between the home and the school. Ideally, there would be a space for parents within the school to meet with teachers, work on school projects, connect with members of community service organizations, or meet with other parents. However many schools, already overcrowded, cannot provide this amenity (Auerbach, 2009).

Parent/family and school-related obstacles can interact to create mistrust and misperceptions among the various actors. Many times parents, the school, and community members have diverging role expectations for each other. Unaligned expectations can in turn lead to misunderstanding and frustration. When frustration on the part of teachers or parents is unresolved, it can lead to withdrawal and disengagement. Many of these problems stem from what psychologists label the fundamental attribution error, or the propensity for people to attribute behavior to personal characteristics instead of situational influences (Kennedy, 2010).

The way that parents conceive of their role within the school varies by socioeconomic status. Middle-class parents typically see their role as being active participants in their child's education, while lower-class parents tend to regard educational staff as experts and thus defer the responsibility of educating their children to the school (Alexander & Entwisle, 1996; Bierman, 1996; Lareau, 1996). This difference in role construction is important because if parents conceive of their role as more active they are more likely to be involved in their child's schooling (Auerbach, 2007). Lower socioeconomic status (SES) parents might disengage from school partnership if they perceive that the school is not doing enough to support their child's academic achievement (Weis, 1990) and/or are confronted with school staff that do not recognize or value their contributions. Thus, to conclude, "each (parents and school personnel), in a sense, blames the other for not taking responsibility for the children of the working class" (Weis, 1990, p. 174).

In addition to unaligned expectations, there can be a misalignment in what each set of actors believes is in the best interest for students. For example, lower-SES and working-class parents tend to value perceived safety above academic rigor when selecting schools (Deluca & Rosenblatt, 2010). Moreover, these same parents tend to take a more hands-off approach to schooling and place the onus for learning on the child, instead of on the teachers or school staff (Deluca & Rosenblatt, 2010; Lareau, 1996). Deluca and Rosenblatt (2010) found that these differences led to lower-SES and middle-class parents engaging with school staff less frequently and focusing more attention on nonacademic issues.

Differences in how parents and school staff think about what constitutes good behavior and appropriate enforcement of rules also exist, and these often follow class and color lines. One example is differences between how lower-SES and working-class parents and middle-class parents view the role of physical force in resolving problems (Lareau, 1996). Lareau (1996) notes that where lower and working-class parents will often use physical force in disciplining their children, and encourage their children to use physical force to resolve issues with other children, middle-class parents are more likely to use and encourage "verbal negotiation" to resolve problems (p. 61). Middle-class conflict resolution strategies are better aligned with the expectations of the school, leading to teachers' more positive perceptions of these students and families, thus fostering deeper connections between school and home.

FOSTERING COMMUNITIES OF ENGAGEMENT FOR PARENTS

In this section, we discuss the following district and school strategies for forming strong linkages between the home and school: setting goals to increase parent involvement, increasing trust through effective communication, and building collaboration. Before we do, we offer a few insights about the importance of context in forming these connections.

Understanding Context

As we have noted throughout this volume, "context matters." Here we add that leaders of schools and districts that are effective at engaging with parents recognize the contextual challenges and assets and attend to them in crafting a vision for building home–school connections (Auerbach, 2009). Context is defined by the characteristics of the family, school, and community (Bierman, 1996).

Superintendents and principals should be aware of the circumstances of families within their schools, acknowledging the variability in family situations and providing options for all families to participate. The ways that parents are involved in the school can be partially predicted by their personal characteristics. For example, low-income parents and minority parents are more likely to be involved in types of engagement that occur in the home (Auerbach, 2007), whereas white and higher-income parents are also likely to be involved in types of engagement that occur in the school (Eccles & Harold, 1996). Other salient family characteristics are the family's structure (e.g., single parent household, household with stepparents, multigenerational household), cultural background, language proficiency, education level, employment status, and home educational culture.

A principal highlighted in a study by Kochanek (2005) illustrates how a leader can build a culture of engagement while attending to contextual factors. To engage with her low-income parents with limited English proficiency, she began by providing English language instruction to parents after school. Then she employed those very parents who had benefited from the program as aides in the school. She then created multiple opportunities for parents to participate within the school. Finally, she changed the timing of programming to be more flexible so that working parents could participate. What is key to this story is not *what* the principal did, but the fact that she shaped her program for parent involvement according to the needs of the families in her schools. No single practice was expected to solve the problem of low parent engagement; instead, the policies and practices she used in her school were multiple, flexible, and adaptable.

Important school contextual factors include level (elementary, middle, high school), size, mobility rate, and existing teacher capacity. To begin with, we know that parent involvement looks different as students age, and schools should be responsive to how parents can and will be involved at each level of student development. Research indicates that parents are most involved in their child's education in the home in elementary school, and even through middle school, but that in later years this type of participation begins to ebb (Eccles & Harold, 1996; Murphy, 2016). Eccles and Harold (1996) posit that this change may be due to school structure, a decreased sense of parent efficacy as content becomes more difficult, a desire on the part of parents to give children more independence as they age, and/or a decreased sense of attachment to a school that is not located as close to the home.

Teachers and school staff are also less likely to reach out to parents as students age (Eccles & Harold, 1996; Auerbach, 2007). This is due in part to the structure of middle and high schools, in which teachers instruct many more students in departmentalized programs than elementary teachers do in self-contained classrooms. In addition, high school teachers tend to regard themselves as subject area experts, and as such, not responsible for engaging with parents beyond managing specific classroom problems (Levine & Marcus, 2007).

For leaders in middle and high schools, there is less research on building connections with parents from which to learn; however, there is evidence of effective strategies for parental involvement at these levels. For instance, middle schools that coordinate transition efforts that bridge the jump from elementary school tend to have more parent engagement (Epstein, 1996). Additionally, effective secondary schools create structures that enable closer collaboration among teachers around a smaller group of students, such as a student house or cohort system, in order to mitigate obstacles to parental engagement (Eccles & Harold, 1996).

School size and family mobility rate can also impact the relationship between parents and teachers within a school (Bryk et al., 2010). Some research shows that smaller schools are better able to attend to students and develop a culture of caring (Cotton, 1996; Stewart, 2008). School staff in smaller schools are likely to teach fewer students and thus may be better able to develop connections with parents (Gardner, Ritblatt, & Beatty, 1999). Mobile parents are less likely to reach out to school staff and teachers may be less able to develop deep connections with students who are not a consistent part of the school community. Schools with a high level of student mobility often demonstrate higher levels of teacher and principal mobility as well that can have adverse effects on school culture and parental support systems (Murphy, 2010).

Knowledge of how to effectively involve parents also varies across schools (Chavis et al., 1997). Leaders need to assess their own capacity and the capacity among their staff for how to engage with parents (Auerbach, 2007, 2009). One dimension of this is investing teachers in the vision for parent involvement. Their dedication to increasing parent engagement is the lynchpin of effective implementation. It is important that teachers, not outside consultants or program staff, lead the charge in building relation-ships with parents as ultimately it is the teachers who must learn from and engage with parents about their children (Auerbach, 2009).

Leaders must also heed community characteristics that are relevant to the task of building community for parents. Community characteristics describe the resources, conditions, and physical space in the neighborhood where the school's students live, what we describe as "community capi-tal." Specifically, Bryk et al. (2010) discuss community characteristics that include the resources available to community members, the safety of the community, and the strength of social networks (both within the commu-nity and extending outside of the community). Bryk and his team found that when these community characteristics were more positive, school change was more likely to be successful.

The quality of available community resources is related to a family's ability to nurture their children. Effective school leaders seek out and use the resources within the community to support their visions, whereas inef-fective principals at best ignore these resources, and at worst eschew them (Leithwood & Montgomery, 1982). We take up the issue of community beyond parents in the following chapter.

Developing a Vision for a Culture of Engagement

Leaders who operate schools effective at engaging with parents tend to be mission driven. That is, the leaders are strongly motivated by the will to change and make choices that support parent engagement goals. These leaders understand that parent involvement is key to student success and inspire parents and school staff to buy in to this belief. Their hopes for students and parents stem from a connection with the families in the schools powered by their compassion and dedication. Auerbach (2009, p. 24) relates the sense of possibility expressed by one principal:

[She] insisted that leadership for family engagement begins with a belief, what she called "a natural feeling" for the role of parents in education and a sense of collective responsibility for children. The administrator has to believe that family engagement can happen in what she termed a "ghetto school" like hers and understand that low-income, immigrant parents are "devoted parents, hardwork-ing, trusting, compassionate, and very open. Very open to change."

Research tells us that most parents *want* to be involved, regardless of socioeconomic status, race, or ethnicity (Eccles & Harold, 1996; Hoover-Dempsey et al., 2005). District and school-based leaders must have faith in this truth and demonstrate a concerted will to involve parents in the schooling of their children. The vision for parent involvement is driven by the leader's dedication to making parents an integral part of the school community. This means that leaders must be deeply involved in planning and implementing the vision for parent engagement.

Leaders with the will to involve parents know that they need to develop a comprehensive program for parent involvement that addresses the specific requirements of the parents and children in their school. These programs should be multifaceted, involve parents at all levels of the school's operation, acknowledge the multiple ways that parents can be involved in their child's education, and underscore program elements described in research studies (Goldenberg, 2004).

Leaders show their commitment to parent involvement by offering a diverse array of programs and policies to attract all parents and overcome practical constraints (Auerbach, 2007; Johnson & Asera, 1999). While any individual policy or program might not be sufficient to reshape parent involvement, a comprehensive vision will feature multiple avenues for parents to become more deeply involved. Just as teachers should incorporate student interests when differentiating their lessons, schools should incorporate parent interests in differentiating their programs for parental involvement. A powerful vision will underscore multiple opportunities for parents to be involved both at the school site and in the home (Cotton, 2000; Goldenberg, 2004).

Being committed also entails that leaders are personally involved in efforts to involve parents (Auerbach, 2009). Leaders of effective schools spend considerably more time building relationships with the parents and the community (Cotton, 2003). The involvement of school leaders also reinforces the symbolic aspects of the vision, signaling to school staff and parents that they are committed to increasing parent participation and ownership (Auerbach, 2007).

Commitment also means resourcing the work. Leaders in effective schools do not simply rely on existing capital, but seek out additional resources from the district and the community. These can be in the form of additional human resources, physical resources, or time (Desimone, 2002). A principal in Auerbach's (2007, p. 719) study captured this type of commitment as follows:

> At the school level, I think only the principal can set the stage for parent engagement to occur because the principal's got to include it on the calendar . . . the principal has got to deploy resources to make it happen when they're planning the budget, when they're making assignments of staff, when they make their own time available to work with parents.

Change takes time and setbacks can be frustrating to school staff (Bryk et al., 2010). However, in schools that are successful at creating community for parents, there is a norm of continuous improvement. Setbacks in implementation are met with different strategies or with patience and the commitment to see the effort through. Policies and practices implemented in an effort to increase parent engagement must become an integral part of the school program so that in times of financial strain or other external shocks they remain central to the vision (Powell, 1991).

Finally, a culture of parental engagement includes collective responsibility shared by the school, family, and community to educate children (Auerbach, 2009; Cotton, 2003) because these three entities make up overlapping spheres of influence that together shape the education of a child (Epstein, 1996).

Bringing a vision of community for parents to life necessitates formal leaders and school staff setting goals and creating expectations. Goals and expectations must be context specific, strategic, and integrated. A plan that is context specific begins with data collection. In order to create a strategic plan for reaching goals related to parental involvement, leaders should collect and use data on related parent and teacher needs. These data can serve several purposes: (1) to assess the types of existing parent engagement efforts, (2) to gauge the level of teacher capacity for parent outreach, and (3) to evaluate the quality and effectiveness of current efforts to build a culture of meaningful parental involvement.

The literature to date does not speak much to this issue, but as accountability structures continue to become ingrained in schools, it only makes sense that data on parent involvement would be collected and analyzed. Documents, artifacts, surveys, interviews, and focus groups can be used to assess effectiveness. These data can then be used to refine goals and strategies to address deficiencies and build on existing assets (Hayes et al., 2004; Leithwood, Jantzi, & Steinbach, 1999). There are some accounts of informal data collection guiding leader actions regarding parent engagement (Dinham, Cairney, Craigie, & Wilson, 1995), but nothing as structured as the sort of data mechanisms commonly used to assess student achievement or teacher effectiveness.

Building Trust

When working to build buy-in from parents for a vision of community of engagement, it is imperative that district and school leaders build trust and strong lines of communication. As discussed above, mistrust between school actors and parents is a major obstacle to the development of a participatory culture. Leaders who effectively engage with parents overcome mistrust and misperceptions by both actively reaching out to parents and communicating their vision and expectations.

Policies and practices that bring parents, students, and teachers together can help build trust among the three parties. Activities can be located in the school (Auerbach, 2009; Johnson & Asera, 1999), in the home (Lloyd, 1996), or in community spaces. Schools that effectively involve parents welcome parents into the school by allowing for observations of classes (Johnson & Asera, 1999), or by creating spaces for parents within the school building (Epstein, 1996; Leithwood, 2008; Leithwood et al., 2010). Leithwood and Montgomery (1982) highlight other strategies used by principals to nurture participatory community, including holding community meetings, facilitating parent-teacher groups, and being visible within the school and community themselves. By welcoming parents into the school, school staff reaffirm respect and appreciation for parents, characteristics imperative to building trusting relationships (Scheurich, 1998).

Simply reaching out to parents can promote a culture of engagement. Eccles and Harold (1996) found a positive association between how often teachers reached out to parents and how involved those parents were in the school community. This is true at the elementary, middle, and high school levels (Epstein, 1996) and especially so for low-income or minority parents (Auerbach, 2007). Schools see the most success engaging with parents when they (1) include parents in crafting the vision to make sure that parents are a voice in the process from the beginning and (2) ensure that expectations of all parties are clear (Cotton, 2003; Scanlan & Lopez, 2012). Principals can enhance trust by reaching out to parents before enacting reforms (Cooper, 1996; Leithwood et al., 1999).

Many schools use parent coordinators to ensure that parents are being contacted regularly by someone other than the classroom teacher. Parent coordinators can be especially effective for fostering trust among parents who are culturally and linguistically diverse (Epstein, 1996). Parent coordinators can be used to reach out to parents, build social networks among the parents, and represent parent interests at the school (Kochanek, 2005). Having parent voices be heard and represented by the coordinator can help leaders craft strategies of engagement that are tailored to the interests of the parent community (Haynes & Ben-Avie, 1996).

Leaders also build trust by practicing asset-based thinking. Researchers have defined some of the assets existing within families as "rituals, traditional values, family dreams and aspirations, cultural norms for student behavior, racial identity development, practices that involve families in their children's education and schools, and formal and informal community organizations that support families" (Epstein, 1996, pp. 231–232).

Asset-based thinking about parents is present in the manner in which school staff communicates with parents. When school staff see parents as important members of the school community, they treat them with respect and find ways to meet their needs (Auerbach, 2007). Leaders in effective schools focus on points of commonality shared by school staff and parents rather than on differences (Goldenberg, 2004).

Extant social networks that often overlap with kinship networks that parents already look to for support represent an important asset that can be used by schools building cultures of parental engagement (Bierman, 1996). This work can include actively seeking the support of grandparents, who are more likely to be an integral part of the family unit in low-income and minority neighborhoods (Bryk et al., 2010).

Leaders of schools with a strong culture of engagement recognize and honor parents' desire to be involved as an asset. These leaders do not leave the formation of this culture to the parents themselves, but know that the onus of involving parents, especially in schools serving low-income and minority parents, lies with the school (Auerbach, 2009). In these schools, leaders act as boundary spanners, trying to bridge the divide between the home and the school, instead of as a buffer against parental involvement (Hallinger & Heck, 1998). They lead parents through a process of socialization in which they engage with parents to build buy-in and trust, and help them see that their engagement is a prerequisite not only for the achievement of their own student, but for the success of the school (Haynes & Ben-Avie, 1996).

Building Collaboration

To create a culture of engagement, leaders implement policies and practices that accommodate varied family structures and needs. This includes extending available times for conferences to allow working parents to participate, hiring interpreters to aid with communication with non-English speaking parents, implementing culturally responsive family nights, and/or providing transportation to school events.

Activities for parent involvement can be academic or nonacademic. Their purpose is to nurture collaboration among parents and students, parents and teachers, and students and teachers. Academic activities can include content-related nights where students are able to share the work they do at school with parents and teachers are able to explain the content being taught in the classroom. Nonacademic activities could include recreational activities, such as participation in sports, games, or movies. Both types of activities open the lines of communication between parents and school staff and help bolster mutual understanding.

To increase involvement within the school, leaders must collaborate with parents to devise coherent ways for parents to volunteer. Collaboration is essential for matching parent assets to the needs of the school. Volunteer opportunities within the school should be managed by school staff and parents to maximize the impact of the parent's time and effort. Ideally, volunteers would help where their particular skills were most beneficial, would have clear guidelines for what they should be doing, and would become an integral part of the classroom (Haynes & Ben-Avie, 1996).

School leaders may also work collaboratively to help parents strengthen the educational environment in the home. Policies and practices that may influence change in the home environment, which include parenting classes, are aimed at helping parents help their children academically in the home. These classes might cover academic topics like how to support children in specific content areas (Auerbach, 2007). They may also be aimed at building the skills of the parents themselves by providing General Educational Development (GED), computer literacy, job search, or literacy classes (Auerbach, 2007; Bryk et al., 2010). Classes may also be used to provide information on nonacademic topics such as health, community issues, laws, and political issues (Auerbach, 2009). Some schools direct programs toward helping parents change their sense of efficacy in regard to helping their children. Other programs help parents understand their role in the school (Griffith, 2001). Programs and polices meant to educate parents or change the home learning environment should focus on making sure that parents hold high expectations for their students and then give parents the information and training they need to turn those expectations into reality (Hattie, 2009). Effective educational programs for parents are concrete. They provide parents with specific strategies to target adult or student needs in particular areas. Ostensibly, better educated and better informed parents will be better able to support their students (Dauber & Epstein, 1993).

Teacher requests for parents to help students at home with homework or school projects, sending home newsletters informing parents of what content is being covered, and explaining strategies for helping students in those areas are common ways that school staff work collaboratively to influence home educational culture (Bryk et al., 2010; Cotton, 2000; Eccles & Harold, 1996). Homework can be an effective means for teachers to encourage parents to help their children academically at home (Goldenberg, 2004). Teachers can request parents to sign student assignments on a regular basis (Kochanek, 2005) or call parents when students do not complete their homework (Goldenberg, 2004). In addition to teachers reaching out to parents with generalized information about how to help their children, teachers should also provide individualized information to parents to help parents monitor the specific learning needs of their child (Bierman, 1996). School staff should guide parents in understanding the information they provide so that it is meaningful and results in building trusting relationships and collaborative efforts instead of being a source of frustration that ultimately fosters mistrust (Bierman, 1996).

11

Operations: Staffing, Time, and Material Resources

Elsewhere, we reported that teachers are the essential resources in schools. Here we deepen that position concluding that since "organizations depend on the quality of their people" (Bryk, Sebring, Allensworth, Luppescu, & Easton, 2010, p. 54) instructional capacity is the most significant theme in the school improvement narrative. Researchers and developers here often refer to issues like human and social capital. Inside the education profession, it is best to link this concept more concretely to our own work, that is, to employ the idea of instructional capital or capacity. Or stated more directly, "a primary channel through which principals can be expected to improve the quality of teachers is through teacher transitions that improve the caliber of the workforce" (Branch, Rivkin, & Hanushek, 2003, p. 5).

In Chapter 9 we looked at professional capacity in considerable detail. We partitioned the concept into four buckets: staffing, time and material resources, and support was addressed in Chapter 8 and personnel development in Chapter 9. However, we also provided some important contextual comments. First, what Bryk (2010, p. 54) and colleagues refer to as the "human resources subsystem" is especially critical in high human, low technology-based industries. Remember here that over eighty percent of each school dollar is devoted to people. Second, instructional capacity is particularly important in schools with large numbers of students in peril. It is also more difficult to grow in these schools. Third, and relatedly, capacity building is extremely important for schools in difficult circumstances. Fourth, leaders are a key lever in fostering instructional capacity, or as Branch and associates (2003, p. 5) capture it, "the management of teacher quality is an important pathway through which principals affect school quality."

STAFFING

To begin with, there is abundant evidence that "the collective capacity of a school-based professional community is contingent on the quality of the staff recruited into the school" (Bryk et al., 2010, p. 57) and that "recruiting capable teachers is critical to the breadth and depth of expertise needed to undertake school improvement" (pp. 54–55). That is, "it is difficult to produce positive discernments of competence and integrity when teachers are not competent" (Kochanek, 2005, p. 21; see Table 11.1).

What is true for teacher recruitment is true for teacher selection as well. Indeed, research informs us that "the teacher selection process [has] a sizeable, statistically significant effect on student achievement gains" (Brewer, 1993, p. 282). And again, across thirty-five years of research we find that effective leaders are personally and deeply involved with well thought out teacher selection processes.

Research helps us see that capacity building extends beyond recruitment and selection. For example, it shows us that capacity building addresses retention and that leadership, as it was in previous functions, is a critical element here (Sather, 1999). Capacity building also captures the allocation or assignment of teacher talent. As York-Barr and Duke (2004, p. 290) inform us, at one level this occurs through the thoughtful matching of "the unique and varied leadership capacities of individual teachers with the unique and varied leadership functions" in the school. Careful attention to mentoring assignments is important here (Youngs, 2007). So too are additional training opportunities for teachers assigned to help people schoolwide with functions such as managing data or facilitating technology use or roles such as instructional coaches (Goldstein, 2004; Wohlstetter, Datnow, & Park, 2008). So too is the assignment of teachers to important cross-class responsibilities. We describe all this as the allocation of teachers to other teachers and to schoolwide improvement work (Murphy, 2005a; Timperley, 2009).

At a second level, allocation occurs as leaders move teachers to "assignments that result in a better fit between the needs of the students and the talents of teachers" (Leithwood & Montgomery, 1982, p. 325). Important here is the assignment of teachers to subjects and grade levels for which they are formally prepared and in which they are certified (Cosner, 2011). The major conclusion on this second dimension of allocation is that "the careful assignment of teachers to classes is unquestionably a critical leadership function" (Blase & Kirby, 2009, p. 68)—"at the classroom level, effective leaders are directly involved in matching teachers with students"

(Leithwood & Montgomery, 1982, p. 334). This leadership assignment function takes on added significance for students placed at risk (Oakes & Guiton, 1995; Quint, 2006).

There is a growing body of evidence that effective leaders bolster instructional capacity by moving less-than-successful, inadequate, and uncaring teachers from their schools, either through transfer or termination (Finnigan & Gross, 2007). They understand that "high performing teams do not carry C players for long" (Tichy & Cardwell, 2004, p. 9), that "incompetent teachers not only harm the children in their classrooms, but they also call into question the dedication and competence of the entire staff" (Kochanek, 2005, p. 91). Transfer is used as a capacity-building tool in two ways by school leaders. To begin with, leaders counsel teachers to move to positions that provide a better fit for their skills and/or values and points of view about teaching and learning. They also exert pressure so that teachers understand that it is in their best interest to teach elsewhere, or perhaps seek out different lines of work or retire (Cotton, 2003; Goldstein, 2004). Effective leaders are also less reluctant than their peers to terminate teachers' employment in their schools (Johnson & Asera, 1999; Spillane et al., 2001b).

Capacity building is enhanced when leaders are aggressive in not accepting weak teachers and teachers who do not fit with the district's and the school's vision and values. They push back against requests from the district that would undermine school cohesion and student learning.

Finally, instructional capacity is about leaders carrying out efforts to ensure that effective teachers stay at their schools. We know in general that teachers remain at their schools because they have effective principals. In addition, effective leaders use a plethora of strategies to hold good teachers. We present some of these below.

It is one thing to report that instructional capacity is critical in improving outcomes for children and that leaders are essential in making the human capital aspects of the system function well. But the question of what the criteria for this work should be requires probing. We know that leaders at all levels need to make staffing a priority. Leaders model what is important by how they spend their time more so than by what they say. So to begin with, considerable time needs to be allotted to the staffing functions, greater "regard for the human resources necessary to make the system actually work" (Bryk et al., 2010, p. 206) is required. Second, leaders need to carve out as much autonomy and influence over staffing functions as possible. They cannot allow bureaucratic and political considerations to hold the high ground. Rather, they need to be powerful advocates for their districts and schools and their students. If there is one venue where it is wise to be the squeaky wheel, this is it.

Diving deeper, leaders need to look carefully at criteria that make a difference while pushing aside those that are less influential. And all the while they must hold firm to the knowledge that (1) there is no single criteria that can carry the day, and (2) a collection of smaller forces can bring large impacts. Let us start with an examination of what is often minimized in staffing positions. We know that a number of the key indicators historically employed here are not particularly robust. Included here are educational degrees, coursework, grades earned, teacher evaluations, and certification in general (Borman & Kimball, 2005; Hattie, 2009; Nye, Konstantopoulos, & Hedges, 2004; Wayne & Youngs, 2003). Attention to less visible and rarely used background factors makes more empirical sense. Here scholars highlight (1) ratings of the universities from which candidates graduate; (2) intellectual ability or scores on standardized measures of achievement, especially verbal ability (Thompson & O'Quinn, 2001; Wayne & Youngs, 2003); and (3) subject matter knowledge (Hattie, 2009; Hill, Rowan, & Ball, 2005). In the world of instructional capacity, these are stronger measures than the ones we have relied on for so long (Flanagan & Grissmer, 2002; Grissmer, Flanagan, & Williamson, 1998).

Moving beyond background characteristics, research confirms the hallmark place in terms of student learning of a number of "softer" elements that teachers do (or do not) bring to the job. Passion for the work in general and a deep sense of caring for children and young persons are critically important (Johnson & Asera, 1999) as is the ability to turn that passion and caring into trusting relationships (Murphy & Torre, 2014). There is also considerable evidence that the care and specificity with which schools and districts define their values and vision and the ability of leaders to use staffing to align human resources with those missions is related to more pronounced student learning (Desimone, 2002; Huberman, Parrish, Hannan, Arellanes, & Shambaugh, 2011). Attention to staffing in regard to fluency with culturally appropriate pedagogy seems important (Auerbach, 2007).

TIME AND MATERIAL RESOURCES

Time

Leaders impact instructional capacity by how they value and address the essential resource of time, "a potent variable affecting student learning" (Firestone & Wilson, 1985, p. 12; see Table 11.1). Effective leaders have a sixth sense for the importance of this scarce resource (Blase & Kirby, 2009). They understand "that it is a finite and valuable resource that is sometimes squandered by competing demands and conflicting priorities" (Leithwood et al., 2004, p. 57). For example, when one computes the academic learning time (academic content and rate of engagement and of success) the big number of 420 minutes per day drops dramatically. Principals who see "real" time in schools in this manner understand that it is a resource that needs to be safeguarded (Creemers & Reezigt, 1996; Yair, 2000).

Table 11.1 Building Instructional Capacity: Staffing, Time, and Material Resources

Staffing
Recruitment
Selection
Assigning
Removing
Retaining
Time
Extend
Allocate
Protect
Use
Support
Emotional Support
Appraisal Support

Effective school leaders also insure that the significant variability in the use of time in schools is compressed (Bryk et al., 2010). They allocate their own time in ways that enhance the quality of teaching and learning in the school (Johnson & Asera, 1999). As is the case with other resources like funding, because "daily, weekly, and annual schedules have a substantial impact on the time available for instruction" (Firestone & Wilson, 1985 p. 12), effective leaders at all levels are proactive in their efforts to add to available time in the school (Cotton, 2003). Strategies here include lengthening the school day, week, and/or year (Conchas, 2001; Johnson & Asera, 1999), either for all children or for the most in need of extra assistance (Murphy, 2010).

Effective leaders are also planful about adding time within the school day for subject areas deemed most essential for student success, generally English (reading) and mathematics (Balfanz, Herzog, & MacIver, 2007). Again, we see that this strategy can apply to all children or children with the greatest needs (Auerbach, 2009; Betts, Zau, & Koedel, 2010). Equally important, effective leaders are attentive to how time is allocated within the school day. Most importantly, "they allocate more time to tasks directly related to the teaching-learning process" (Goldring & Pasternack, 1994, p. 241) and work to ensure that time is devoted to engagement with challenging academic materials (Hattie, 2009; Yair, 2000).

On a third front, leaders in effective schools are diligent in protecting overall allotment of available time. As noted above, they work with tenacity to ensure that time is not squandered. Researchers have uncovered a number of general and specific strategies in play here. On one hand, these

Chapter 11

leaders buffer teachers from "intrusive forces" (Dannetta, 2002, p. 162) that usurp time: "They give teachers time to teach" (Blase & Kirby, 2009, p. 73). They protect teaching time from district, school management, and community actions that negatively impact learning time. They also protect time by establishing a safe and supportive culture that minimizes student disruptions (Leithwood, Anderson, Mascall, & Strauss, 2011; Robinson, Lloyd, & Rowe, 2008).

Finally, effective leaders are proactive in shaping the use of time in classrooms (Hallinger & Murphy, 1985; Murphy, 1990). They forge consistent district and schoolwide understandings about time use (Creemers & Reezigt, 1996). They cooperate with and support teachers to ensure that classes begin and end on time and that minimal amounts of time are lost due to transitions during class periods (O'Donnell & White, 2005; Scanlan & Lopez, 2012). Since the average student is actively attending in class only about half the time (Murphy & Torre, 2014), principals are diligent in helping teachers use strategies to enhance engagement. They work to ensure that teachers present students with meaningful and challenging material, "active and energizing pedagogies" (Balfanz et al., 2007, p. 231), not continuous teacher talk (Goodlad, 1984; Hattie, 2009), and authentic assessments.

Material Resources

To this point in Chapter 11, we have examined "staffing" and "time." Here we focus on "material resources." As was the case with staffing and time, we know that leaders' attention to materials is important for the implementation and improvement of instruction and student learning (Desimone, 2002; Spillane et al., 2001b). There is extensive evidence that effective leaders are proactive in identifying material resources to strengthen their schools (Blase & Blase, 2004; Eilers & Camacho, 2007), and classroom instruction in particular (Cotton, 2003). They turn up more community, grant-based, and district resources (Beachum & Dentith, 2004), oftentimes because they have invested the time to develop positive and trusting relationships with the actors in these three sectors (Eilers & Camacho, 2007). Equally important, effective leaders understand that it is not about securing resources per se, but rather about securing resources that are linked to school goals (Robinson et al., 2008). Material resources sought and garnered include instructional material, such as books, tools, equipment, technology, and supplies (Clark, Dyson, Millward, & Robson, 1999; Supovitz & Christman, 2003).

Again, as was the case with time, the role of the leader is only half completed with the identification and securing of additional resources. Equally important is the fact that effective school leaders are adept at the employment of material resources (Sweeney, 1982). Here we learn that because "the possession of resources does not automatically translate into their use in efforts to lead change in instruction" (Spillane et al., 2001b,

p. 927); that is, it is the use or activation of material resources that is most important (Sweeney, 1982). As Spillane and his team (2001b, p. 937) note, "the skills with which these resources are configured by school leaders" is the central issue.

We see here that effective leaders ensure that materials are used in the manner intended (Newmann, Smith, Allensworth, & Bryk, 2001), including customization to the local context (Supovitz & Christman, 2003). "Creative configuration and activation of resources is critical" (Spillane et al., 2001b, p. 921). Robinson (2007) refers to this as the strategic dimension of resource allocation. The critical issue is the ability of leaders to integrate material resources "with regard for the coherence and strategic alignment of resulting activities" (Robinson, 2007, p. 13), what Malen and Rice (2004, p. 636) describe as "the degree of correspondence between resources that are available and the resources that are required to accomplish organizational goals."

SUPPORT

Here we continue our discussion of how leaders can help build instructional capacity in their districts and schools. The spotlight is on support for teachers, support in addition to materials and time treated in Table 11.1. The perhaps obvious, but still needed to be made point is that leader support is a cardinal element in the equation of leadership effectiveness (Cotton, 2003). Indeed, teachers often inform us that it is the hallmark element (Leithwood, Patten, & Jantzi, 2010).

A few notes are helpful before we unpack the concept of leader support for teachers. We know from research studies and the wisdom of practice that it is a difficult construct to corral. Or, as Mangin notes (2007, p. 326), the "notion of support is inherently elusive owing to its subjective manner." And as Littrell, Billingsley, and Cross (1994, p. 297) extend this point, "defining support is a multidimensional concept that includes a wide range of behaviors." Metaphorically, support is more akin to a stew than it is a dish of distinct foods (Murphy, Beck, Crawford, & Hodges, 2001).

It is also helpful to expose some of the embedded concepts in the narrative around leader support, insights that are easy to lose sight of in the rush of leaders' frenetic work schedules. We know, for example, that not all support work is equal. Supports can be categorized across the continuum from low-level to high-level activities (May & Supovitz, 2011). Researchers and practitioners also remind us that support is often informal as well as formal in design (Leithwood, Jantzi, & Steinbach, 1999; Penuel et al., 2010). Supovitz and Poglinco (2001, p. 16), in turn, reinforce one of the essential conclusions here. That is, context is always critical. In this case, they confirm that support is "dependent on the personality and

Chapter 11

temperament of the principal, the particular needs of individual teachers, and the environment of the school."

The literature helps us see that support is bifurcated. At times the focus is on subtraction—taking away problems, reducing ambiguities, buffering unhelpful forces, and removing organizational barriers. At other times, the focus is on additions—augmenting actions. As with most issues in schools, there is a difference between assessments of the amount of support teachers desire and the amount of support they see coming their way from school leaders (Littrell et al., 1994).

Researchers, developers, and practitioners have developed a variety of frames to array support. Crum and Sherman (2008) define principal support as understanding, encouraging, and empowering teachers. Leithwood and colleagues (1999) employ the concept as individualized support, a construct that stands above others in the platform of transformational leadership practices. Supovitz and Poglinco (2001) suggest that principals' support for teachers materializes through the provision of resources, counseling, and encouragement. Gurr, Drysdale, and Mulford (2005, p. 4) find that leaders provide three types of support: one-off or cross crisis support, support for individuals as they undergo change processes, and ongoing support in the form of acknowledging others. Finally, House (cited in Littrell et al., 1994) created a four-dimensional framework to describe support: emotional support, instrumental support, informational support, and appraisal support. Building on these different formulations, we examine support below in three main categories: emotional and environmental support, appraisal support, and organizational systems support. Before we do so, however, we make explicit the power of the support tool for school leaders.

Support has been shown to have powerful, positive effects across an array of organizational conditions and outcomes, including the following:

- Augmentation of teacher leadership (York-Barr & Duke, 2004)
- Positive sense of self for teachers (Littrell et al., 1994)
- Teacher commitment to school goals (Riehl & Sipple, 1996)
- Teacher personal health (Littrell et al., 1994)
- Quality and range of instruction (Blase & Blase, 2004; Mangin, 2007)
- Implementation of change efforts (Datnow & Castellano, 2001; Louis & Miles, 1990)
- Increased emphasis on student achievement (Sweeney, 1982)
- Enhancement of teacher trust (Youngs, 2007)
- School culture and climate (Supovitz, Sirinides, & May, 2010)
- Teacher morale (Leithwood et al., 1999)
- Student learning outcomes (Hoy, Hannum, & Tschannen-Moran, 1998; Mulford & Silins, 2003)
- Overall school performance (Heck, 2000; Robinson, 2007)

Emotional Support

Emotional support is at the heart of capacity-building work. Analysts describe emotional support in a variety of ways and with varying tones. The overarching idea that gives meaning to the subdimensions of support is trust (Youngs, 2007), or more specifically caring and trusting relationships between the principal and the teacher (Murphy & Torre, 2014). Scholars reveal that trust can be described in a number of overlapping ways, that is, through assorted behaviors that "communicate the leader's respect for his or her colleagues and concerns about their personal feelings and needs" (Leithwood, 2006, p. 31)—"being open, supportive, and friendly" (Leithwood et al., 2011, p. 16). It includes actions that convey an openness to new ideas and the freedom to learn from mistakes (Blase & Blase, 2000), as well as the sense that the leader is clearly part of the team (Supovitz & Poglinco, 2001). It encompasses efforts to recognize accomplishments (Chavis, Ward, Elwell, & Barret, 1997).

Nurturing is an essential aspect of trusting relations (Blase & Kirby, 2009). It includes elements such as "going to bat" for teachers (Chavis et al., 1997) or moral support (Leithwood et al., 1999), showing concern (Barnett, McCormick, & Conners, 2001), consideration (Walker & Slear, 2011), and sensitivity (Mayrowetz & Weinstein, 1999). Listening to the personal needs of teachers and treating each teacher uniquely (May & Supovitz, 2011) are often treated in the literature on emotional support. Affording respect is part of the narrative. So too are providing voice and hearing opinions (Hayes, Christie, Mills, & Lingard, 2004). Using an inquiry approach to working with staff is supportive (Blase & Blase, 2004). Undergirding nurturing are the principles of fairness in dealing with staff (Kochanek, 2005), asset-based understandings of teacher colleagues (Wohlstetter et al., 2008), and personal approachability (Lomotey, 1989).

We learn from an assortment of investigations that leader interpersonal leadership skills are essential in fostering nurturing relationships. Communication skills are particularly important (Walker & Slear, 2011), especially authentic hearing (Beachum & Dentith, 2004). The ability to resolve conflicts rather than allowing them to undermine relationships is also highlighted in the research (Robinson, 2008).

There is a thick line of research over the past forty years on the importance of principal involvement, attentiveness, and visibility in promoting nurturing relationships (Johnson & Asera, 1999; Murphy & Torre, 2014). Supportive leaders are approachable (Kockanek, 2005). They interact in both formal and informal ways with staff (Youngs, 2007). In the process, they foster trust and grow a "more productive and stimulating environment" (Littrell et al., 1994, p. 306).

Embedded in our analysis is the fact that in the domain of emotional support "the most powerful example is the principal herself or himself" (Blase & Kirby, 2009, p. 27). Thus we find role modeling at the heart of emotional support (Crum & Sherman, 2008), "providing appropriate models of best practice and beliefs considered fundamental to the organization" (Littrell et al., 1994, p. 9). Indeed, in effective schools staff report that school leaders are "sources of advice about teaching problems" (Robinson et al., 2008, p. 667). In these schools, "teachers discern an ability and willingness on the principal's part to model appropriate behavior" (Blase & Kirby, 2009, p. 29). Such modeling leads to improvements in teacher's thinking, instruction in classrooms, and school culture (May & Supovitz, 2011). The obverse is true as well. When principals are "absent from the daily life of the school" (Youngs, 2007, p, 122) and this modeling is absent, teachers often struggle (Cooper, 1996). Modeling in the literature includes discussing instructional expectations (Walker & Slear, 2011); developing and using protocols (Johnson & Asera, 1999); demonstrating teaching techniques with and for teachers (Blanc et al., 2010); making suggestions (Blase & Blase, 2004); being personally involved in problem solving and implementation work (Louis & Miles, 1990); sharing one's own personal experiences (Blase & Blase, 2004); and encouraging teacher leadership (Blase & Blase, 2004).

In a similar vein, emotional support occurs when principals act as facilitators and counselors for teachers (Bryk et al., 2010). As Robinson and team (2008, p. 663) discovered, principals are "significantly more likely to be nominated as sources of advice in higher achieving schools." The involvement and accessibility discussed earlier, in turn, provide avenues for principals to shape teaching activity (Mangin, 2007). A "key dimension of this advisory role is an accessible, nonintrusive attentiveness to teachers' concerns" (Friedkin & Slater, 1994, p. 150).

Appraisal Support

In their study, Littrell and associates (1994) found that appraisal support was second to emotional support in importance. For purposes of analysis, we partition appraisal support into two dimensions, acknowledging that they are two intertwined elements rather than discrete categories: feedback and praise/recognition. As we report below, each is highly valued by teachers, associated with effective school leaders, and linked to important organizational outcomes. In his cardinal analysis, Hattie (2009, p. 12) lays out the significance of the first aspect of our chronicle here when he reports "that the most powerful single influence on achievement is feedback, . . . that the most important feature [is] the creation of situations in classrooms for the teachers to receive more feedback about their teaching." It is clear then that leaders must be aggressive in this area, including making themselves accessible to discuss classroom-based work.

While this is not the place to lay out all of the qualities of positive feedback in general, those characteristics that find a home in the appraisal system do merit some attention. We learn from the research, for example, that feedback addressed in a collaborative stance, or that offers "mutual engagement" (Coldren & Spillane, 2007, p. 376) is desirable (Blase & Blase, 2004). "Thoughtful discourse" (Blase & Blase, 2000, p. 133) is important as well, with time for explanatory back and forth among participants (Blase & Blase, 2004). It is critically important that the principal is viewed as knowledgeable and credible (Leithwood et al., 1999). Blase and Blase (2004, p. 22) provide specificity to this characteristic when they describe credibility as "knowledge and mastery of a number of complex prerequisite skills and processes." Appraisal feedback should be specific and anchored in care and individual consideration (Blase & Blase, 2000). It should be provided in a nonthreatening manner (Hayes et al., 2004). It should provide salient and actionable information, information about teachers' efforts to enhance student learning (Robinson, 2007). Thus appraisal feedback should be "detailed and descriptive" (Blase & Blase, 2004, p. 39) and provide teachers "with alternative suggestions to what they [are] doing" (p. 135). Robinson (2007, p. 15) concludes that not all leader feedback is equal: "feedback about learning processes may be more effective than feedback about outcomes and feedback that is linked to a corrective strategy is more helpful than one that is not."

Absent or infrequent feedback is unhelpful. So too is punitive feedback and feedback that threatens the self-esteem of teachers (Blase & Blase, 2004). Feedback that fails to promote self-reflection is also of limited value. For example, in the Blase and Blase (2004, p. 46) study, "teachers explained that ineffective principals who did post observation conferences frequently failed to provide any growth-promoting constructive feedback about their observations." Such activity causes teacher to lose "respect and trust in their principals, causes a drop in teacher motivation and self-esteem, [and] increases anger and sense of futility" (p. 48).

On the other hand, feedback that includes the positive characteristics outlined above produces gains in "teacher motivation, self-esteem, confidence, and sense of security" (Blase & Blase, 2004, pp. 143–144). Positive feedback is "potentially transforming" (Leithwood et al., 1999, p. 144). Feedback with positive elements is also associated with stronger school improvement measured in terms of student achievement gains (Mulford & Silins, 2003).

The other stem of appraisal support is praise and recognition (Hallinger & Heck, 1998), a construct heavily intertwined with feedback. Teachers consistently report that praise is of special importance, one of the most powerful tools that principals possess for affecting teachers and teaching (Blase & Kirby, 2009). Reviewers here find that "it is clear that effective principals build time for praise into their busy schedules" (Blase & Kirby, 2009, p. 20)—an "ongoing support in the form of acknowledging others" (Gurr, Drysdale, & Mulford, 2006, p. 375). At times in the research, we see that recognition is expressed in terms of incentives and rewards (Leithwood et al., 2004), often in domains such as resources for professional development, career opportunities, and additional pay (Leitner, 1994; O'Donnell & White, 2005).

As was the case with feedback, there are elements that make praise work well or poorly. On the downside, leader praise is much less productive if it is laced with heavy doses of criticism (Blase & Blase, 2004). Praise that is seen as insensitive, inauthentic, or ritualistic is viewed by teachers as not helpful at best and harmful at worst (Blase & Blase, 2004). Fairness is seen as critical to teachers. When teachers perceive that principals are playing favorites, feedback often loses its meaning (Blase & Blase, 2004). It is the task of principals to pound meaning into praise. They move in this manner by providing praise that is "focused on specific and concrete teaching behaviors" (Blase & Blase, 2000, p. 136), that is "being specific about what is being praised as 'good work'" (Leithwood et al., 1999, p. 73), and by using both public and private and formal and informal praise. Sincerity is a hallmark element of praise and recognition (Blase & Kirby, 2009). Public feedback should focus on individual and school anchored achievements. Blase and Kirby (2009, p. 17) direct the spotlight to the essence of productive praise when they report that "teachers indicated that the praise that influenced them most was evoked by their work, that is, is related to professional performance."

As was the case with feedback, recognition is not an outcome in itself. At the group level, it is a tool for reinforcing school goals (Leitner, 1994), building a positive school culture (Blase & Kirby, 2009), promoting school reform (Mayrowetz & Weinstein (1999), and improving student learning (Sather, 1999). On the individual front, scholars confirm that leader praise is linked to teacher pride, self-esteem, and efficacy (Blase & Blase, 1999). It has been linked to enhanced instructional performance. Specifically, praise has been shown to influence "teacher reflective behavior, including refinement of effective teaching strategies, risk taking, and innovation/creativity" (Blase & Blase, 1999, p. 363).

Systems Support

As we saw with emotional and appraisal support, organizational systems support is comprised of various defining elements. One key element is buffering, finding ways to protect teachers from intrusions (Foster & St. Hilaire, 2003; Gray et al., 1999). Researchers over the last three decades have routinely found "that teachers in effective schools [are] buffered to a far greater extent than teachers in ineffective schools" (Rossmiller, 1992, p. 133). Leaders in effective districts and schools see themselves as protectors (Supovitz & Poglinco, 2001). Particularly important is buffering the technical core (Leithwood et al., 1999) or "intrusions on teaching" (Riehl & Sipple, 1996, p. 883). On this topic, Leithwood, Day, Sammons, Harris, and Hopkins (2006a, p. 37) remind us, "the buffering function acknowledges the open nature of schools and the constant bombardment of staff with expectations from parents, the media, special interest groups and the government."

Analysts of support via buffering expose an assortment of ways that leaders protect teachers from intrusion. The core idea here is eliminating competing agendas (Bryk et al., 2010). One strategy is keeping required paperwork to a minimum (Lomotey, 1989). Another is not interrupting classes via the intercom systems or via messengers (Blase & Blase, 2004). A third is reducing teacher time committed to work outside their classrooms, especially meetings (Blase & Kirby, 2009). A fourth is "not burdening teachers with bureaucratic tasks and busy work" (Leithwood et al., 2011, p. 16) and "unreasonable demands from the policy environment (Leithwood et al., 2010, p. 678). Finally, buffering includes protecting "teachers from excessive pupil disciplinary activity" (Leithwood et al., 2006a, p. 37). Like the other types of support examined above, buffering is linked to higher staff commitment to school goals (Riehl & Sipple, 1996).

Systems support is also about providing teachers with help when assistance is needed. Researchers affirm that both internal and external assistance are important (Louis & Miles, 1990). Helping teachers in implementing reforms is valuable (Louis & Miles, 1990). So too is securing mentoring assistance, especially for newly hired teachers (Youngs, 2007). The personal effort of district and school leaders is noted across all the dimensions of assistance (Supovitz & Poglinco, 2001).

Systems support also includes the two pillars of methods of work and structures (Blanc et al., 2010; Jackson, 2000). Of particular importance here are the creation and use of collective decision making that promotes meaningful involvement, discretion, and authentic autonomy (not simply isolation) (Mangin, 2007; Murphy, 2005a). Assorted scholars refer to this as "time and opportunities for peer connections among teachers" (Blase & Blase, 2000, p. 138), both during and outside the school day (Eilers & Camacho, 2007). Supovitz and Christman (2003, p. 7) conclude, for example, that

> Not only do communities need protected time that frees them to investigate instruction together, they also need structures to capitalize on the opportunities created by time together in order to have disciplined conversations about the connections between their instructional strategies and student learning.

Penuel, Riel, Krause, and Frank (2009) and Penuel and team (2010) conclude that social structure support is highly valuable in school implementation efforts, in energizing instructional change, and in generating "consistent forms of practice across a variety of settings" (2010, p. 87).

Structural systems that provide personal assistance to teachers, such as mentors and coaches are helpful (Huberman et al., 2011). Programs are also valuable (Auerbach, 2009). Noteworthy here are programs that create agreement on the boundaries of appropriate teaching practices, a reigning in of variation to enhance alignment and cohesion across classes

(Newmann et al., 2001; Rowan & Miller, 2007). Operating schedules can also act as a form of systems support (McDougall, Saunders, & Goldenberg, 2007). Systems focused on "teaching workloads represent an[other] important resource that allows teachers to do their work" (Riehl & Sipple, 1996, p. 887). "Deploying staff creatively so as to keep classes as small as possible" (Cotton, 2003, p. 37) can be a powerful support (Newmann, Wehlage, & Lamburn, 1992). As we touched on above, attention is directed in the research to systems that provide teachers with support on student discipline issues (Blase & Kirby, 2009).

Chapter 11

12

School Improvement

For over forty years, beginning with the early teacher effects and school effectiveness studies, academics, practitioners, developers, and policy makers have been struggling with the task of building good schools. During that time, we have passed through different eras of school improvement work, such as effective schools, systemic school improvement, school restructuring, comprehensive school reform, school turnaround, scaling up, the improvement sciences, and so forth. We have been supplied with an amazing variety of specific interventions designed to assist leaders in helping all students achieve ambitious targets of performance. Over that time, I have been engaged in accumulating and making sense of all that work. My colleagues and I have reaffirmed some well accepted canons of school improvement and added layers of depth to others. We have also uncovered some new insights about dimensions of school improvement that have been insufficiently investigated. But most importantly, I believe that we have created a comprehensive and integrated way for school leaders to think about and then build productive schools—what we call the architecture of school improvement.

The purpose of this chapter is to capture that work. In the first half of the chapter, I explore what we mean when we talk about school improvement, exposing the central reality that school improvement needs to be understood in terms of the larger political, social, and economic forces in play at any given time. Context matters. It shapes the definition of school improvement. I also suggest that our understanding of school improvement is defined by changes in the center of gravity within the education industry itself. That is, it is only by discerning major changes in what counts as schooling, changes influenced by larger economic, political, and social forces, that we know what school improvement means. In short, the construct of school improvement has varied over time. At the end of this introductory section, the reader should have a good understanding of the seedbed from which current efforts at school improvement grow—and why those efforts look the way they do.

In the second half of the chapter, I review what scholars have uncovered about how to build productive schools in a postindustrial world. I present this as a framework for school improvement work. I begin with the basic equation of school improvement. I then deepen the narrative around that essential algorithm. I accomplish this by exposing and populating the key dimensions of the school improvement framework in the service of the first nine Professional Standards for Educational Leaders (PSEL): the building material, the construction principles, the supporting frames, and the integrative dynamic.

The Postindustrial World

Over the last few decades, I have combined two frames to hammer out a way to think broadly about the evolution and growth of school improvement. One frame is historical analysis, studying school improvement over long stretches of time (Murphy, 1991, 2012; Murphy, Beck, Crawford, & Hodges, 2001). The other frame is Tushman and Romanelli's (1985) seminal theory of organizational evolution, the punctuated equilibrium model of organizational change. The historical analysis provides the content of the narrative; the punctuated equilibrium model provides the frames to make sense of that content.

At the heart of their model, Tushman and Romanelli hypothesize that "organizations progress through *convergent* periods punctuated by *reorientations* which demark and set the bearings for the next convergent period" (p. 173). According to the theory, convergent periods cover long time spans during which incremental and marginal shifts that refine and elaborate organizational elements toward increased alignment dominate. Reorientations, on the other hand, encompass "periods of discontinuous change where strategies, power, structure, and systems are fundamentally transformed toward a new basis of alignment" (p. 173). According to the model, the critical driver of fundamental change is upheaval in the environment of the institution. In particular, the punctuated equilibrium theory of organizational evolution posits that two forces provide the impetus for change in institutions, that is, for punctuating a reorientation that disrupts a period of convergence: (1) "sustained low performance . . . and (2) major changes in competitive, technological, social, and legal conditions in the environment" (p. 178) that make existing arrangements increasingly ineffective. Tushman and Romanelli maintain that shock from the environment can be addressed either through anticipatory actions or skilled work after impact, and that the internal dimensions of the organization can be brought into congruence with external forces. They maintain that effective or improving organizations are those that create this alignment (Tushman, Newman, & Romanelli, 1988). They and other scholars also routinely find that leadership mediates, effectively or ineffectively, between internal forces promoting inertia and the demands for fundamental change that emanate from the environment. We return to this hallmark conclusion in our discussion of the integrative dynamic of school improvement below.

The Education Narrative

When we bring our two frames together in education, we learn that our industry has indeed experienced long eras of convergence followed by much shorter periods of reorientation. We confirm Tushman and Romanelli's (1985) theory that we have been pushed out of convergence (or into reorientation) by external changes in the environment, that is, by economic, political, and social forces. We also see that "what counts" for school improvement changes during these periods of transition and solidifies as new eras of convergence firm up.

Peering a bit deeper, we learn that we are in the end stage of a period of reorientation at the current time, being pushed from a long era of convergence (1920–1990) that formed after the last period of reorientation (1890–1920). We see also that, consistent with the punctuated equilibrium model, forces external to education are powering much of the unsettling of the status quo, most importantly for us in the definition of effective school leadership.

Economic Forces To begin with, it is almost a fundamental law that the economy is undergoing a significant metamorphosis. There is widespread agreement that we have been and continue to be moving from an industrial to a postindustrial or information economy. Key aspects of the new economy include the globalization of economic activity, the demise of the mass production economy, a privileging of information technology, an increase in the skills required to be successful, and an emphasis on the service dimensions of the marketplace (National Center on Education and the Economy, 2006). It is also becoming clear to many analysts that with the arrival of the postindustrial society, we are experiencing a breakdown of the social structure associated with industrialism (Hood, 1994). The ascent of the global economy has brought an emphasis on new markets. There is a growing belief in "the assumption that left to itself economic interaction between rationally self-interested individuals in the market will spontaneously yield broad prosperity, social harmony, and all other manner of public and private good" (Himmelstein, 1983, p. 16). Supported by market theory and theories of the firm and by the public choice literature, there is a renewed interest in private market.

Social and Political Forces The political and social environments also appear to be undergoing important changes. There has been a loosening of bonds of democracy (Elshtain, 1995). The infrastructure of civil society also has been impaired. Analysts discern fairly significant tears in the fabric known as "modern civil society" (Dahrendorf, 1995, p. 23).

As a consequence of these basic shifts—the weakening of democracy and the deterioration of civil society, especially in conjunction with the ideological space that they share with economic fundamentalism— important sociopolitical trends have begun to emerge: (1) an increasing sense of personal insecurity and unease in the population at large, (2) the deterioration of essential features of community life, (3) shifts in the boundaries—both real and symbolic—between the state and alternative sociopolitical structures, and (4) an expanding belief that the enhancement of social justice through collective action, especially public action, is unlikely.

One strand of this evolving sociopolitical mosaic is plummeting public support for government. Citizens are becoming disconnected from and frustrated with government and politics. They lack faith in public officials, and they are skeptical of the bureaucratic quagmire of professional control that defined education for almost all of the twentieth century.

The ideological footings of the emerging sociopolitical infrastructure are also becoming increasingly visible. The one piece of the foundation that shines most brightly is what Tomlinson (1986) describes as the "ascendancy of the theory of the social market" (p. 211)—a theory that is anchored on the "supreme value [of] individual liberty" (p. 211). This emerging high regard for individualism and liberty is both an honoring of the individual and a discrediting of collective action. Social market theory suggests a "reduced role for government, greater consumer control, and a belief in efficiency and individuality over equity and community" (Bauman, 1996, p. 627). It includes the privileging of private over public delivery and a diminution in the power of government agents and professional experts (Murphy, 2012).

Postindustrial School Improvement

As I have documented over the last quarter century, school improvement in a postindustrial educational world looks differently than it did during the long era of convergence between 1920 and 1990. We see the reforged concept in each of the three critical domains of schools: goals and the core technology, management and organization, and linkages to external constituents (the institutional level).

Goals and the Core Technology

There is some evidence that a more robust understanding of the education production function is beginning to be translated into new ways of thinking about learning and teaching. Indeed, a century of focus on teaching is giving way to a focus on learning. In addition, the strongest theoretical and disciplinary influence on education—behavioral psychology—is being supplemented by constructivist psychology and newer sociological perspectives on learning—in much the same way that behavioral psychology pushed mind psychology aside in the early 1900s. This shift toward research on cognition and learning offers quite different understandings of school improvement work. Underlying these changes are profoundly different ways of thinking about the educability of children. Those at the forefront of this reorientation away from schools that were historically organized to produce results consistent with the normal curve, to sort youth into the various strata needed to fuel the economy, see education being transformed around the new definition of equal opportunity for learners that we discussed in Chapter 3—equal access to high-status knowledge.

School Organization

At the organizational level, reorientation has thrown into question the operant organizational and management models and structures of the twentieth century. There is a growing sentiment that the existing administrative structure is failing, that the last century produced "bureaucratic arteriosclerosis, insulation from parents and patrons, and the low productivity of a declining industry protected as a quasi-monopoly" (Tyack, 1993, p. 3). It is increasingly being concluded that the existing bureaucratic system of administration is incapable of addressing the needs of a postindustrial education system.

In particular, the institutional and hierarchical system of management has come under sharp criticism from (a) those who argue that schools are so covered with bureaucratic sediment that initiative, creativity, and professional judgment have all been paralyzed and the likely success of reforms has been neutralized, (b) critics who maintain that bureaucratic management practices are interfering with learning, (c) analysts who believe that bureaucracy is counterproductive to the needs and interests of educators within schools, (d) critics who suggest that bureaucratic management is inconsistent with the sacred values of education, (e) scholars who view bureaucracy as a form of operation that inherently forces attention away from the core technology of schooling, (f) reform proponents who hold that the existing organizational structure of schools is neither sufficiently flexible nor sufficiently robust to meet the needs of students in a postindustrial society, and (g) analysts who believe that the rigidities of bureaucracy impede the ability of parents and citizens to govern and reform schooling.

This tremendous attack on the institutional and bureaucratic infrastructure of schools has led to alternative methods of operating that are grounded on new values and principles. Concomitantly, new forms of school organization and management are emerging. The basic organizing and management principles of schooling are giving way to more proactive attempts to lead educational systems. Forms to significantly change the nature of social relationships in schools are emerging (see Chapter 9). The hierarchical, bureaucratic organizational structures that have defined schools since the onslaught of scientific management in the early 1900s are giving way to more decentralized and more professionally controlled systems that create new designs for school management. In these new postindustrial organizations, there are important shifts in roles, relationships, and responsibilities: Traditional patterns of relationships are altered, authority flows are less hierarchical, role definitions are both more general and more flexible, leadership is connected to competence for needed tasks rather than to formal position, and independence and isolation are replaced by cooperative work. Furthermore, the structural orientation implanted during the reign of scientific management is being overshadowed by a focus on the human element. The operant goal is no longer maintenance of the organizational infrastructure, but rather the development of human resources. Learning climates and organizational adaptivity are being substituted for the more traditional emphasis on uncovering and applying the one best model of performance.

Institutional Level

Most analysts of the institutional level of schooling—the interface of the school with its larger (generally immediate) environment—have concluded that the public monopoly approach to education is being recast at the current time, that is, during the current period of reorientation. They envision the demise of schooling as a sheltered government monopoly heavily controlled by professionals. In its stead, they forecast the emergence of a system of schooling and improvement designs driven by economic and political forces that substantially increase the saliency of the market. Embedded in this conception are a number of interesting dynamics, all of which gain force from a realignment of power and influence between professional educators and consumers. The most important is that the traditional dominant relationship—with professional educators on the playing field and parents on the sidelines acting as cheerleaders or agitators or, more likely, passive spectators—is replaced by rules that advantage the consumer (see Chapter 10).

Four elements of this emerging portrait of transformed governance for consumers are most prevalent: choice in selecting a school, voice in school governance, partnership in the education of their children, and enhanced membership in the school community. Central to all four is a blurring of the boundaries between the home and the school, between the school and the community, and between professional staff and lay constituents. Collectively, these components lend support to the grassroots political and

Figure 12.1   The Architecture of School Improvement

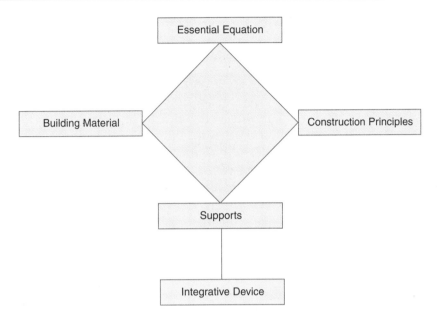

competitive economic arguments that support the calls for more locally controlled organizations and to market-anchored conceptions of school improvement.

As noted in the introduction, our assignment in this section, our goal if you will, is to present a way of thinking about school improvement that both honors our reoriented view of education and grounds its conclusions on the best empirical evidence from the last three decades. We lay out a framework that accomplishes this in five parts: an essential equation, building material, construction principles, enabling supports, and integrative device (see Figure 12.1).

The Essential School Improvement Equation

As discussed in the Introduction, the evidence directs me to the position that there is an essential school improvement algorithm, one that is both simple and elegant:

$$\text{School Improvement} = \text{Academic Press} + \text{Supportive Community}$$

The equation represents the core of school improvement work in the modern era. Another parsimonious model for this narrative is the double helix. Both encapsulations inform us that (1) these are the two critical components of school improvement, (2) they are most powerful in tandem, and (3) they work best when they wrap around each other like strands in a rope.

Building Material

The question at hand is, How can academic press and supportive culture be created in schools, how can school improvement be realized? My work over the years has convinced me that the answer is contained in the other four pieces of the framework.

The first of these pieces, the content, involves identifying and bringing the right materials to the school improvement building site. This is the aspect of the framework that has been most deeply explored over the last three decades. During that time, researchers have been quite active in mining for the raw materials of school improvement. In addition, using this material, numerous content-based taxonomies have been forged, beginning around 1980 with the correlates of effective schools and carrying through to today as seen in the recent comprehensive review of meta-analyses by Hattie (2009), the hallmark study by Bryk, Sebring, Allensworth, Luppescu, and Easton (2010) on the essential elements of school improvement, and the important new analysis from the National Center on Scaling up Effective Schools (Preston, Goldring, Guthrie, & Ramsey, 2012).

The good news here is that while lists and taxonomies often feature different terms and place ideas in different categories, there is an astonishing amount of agreement on the material contained in these categorizations—that is, on the ingredients of school improvement. It is beyond the scope of this article to provide a comprehensive and integrative analysis of this thirty years of scholarship. Rather, based on that work, I simply offer a taxonomy constructed from those studies, one that captures the "right stuff" of school improvement—and thus the scaffolding for PSEL (see Chapters 4 through 11).

Construction Principles

While attention has been lavished on uncovering the best materials (content) to use to forge school improvement initiatives—that is, to help create schools defined by academic press and supportive culture—our understanding of the rules that need to be followed in putting the content pieces together is much less well developed. What we do know is often embedded in or threaded across the content narrative. Principles rarely have a starring role in the school improvement play. One often has to read between the lines to discover these ideas. The art of "seeing the missing" is also essential in developing an understanding of these guiding principles. Forensic school improvement work is generally a good method of identifying the pieces of this critical component of the school improvement framework.

Based on a close reading of school improvement research over a long period of time, my assessment mirrors that of Michael Fullan, which is that the construction principles are as important as the content elements in

Table 12.1   The Building Material of School Improvement

Quality Instruction • Effective teachers • Quality pedagogy
Curriculum • Content coverage • Time • Rigor • Relevance
Personalized Learning Environment for Students • Safe and orderly climate • Meaningful connections • Opportunities to participate
Professional Learning Environment for Educators • Collaborative culture of work • Participation and ownership • Shared leadership
Learning-Centered Leadership • Forging academic press • Developing supportive culture
Learning-Centered Linkages to the School Community • Connections to parents • Linkages to community agencies and organizations
Monitoring of Progress and Performance Accountability • Performance-based goals • Systematic use of data • Shared accountability

school improvement work. Working on the latter without attending to the former is a recipe for failure, akin to building beautiful rooms on the third floor of a house without load-bearing walls. While it is beyond the scope of this chapter to compile and describe the universe of these principles, given the impoverished state of knowledge in this area of the framework, simply providing a taxonomy is insufficient. Instead, I illustrate the idea of "construction principles" with three examples.

Structure Does Not Predict Performance

Almost all school improvement work involves structural changes. This is appropriate, for as Kirst and Meister (1985) documented in their cardinal analysis, structural changes are needed to capture and hold reform initiatives. However, the prevalent assumption that structure (e.g., block scheduling) will provide desired results (e.g., better instruction, more student engagement) is without foundation (Elmore, 1995; Murphy, 1991). Thus we see the essential paradox of school improvement construction work: structural changes almost never predict outcomes, but they are essential for initiatives to take root and develop.

Here is the essence of the problem. Educators in their attempts to improve their schools identify activities that worked elsewhere and then bring them home. These are almost universally structural transfers (e.g., academies, looping, charter schools, ungraded classrooms, detracking, and so forth). School leaders are often masters at brokering such transfers. Policy at all levels bolsters this approach to school improvement as well. The disheartening reality is that the DNA of these interventions, that is, what made them work elsewhere, rarely makes the voyage as the structures are transferred. What schools end up with are empty shells of change, structures without the fuel to power improvement.

Another encapsulation of the structural principle is that form follows function. Or alternatively, school improvement work is first and foremost about identifying the DNA of improvement, then building out structures to contain that material. Violation of this construction principle is the norm in schools. It dooms a good deal of all improvement work, much more so than the selection of the wrong building materials.

Context Always Matters

Research from every sector of the school reform landscape confirms that context is critical. History and experience, type of school, nature of the community and the district, level of schooling, and an assortment of other contextual factors are important in the development of academic press and supportive culture. For example, creating personalized learning environments is somewhat different work in high schools than in elementary schools. Interventions, built or imported (even when they carry the right DNA), need to be shaped and contoured to fit the school context. When they are not, they tend not to fit. And when improvement efforts do not fit at the school, they rarely flourish.

Cohesion and Alignment Are Essential Nearly four decades ago Richard Elmore first helped me understand the meaning of cohesion in school improvement work when he noted that pretty much anything (from the right content categories) done well will work. Since that time, other scholars have added some nuances to this important lesson and helped form it into an essential school improvement construction principle. Creating separate galaxies for content elements and their related anchor programs is a poor way to pursue school improvement. The better approach, and the only one with real hope of promoting successful change, is to bring whatever content is engaged into one galaxy with a common center of gravity.

Employing building material that is of medium quality (i.e., has only medium effect sizes), but that is universally supported and richly linked to other elements in the school will ensure greater improvement than using high quality content elements that are poorly connected.

We close this section by returning to the core message: construction principles are an essential component of the school improvement framework. Yet they receive only limited attention in scholarly analysis and are often conspicuous by their absence from school improvement work. This fact explains the failure of school improvement efforts to a much greater extent than do poor choices in selecting building materials.

Supports

We have also learned, again from examining embedded patterns in the school improvement mosaic, that "organizational tools" need to be thoughtfully used if school improvement efforts are to bear fruit. They are the fourth component of the framework.

All of the building materials and guiding principles by definition carry a positive charge, each is a hero or heroine in the school improvement narrative, although, as we noted above, with limited powers when working alone. Organizational supports, on the other hand, are neutral. They can carry either a positive or negative charge; that is, they can be employed to help or hinder school improvement work.

There are a variety of ways to think about these supports or tools. For example, there is the well-established framework of "capital": human capital, financial capital, social capital, and so forth, with each form of capital composed of numerous subdimensions (e.g., leadership capital in the human capital area). However, in employing the idea of "neutral charge" we underscore a design that is more compact and considerably less likely to bleed into "material" and "principles" than other support taxonomies. Here we include: organizational structures (e.g., grade-level academies, K-2 schools), operating systems (e.g., procedures for assigning children to teachers and classes), policies (e.g., assigning struggling students to mandatory after-school tutoring), and practices (e.g., the way the principal interacts with children in the school hallways). We find considerable evidence in the school improvement research that the tools to mix quality material and construction principles in a productive fashion are found in these categories (see Chapter 8).

The Integrative Dynamic

Since the first studies of effective schools and districts and investigations of successful change, leadership has enjoyed a central role in the school improvement narrative. It is prominently displayed in Table 12.1. My work with my colleague Philip Hallinger over the last thirty years

Chapter 12

has taken me beyond that conclusion, however. I see a deeper pattern of leadership in the school improvement tapestry and a more central location for that pattern. The storyline is one in which school leaders provide the dynamism to make all the components of the framework function. The recent cardinal volume by Bryk and colleagues (2010) affirms leadership as the integrative dynamic. More specifically, they conclude that leadership is the essential enabling element of school improvement work, thus the focus on PSEL.

We began this analysis with a robust treatment of the meaning of school improvement in the postindustrial world of education. We undertook this exploration because it is foundational to school improvement work yet receives only passing notice, at best, in the literature. School improvement, we saw, is not a fixed concept. It takes on different meanings in different times. We argued above that current perspectives on school improvement have been heavily shaped by powerful forces external to the business of education as well as an ongoing reorientation of schooling that is pushing the profession off the footings on which it sat for almost all of the twentieth century.

We then exposed the architecture that captures the universe of school improvement, or alternatively the scaffolding that undergirds all effective improvement efforts. At the heart of that framework is the essential school improvement equation, one that defines school improvement as academic press and supportive culture. We saw that concepts and materials from the other components of the framework come together to energize the essential equation. We discussed the component that is best understood, the content of school improvement or the right building material. Here I argued that a near myopic focus on content has limited our ability to secure the end goal of improvement. I then introduced the third component of the framework, school improvement construction principles. I reported that the inability to understand and operationalize these principles has been largely responsible for the frustration and ineffectiveness of much school improvement work. A parsimonious and neutrally charged set of the tools that need to be used in school improvement work was then layered into the framework. We closed with the empirically anchored conclusion that leadership is the integrative dynamic in fostering school improvement.

References

Ackerman, R. H., & Maslin-Ostrowski, P. (2002). *The wounded leader: How real leadership emerges in times of crisis.* San Francisco, CA: Jossey-Bass.

Adams, C. (2010). Social determinants of student trust in high poverty elementary schools. In W. K. Hoy & M. DiPaola (Eds.), *Analyzing school contexts: Influences of principals and teachers in the service of students* (pp. 255–280). Charlotte, NC: Information Age.

Adams, C., & Forsyth, P. (2009). Conceptualizing and validating a measure of student trust. In W. K. Hoy & M. DiPoala (Eds.), *Studies in School Improvement* (pp. 263–277). Charlotte, NC: Information Age.

Ainscow, M., & Southworth, G. (1996). School improvement: A study of the roles of leaders and external consultants. *School Effectiveness and School Improvement, 7*(3), 229–251.

Alcoff, L. (1991–1992, Winter). The problem of speaking for others. *Cultural Critique, 20,* 5–32.

Alder, N. (2000). Teaching diverse students. *Multicultural Perspectives, 2*(2), 28–31.

Alexander, K., & Entwisle, D. (1996). Schools and children at risk. In A. Booth & J. Dunn (Eds.), *Family-school links: How do they affect educational outcomes?* (pp. 67–88). Mahwah, NJ: Erlbaum.

Alexander, K., Entwisle, D., & Horsey, C. (1997). From first grade forward: Early foundations of high school dropout. *Sociology of Education, 70*(2), 87–107.

Alexander, K. L., & Cook, M. A. (1982). Curricula and coursework: A surprise ending to a familiar story. *American Sociological Review, 47*(5), 626–640.

Alexander, K. L., Cook, M., & McDill, E. L. (1978). Curriculum tracking and educational stratification: Some further evidence. *American Sociological Review, 43,* 47–66.

Alexander, K. L., & McDill, E. L. (1976). Selection and allocation within schools: Some causes and consequences of curriculum placement. *American Sociological Review, 41,* 936–980.

Allensworth, E. M., & Easton, J. Q. (2005). *The on-track indicator as a predictor of high school graduation.* Chicago, IL: Consortium on Chicago School Research at the University of Chicago.

Allington, R. (1983). The reading instruction provided readers of differing reading ability. *Elementary School Journal, 83*(5), 548–559.

Alvermann, D. E., Young, J. P., Weaver, D., Hinchman, K. A., Moore, D. W., Phelps, S. F., & Zalewski, P. (1996). Middle and high school students' perceptions of how they experience text-based discussions: A multicase study. *Reading Research Quarterly, 31*(3), 244–267.

American Association of School Administrators. (2007). *Statement of ethics for school administrators.* Arlington, VA: Author.

Ancess, J. (2000). The reciprocal influence of teacher learning, teaching practice, school restructuring, and student learning outcomes. *The Teachers College Record, 102*(3), 590–619.

Ancess, J. (2003). *Beating the odds: High schools as communities of commitment.* New York, NY: Teachers College Press.

Anderman, E. M., Maehr, M. L., & Midgley, C. (1999). Declining motivation after the transition to middle school: Schools can make a difference. *Journal of Research & Development in Education, 32*(3), 131–147.

Anderman, L. H. (2003). Academic and social perceptions as predictors of change in middle school students' sense of school belonging. *The Journal of Experimental Education, 72*(1), 5–22.

Anderson, R. C., Hiebert, E. H., Scott, J. A., & Wilkinson, I. A. G. (1985). *Becoming a nation of readers: The report of the Commission on Reading.* Washington, DC: The National Institute of Education. U.S. Department of Education.

Anderson, S., Moore, S., & Sun, J. (2009). Positioning the principals in patterns of school leadership distribution. In K. Leithwood, B. Mascall, & T. Strauss (Eds.), *Distributed leadership according to the evidence* (pp. 111–136). London, UK: Routledge.

Antrop-González, R. (2006). Toward the "school as sanctuary" concept in multicultural urban education: Implications for small high school reform. *Curriculum Inquiry, 36*(3), 273–301.

Antrop-González, R., & De Jesús, A. (2006). Toward a theory of critical care in urban small school reform: Examining structures and pedagogies of caring in two Latino community based schools. *International Journal of Qualitative Studies in Education, 19*(4), 409–433.

Apple, M. W. (2003). *The state and the politics of knowledge.* New York, NY: Routledge Falmer.

Arnot, M., McIntyre, D., Pedder, D., & Reay, D. (2004). *Consultation in the classroom: Developing dialogue about teaching and learning.* Cambridge, UK: Pearson.

Askew, B. J., Fountas, I. C., Lyons, C. A., Pinnell, G. S., & Schmitt, M. C. (2000). A review of reading recovery. In R. D. Robinson, M. C. McKenna, & J. M. Wedman (Eds.), *Issues and trends in literacy education* (2nd ed., pp. 284–303). Needham Heights, MA: Allyn & Bacon.

Askew, B. J., & Gaffney, J. S. (1999). Reading recovery: Waves of influence on literacy education. In J. S. Gaffney & B. J. Askew (Eds.), *Stirring the waters: The influence of Marie Clay* (pp. 75–98). Portsmouth, NH: Heinemann.

Atweh, B., & Burton, L. (1995). Students as researchers: Rationale and critique. *British Educational Research Journal, 21*(5), 561–575.

Au, K. H. (2002). Communities of practice: Engagement, imagination, and alignment in research on teacher education. *Journal of Teacher Education, 53*(3), 222–227.

Au, K. H., & Asam, C. L. (1996). Improving the literacy achievement of low-income students of diverse backgrounds. In M. F. Graves, P. van den Broek, & B. M. Taylor (Eds.), *The first R: Every child's right to read* (pp. 199–223). New York, NY: Teachers College Press.

Auerbach, S. (2007). Visioning parent engagement in urban schools. *Journal of School Leadership, 17*(6), 699–734.

Auerbach, S. (2009). Walking the walk: Portraits in leadership for family engagement in urban schools. *School Community Journal, 19*(1), 9–32.

Baker, J. A., Terry, T., Bridger, R., & Winsor, A. (1997). Schools as caring communities: A relational approach to school reform. *The School Psychology Review, 26*(4), 586–602.

Balfanz, R., & Byrnes, V. (2006). Closing the mathematics achievement gap in high-poverty middle schools: Enablers and constraints. *Journal of Education for Students Placed at Risk, 11*(2), 143–159.

Balfanz, R., Herzog, L., & MacIver, D. (2007). Preventing student disengagement and keeping students on the graduation path in urban middle-grades schools: Early identification and effective interventions. *Educational Psychologist, 42*(4), 223–235.

Bali, V.A., & Alvarez, R. M. (2003). Schools and educational outcomes: What causes the 'race gap' in student test scores? *Social Science Quarterly, 84*(3), 485–507.

Bandura, A. (1993). Perceived self-efficacy in cognitive development and functioning. *Educational Psychologist, 28*(2), 117–148.

Barascout, R. (2016). A bullied boy who grew up to change school climate. In S. J. Gross & J. P. Shapiro (Eds.), *Democratic ethical educational leadership: Reclaiming school reform* (pp. 144–148). New York, NY: Routledge.

Barker, B. (2001). Do leaders matter? *Educational Review, 53*(1), 65–76.

Barnes, C. A., Camburn, E., Sanders, B. R., & Sebastian, J. (2010). Developing instructional leaders: Using mixed methods to explore the black box of planned change in principals' professional practice. *Educational Administration Quarterly, 46*(2), 241–279.

Barnett, K., & McCormick, J. (2004). Leadership and individual principal-teacher relationships in schools. *Educational Administration Quarterly, 40*(3), 406–434.

Barnett, K., McCormick, J., & Conners, R. (2001). Transformational leadership in schools: Panacea, placebo, or problem? *Journal of Educational Administration, 39*(1), 24–46.

Baron, R., Tom, D., & Cooper, H. (1985). Social class, race, and teacher expectations. In J. Dusek (Ed.), *Teacher expectancies* (pp. 251–269). Hillsdale, NJ: Erlbaum.

Barth, R. S. (1988). School: A community of leaders. In A. Lieberman (Ed.), *Building a professional culture in schools* (pp. 129–147). New York, NY: Teachers College Press.

Barton, P. E. (2003). *Parsing the achievement gap* (Policy Information Report). Princeton, NJ: Educational Testing Service.

Bates, R. J. (1984). Toward a critical practice of educational administration. In T. J. Sergiovanni & J. E. Corbally (Eds.), *Leadership and organizational culture: New perspectives on administrative theory and practice* (pp. 260–274). Urbana, IL: University of Illinois Press.

Battistich, V., Solomon, D., Kim, D., Watson, M., & Schaps, E. (1995). Schools as communities, poverty levels of student populations, and students' attitudes, motives, and performance: A multilevel analysis. *American Educational Research Journal, 32*(3), 627–658.

Battistich, V., Solomon, D., Watson, M., & Schaps, E. (1997). Caring school communities. *Educational Psychologist, 32*(3), 137–151.

Bauman, P. C. (1996). Governing education in an antigovernment environment. *Journal of School Leadership, 6*(6), 625–643.

Beachum, F., & Dentith, A. M. (2004). Teacher leaders creating cultures of school renewal and transformation. *Educational Forum, 68*(3), 276–286.

Beauchamp, T. L., & Childress, J. F. (1984). Morality, ethics and ethical theories. In P. Sola (Ed.), *Ethics, education, and administrative decisions: A book of readings* (pp. 39–67). New York, NY: Peter Lang.

Beck, L. G. (1994). *Reclaiming educational administration as a caring profession.* NewYork, NY: Teachers' College Press.

Beck, L. G., & Foster, W. (1999). Administration and community: Considering challenges, exploring possibilities. In J. Murphy & K. S. Louis (Eds.), *Handbook of research on educational administration* (pp. 337–358). San Francisco, CA: Jossey-Bass.

Beck, L. G., & Murphy, J. (1992). *Understanding the principalship: A metaphorical analysis, 1960–1990.* San Francisco, CA: Jossey-Bass.

Beck, L. G., & Murphy, J. (1994). *Ethics in educational leadership programs: An expanding role.* Newbury Park, CA: Corwin.

Beck, L. G., & Murphy, J. (1996). *The four imperatives of a successful school.* Newbury Park, CA: Corwin.

Beck, L. G., Murphy, J., & Associates. (1997a). *Ethics in educational leadership programs: Emerging models.* University Park, CA: University Council for Educational Administration.

Beck, L. G., Murphy, J., & Assocs. (1997b). *Ethics in educational leadership programs: An expanding role.* Columbia, MO: UCEA.

Becker, B. E., & Luthar, S. S. (2002). Social-emotional factors affecting achievement outcomes among disadvantaged students: Closing the achievement gap. *Educational Psychologist, 37*(4), 197–214.

Beckner, W. (2004). *Ethics for educational leaders.* Boston, MA: Pearson Education.

Begley, P. T. (2006). Self-knowledge, capacity and sensitivity: Prerequisites to authentic leadership by school principles. *Journal of Educational Administration, 44*(6), 570–589.

Begley, P. T., & Johansson, O. (Eds.). (2003). *The ethical dimensions of school leadership.* Boston, MA: Kluwer Academic.

Beishuizen, J. J., Hof, E., Putten, C. M., Bouwmeester, S., & Asscher, J. J. (2001). Students' and teachers' cognitions about good teachers. *British Journal of Educational Psychology, 71*(2), 185–201.

Bempechat, J. (1992). *Fostering high achievement in African American children: Home, school, and public policy influences* (ERIC Clearinghouse of Urban Education). Columbia, NY: Teachers College, Columbia University, Office of Educational Research and Improvement, Institute for Urban and Minority Education, and U.S. Department of Education (Contract No. R188062013).

Bempechat, J., & Ginsburg, H. (1989). *Underachievement and educational disadvantage: The home and school experiences of at-risk youth.* Urban Diversity Series No. 99. New York, NY: ERIC Clearinghouse on Urban Education and Institute for Urban and Minority Education, Teachers College, Columbia University (ED 315 485).

Bennett, A., Bridglall, B. L., Cauce, A.M., Everson, H. T., Gordon, E.W., Lee, C.D., . . . Stewart, J. K. (2007). Task force report on the affirmative development of academic ability: All students reaching the top: Strategies for closing academic achievement gaps. In E. W. Gordon & B. L. Bridglall (Eds.), *Affirmative development: Cultivating academicability* (pp. 239–275). Lanham, MD: Rowman and Littlefield.

Berends, M., Bodilly, S., & Kirby, S. (2003). New American schools: District and school leadership for whole-school reform. In J. Murphy & A. Datnow (Eds.), *Leadership lessons from comprehensive school reforms* (pp. 109–131). Thousand Oaks, CA: Corwin.

Berends, M., Lucas, S. R., Sullivan, T., & Briggs, R. J. (2005). *Examining gaps in mathematics achievement among racial-ethnic groups, 1972–1992.* Santa Monica, CA: Rand.

Berry, B., & Ginsberg, R. (1990, April). Creating lead teachers: From policy to implementation. *Phi Delta Kappan, 71*(8), 616–621.

Betts, J., Zau, A., & Koedel, C. (2010). *Lessons in reading reform: Finding what works.* San Francisco, CA: Public Policy Institute of California.

Bidwell, C. E., & Yasumoto, J. Y. (1999). The collegial focus: Teaching fields, collegial relationships, and instructional practice in American high schools. *Sociology of Education, 72*(4), 234–256.

Bierman, K. L. (1996). Family-school linkages: An overview. In A. Booth & J. Dunn (Eds.), *Family-school links: How do they affect educational outcomes?* (pp. 328–365). Hillsdale, NJ: Erlbaum.

Bingham, C. S. (1994, February). *Class size as an early intervention strategy in white-minority achievement gap reduction.* Paper presented at the annual meeting of the American Association of School Administrators, San Francisco, California.

Birch, S. H., & Ladd, G. W. (1997). The teacher-child relationship and children's early school adjustment. *Journal of School Psychology, 35*(1), 61–79.

Bishop, H. L., Tinley, A., & Berman, B. T. (1997). A contemporary leadership model to promote teacher leadership. *Action in Teacher Education, 19*(3), 77–81.

Blair, L. (2016). Rachel's challenge: A caring connection. In S. J. Gross & J. P. Shapiro (Eds.), *Democratic ethical educational leadership: Reclaiming school reform* (pp. 103–106). New York, NY: Routledge.

Blair, M. (2002). Effective school leadership: The multi-ethnic context. *British Journal of Sociology of Education,* 179–191.

Blanc, S., Christman, J. B., Liu, R., Mitchell, C., Travers, E., & Bulkley, K. E. (2010). Learning to learn from data: Benchmarks and instructional communities. *Peabody Journal of Education, 85*(2), 205–225.

Blase, J., & Blase, J. (1999). Principals' instructional leadership and teacher development: Teachers' perspectives. *Educational Administration Quarterly, 35*(3), 349–378.

Blase, J., & Blase, J. (2000). Effective instructional leadership: Teachers' perspectives on how principals promote teaching and learning in schools. *Journal of Educational Administration, 38*(2), 130–141.

Blase, J., & Blase, J. (2004). *Handbook of instructional leadership: How really good principals promote teaching and learning.* Thousand Oaks, CA: Corwin.

Blase, J., & Kirby, P. (2009). *Bringing out the best in teachers: What effective principals do.* Thousand Oaks, CA: Corwin.

Blegen, M. B., & Kennedy C. (2000). Principals and teachers, leading together. *NASSP Bulletin, 84*(616), 1–6.

Bloomberg, L., Ganey, A., Alba, V., Quintero, G., & Alvarez-Alcantara, L. (2003). Chicano-Latino youth leadership institute: An asset-based program for youth. *American Journal of Health Behavior, 27*(1), 45–54.

Blumenfeld, P., Fishman, B. J., Krajcik, J., Marx, R. W., & Soloway, E. (2000). Creating usable innovations in systemic reform: Scaling up technology embedded project-based science in urban schools. *Educational Psychologist, 35*(3), 149–164.

Boekaerts, M. (1993). Being concerned with well-being and with learning. *Educational Psychologist, 28*(2), 149–167.

Bol, L., & Berry, R. O. (2005, April/May). Secondary mathematics teachers' perceptions of the achievement gap. *The High School Journal, 88*(4), 32–45.

Boles, K., & Troen, V. (1996). Teacher leaders and power: Achieving school reform from the classroom. In G. Moller & M. Katzenmeyer (Eds.), *Every teacher as a leader: Realizing the potential of teacher leadership* (pp. 41–62). San Francisco, CA: Jossey-Bass.

Borko, H. (2004). Professional development and teacher learning: Mapping the terrain. *Educational Researcher, 33*(8), 3–15.

Borman, G. D. (2005). National efforts to bring reform to scale in high-poverty schools: Outcomes and implications. *Review of Research in Education, 29*(1), 1–27.

Borman, G. D., & Kimball, S. M. (2005). Teacher quality and educational equality: Do teachers with higher standards-based evaluation ratings close student achievement gaps? *The Elementary School Journal, 106*(1), pp. 3–20.

Boyan, N. J. (1963). Common and specialized learnings for administrators and supervisors: Some problems and issues. In D. J. Leu & H. C. Rudman (Eds.), *Preparation programs for school administrators: Common and specialized learnings* (pp. 1–23). East Lansing, MI: Michigan State University.

Boyer, E. L. (1983). *High school: A report on secondary education in America.* New York, NY: Harper and Row.

Bragg, S. (2007). "It's not about systems, it's about relationships": Building a listening culture in a primary school. In D. Thiessen & A. Cook-Sather (Eds.), *International handbook of student experience in elementary and secondary school* (pp. 659–680). Dordrecht, Netherlands: Springer.

Branch, G., Hanushek, E., & Rivkin, S. (2012). *Estimating the effect of leaders on public sector productivity: The case of school principals* (Working Paper 66). Washington, DC: National Center for Analysis of Longitudinal Data in Education Research.

Branch, G., Rivkin, S., & Hanushek, E. (2003). School leaders matter: Measuring the impact of effective principals. *Education Next, 13*(1), 1–8.

Branson, C. (2009). *Leadership for age of wisdom.* Dordrecht, Netherlands: Springer Education.

Branson, C. (2010, March). Ethical decision making: Is personal moral integrity the missing link? *Journal of Authentic Leadership in Education, 1*(1), 1–8.

Branson, C., & Gross, S. J. (Eds.). (2014). *Handbook of ethical educational leadership.* New York, NY: Routledge.

Brattesani, K. A., Weinstein, R. S., & Marshall, H. H. (1984). Student perceptions of differential teacher treatment as moderators of teacher expectation effects. *Journal of Educational Psychology, 76*(2), 236–247.

Braxton, J. M., Hirschy, A. S., & McClendon, S. A. (2011). *Understanding and reducing college student departure: ASHE-ERIC higher education report* (Vol. 16). San Francisco, CA: Jossey-Bass.

Braybrook, R. (1985). *The aircraft encyclopedia.* New York, NY: Simon & Schuster.

Bredeson, P. V. (2005, Fall). Building capacity in schools: Some ethical considerations for authentic leadership and learning. *Values and Ethics in Educational Administration, 4*(1), 1–7.

Brewer, D. J. (1993). Principals and student outcomes: Evidence from U.S. high schools. *Economics of Education Review, 12*(4), 281–292.

Brewster, C., & Fager, J. (2000). *Increasing student engagement and motivation: From time-on-task to homework.* Portland, OR: Northwest Regional Educational Laboratory.

Bridges, E. M. (1977). The nature of leadership. In L. L. Cunningham, W. G. Hack, & R. O. Nystrand (Eds.), *Educational administration: The development decades* (pp. 202–230). Berkeley, CA: McCutchan.

Brigg, P. (2016). Mr. Murray vs. merit pay. In S. J. Gross & J. P. Shapiro (Eds.), *Democratic ethical educational leadership: Reclaiming school reform* (pp. 116–120). New York, NY: Routledge.

Brookover, W. B., Beady, C., Flood, P., Schweitzer, J., & Wisenbaker, J. (1979). *School social systems and student achievement: Schools can make a difference.* New York, NY: Praeger.

Brookover, W. B., Brady, N. V., & Warfield, M. (1981). *Educational policies and equitable education: A report of studies of two desegregated school systems.* East Lansing, MI: Center for Urban Affairs, Michigan State University.

Brookover, W. B., & Lezotte, L. W. (1977). *Changes in school characteristics coincident with changes in student achievement.* East Lansing, MI: College of Urban Development, Michigan State University.

Brookover, W. B., Schweitzer, J. J., Schneider, J. M., Beady, C. H., Flood, P. K., & Wisenbaker, J. M. (1978). Elementary school social climate and school achievement. *American Educational Research Journal, 15*(2), 301–318.

Brooks, R., Milburn, N., Rotheram-Borus, M., & Witkin, A. (2004). The system-of-care for homeless youth: Perceptions of service providers. *Evaluation and Program Planning, 27*(4), 443–451.

Brown, J., & Sheppard, B. (1999). *Leadership, organizational learning, and classroom change.* Paper presented at the annual meeting of the American Educational Research Association, Montreal, Quebec, Canada.

Broyles, I. L. (1991, April). *Transforming teacher leadership through action research.* Paper presented at the annual meeting of the New England Educational Research Association, Portsmouth, NH.

Bru, E., Stephens, P., & Torsheim, T. (2002). Students' perceptions of class management and reports of their own misbehavior. *Journal of School Psychology, 40*(4), 287–307.

Bruggencate, G., Luyten, H., Scheerens, J., & Sleegers, P. (2012). Modeling the influence of school leaders on student achievement: How can school leaders make a difference? *Educational Administration Quarterly, 48*(4), 699–732.

Brunner, C., Fasca, C., Heinze, J., Honey, M., Light, D., Mandinach, E., & Wexler, D. (2005). *Linking data and learning: The grow network study.* New York, NY: Education Development Center.

Bryk, A. S., Lee, V., & Holland, P. B. (1993). *Catholic schools and the common good.* Cambridge, MA: Harvard University Press.

Bryk, A. S., Sebring, P. B., Allensworth, E., Luppescu, S., & Easton, J. (2010). *Organizing schools for improvement: Lessons from Chicago.* Chicago, IL: University of Chicago Press.

Bryman, A. (2004). Qualitative research on leadership: A critical but appreciative review. *The Leadership Quarterly, 15*(6), 729–769.

Bulkley, K. E., & Hicks, J. (2005). Managing community: Professional community in charter schools operated by educational management organizations. *Educational Administration Quarterly, 41*(2), 306–348.

Burch, P., & Spillane, J. P. (2003). Elementary school leadership strategies and subject matter: Reforming mathematics and literacy instruction. *The Elementary School Journal,* 519–535.

Burke, C., & Grosvenor, I. (2003). *The school I'd like: Children and young people's reflections on an education for the 21st century.* London, UK: Routledge.

Burns, R., Keyes, M., & Kusimo, P. (2005). *Closing achievement gaps by creating culturally responsive schools.* Charleston, WV: Appalachia Educational Lab.

Burris, C. C., & Welner, K. G. (2005, April). Closing the achievement gap by detracking. *Phi Delta Kappan, 86*(6), 594–598.

Cabello, B., & Terrell, R. (1994). Making students feel like family: How teachers create warm and caring classroom climates. *Journal of Classroom Interaction, 29*(1), 17–23.

Caldwell, B. J. (1998). Strategic leadership, resource management and effective school reform. *Journal of Educational Administration, 36*(5), 445–461.

California State Department of Education. (1984). *Time and learning in California Public Schools.* Sacramento, CA: Author.

Callahan, R. E. (1962). *Education and the cult of efficiency.* Chicago, IL: University of Chicago Press.

Camara, W. J., & Schmidt, A. E. (1999). *Group differences in standardized testing and social stratification.* Cambridge, MA: The Civil Rights Project at Harvard University.

Camburn, E., Rowan, B., & Taylor, J. E. (2003). Distributed leadership in schools: The case of elementary schools adopting comprehensive school reform models. *Educational Evaluation and Policy Analysis, 25*(4), 347–373.

Campbell, R. F., Fleming, T., Newell, L., & Bennion, J. W. (1987). *A history of thought and practice in educational administration.* New York, NY: Teachers College Press.

Carbonaro, W., & Gamoran, A. (2002). The production of achievement inequality in high school English. *American Educational Research Journal, 39*(4), 801–827.

Carnegie Forum on Education and the Economy. (1986, May). *A nation prepared: Teachers for the 21st century.* Washington, DC: Author.

Catalano, R. F., Loeber, R., & McKinney, K. C. (1999). School and community interventions to prevent serious and violent offending. *Juvenile Justice Bulletin,* 1–12.

Center for Teaching Quality. (2007). *Teaching and learning conditions improve high school reform efforts.* Chapel Hill, NC: Author.

Chaplain, R. (1996a). Making a strategic withdrawal: Disengagement and self-worth protection in male pupils. In J. Rudduck, R. P. Chaplain, & G. Wallace (Eds.), *School improvement: What can pupils tell us?* (pp. 97–111). London, UK: Routledge.

Chaplain, R. (1996b). Pupils under pressure: Coping with stress at school. In J. Rudduck, R. P. Chaplain, & G. Wallace (Eds.), *School improvement: What can pupils tell us?* (pp. 116–127). London, UK: Routledge.

Chavis, G., Ward, L., Elwell, T., & Barret, C. (1997). *Improving student performance in high poverty schools.* (Report Number: 96–86). Tallahassee, FL: Office of Program Policy Analysis and Government Accountability.

Cheney, D., Blum, C., & Walker, B. (2004). An analysis of leadership teams' perceptions of positive behavior support and the outcomes of typically developing and at-risk students in their schools. *Assessment for Effective Intervention, 30*(1), 7–24.

Childs-Bowen, D., Moller, C., & Scrivner, J. (2000, May). Principals: Leaders of leaders. *NASSP Bulletin, 84*(6), 27–34.

Chin, T., & Phillips, M. (2004, July). Social reproduction and child-rearing practices: Social class, children's agency, and the summer activity gap. *Sociology of Education, 77*(3), 185–210.

Christensen, J. C. (1987). Roles of teachers and administrators. In P. R. Burden (Ed.), *Establishing career ladders in teaching: A guide for policy makers* (pp. 88–110). Springfield, IL: Charles C Thomas.

Christle, C. A., Jolivette, K., & Nelson, C. M. (2005). Breaking the school to prison pipeline: Identifying school risk and protective factors for youth delinquency. *Exceptionality, 13*(2), 69–88.

Clark, C., Dyson, A., Millward, A., & Robson, S. (1999). Theories of inclusion, theories of schools: Deconstructing and reconstructing the "inclusive school." *British Educational Research Journal, 25*(2), 157–177.

Clark, D. L., Lotto, L. S., & Astuto, T. A. (1984). Comparative analysis of two lines of inquiry. *Educational Administration Quarterly, 20*(3), 41–68.

Clark, D. L., Lotto, L. S., & McCarthy, M. M. (1980). *Why do some urban schools succeed?* Bloomington, IN: Phi Delta Kappa.

Clift, R., Johnson, M., Holland, P., & Veal, M. L. (1992). Developing the potential for collaborative school leadership. *American Educational Research Journal, 29*(4), 877–908.

Clotfelter, C. T., Ladd, H. F., & Vigdor, J. (2005). Who teaches whom? Race and the distribution of novice teachers. *Economics of Education Review, 24*(4), 377–392.

Cochran-Smith, M., & Lytle, S. (1999). Relationship of knowledge and practice: Teacher learning in communities. In A. Iran-Nejad & C. D. Pearson (Eds.), *Review of research in education* (Vol. 24, pp. 249–306). Washington, DC: American Educational Research Association.

Cohen, M. D., March, J. G., & Olsen, J. P. (1972, March). A garbage can model of organizational choice. *Administrative Science Quarterly, 17*(1), 1–26.

Coldren, A. F., & Spillane, J. P. (2007). Making connections to teaching practice: The role of boundary practices in instructional leadership. *Educational Policy, 21*(2), 369–396.

Collins, J., & Valentine J. (2010). *Testing the impact of student engagement on standardized achievement: An empirical study of the influence of classroom engagement on test scores across school types.* Paper presented at the Annual Meeting of the University Council for Education Administration, New Orleans, LA. Retrieved from ERIC database.

Collins, P. H. (1997). Comment on Hedeman's "The truth and method: Feminist standpoint theory revisited": Where's the power? *Signs, 22*(2), 375–381.

Commeyras, M. (1995). What can we learn from students' questions? *Theory Into Practice, 34*(2), 101–106.

Conchas, G. Q. (2001). Structuring failure and success: Understanding the variability in Latino school engagement. *Harvard Educational Review, 71*(3), 475–505.

Conley, D. T. (1997). *Roadmap to restructuring: Charting the course of change in American education.* Eugene, OR: ERIC Clearinghouse on Educational Management.

Conley, S. (1991). Review of research on teacher participation in school decision making. *Review of Research in Education, 17*, 225–266.

Connell, J. P., & Wellborn, J. G. (1991). Competence, autonomy, and relatedness: A motivational analysis of self-system processes. In M. R. Gunnar & L. A. Sroufe (Eds.), *Self-processes and development. The Minnesota symposia on child psychology* (Vol. 23, pp. 43–77). Hillsdale, NJ: Erlbaum.

Connolly, M., & James, C. (2006). Collaboration for school improvement: A resource dependency and institutional framework of analysis. *Educational Management, Administration & Leadership, 34*(1), 69–87.

Cook-Sather, A. (2002). Authorizing students' perspectives: Toward trust, dialogue, and change in education. *Educational Researcher, 31*(4), 3–14.

Cook-Sather, A. (2006). 'Change based on what students say': Preparing teachers for a paradoxical model of leadership. *International Journal of Leadership in Education, 9*(4), 345–358.

Cook-Sather, A., & Shultz, J. (2001). Starting where the learner is: Listening to students. In J. Shultz & A. Cook-Sather (Eds.), *In Our Own Words: Students' Perspectives on School* (pp. 1–17). New York, NY: Rowman & Littlefield.

Cooley, V. E., & Shen, J. (2003). School accountability and professional job responsibilities: A perspective from secondary principals. *NASSP Bulletin, 87*(634), 10–25.

Cooper, J. E., Ponder, G., Merritt, S., & Matthews, C. (2005). High-performing high schools: Patterns of success. *NASSP Bulletin, 89*(645), 2–23.

Cooper, R. (1996). Detracking reform in an urban California high school: Improving the schooling experiences of African American students. *Journal of Negro Education, 65*(2), 190–208.

Cooper, R. (2000, January). Urban school reform from a student-of-color perspective. *Urban Education, 34*(5), 597–622.

Cosner, S. (2009). Building organizational capacity through trust. *Educational Administration Quarterly, 45*(2), 248–291.

Cosner, S. (2011). Supporting the initiation and early development of evidence-based grade-level collaboration in urban elementary schools: Key roles and strategies of principals and literacy coordinators. *Urban Education, 46*(4), 786–827.

Cotton, K. (1996). *School size, school climate, and student performance.* Portland, OR: Northwest Regional Educational Laboratory.

Cotton, K. (2000). *The schooling practices that matter most.* Alexandria, VA: Association for Supervision and Curriculum Development.

Cotton, K. (2003). *Principals and student achievement: What the research says.* Alexandria, VA: Association for Supervision and Curriculum Development.

Craig, C. (2009). Research in the midst of organized school reform: Versions of teacher community in tension. *American Educational Research Journal, 46*(2), 598–619.

Cranston, N., Ehrich, L. C., & Kimber, M. (2014). Managing ethical dilemmas. In C. M. Branson & S. J. Gross. (Eds.), *Handbook of ethical educational leadership* (pp. 229–245). New York, NY: Routledge.

Creemers, B. P. M., & Reezigt, G. J. (1996). School level conditions affecting the effectiveness of instruction. *School Effectiveness and School Improvement, 7*(3), 197–228.

Croninger, R., & Lee, V. (2001). Social capital and dropping out of high school: Benefits to at-risk students of teachers' support and guidance. *Teachers College Record, 103*(4), 548–581.

Crosnoe, R. (2011). *Fitting in, standing out: Navigating the social challenges of high school to get an education.* Cambridge, UK: Cambridge University Press.

Crow, G. M., & Pounder, D. G. (2000, April). Interdisciplinary teacher teams: Context, design, and process. *Educational Administration Quarterly, 36*(2), 216–254.

Crowther, F. (1997). The William Walker oration, 1996: Unsung heroes: The leaders in our classrooms. *Journal of Educational Administration, 35*(1), 5–17.

Crowther, F., Kaagan, S. S., Ferguson, M., & Hann, L. (2002). *Developing teacher leaders: How teacher leadership enhances school success.* Thousand Oaks, CA: Corwin.

Crowther, F., & Olsen, P. (1997). Teachers as leaders—an exploratory framework. *International Journal of Educational Management, 11*(1), 6–13.

Cruddas. (2001). Rehearsing for reality: Young women's voices and agendas for change. *Forum, 43*(2), 62–66.

Crum, K. S., & Sherman, W. H. (2008). Facilitating high achievement: High school principals' reflections on their successful leadership practices. *Journal of Educational Administration, 46*(5), 562–580.

Csikszentmihalyi, M., & Larson, R. (1984). *Being adolescent: Conflict and growth in the teenage years.* New York, NY: Basic Books.

Csikszentmihalyi, M., & Larson, R. (1986). *Being adolescent: Conflict and growth in the teenage years* (2nd ed.). New York, NY: Basic Books.

Cuban, L. (1988). *The managerial imperative and the practice of leadership in schools.* Albany, NY: State University of New York Press.

Curry, M. (2008). Critical friends groups: The possibilities and limitations embedded in teacher professional communities aimed at instructional improvement and school reform. *The Teachers College Record, 110*(4), 733–774.

Cusick, P. A. (1983). *The egalitarian ideal and the American high school: Studies of three schools.* New York, NY: Longman.

Dahl, K. L. (1995). Challenges in understanding the learner's perspective. *Theory Into Practice, 34*(2), 124–130.

Dahrendorf, R. (1995). A precarious balance. Economic opportunity, civil society, and political liberty. *The Responsive Community,* 13–39.

Dannetta, V. (2002). What factors influence a teacher's commitment to student learning? *Leadership and Policy in Schools, 1*(2), 144–171.

Darity, W. Jr., Castellino, D., Tyson, K., Cobb, C., & McMillen, B. (2001). *Increasing opportunity to learn via access to rigorous courses and programs: One strategy for closing the achievement gap for at-risk and ethnic minority students.* Raleigh, NC: North Carolina State Dept. of Public Instruction, Raleigh. Div. of Accountability.

Darling-Hammond, L., Ancess, J., & Ort, S. (2002). Reinventing high school: Outcomes of the coalition campus schools project. *American Educational Research Journal, 39*(3), 639–673.

Darling-Hammond, L., Bullmaster, M. L., & Cobb, V. L. (1995). Rethinking teacher leadership through professional development schools. *The Elementary School Journal, 96*(1), 87–107.

Darling-Hammond, L., & McLaughlin, M. W. (1995). Policies that support professional development in an era of reform. *Phi Delta Kappan, 76*(8), 597–604.

Darling-Hammond, L., & Post, L. (2000). Inequality in teaching and schooling: Supporting high-quality teaching and leadership in low-income schools.

In R. D. Kahlenberg (Ed.), *A notion at risk: Preserving public education as an engine of social mobility* (pp. 127–167). New York, NY: The Century Foundation Press.

Datnow, A., Borman, G. D., Stringfield, S., Overman, L. T., & Castellano, M. (2003). Comprehensive school reform in culturally and linguistically diverse contexts: Implementation and outcomes from a four-year study. *Educational Evaluation and Policy Analysis, 25*(2), 143–170.

Datnow, A., & Castellano, M. E. (2001). Managing and guiding school reform: Leadership in success for all schools. *Educational Administration Quarterly, 37*(2), 219–249.

Datnow, A., Park, V., & Kennedy, B. (2008). *Acting on data: How urban high schools use data to improve instruction.* Los Angeles, CA: Center on Educational Governance.

Dauber, S. L., & Epstein, J. L. (1993). Parents' attitudes and practices of involvement in inner-city elementary and middle schools. *Families and Schools in a Pluralistic Society,* 53–71.

Davis, H. A. (2003). Conceptualizing the role and influence of student-teacher relationships on children's social and cognitive development. *Educational Psychologist, 38*(4), 207–234.

Davis, S., Leon, R., & Fultz, M. (2013). How principals learn to learn: The comparative influence of on-the-job experiences, administrator credential programs, and the ISLLC standards in the development of leadership expertise among urban public school principals. *Version, 1*(3), 1–30.

Day, C. (2005). Sustaining success in challenging contexts: Leadership in English schools. *Journal of Educational Administration, 43*(6), 573–583.

Delgado-Gaitan, C. (1992). School matters in the Mexican-American home: Socializing children to education. *American Educational Research Journal, 29*(3), 495–513.

DeLuca, S., & Rosenblatt, P. (2010). Does moving to better neighborhoods lead to better schooling opportunities? Parental school choice in an experimental housing voucher program. *The Teachers College Record, 112*(5), 1443–1491.

Demaray, M. K., & Malecki, C. K. (2002a). The relationship between perceived social support and maladjustment for students at risk. *Psychology in the Schools, 39*(3), 305–316.

Demaray, M. K., & Malecki, C. K. (2002b). Critical levels of perceived social support associated with student adjustment. *School Psychology Quarterly, 17*(3), 213–214.

DeRidder, L. M. (1991). How suspension and expulsion contribute to dropping out. *Education Digest, 56*(6), 44–47.

Desimone, L. (2002). How can comprehensive school reform models be successfully implemented? *Review of Educational Research, 72*(3), 433–479.

Desimone, L. M., Porter, A. C., Garet, M. S., Yoon, K. S., & Birman, B. F. (2002). Effects of professional development on teachers' instruction: Results from a three-year longitudinal study. *Educational Evaluation and Policy Analysis, 24*(2), 81–112.

Dillon, D. R. (1989). Showing them that I want them to learn and that I care about who they are: A microethnography of the social organization of a secondary low-track English-reading classroom. *American Educational Research Journal, 26*(2), 227–259.

Dinham, S. (2005). Principal leadership for outstanding educational outcomes. *Journal of Educational Administration, 43*(4), 338–356.

Dinham, S., Cairney, T., Craigie, D., & Wilson, S. (1995). School climate and leadership: Research into three secondary schools. *Journal of Educational Administration, 33*(4), 36–58.

Dirks, K., & Ferrin, D. (2002). Trust in leadership: Meta-analytic findings and implications for research and practice. *Journal of Applied Psychology, 87*(4), 611–628.

Dishion, T. J., Poulin, F., & Barraston, B. (2001). Peer group dynamics associated with iatrogenic effects in group interventions with high-risk adolescents. *New Directions for Child and Adolescent Development, 2001*(91), 79–92.

Dornbusch, S. M. (1996). The structural context of family-school relations. In A. Booth & J. Dunn (Eds.), *Family-school links: How do they affect educational outcomes?* (pp. 35–44). Mahwah, NJ: Erlbaum.

Downey, D. B., von Hippel, P. T., & Broh, B. A. (2004, October). Are schools the great equalizer? Cognitive inequality during the summer months and the school year. *American Sociological Review, 69*, 613–635.

Doyle, M. (2000). *Making meaning of teacher leadership in the implementation of a standards-based mathematics curriculum.* Paper presented at the annual meeting of the American Educational Research Association, New Orleans, LA.

Drago-Severson, E. (2004). *Helping teachers learn: Principal leadership for adult growth and development.* Thousand Oaks, CA: Corwin.

Duffy-Hester, A. M. (1999). Teaching struggling readers in elementary school classrooms: A review of classroom reading programs and principles for instruction. *The Reading Teacher, 52*(5), 480–495.

DuFour, R., & Eaker, R. (1992). *Creating the new American school: A principal's guide to school improvement.* Bloomington, IN: National Education Service.

DuFour, R., & Eaker, R. (1998). *Professional learning communities at work: Best practices for enhancing student achievement.* Bloomington, IN: Association for Supervision and Curriculum Development.

Dumay, X. (2009). Origins and consequences of schools' organizational culture for student achievement. *Educational Administration Quarterly, 45*(4), 523–555.

Eccles, J. S., & Harold, R. D. (1996). Family involvement in children's and adolescents' schooling. In A. Booth & J. Dunn (Eds.), *Family-school links: How do they affect educational outcomes?* (pp. 3–34). Mahwah, NJ: Erlbaum.

Eccles-Parsons, J., Adler, T. F., Futterman, R., Goff, S. B., Kaczala, C. M., Meece, J. L., & Midgley, C. (1983). Expectancies, values, and academic behaviors. In J. T. Spence (Ed.), *Achievement and achievement motivation* (pp. 75–149). San Francisco, CA: W. H. Freeman.

Eckert, P. (1989). *Jocks and burnouts: Social categories and identity in the high school.* New York, NY: Teachers College Press.

Eder, D. (1981). Ability grouping as a self-fulfilling prophecy: A micro-analysis of teacher-student interaction. *Sociology of Education, 54*(3), 151–161.

Edmonds, R. (1978). *Search for effective schools: The identification and analysis of city schools that are instructionally effective for poor children.* Cambridge, MA: Center for Urban Studies, Harvard University.

Edmonds, R. (1979). Effective schools for the urban poor. *Educational Leadership, 37*(1), 15–24.

Edmonds, R., & Frederiksen, J. R. (1978). *Search for effective schools: The identifica-tion and analysis of city schools that are instructionally effective for poor children.* Cambridge, MA: Center for Urban Studies, Harvard University.

Eggert, L. L., Thompson, E. A., Herting, J. R., & Nicholas, L. J. (1995). Reducing suicide potential among high-risk youth: Tests of a school-based prevention program. *Suicide and Life-Threatening Behavior, 25*(2), 276–296.

Eilers, A. M., & Camacho, A. (2007). School culture change in the making: Leadership factors that matter. *Urban Education, 42*(6), 616–637.

Ellwood, C. M. (1993). Can we really look through our students' eyes? An urban teacher's perspective. *Educational Foundations, 7*(3), 63–78.

Elmore, R. F. (1995). Structural reform and educational practice. *Educational Researcher, 24*(9), 23–26.

Elshtain, J. J. (1995). *Democracy on trial.* New York, NY: Basic Books.

English, F. (2000). Psst! What does one call a set of non-empirical beliefs required to be accepted on faith and enforced by authority? [Answer: a religion, aka the ISLLC standards]. *International Journal of Leadership in Education, 3*(2), 159–167.

Ensminger, M., & Slusarcick, A. (1992). Paths to high school graduation or drop-out: A longitudinal study of a first-grade cohort. *Sociology of Education, 65*(2), 95–113.

Entwisle, D. R., Alexander, K. L., & Olson, L. S. (2000). Summer learning and home environment. In R. D. Kahlenberg (Ed.), *A notion at risk: Preserving public education as an engine for social mobility* (pp. 9–30). New York, NY: The Century Foundation Press.

Epstein, J. (1981a). Introduction and overview. In J. L. Epstein & P. W. Jackson (Eds.), *The quality of school life* (pp. 1–17). Lexington, MA: Lexington Books.

Epstein, J. (1981b). Patterns of classroom participation, student attitudes, and achievements. In J. L. Epstein & P. W. Jackson (Eds.), *The quality of school life* (pp. 81–115). Lexington, MA: Lexington Books.

Epstein, J. (1996). Perspectives and previews on research and policy for school, family, and community partnerships. In A. Booth & J. Dunn (Eds.), *Family-school links: How do they affect educational outcomes?* (pp. 209–246). Mahwah, NJ: Erlbaum.

Epstein, J., & McPartland, J. (1976). The concept and measurement of the quality of school life. *American Educational Research Journal, 13*(1), 15–30.

Erickson, D. A. (1977). An overdue paradigm shift in educational administration, or how can we get that idiot off the freeway. In L. L. Cunningham, W. G. Hack, & R. O. Nystrand (Eds.), *Educational administration: The developing decades* (pp. 114–143). Berkeley, CA: McCutchan.

Erickson, D. A. (1979). Research on educational administration: The state-of-the-art. *Educational Researcher, 8,* 9–14.

Ermeling, B. A. (2010). Tracing the effects of teacher inquiry on classroom practice. *Teaching and Teacher Education, 26*(3), 377–388.

Etheridge, C. P., Valesky, T. C., Horgan, D. D., Nunnery, J., & Smith, D. (1992). *School-based decision making: An investigation into effective and ineffective decision making processes and the impact on school climate variables.* Paper presented at the annual meeting of the American Educational Research Association, San Francisco, CA.

Evans, R. (1991). *Ministrative insight: Education administration as pedagogic practice.* Paper presented at the annual meeting of the American Educational Research Association, Chicago, IL.

Evertson, C. (1982). Differences in instructional activities in higher- and lower-achieving junior high English and math classes. *Elementary School Journal, 82*(4), 329–350.

Farkas, G. (2003). Racial disparities and discrimination in education: What do we know, how do we know it, and what do we need to know? *Teachers College Record, 105*(6), 1119–1146.

Farkas, G., Grobe, R. P., Sheehan, D., & Shuan, Y. (1990). Cultural resources and school success: Gender, ethnicity, and poverty groups within an urban school district. *American Sociological Review, 55*(1), 127–142.

Farquhar, R. (1981). Preparing educational administrators for ethical practice. *The Alberta Journal of Educational Research, 27*(2), 192–204.

Farrell, E. (1990). *Hanging in and dropping out: Voices of at-risk high school students.* New York, NY: Teachers College Press.

Fay, C. (1992). Empowerment through leadership: In the teachers' voice. In C. Livingston (Ed.), *Teachers as leaders: Evolving roles* (pp. 57–90). Washington, DC: National Education Association.

Feldlaufer, H., Midgley, C., & Eccles, J. S. (1988). Student, teacher, and observer perceptions of the classroom environment before and after the transition to junior high school. *The Journal of Early Adolescence, 8*(2), 133–156.

Feldman, A., & Matjasko, J. (2005). The role of school-based extracurricular activities in adolescent development: A comprehensive review and future directions. *Review of Educational Research, 75*(2), 159–210.

Felner, R., Seitsinger, A., Brand, S., Burns, A., & Bolton, N. (2007). Creating small learning communities: Lessons from the project on high-performing learning communities about "what works" in creating productive, developmentally enhancing, learning contexts. *Educational Psychologist, 42*(4), 209–221.

Ferguson, R. F. (1991). Racial patterns in how school and teacher quality affect achievement and earnings. *Challenge: A Journal of Research on Black Males, 2*(1), 1–35.

Ferguson, R. F. (1998). Can schools narrow the black-white test score gap? In C. Jencks and M. Phillips (Eds.), *The black-white test score gap* (pp. 318–374). Washington, DC: Brookings Institution Press.

Ferguson, R. F. (2003, July). Teachers' perceptions and expectations and the black-white test score gap. *Urban Education, 38*(4), 460–507.

Fessler, R., & Ungaretti, A. (1994). Expanding opportunities for teacher leadership. In D. R. Walling (Ed.), *Teachers as leaders: Perspectives on the professional development of teachers* (pp. 211–222). Bloomington, IN: Phi Delta Kappa.

Fine, M. (1986). Why urban adolescents drop into and out of public high school. *The Teachers College Record, 87*(3), 393–409.

Fine, M., Torre, M. E., Burns, A., & Payne, Y. A. (2007). Youth research/participatory methods for reform. In D. Thiessen & A. Cook-Sather (Eds.), *International handbook of student experience in elementary and secondary school* (pp. 805–828). New York, NY: Springer Netherlands.

Finn, J. D., & Rock, D. (1997). Academic success among students at risk for school failure. *Journal of Applied Psychology, 82*(2), 221–234.

Finnigan, K. S., & Gross, B. (2007). Do accountability policy sanctions influence teacher motivation? Lessons from Chicago's low-performing schools. *American Educational Research Journal, 44*(3), 594–630.

Firestone, W. A., & Martinez, M. C. (2007). Districts, teacher leaders, and distributed leadership: Changing instructional practice. *Leadership and Policy in Schools, 6*(1), 3–35.

Firestone, W. A., & Martinez, M. C. (2009). Districts, teacher leaders, and distributed leadership: Changing instructional practice. In K. Leithwood, B. Mascall, & T. Strauss (Eds.), *Distributed leadership according to the evidence* (pp. 61–86). London, UK: Routledge.

Firestone, W. A., & Wilson, B. L. (1985). Using bureaucratic and cultural linkages to improve instruction: The principal's contribution. *Educational Administration Quarterly, 21*(2), 7–30.

First, J. M., & Carrera, J. W. (1988). *New voices: Immigrant students in U.S. public schools.* Boston, MA: National Coalition of Advocates for Students.

Flanagan, A., & Grissmer, D. (2002). The role of federal resources in closing the achievement gap. In J. E. Chubb & T. Loveless (Eds.), *Bridging the achievement gap* (pp. 199–225). Washington, DC: Brookings Institution Press.

Flutter, J., & Rudduck, J. (2004). *Consulting pupils: What's in it for schools?* London, UK: Routledge.

Ford, D. Y., Grantham, T. C., & Whiting, G. W. (2008, March). Another look at the achievement gap: Learning from the experiences of gifted Black students. *Urban Education, 43*(2), 216–239.

Fordham, S., & Ogbu, J. U. (1986). Black students' school success: Coping with the "burden of 'acting white.'" *The Urban Review, 18*(3), 176–206.

Forster, E. M. (1997, Fall). Teacher leadership: Professional right and responsibility. *Action in Teacher Education, 19*(3), 82–94.

Forsyth, P. (1999). A brief history of scholarship on educational administration. In J. Murphy & P. Forsyth (Eds.), *Educational administration: A decade of reform* (pp. 71–92). Newbury Park, CA: Corwin.

Foster, R., & St. Hilaire, B. (2003). Leadership for school improvement: Principals' and teachers perspectives. *International Electronic Journal for Leadership in Learning, 7*(3), 1–18.

Foster, W. (1988). Educational administration: A critical appraisal. In D. E. Griffiths, R. T. Stout, & P. B. Forsyth (Eds.), *Leaders for America's schools: The report and papers of the National Commission on Excellence in Educational Administration* (pp. 68–81). Berkeley, CA: McCutchan.

Franke, M. L., Carpenter, T. P., Levi, L., & Fennema, E. (2001). Capturing teachers' generative change: A follow-up study of professional development in mathematics. *American Educational Research Journal, 38*(3), 653–689.

Franklin, C., & Streeter, C. (1995). School reform: Linking public schools with human services. *Social Work, 40*(6), 773–782.

Fredricks, J. A., Blumenfeld, P. C., & Paris, A. H. (2004). School engagement: Potential of the concept, state of the evidence. *Review of Educational Research, 74*(1), 59–109.

Freiberg, H. J., Huzinec, C. A., & Templeton, S. M. (2009). Classroom management—a pathway to student achievement: A study of fourteen inner-city elementary schools. *The Elementary School Journal, 110*(1), 63–80.

Freire, P. (1970). *Pedagogy of the oppressed* (M. B. Ramos, Trans.). New York, NY: Continuum.

Frick, W. C., Faircloth, S. C., & Little, K. S. (2013, March). Responding to the collective and individual 'Best Interests of Students': Revisiting the tension between administrative practice and ethical imperatives in special education leadership. *Educational Administration Quarterly, 49*(2), 207–242.

Friedkin, N. E., & Slater, M. R. (1994). School leadership and performance: A social network approach. *Sociology of Education, 67*(2), 139–157.

Frost, D., & Durrant, J. (2003, May). Teacher leadership: Rationale, strategy, and impact. *School Leadership & Management, 23*(2), 173–186.

Fryer, R., & Levitt, S. D. (2004, May). The black-white test score gap in the first two years of school. *Review of Economics and Statistics, 86*(2), 447–464.

Fullan, M. (1982). *The meaning of educational change.* New York, NY: Teachers College Press.

Fullan, M. (1993). *Change forces: Probing the depths of educational reform.* London, UK: Falmer.

Fullan, M. (1994). Teacher leadership: A failure to conceptualize. In D. R. Walling (Ed.), *Teachers as leaders: Perspectives on the professional development of teachers* (pp. 241–254). Bloomington, IN: Phi Delta Kappa.

Fullan, M. (2002). Leadership and sustainability. *Principal Leadership, 3*(4), 13–17.

Fullan, M., & Ballew, A. C. (2002). *Leading in a culture of change.* San Francisco, CA: Jossey-Bass.

Furman, G. C. (2004). The ethic of community. *Journal of Educational Administration, 42*, 215–235.

Furman-Brown, G. (Ed.). (2002). *School as community: From promise to practice.* New York, NY: SUNY Press.

Galletta, A., & Ayala, J. (2008). Erasure and survival: Creating a future and managing a past in a restructuring high school. *Teachers College Record, 110*(9), 1959–1985.

Gamoran, A. (1996). Effects of schooling on children and families. In A. Booth & J. Dunn (Eds.), *Family-school links: How do they affect educational outcomes?* (pp. 107–114). Mahwah, NJ: Erlbaum.

Gamoran, A. (2000). High standards: A strategy for equalizing opportunities to learn. In R. D. Kahlenberg (Ed.), *A notion at risk: Preserving public education as an engine for social mobility* (pp. 93–126). New York, NY: The Century Foundation Press.

Gandara, P., Maxwell-Jolly, J., & Driscoll, A. (2005). *Listening to teachers of English language learners: A survey of California teachers' challenges, experiences, and professional development needs.* Berkeley, CA: University of California Linguistic Minority Research Institute. Retrieved from http://escholarship.org/uc/item/6430628z

Garcia, F., Kilgore, J., Rodriguez, P., & Thomas, S. (1995). "It's like having a metal detector at the door": A conversation with students about voice. *Theory Into Practice, 34*(2), 138–144.

Gardner, P. W., Ritblatt, S. N., & Beatty, J. R. (1999). Academic achievement and parental school involvement as a function of high school size. *The High School Journal, 83*(2), 21–27.

Garet, M. S., Porter, A. C., Desimone, L., Birman, B. F., & Yoon, K. S. (2001). What makes professional development effective? Results from a national sample of teachers. *American Educational Research Journal, 38*(4), 915–945.

Garmezy, N. (1991). Resiliency and vulnerability to adverse developmental outcomes associated with poverty. *American Behavioral Scientist, 34*(4), 416–430.

Gault, A., & Murphy, J. (1987, Winter). The implications of high expectations for bilingual students. *Journal of Educational Equity and Leadership, 7*(4), 301–317.

Geijsel, F., Sleegers, P., Leithwood, K., & Jantzi, D. (2003). Transformational leadership effects on teachers' commitment and effort toward school reform. *Journal of Educational Administration, 41*(3), 228–256.

Ginsberg, A. E., Shapiro, J. P., & Brown, S. P. (2004). *Gender in urban education: Strategies for student achievement.* Portsmouth, NH: Heinemann.

Giroux, H. A. (2006). *America on the edge: Henry Giroux on politics, education and culture.* New York, NY: Palgrave Macmillan.

Goddard, H., & Goff, B. (1999). Terminal core values associated with adolescent problem behaviors. *Adolescence, 34*(133), 47–54.

Goddard, R. D. (2003). Relational networks, social trust, and norms: A social capital perspective on students' chances of academic success. *Educational Evaluation and Policy Analysis, 25*(1), 59–74.

Goddard, R. D., Hoy, W. K., & Hoy, A. W. (2000). Collective teacher efficacy: Its meaning, measure, and impact on student achievement. *American Educational Research Journal, 37*(2), 479–507.

Goddard, R. D., Salloum, S. J., & Berebitsky, D. (2009). Trust as a mediator of the relationships between poverty, racial composition, and academic achievement: Evidence from Michigan's public elementary schools. *Educational Administration Quarterly, 45*(2), 292–311.

Goldenberg, C. N. (1996). Schools, children at risk, and successful interventions. In A. Booth & J. Dunn (Eds.), *Family-school links: How do they affect educational outcomes?* (pp. 115–124). Mahwah, NJ: Erlbaum.

Goldenberg, C. N. (2004). *Successful school change: Creating settings to improve teaching and learning.* New York, NY: Teachers College Press.

Goldring, E. B., & Pasternack, R. (1994). Principals' coordinating strategies and school effectiveness. *School Effectiveness and School Improvement, 5*(3), 239–253.

Goldstein, J. (2004). Making sense of distributed leadership: The case of peer assistance and review. *Educational Evaluation and Policy Analysis, 26*(2), 173–197.

Goldstein, L. S. (1999). The relational zone: The role of caring relationships in the co-construction of mind. *American Educational Research Journal, 36*(3), 647–673.

González, R., & Padilla, A. (1997). The academic resilience of Mexican American high school students. *Hispanic Journal of Behavioral Sciences, 19*(3), 301–317.

Good, T. L., & Marshall, S. (1984). Do students learn more in heterogeneous or homogeneous groups? In P. L. Peterson, L. C. Wilkinson, & M. Hallinan (Eds.), *The social context of instruction: Group organization and group processes* (pp. 15–38). Orlando, FL: Academic Press.

Goodenow, C. (1993). Classroom belonging among early adolescent students relationships to motivation and achievement. *The Journal of Early Adolescence, 13*(1), 21–43.

Goodenow, C., & Grady, K. E. (1993). The relationship of school belonging and friends' values to academic motivation among urban adolescent students. *The Journal of Experimental Education, 62*(1), 60–71.

Goodlad, J. I. (1984). *A place called school: Prospects for the future.* New York, NY: McGraw-Hill.

Grafton, J. (Ed.). (1999). *Franklin Delano Roosevelt: Great speeches.* Mineola, NY: Dover.

Gray, J., Hopkins, D., Reynolds, D., Wilcox, B., Farrell, S., & Jesson, D. (1999). *Improving schools: Performance and potential.* Philadelphia, PA: Open University Press.

Greene, J. C., & Lee, J. H. (2006). Quieting educational reform . . . with educational reform. *American Journal of Evaluation, 27*(3), 337–352.

Greenfield, T. B. (1988). The decline and fall of science in educational administration. In D. E. Griffiths, R. T. Stout, & P. B. Forsyth (Eds.), *Leaders for America's schools: The report and papers of the National Commission on Excellence in Educational Administration* (pp. 131–159). Berkeley, CA: McCutchan.

Greenfield, W. D. (2004). Moral leadership in schools. *Journal of Educational Administration, 42*(2), 174–196.

Greenwood, G. E., & Hickman, C. W. (1991). Research and practice in parent involvement: Implications for teacher education. *The Elementary School Journal,* 279–288.

Griffin, G. A. (1995). Influences of shared decision making on school and classroom activity: Conversations with five teachers. *The Elementary School Journal, 96*(1), 29–45.

Griffith, J. (2001). Principal leadership of parent involvement. *Journal of Educational Administration, 39*(2), 162–186.

Griffiths, D. E. (1988). *Educational administration: Reform PDQ or RIP* (Occasional paper, No. 8312). Tempe, AZ: University Council for Educational Administration.

Griffiths, D. E., Stout, R. T., & Forsyth, P. B. (Eds.). (1988). *Leaders for America's schools: The report and papers of the National Commission on Excellence in Educational Administration.* Berkeley, CA: McCutchan.

Grissmer, D., Flanagan, A., & Williamson, S. (1998). Why did the black-white score gap narrow in the 1970s and 1980s? In C. Jencks & M. Phillips (Eds.), *The black-white test score gap* (pp. 182–226). Washington, DC: Brookings Institution Press.

Grissom, J., & Keiser, L. (2011). A supervisor like me: Race, representation, and the satisfaction and turnover decisions of public sector employees. *Journal of Policy Analysis and Management, 30*(3), 557–580.

Gronn, P. (2009). Hybrid leadership. In K. Leithwood, B. Mascall, & T. Strauss (Eds.), *Distributed leadership according to the evidence* (pp. 17–39). London, UK: Routledge.

Gross, S. J. (1998). *Staying centered: Curriculum leadership in a turbulent era.* Alexandria, VA: Association for Supervision and Curriculum Development.

Gross, S. J. (2000, October). *From turbulence to tidal wave: Understanding the unraveling of reform at one innovative and diverse urban elementary school for children at risk.* Paper presented at the Northeast Educational Research Association annual conference, Ellenville, New York.

Gross, S. J. (2001). Navigating a gale: Sustaining curriculum-instruction-assessment innovation in an urban high school for immigrants. *Journal of Research in Education, 11*(1), 74–87.

Gross, S. J. (2004). *Promises kept: Sustaining school and district innovation in a turbulent era.* Alexandria, VA: Association of Supervision and Curriculum Development.

Gross, S. J. (2006). *Leadership mentoring: Maintaining school improvement in turbulent times.* Lanham, MA: Rowman & Littlefield.

Gross, S. J. (2014a). Using turbulence theory to guide actions. In C. M. Branson & S. J. Gross (Eds.), *Handbook on ethical educational leadership* (pp. 246–262). New York, NY: Routledge.

Gross, S. J. (2014b, April 25–26). *Profiles in democratic ethical leadership: Educating for moral literacy through the power of exemplars.* Paper presented at the 10th Annual Moral Literacy Colloquium at Pennsylvania State University, University Park, PA.

Gross, S. J., & Shapiro, J. P. (2016). *Democratic ethical educational leadership: Reclaiming school reform.* New York, NY: Routledge.

Grossman, P., Wineburg, S., & Woolworth, S. (2001). Toward a theory of teacher community. *Teachers College Record, 103*(6), 942–1012.

Grubb, W. N., & Flessa, J. J. (2006, Oct). "A job too big for one": Multiple principals and other nontraditional approaches to school leadership. *Educational Administration Quarterly, 42*(4), 518–550.

Gryskiewicz, S. S. (1999). *Positive turbulence: Developing climates for creativity, innovation, and renewal.* San Francisco, CA: Jossey-Bass.

Guest, A., & Schneider, B. (2003). Adolescents' extracurricular participation in context: The mediating effects of schools. *Sociology of Education, 76*(2), 89–109.

Gurr, D., Drysdale, L., & Mulford, B. (2005). Successful principal leadership: Australian case studies. *Journal of Educational Administration, 43*(6), 539–551.

Gurr, D., Drysdale, L., & Mulford, B. (2006). Models of successful principal leadership. *School Leadership and Management, 26*(4), 371–395.

Guskey, T. R. (2003). Analyzing lists of the characteristics of effective professional development to promote visionary leadership. *NASSP Bulletin, 87*(637), 4–20.

Haiyan, Q., & Walker, A. (2014). Leading with empathy. In C. Branson & S. J. Gross (Eds.), *Handbook of ethical educational leadership.* New York, NY: Routledge.

Hale-Benson, J. (1990). Achieving equal educational outcomes for black children. In A. Barona & E. E. Garcia (Eds.), *Children at risk: Poverty, minority status, and other issues in educational equity* (pp. 201–215). Washington, DC: National Association of School Psychologists.

Hall, P. M. (2001). Social class, poverty, and schooling: Social contexts, educational practices and policy options. In B. J. Biddle (Ed.), *Social class, poverty, and education: Policy and practice* (pp. 213–242). New York, NY: Routledge.

Hallinan, M. T. (1984). *A place called school: Prospects for the future.* New York, NY: McGraw-Hill.

Hallinan, M. T. (2001). Sociological perspectives on black-white inequalities in American schooling. *Sociology of Education, 74*(0), 50–70.

Hallinan, M. T., & Kubitschek, W. N. (1999). Curriculum differentiation and high school achievement. *Social Psychology of Education, 3*(1), 41–62.

Hallinger, P. (1992). The evolving role of American principals. From managerial to instructional and transformational leaders. *Journal of Educational Administration, 30*(3), 94–112.

Hallinger, P. (2003). Leading educational change. Reflection on the practice of instructional and transformational leadership. *Cambridge Journal of Education, 33*(3), 329–352.

Hallinger, P., Bickman, L., & Davis, K. (1996). School context, principal leadership, and student reading achievement. *The Elementary School Journal, 96*(5), 527–549.

Hallinger, P., & Heck, R. (1996). Reassessing the principal's role in school effectiveness: A review of empirical research, 1980–1995. *Educational Administration Quarterly, 32*(1), 5–44.

Hallinger, P., & Heck, R. (1998). Exploring the principal's contribution to school effectiveness: 1980–1995. *School Effectiveness and School Improvement, 9*(2), 157–191.

Hallinger, P., & Murphy, J. (1985). Assessing the instructional management behavior of principals. *Elementary School Journal, 86*(2), 217–247.

Hallinger, P., & Murphy, J. (1986). The social context of effective schools. *American Journal of Education, 94*(3), 328–355.

Hallinger, P., & Murphy, J. (2013). Running on empty: Finding the time and capacity to lead learning. *NASSP Bulletin, 97*(1), 5–21.

Hallinger, P., Murphy, J., & Hausman, C. (1992, August). Restructuring schools: Principals' perceptions of fundamental educational reform. *Educational Administration Quarterly, 28*(3), 330–349.

Halverson, R., Grigg, J., Prichett, R., & Thomas, C. (2007). The new instructional leadership: Creating data-driven instructional systems in school. *Journal of School Leadership, 17*(2), 159–194.

Hamilton, L. S., McCaffrey, D. F., Stecher, B. M., Klein, S. P., Abby, R., & Bugliari, D. (2003). Studying large-scale reforms of instructional practice: An example from mathematics and science. *Educational Evaluation and Policy Analysis, 25*(1), 1–29.

Hamilton, S. F. (1983). The social side of schooling: Ecological studies of classrooms and schools. *The Elementary School Journal, 83*(4), 313–334.

Harris, A. (2003). Teacher leadership as distributed leadership: Heresy, fantasy or possibility? *School Leadership & Management, 23*(3), 313–324.

Harris, A. (2004). Distributed leadership and school improvement. *Educational Management Administration & Leadership, 32*(1), 11–24.

Harris, A. (2009). Distributed leadership and knowledge creation. In K. Leithwood, B. Mascall, & T. Strauss (Eds.), *Distributed leadership according to the evidence.* London, UK: Routledge.

Harris, D. N., & Herrington, C. D. (2006, February). Accountability, standards, and the growing achievement gap: Lessons from the past half-century. *American Journal of Education, 112*(2), 209–238.

Harrison, J. W., & Lembeck, E. (1996). Emergent teacher leaders. In G. Moller & M. Katzenmeyer (Eds.), *Every teacher as a leader: Realizing the potential of teacher leadership* (pp. 101–116). San Francisco, CA: Jossey-Bass.

Hart, A. W. (1990). Impacts of the school social unit on teacher authority during work redesign. *American Educational Research Journal, 27*(3), 503–532.

Hart, A. W. (1994, November). Creating teacher leadership roles. *Educational Administration Quarterly, 30*(4), 472–497.

Hart, A. W. (1995, September). Reconceiving school leadership: Emergent view. *The Elementary School Journal, 96*(1), 9–28.

Hart, R., & Baptist, B. (1996). Developing teacher leaders: A state initiative. In G. Moller & M. Katzenmeyer (Eds.), *Every teacher as a leader: Realizing the potential of teacher leadership* (pp. 85–100). San Francisco, CA: Jossey-Bass.

Harter, S. (1996). Teacher and classmate influences on scholastic motivation, self-esteem, and level of voice in adolescents. In J. Juvonen & K. Wentzel (Eds.), *Social motivation: Understanding children's school adjustment* (pp. 11–42). New York, NY: Cambridge Studies in Social and Emotional Development.

Harter, S., Waters, P. L., & Whitesell, N. R. (1997). Lack of voice as a manifestation of false self-behavior among adolescents: The school setting as a stage upon which the drama of authenticity is enacted. *Educational Psychologist, 32*(3), 153–173.

Hatfield, R. C., Blackman, C. A., & Claypool, C. (1986). *Exploring leadership roles performed by teaching in K-12 schools.* Paper presented at the annual conference of the American Association of Colleges of Teacher Education, Chicago, IL.

Hattie, J. (2009). *Visible learning: A synthesis of over 800 meta-analyses relating to achievement.* New York, NY: Routledge.

Hauser, M. E. (1997). How do we really work? A response to "Locked in uneasy sisterhood: Reflections on feminist methodology and research relationships." *Anthropology & Education Quarterly, 28*(1), 123–126.

Hawley, W. D., & Valli, L. (1999). The essentials of effective professional development: A new consensus. In L. Darling-Hammond & G. Sykes (Eds.), *Teaching as the learning profession: Handbook of policy and practice* (pp. 127–150). San Francisco, CA: Jossey-Bass.

Haycock, K. (1998). Good teaching matters: How well-qualified teachers can close the education gap. *The Education Trust, 31*(2).

Haycock, K. (2001, March). Closing the achievement gap. *Educational Leadership, 58*(6), 6–11.

Hayes, C. B., Ryan, A., & Zseller, E. B. (1994). The middle school child's perceptions of caring teachers. *American Journal of Education, 103*(1), 1–19.

Hayes, D., Christie, P., Mills, M., & Lingard, B. (2004). Productive leaders and productive leadership: Schools as learning organisations. *Journal of Educational Administration, 42*(5), 520–538.

Haynes, N. M., & Ben-Avie, M. (1996). Parents as full partners in education. In A. Booth & J. Dunn (Eds.), *Family-school links: How do they affect educational outcomes?* (pp. 45–55). Mahwah, NJ: Erlbaum.

Heck, R. H. (1992). Principals' instructional leadership and school performance: Implications for policy development. *Educational Evaluation and Policy Analysis, 14*(1), 21–34.

Heck, R. H. (2000). Examining the impact of school quality on school outcomes and improvement: A value-added approach. *Educational Administration Quarterly, 36*(4), 513–552.

Heck, R. H., & Hallinger, P. (n.d). *Assessing the contribution of principal and collaborative leadership.* Unpublished manuscript.

Heck, R. H., & Hallinger, P. (2009). Assessing the contribution of distributed leadership to school improvement and growth in math achievement. *American Educational Research Journal, 46*(3), 659–689.

Heck, R. H., & Hallinger, P. (2010). Leadership: School improvement. In P. L. Peterson, E. L. Baker, & B. McGaw (Eds.), *International Encyclopedia of Education* (3rd ed., pp. 135–142). Oxford, UK: Elsevier.

Heck, R. H., & Hallinger, P. (2014). Modeling the effects of school leadership on teaching and learning over time. *Journal of Educational Administration, 52*(5), 653–681.

Heck, R. H., & Marcoulides, G. A. (1996). School culture and performance: Testing the invariance of an organizational model. *School Effectiveness and School Improvement, 7*(1), 76–95.

Hegel, G. W. F. (1892). *The logic of Hegel.* Oxford, UK: Clarendon.

Heller, M. F., & Firestone, W. A. (1995). Who's in charge here? Sources of leadership for change in eight schools. *The Elementary School Journal, 96*(1), 65–86.

Hertert, L., & Teague, J. (2003). *Narrowing the achievement gap: A review of research, policies, and issues* [Report]. Palo Alto, CA: EdSource, Inc. (ED 473 724)

Hess, F. M. (2003, January). *A license to lead: A new leadership agenda for America's schools.* Washington, DC: Progressive Policy Institute.

Heyns, B. (1974). Social selection and stratification within schools. *American Journal of Sociology, 79*(6), 1434–1451.

Hiebert, E. H., & Pearson, P. D. (1999). *Building on the past, bridging to the future: A research agenda for the Center for the Improvement of Early Reading Achievement.* Ann Arbor, MI: University of Michigan, Center for the Improvement of Early Reading Achievement.

Hill, H. C., Rowan, B., & Ball, D. L. (2005). Effects of teachers' mathematical knowledge for teaching on student achievement. *American Educational Research Journal, 42*(2), 371–406.

Himmelstein, J. L. (1983). The new right. In R. C. Liebman & R. Wuthnow (Eds.), *The new Christian right: Mobilization and legitimization* (pp. 13–30). New York, NY: Aldine.

Hoge, D. R., Smit, E. K., & Hanson, S. L. (1990). School experiences predicting changes in self-esteem of sixth- and seventh-grade students. *Journal of Educational Psychology, 82*(1), 117–127.

The Holmes Group. (1986). *Tomorrow's teachers: A report of the Holmes Group.* East Lansing, MI: Author.

Hood, C. (1994). *Explaining economic policy reversals.* Buckingham, England: Open University Press.

Hoover-Dempsey, K. V., Walker, J. M. T., Sandler, H. M., Whetsel, D., Green, C. L., Wilkins, A. S., & Clossen, K. E. (2005). Why do parents become involved? Research findings and implications. *Elementary School Journal, 106*(2), 105–130.

Horn, I. S. (2005). Learning on the job: A situated account of teacher learning in high school mathematics departments. *Cognition and Instruction, 23*(2), 207–236.

Horn, I. S. (2010). Teaching replays, teaching rehearsals, and re-visions of practice: Learning from colleagues in a mathematics teacher community. *Teachers College Record, 112*(1), 225–259.

Howard, T. C. (2001). Telling their side of the story: African-American students' perceptions of culturally relevant teaching. *The Urban Review, 33*(2), 131–149.

Howard, T. C. (2002). Hearing footsteps in the dark: African American students' descriptions of effective teachers. *Journal of Education for Students Placed at Risk, 7*(4), 425–444.

Hoy, W., Hannum, J., & Tschannen-Moran, M. (1998). Organizational climate and student achievement: A parsimonious and longitudinal view. *Journal of School Leadership, 8*(4), 336–359.

Huberman, M., Parrish, T., Hannan, S., Arellanes, M., & Shambaugh, L. (2011). *Turnaround schools in California: Who are they and what strategies do they use?* San Francisco, CA: WestEd.

Hughes, S. (2003). An early gap in black-white mathematics achievement: Holding school and home accountable in an affluent city school district. *The Urban Review, 35*(4), 297–322.

Hulpia, H., Devos, G., & Rosseel, Y. (2009). Development and validation of scores on the distributed leadership inventory. *Educational and Psychological Measurement, 69*(6), 1013–1034.

Iatarola, P., Schwartz, A., Stiefel, L, & Chellman, C. (2008). Small schools, large districts: Small-school reform and New York City's students. *Teachers College Record, 110*(9), 1837–1878.

Ingram, D., Seashore Louis, K., & Schroeder, R. (2004). Accountability policies and teacher decision making: Barriers to the use of data to improve practice. *Teachers College Record, 106*(6), 1258–1287.

Interstate School Leaders Licensure Consortium (ISLLC). (1996). *Standards for school leaders.* Washington, DC: Council of Chief State School Officers.

Irvine, J. J. (1990). *Black students and school failure: Policies, practices, and prescriptions.* New York, NY: Greenwood.

Jackson, D. S. (2000). The school improvement journey: Perspectives on leadership. *School Leadership and Management, 20*(1), 61–78.

Jackson, Y., & Warren, J. S. (2000). Appraisal, social support, and life events: Predicting outcome behavior in school-age children. *Child Development, 71*(5), 1441–1457.

Jagers, R. J., & Carroll, G. (2002). Issues in educating African American children and youth. In S. Stringfield & D. Land (Eds.), *Educating at-risk students. 101st yearbook of the National Society for the Study of Education. Part II* (pp. 49–65). Chicago, IL: University of Chicago Press.

Jencks, C., & Phillips, M. (1998). America's next achievement test. *The American Prospect, 40*, 44–53.

Johnson, J. F., Jr., & Asera, R. (1999). *Hope for urban education: A study of nine high-performing, high-poverty, urban elementary schools.* Washington, DC: U.S. Department of Education, Planning and Evaluation Services.

Johnson, J., & Hynes, M. C. (1997, Fall). Teaching/learning/leading: Synonyms for change. *Action in Teacher Research, 19*(3), 107–119.

Johnson, L. S. (2009). School contexts and student belonging: A mixed methods study of an innovative high school. *School Community Journal, 19*(1), 99–118.

Johnson, S. M. (1989). Schoolwork and its reform. In J. Hannaway & R. Crowson (Eds.), *The politics of reforming school administration. 1989 yearbook of the Politics of Education Association* (pp. 95–112). New York, NY: Falmer Press.

Johnston, P. H., & Nicholls, J. G. (1995). Voices we want to hear and voices we don't. *Theory Into Practice, 34*(2), 94–100.

Jordan, W., & Cooper, R. (2003). High school reform and black male students: Limits and possibilities of policy and practice. *Urban Education, 38*(2), 196–216.

Joselowsky, F. (2007). Youth engagement, high school reform, and improved learning outcomes: Building systemic approaches for youth engagement. *NASSP Bulletin, 91*(3), 253–276.

Katzenmeyer, M., & Moller, G. (2001). *Awakening the sleeping giant: Helping teachers develop as leaders.* Newbury Park, CA: Corwin.

Keedy, J. L. (1999). Examining teacher instructional leadership within the small group dynamics of collegial groups. *Teaching and Teacher Education, 15*(7), 785–799.

Kelley, J. A. (1994). The National Board for Professional Teaching Standards: Toward a community of teacher leaders. In D. R. Walling (Ed.), *Teachers as leaders: Perspectives on the professional development of teachers* (pp. 299–313). Bloomington, IN: Phi Delta Kappa.

Kennedy, M. M. (2010). Attribution error and the quest for teacher quality. *Educational Researcher, 39*(8), 591–598.

Kensler, L. A. W., & Uline, C. L. (2016). The transformation of a school district from energy hog to energy star. In S. J. Gross & J. P. Shapiro (Eds.), *Democratic ethical educational leadership: Reclaiming school reform* (pp. 54–58). New York, NY: Routledge.

Kerr, K., Marsh, J., Ikemoto, G., Darilek, H., & Barney, H. (2006). Strategies to promote data use for instructional improvement actions, outcomes, and lessons from three urban districts. *American Journal of Education, 112*(4), 496–520.

Kershner, R. (1996). The meaning of "working hard" in school. In J. Rudduck, R. P. Chaplain, & G. Wallace (Eds.), *School improvement: What can pupils tell us?* (pp. 66–81). London, UK: Routledge.

Kezar, A. (2000). Pluralistic leadership: Incorporating diverse voices. *Journal of Higher Education, 71*(6), 722–743.

Kilcher, A. (1992). Becoming a change facilitator: The first-year experience of five teacher leaders. In C. Livingston (Ed.), *Teachers as leaders: Evolving roles* (pp. 91–113). Washington, DC: National Education Association.

Killion, J. P. (1996). Moving beyond the school: Teacher leaders in the district office. In G. Moller & M. Katzenmeyer (Eds.), *Every teacher as a leader: Realizing the potential of teacher leadership* (pp. 63–84). San Francisco, CA: Jossey-Bass.

King, M. (2001). Professional development to promote schoolwide inquiry. *Teaching and Teacher Education, 18*(3), 243–257.

Kirst, M., & Meister (1985). Turbulence in American secondary schools: What reforms last? *Curriculum Inquiry, 15*(2), 169–186.

Klecker, B. J., & Loadman, W. E. (1998, Spring). Defining and measuring the dimensions of teacher empowerment in restructuring public schools. *Education, 118*(3), 358–371.

Kleiner, B., & Lewis, L. (2005). *Dual enrollment of high school students at postsecondary institutions: 2002–03.* (NCES 2005–008). U.S. Department of Education. Washington, DC: National Center for Education Statistics.

Kleinfeld, J. (1975). Effective teachers of Eskimo and Indian students. *The School Review,* 301–344.

Kliebard, H. M. (1995). *The struggle for the American curriculum 1893–1958* (2nd ed.). New York, NY: Routledge.

Kober, N. (2001, April). *It takes more than testing: Closing the achievement.* A report of the Center on Education Policy. Washington, DC: The Center on Education Policy.

Kochanek, J. R. (2005). *Building trust for better schools: Research-based practices.* Thousand Oaks, CA: Corwin.

Kowalski, T. J. (1995). Preparing teachers to be leaders: Barriers in the workplace. In M. J. O'Hair & S. J. Odell (Eds.), *Educating teachers for leadership and change* (pp. 243–256). Thousand Oaks, CA: Corwin.

Krug, E. A. (1964). *The shaping of the American high school.* New York, NY: Harper & Row.

Krug, E. A. (1972). *The shaping of the American high school, 1920–1941*. Madison, WI: University of Wisconsin Press.

Kruse, S., Seashore Louis, K., & Bryk, A. (1995). An emerging framework for analyzing school-based professional community. In K. Seashore Louis & S. Kruse (Eds.), *Professionalism and community: Perspectives on reforming urban schools* (pp. 23–44). Thousand Oaks, CA: Corwin.

Kurlansky, M. (2004). *1968: The year that rocked the world*. New York, NY: Ballantine Books.

Lachat, M. A., & Smith, S. (2005). Practices that support data use in urban high schools. *Journal of Education for Students Placed at Risk, 10*(3), 333–349.

Ladson-Billings, G. (1994). *The dream keepers: Successful teachers of African American children*. San Francisco, CA: Jossey-Bass.

Laffey, J. (1982). The assessment of involvement with school work among urban high school students. *Journal of Educational Psychology, 74*(1), 62–71.

Land, D., & Legters, N. (2002). The extent and consequences of risk in U.S. education. In S. Stringfield & D. Land (Eds.), *Educating at-risk students. 101st yearbook of the National Society for the Study of Education. Part II* (pp. 1–28). Chicago, IL: University of Chicago Press.

Lareau, A. (1996). Assessing parent involvement in education. In A. Booth & J. Dunn (Eds.), *Family-school links: How do they affect educational outcomes?* (pp. 57–63). Mahwah, NJ: Erlbaum.

Larkin, R. W. (1979). *Suburban youth in cultural crisis*. New York, NY: Oxford University Press.

Learning Point Associates. (2004). *All students reaching the top: Strategies for closing academic achievement gaps*. Naperville, IL: Author.

LeBlanc, P. R., & Shelton, M. M. (1997, Fall). Teacher leadership: The needs of teachers. *Action in Teacher Education, 19*(3), 32–48.

Lee, J. (2006). *Tracking achievement gaps and assessing the impact of NCLB on the gaps: An in-depth look into national and state reading and math outcome trends*. Cambridge, MA: The Civil Rights Project at Harvard University.

Lee, P. W. (1999). In their own voices: An ethnographic study of low-achieving students within the context of school reform. *Urban Education, 34*(2), 214–244.

Lee, V. E., & Burkam, D. T. (2002). *Inequality at the starting gate. Social background differences in achievement as children begin schools*. Washington, DC: Economic Policy Institute.

Lee, V. E., & Burkam, D. T. (2003). Dropping out of high school: The role of school organization and structure. *American Educational Research Journal, 40*(2), 353–393.

Lehr, C. A., Sinclair, M. F., & Christenson, S. L. (2004). Addressing student engagement and truancy prevention during the elementary school years: A replication study of the check & connect model. *Journal of Education for Students Placed at Risk, 9*(3), 279–301.

Leithwood, K. (2005). Understanding successful principal leadership: Progress on a broken front. *Journal of Educational Administration, 43*(6), 619–629.

Leithwood, K. (2006). *Teacher working conditions that matter: Evidence for change*. Toronto, Ontario: Elementary Teachers' Federation of Ontario.

Leithwood, K. (2008). *School leadership, evidence-based decision making and large-scale student assessment*. Paper presented at International Perspectives on Student Assessment Lecture Series. University of Calgary, Alberta, Canada.

Leithwood, K., Anderson, S., Mascall, B., & Strauss, T. (2011). School leaders' influences on student learning: The four paths. In T. Bush, L. Bell, & D. Middlewood (Eds.), *The principles of educational leadership and management* (pp. 13–30). Thousand Oaks, CA: Sage.

Leithwood, K., Day, C., Sammons, P., Harris, A., & Hopkins, D. (2006). *Successful school leadership. What it is and how it influences pupil learning.* London, UK: Department of Education and Skills.

Leithwood, K., & Jantzi, D. (2000a). Principal and teacher leadership effects: A replication. *School Leadership & Management, 20*(4), 415–434.

Leithwood, K., & Jantzi, D. (2000b). The effects of transformational leadership on organizational conditions and student engagement with school. *Journal of Educational Administration, 38*(2), 112–129.

Leithwood, K., & Jantzi, D. (2005). A review of transformational school leadership research 1996–2005. *Leadership and Policy in Schools, 4*(3), 177–199.

Leithwood, K., & Jantzi, D. (2006). Transformational school leadership for large-scale reform: Effects on students, teachers, and their classroom practices. *School Effectiveness and School Improvement, 17*(2), 201–227.

Leithwood, K., Jantzi, D., & McElheron-Hopkins, C. (2006). The development and testing of a school improvement model. *School Effectiveness and School Improvement, 17*(4), 441–464.

Leithwood, K., Jantzi, D., & Steinbach, R. (1999). *Changing leadership for changing times.* Philadelphia, PA: Open University Press.

Leithwood, K., Louis, K. S., Anderson, S., & Wahlstrom, K. (2004). *Review of research: How leadership influences student learning.* New York, NY: The Wallace Foundation, Center for Applied Research and Educational Improvement and Ontario Institute for Studies in Education.

Leithwood, K., & Mascall, B. (2008). Collective leadership effects on student achievement. *Educational Administration Quarterly, 44*(4), 529–561.

Leithwood, K., & Montgomery, D. J. (1982). The role of the elementary school principal in program improvement. *Review of Educational Research, 52*(3), 309–339.

Leithwood, K., Patten, S., & Jantzi, D. (2010). Testing a conception of how school leadership influences student learning. *Educational Administration Quarterly, 46*(5), 671–706.

Leithwood, K., & Steinbach, R. (2005). Toward a second generation of school leadership standards (pp. 257–283). In P. Hallinger (Ed.), *Global trends in school leadership.* Lisse, The Netherlands: Swets and Zetlinger.

Leithwood, K., Steinbach, R., & Ryan, S. (1997). Leadership and team learning in secondary schools. *School Leadership & Management, 17*(3), 303–325.

Leitner, D. (1994). Do principals affect student outcomes?: An organizational perspective. *School Effectiveness and School Improvement, 5*(3), 219–238.

Lester, P. F. (1994). *Turbulence: A new perspective for pilots.* Englewood, CO: Jeppesen.

Levin, J. A., & Datnow, A. (2012). The principal role in data-driven decision making: Using case-study data to develop multi-mediator models of educational reform. *School Effectiveness and School Improvement, 23*(2), 179–201.

Levine, T. H., & Marcus, A. S. (2007). Closing the achievement gap through teacher collaboration: Facilitating multiple trajectories of teacher learning. *Journal of Advanced Academics, 19*(1), 116–138.

Levine, T. H., & Marcus, A. S. (2010). How the structure and focus of teachers' collaborative activities facilitate and constrain teacher learning. *Teaching and Teacher Education, 26*(3), 389–398.

Lewin, K. (1947). Frontiers in group dynamics II. *Human Relations, 1*(3), 443–453.

Lewis, A. (2008). *Add it up. Using research to improve education for low-income and minority students.* Washington, DC: Poverty and Race Research Action Council. Available from http://www.prrac.org/pubs_aiu.pdf

Lezotte, L., Hathaway, D. V., Miller, S. K., Passalacque, J., & Brookover, W. B. (1980). *School learning climate and student achievement: A social system approach to increased student learning.* Tallahassee, FL: The Site Specific Technical Assistance Center, Florida State University Foundation.

Lieberman, A. (1992). Teacher leadership: What are we learning? In C. Livingston (Ed.), *Teachers as leaders: Evolving roles* (pp. 159–165). Washington, DC: National Education Association.

Lieberman, A., & Miller, L. (1999). *Teachers—Transforming their world and their work.* New York, NY: Teachers College Press.

Lieberman, A., Saxl, E. R., & Miles, M. B. (1988). Teacher leadership: Ideology and practice. In A. Lieberman (Ed.), *Building a professional culture in schools* (pp. 148–166). New York, NY: Teachers College Press.

Lincoln, Y. S. (1995). In search of students' voices. *Theory Into Practice, 34*(2), 88–93.

Lipman, P. (1995). "Bringing out the best in them": The contribution of culturally relevant teachers to educational reform. *Theory Into Practice, 34*(3), 202–208.

Little, J. W. (1982). Norms of collegiality and experimentation: Workplace conditions of school success. *American Educational Research Journal, 19*(3), 325–340.

Little, J. W. (1985, November). Teachers as teacher advisors: The delicacy of collegial leadership. *Educational Leadership, 43*(3), 34–36.

Little, J. W. (1987). Teachers as colleagues. In V. Richardson-Koehler (Ed.), *Educators' handbook: A research perspective* (pp. 491–518). White Plains, NY: Longman.

Little, J. W. (1988). Assessing the prospects for teacher leadership. In A. Lieberman (Ed.), *Building a professional culture in schools* (pp. 78–105). New York, NY: Teachers College Press.

Little, J. W. (1995, September). Contested ground: The basis of teacher leadership in two restructuring high schools. *The Elementary School Journal, 96*(1), 47–63.

Littrell, P. C., Billingsley, B. S., & Cross, L. H. (1994). The effects of principal support on special and general educators' stress, job satisfaction, school commitment, health, and intent to stay in teaching. *Remedial and Special Education, 15*(5), 297–310.

Livingston, C. (1992). Teacher leadership for restructured schools. In C. Livingston (Ed.), *Teachers as leaders: Evolving roles* (pp. 9–17). Washington, DC: National Education Association.

Lloyd, G. (1996). Research and practical application for school, family, and community partnerships. In A. Booth & J. F. Dunn (Eds.), *Family-school links: How do they affect educational outcomes?* (pp. 276–287). Mahwah, NJ: Erlbaum.

Lodge, C. (2005). From hearing voices to engaging in dialogue: Problematising student participation in school improvement. *Journal of Educational Change, 6*(2), 125–146.

Lomotey, K. (1989). *African-American principals: School leadership and success.* New York, NY: Greenwood Press.

Lortie, D. (1975). *Schoolteacher: A sociological study.* Chicago, IL: University of Chicago Press.

Louis, K. (2007). Trust and improvement in schools. *Journal of Educational Change, 8*(1), 1–24.

Louis, K. S., & Marks, H. M. (1998). Does professional community affect the classroom? Teachers' work and student work in restructuring schools. *American Journal of Education, 106*(4), 532–575.

Louis, K. S., & Miles, M. B. (1990). *Improving the urban high school: What works and why.* New York, NY: Teachers College Press.

Louis, K. S., & Miles, M. B. (1991). Managing reform: Lessons from urban high schools. *School Effectiveness and School Improvement, 2*(2), 75–96.

Louis, K. S., Dretzke, B., & Wahlstrom, K. (2010, Sept). How does leadership affect student achievement? Results from a national U.S. survey. *School Effectiveness and School Improvement, 21*(3), 315–336.

Louis, K. S., Marks, H. M., & Kruse, S. (1996). Teachers' professional community in restructuring schools. *American Educational Research Journal, 33*(4), 757–798.

Louis, K. S., Mayrowetz, D., Smylie, M., & Murphy, J. (2009). The role of sensemaking and trust in developing teacher leadership. In A. Harris (Ed.), *Distributed leadership: Different perspectives.* New York, NY: Springer.

Lubienski, S. T. (2002, Fall). A closer look at black-white mathematics gaps: Intersection of race and SES in NAEP achievement and instructional practices data. *The Journal of Negro Education, 71*(4), 269–287.

Lucas, S. R., & Gamoran, A. (2002). Tracking and the achievement gap. In J. E. Chubb & T. Loveless (Eds.), *Bridging the achievement gap* (pp. 171–198). Washington, DC: Brookings Institution Press.

Lynch, M., & Strodl, P. (1991). *Teacher leadership: Preliminary development of a questionnaire.* Paper presented at the annual conference of the Eastern Educational Research Association, Boston, MA.

Lyons, C. A., & Pinnell, G. S. (1999). Teacher development: The best investment in literacy education. In J. S. Gaffney & B. J. Askew (Eds.), *Stirring the waters: The influence of Marie Clay* (pp. 197–220). Portsmouth, NH: Heinemann.

Ma, X. (2003). Sense of belonging to school: Can schools make a difference? *The Journal of Educational Research, 96*(6), 340–349.

Ma, X., & Klinger, D. (2000). Hierarchical linear modelling of student and school effects on academic achievement. *Canadian Journal of Education, 25*(1), 41–55.

MacBeath, J. (2005). Leadership as distributed: A matter of practice. *School Leadership and Management, 25*(4), 349–366.

MacBeath, J. (2009). Distributed leadership: Paradigms, policy, and paradox. In K. Leithwood, B. Mascall, & T. Strauss (Eds.), *Distributed leadership according to the evidence* (pp. 41–57). London, UK: Routledge.

Maehr, M. L., & Fyans, L. J., Jr. (1989). School culture, motivation, and achievement. In M. L. Maehr & C. Ames (Eds.), *Advances in motivation and achievement: Motivation enhancing environments* (Vol. 6, pp. 215–247). Greenwich, CT.

Maehr, M. L., & Midgley, C. (1996). *Transforming school cultures.* Boulder, CO: Westview Press.

Magnuson, K. A., & Duncan, G. J. (2006). The role of family socioeconomic resources in the black-white test score gap among young children. *Developmental Review, 26*(4), 365–399.

Maguin, E., & Loeber, R. (1996). Academic performance and delinquency. In M. Tonry (Ed.), *Crime and justice* (Vol. 20, pp. 145–264). Chicago, IL: University of Chicago Press.

Maher, F. A., & Tetreault, M. K. (1993). Frames of positionality: Meaningful dialogues about gender and race. *Anthropological Quarterly, 62*(3), 118–126.

Malen, B., & Rice, J. K. (2004). A framework for assessing the impact of education reforms on school capacity: Insights from studies of high-stakes accountability initiatives. *Educational Policy, 18*(5), 631–660.

Mangin, M. M. (2007). Facilitating elementary principals' support for instructional teacher leadership. *Educational Administration Quarterly, 43*(3), 319–357.

Manning, J. C. (1995). "Ariston metron." *The Reading Teacher, 48*(8), 650–659.

Manthei, J. (1992). *The mentor teacher as leader: The motives, characteristics and needs of seventy-three experienced teachers who seek a new leadership role.* Paper presented at the annual meeting of the American Educational Research Association, San Francisco, CA. (ERIC Document Reproduction Service No. ED346042)

Marks, H. M. (2000). Student engagement in instructional activity: Patterns in the elementary, middle, and high school years. *American Educational Research Journal, 37*(1), 153–184.

Marsh, H. W., & Kleitman, S. (1992). Extracurricular activities: Beneficial extension of the traditional curriculum or subversion of academic goals? *Journal of Educational Psychology, 84*(4), 553–562.

Marsh, H. W., & Kleitman, S. (2002). Extracurricular school activities: The good, the bad, and the nonlinear. *Harvard Educational Review, 72*(4), 464–515.

Marshall, C., & Gerstl-Pepin, C. (2005). *Re-framing educational politics for social justice.* Boston, MA: Allyn & Bacon.

Marshall, C., & Oliva, M. (2006). *Leadership for social justice: Making revolutions in education.* Boston, MA: Allyn & Bacon.

Marzano, R. J., Waters, T., & McNulty, B. A. (2005). *School leadership that works: From research to results.* Alexandria, VA: Association for Supervision and Curriculum Development.

May, H., & Supovitz, J. A. (2006). Capturing the cumulative effects of school reform: An 11-year study of the impacts of America's choice on student achievement. *Educational Evaluation and Policy Analysis, 28*(3), 231–257.

May, H., & Supovitz, J. A. (2011). The scope of principal efforts to improve instruction. *Educational Administration Quarterly, 47*(2), 332–352.

Mayrowetz, D., Murphy, J., Seashore-Louis, K., & Smylie, M. (2009). Conceptualizing distributed leadership as a school reform. In K. Leithwood, B. Mascall, & T. Strauss (Eds.), *Distributed leadership according to the evidence* (pp. 167–195). London, UK: Routledge.

Mayrowetz, D., & Weinstein, C. S. (1999). Sources of leadership for inclusive education: Creating schools for all children. *Educational Administration Quarterly, 35*(3), 423–449.

McCarthy, M. M., Shelton, S., & Murphy, J. (2014). Policy penetration of the ISLLC Standards. *Leadership and Policy for Schools, 14*(3).

McDougall, D., Saunders, W. M., & Goldenberg, C. (2007). Inside the black box of school reform: Explaining the how and why of change at getting results schools. *International Journal of Disability, Development and Education, 54*(1), 51–89.

McIntyre, D., Pedder, D., & Rudduck, J. (2005). Pupil voice: Comfortable and uncomfortable learnings for teachers. *Research Papers in Education, 20*(2), 149–168.

McKee, A. (1984). *Dresden 1945: The devil's tinderbox.* New York, NY: E. P. Dutton.

McKeever, B. (2003). *Nine lessons of successful school leadership teams: Distilling a decade of innovation.* San Francisco, CA: WestEd.

McLaughlin, M. (1994). Somebody knows my name. *Issues in Restructuring Schools, 1*(7), 9–11.

McLaughlin, M. W., & Talbert, J. E. (2001). *Professional communities and the work of high school teaching.* Chicago, IL: University of Chicago Press.

McLaughlin, M. W., & Yee, S. M. L. (1988). School as a place to have a career. In A. Lieberman (Ed.), *Building a professional culture in schools* (pp. 23–44). New York, NY: Teachers College Press.

McLean-Donaldson, K. B. (1994). Through students' eyes. *Multicultural Education, 2*(2), 26–28.

McMahon, S., Wernsman, J., & Rose, D. (2009). The relation of classroom environment and school belonging to academic self-efficacy among urban fourth- and fifth-grade students. *The Elementary School Journal, 109*(3), 267–281.

McQuillan, P. J. (1998). *Education opportunity in an urban, American high school.* Albany, NY: State University of New York Press.

Meehan, M. L., Cowley, K. S., Schumacher, D., Hauser, B., & Croom, N. D. M. (2003, July). *Classroom environment, instructional resources, and teaching differences in high-performing Kentucky schools with achievement gaps.* Charleston, WV: AEL.

Mendez, L. M. R., Knoff, H. M., & Ferron, J. M. (2002). School demographic variables and out-of-school suspension rates: A quantitative and qualitative analysis of a large, ethnically diverse school district. *Psychology in the Schools, 39*(3), 259–277.

Mergendoller, J. R., & Packer, M. J. (1985). Seventh graders' conceptions of teachers: An interpretive analysis. *The Elementary School Journal, 84*(5), 581–600.

Meyer, J. W., & Rowan, B. (1975). *Notes on the structure of educational organizations: Revised version.* Paper presented at the annual meeting of the American Sociological Association, San Francisco, CA.

Mickelson, R. A. (2003). When are racial disparities in education the result of racial discrimination? A social science perspective. *Teachers College Record, 105*(6), 1052–1086.

Mickelson, R. A., & Heath, D. (1999). The effects of segregation and tracking on African American high school seniors' academic achievement. *Journal of Negro Education, 68*(4), 566–586.

Midgley, C., Feldlaufer, H., & Eccles, J. S. (1989). Student/teacher relations and attitudes toward mathematics before and after the transition to junior high school. *Child Development, 60*(4), 981–992.

Miller, L. S. (1995). *An American imperative: Accelerating minority educational advancement.* New York, NY: Minority Education, Teachers College, Columbia University. (ED 315 485).

Miron, L. F., & Lauria, M. (1998). Student voice as agency: Resistance and accommodation in inner-city schools. *Anthropology & Education Quarterly, 29*(2), 189–213.

Mitchell, A. (1997, Fall). Teacher identity: A key to increased collaboration. *Action in Teacher Education, 19*(3), 1–14.

Mitchell, C., & Castle, J. B. (2005). The instructional role of elementary school principals. *Canadian Journal of Education/Revue Canadienne de l'education, 28*(3), 409–433.

Mitchell, C., & Sackney, L. (2006). Building schools, building people: The school principal's role in leading a learning community. *Journal of School Leadership, 16*(5), 627–640.

Mitra, D. L., & Gross, S. J. (2009). Increasing student voice in high school reform: Building partnerships, improving outcomes. *Educational Management Administration & Leadership, 37*(4), 522–543.

Moles, O. (1996). New directions in research and policy. In A. Booth & J. Dunn (Eds.), *Family-school links: How do they affect educational outcomes?* (pp. 247–254). Mahwah, NJ: Erlbaum.

Moller, G., & Katzenmeyer, M. (1996). The promise of teacher leadership. In G. Moller & M. Katzenmeyer (Eds.), *Every teacher as a leader: Realizing the potential of teacher leadership* (pp. 1–18). San Francisco, CA: Jossey-Bass.

Moller, J., & Eggen, A. B. (2005). Team leadership in upper secondary education. *School leadership and management, 25*(4), 331–347.

Moos, R. H. (1978). A typology of junior high and high school classrooms. *American Educational Research Journal, 15*(1), 53–66.

Moos, R. H. (1979). *Evaluating educational environments.* San Francisco, CA: Jossey-Bass.

Morrissey, M. S. (2000). *Professional learning communities: An ongoing exploration.* Austin, TX: Southwest Educational Development Laboratory.

Mukuria, G. (2002). Disciplinary challenges. *Urban Education, 37*(3), 432–452.

Mulford, B., & Silins, H. (2003). Leadership for organisational learning and improved student outcomes—what do we know. *Cambridge Journal of Education, 33*(2), 175–195.

Mullen, C. A., & Hutinger, J. L. (2008). The principal's role in fostering collaborative learning communities through faculty study group development. *Theory Into Practice, 47*(4), 276–285.

Muller, C., Katz, S. R., & Dance, L. J. (1999). Investing in teaching and learning dynamics of the teacher-student relationship from each actor's perspective. *Urban Education, 34*(3), 292–337.

Munoz, M., Ross, S., & McDonald, A. (2007). Comprehensive school reform in middle schools: The effects of different ways of knowing on student achievement in a large urban district. *Journal for Students Placed at Risk, 12*(2), 167–183.

Murdock, T. B., Anderman, L. H., & Hodge, S. A. (2000). Middle-grade predictors of students' motivation and behavior in high school. *Journal of Adolescent Research, 15*(3), 327–351.

Murnane, R. J., & Levy, F. (1996). *Teaching the new basic skills: Principles for educating children to thrive in a changing economy.* New York, NY: The Free Press.

Murphy, J. (1989). Educational reform in the 1980s: Explaining some surprising success. *Educational Evaluation and Policy Analysis, 11*(3), 209–223.

Murphy, J. (1990a). Principal instructional leadership. In L. S. Lotto & P. W. Thurston (Eds.), *Advances in educational administration: Changing perspectives on the school.* (Volume 1, Part B). Greenwich, CT: JAI Press.

Murphy, J. (1990b, April-June). Improving the preparation of school administrators: The National Policy Board's story. *The Journal of Educational Policy, 5*(2), 181–186.

Murphy, J. (1991). *Restructuring schools: Capturing and assessing the phenomena.* New York, NY: Teachers College Press.

Murphy, J. (1992a). *The landscape of leadership preparation: Reframing the education of school administrators.* Newbury Park, CA: Corwin.

Murphy, J. (1992b). School effectiveness and school restructuring: Contributions to educational improvement. *School Effectiveness and School Improvement, 3*(2), 90–109.

Murphy, J. (1996). *The privatization of schooling: Problems and possibilities.* Thousand Oaks, CA: Corwin.

Murphy, J. (1999). New consumerism: The emergence of market-oriented governing structures for schools. In J. Murphy & K. S. Louis (Eds.), *The handbook of research on school administration.* San Francisco, CA: Jossey-Bass.

Murphy, J. (1999a). *The quest for a center: Notes on the state of the profession of educational leadership.* Columbia, MO: University Council for Educational Administration.

Murphy, J. (1999b). Changes in preparation programs: Perceptions of department chairs. In J. Murphy & P. Forsyth (Eds.), *Educational administration: A decade of reform.* Thousand Oaks, CA: Corwin.

Murphy, J. (2000, February). Governing America's schools: The shifting playing field. *Teachers College Record, 102*(1), 57–84.

Murphy, J. (2002, April). Reculturing the profession of educational leadership: New blueprints. *Educational Administration Quarterly, 38*(3), 176–191.

Murphy, J. (2005a). *Connecting teacher leadership and school improvement.* Thousand Oaks, CA: Corwin.

Murphy, J. (2005b, February). Uncovering the foundations of the ISLLC Standards and addressing concerns in the academic community. *Educational Administration Quarterly, 41*(1), 154–191.

Murphy, J. (2006, December). The evolving nature of the American high school: A punctuated equilibrium model of institutional change. *Leadership and Policy in Schools, 5*(4), 1–39, 285–324.

Murphy, J. (2010). *The educator's handbook for understanding and closing achievement gaps.* Thousand Oaks, CA: Corwin Press.

Murphy, J. (2012). *Homeschooling in America.* Thousand Oaks, CA: Corwin.

Murphy, J. (2013). The architecture of school improvement. *Journal of Educational Administration, 51*(3), 252–263.

Murphy, J. (2015a). *Creating instructional capacity.* Thousand Oaks, CA: Corwin.

Murphy, J. (2015b). *Leading school improvement: A framework for action.* West Palm Beach, FL: Learning Sciences International.

Murphy, J. (2016). *Understanding schooling through the eyes of students.* Thousand Oaks, CA: Corwin Press.

Murphy, J. (in press). *Creating instructional capacity.* Thousand Oaks, CA: Corwin.

Murphy, J., & Beck, L. G. (1995, Fall). School-based management: Taking stock. *Kappa Delta Pi Record, 32*(1), 6–10.

Murphy, J., Beck, L. G., Crawford, M., & Hodges, A. (2001). *The productive high school: Creating personalized academic communities.* Thousand Oaks, CA: Corwin.

Murphy, J., & Datnow, A. (2003a). Leadership lessons from comprehensive school reform designs. In J. Murphy & A. Datnow (Eds.), *Leadership for comprehensive school reform*. Thousand Oaks, CA: Corwin.

Murphy, J., & Datnow, A. (2003b). Tracing the development of comprehensive school reform designs. In J. Murphy & A. Datnow (Eds.), *Leadership for comprehensive school reform*. Thousand Oaks, CA: Corwin.

Murphy, J., Elliott, S. N., Goldring, E., & Porter A. (2007, April). Leadership for learning: A research-based model and taxonomy of behaviors. *School Leadership & Management, 27*(2), 179–201.

Murphy, J., & Hallinger, P. (1989, September). A new era in the professional development of school administrators: Lessons from emerging programs. *Journal of Educational Administration, 27*(2), 22–45.

Murphy, J., Hallinger, P., & Lotto, L. S. (1986, November-December). Inequitable allocations of alterable learning variables in schools and classrooms. *Journal of Teacher Education, 37*(6), 21–26.

Murphy, J., Hallinger, P., & Mesa, R. P. (1985, Summer). School effectiveness: Checking progress and assumptions and developing a role for state and federal government. *Teachers College Record, 86*(4), 615–641.

Murphy, J., Hallinger, P., Weil, M., & Mitman, A. (1983, Fall). Problems with research on educational leadership: Issues to be addressed. *Educational Evaluation and Policy Analysis, 5*(3), 297–305.

Murphy, J., Hull, T., & Walker, A. (1987, July-August). Academic drift and curricular debris: An analysis of high school course-taking patterns with implications for local policy makers. *Journal of Curriculum Studies, 19*(4), 341–360.

Murphy, J., & Shipman, N. J. (2003). Developing standards for school leadership development: A process. In P. Hallinger (Ed.), *The changing landscape of educational leadership development: A global perspective*. Lisse, The Netherlands: Swets and Zetlinger.

Murphy, J., Smylie, M., Mayrowetz, D., & Louis, K. S. (2009, April). The role of the principal in fostering the development of distributed leadership. *School Leadership & Management, 29*(2), 181–214.

Murphy, J., & Tobin, K. (2011a). *Homelessness comes to school*. Thousand Oaks, CA: Corwin.

Murphy, J., & Tobin, K. (2011b, November). Homelessness comes to school: Homeless children and youth can succeed. *Phi Delta Kappan, 92*(3).

Murphy, J., & Torre, D. (2014). *Creating productive cultures in schools: For students, teachers, and parents*. Thousand Oaks, CA: Corwin.

Murphy, J., Weil, M., & McGreal, T. L. (1986, September). The basic practice model of instruction. *Elementary School Journal, 87*(1), 83–95.

Murphy, J., Weil, M., Hallinger, P., & Mitman, A. (1982, December). Academic press: Translating high expectations into school policies and classroom practices. *Educational Leadership, 40*(3), 22–26.

Murphy, J., Weil, M., Hallinger, P., & Mitman, A. (1985, Spring). School effectiveness: A conceptual framework. *The Educational Forum, 49*(3), 361–374.

Murphy, J., Yff, J., & Shipman, N. J. (2000, January-March). Implementation of the Interstate School Leaders Licensure Consortium standards. *The International Journal of Leadership in Education, 3*(1), 17–39.

Murtadha, K. (2009). Notes from the (battle) field for equity in education. *Leadership and Policy in Schools, 8*(3), 342–354.

Myers, S. L. Jr., Kim, H., & Mandala, C. (2004, Winter). The effect of school poverty on racial groups in test scores: The case of the Minnesota Basic Standards Tests. *The Journal of Negro Education, 73*(1), 82–98.

National Center on Education and the Economy. (2006). *Tough choices or tough times: The report on the New Commission on the Skills of the American Workforce.* San Francisco, CA: Jossey-Bass.

National Commission for the Principalship. (1990). *Principals for our changing schools: Preparation and certification.* Fairfax, VA: Author.

National Commission for the Principalship. (1993). *Principals for our changing schools: The knowledge and skill base.* Fairfax, VA: Author.

National Policy Board for Educational Administration (NPBEA). (1996). *Educational leadership policy standards: ISLLC 1996.* Washington, DC: Council of Chief State School Officers.

National Policy Board for Educational Administration (NPBEA). (2008). *Educational leadership policy standards: ISLLC 2008.* Washington, DC: Council of Chief State School Officers.

National Policy Board for Educational Administration (NPBEA). (2015). *Professional standards for educational leaders 2015.* Reston, VA: Author.

Natriello, G., McDill, E. L., & Pallas, A. M. (1990). *Schooling disadvantaged children: Racing against catastrophe.* New York, NY: Teachers College Press.

Nelson, B. S., & Sassi, A. (2005). *The effective principal: Institutional leadership in high quality learning.* New York, NY: Teachers College Press.

Neuman, S. B., & Celano, D. (2006, April-June). The knowledge gap: Implications of leveling the playing field for low-income and middle-income children. *Reading Research Quarterly, 41*(2), 176–201.

Newmann, F. M. (1981). Reducing student alienation in high schools: Implications of theory. *Harvard Educational Review, 51*(4), 546–564.

Newmann, F. M. (1989). Student engagement and high school reform. *Educational Leadership, 46*(5), 34–36.

Newmann, F. M. (1992). Conclusion. In F. M. Newmann (Ed.), *Student engagement and achievement in American secondary schools* (pp. 182–217). New York, NY: Teachers College Record.

Newmann, F. M., & Wehlage, G. G. (1994). From knowledge to understanding. In *Issues in restructuring schools* (Issue report No. 7, pp. 15–16). Madison: University of Wisconsin-Madison, Center on Organization and Restructuring of Schools.

Newmann, F. M., & Wehlage, G. G. (1995). *Successful school restructuring.* Madison: University of Wisconsin-Madison, Center of Organization and Restructuring of Schools.

Newmann, F. M., King, M. B., & Youngs, P. (2000). Professional development that addresses school capacity: Lessons from urban elementary schools. *American Journal of Education, 108*(4), 259–299.

Newmann, F. M., Rutter, R. A., & Smith, M. S. (1989). Organizational factors that affect school sense of efficacy, community, and expectations. *Sociology of Education, 62*(4), 221–238.

Newmann, F. M., Smith, B., Allensworth, E., & Bryk, A. S. (2001). Instructional program coherence: What it is and why it should guide school improvement policy. *Educational Evaluation and Policy Analysis, 23*(4), 297–321.

Newmann, F. M., Wehlage, G. G., & Lamburn, S. D. (1992). The significance and sources of student engagement. In F. M. Newmann (Ed.), *Student engagement and achievement in American secondary schools* (pp. 11–39). New York, NY: Teachers College Press.

Nichols, J. D., Ludwin, W. G., & Iadicola, P. (1999). A darker shade of gray: A year-end analysis of discipline and suspension data. *Equity & Excellence in Education, 32*(1), 43–54.

Nieto, S. (1994). Lessons from students on creating a chance to dream. *Harvard Educational Review, 64*(4), 392–427.

Noddings, N. (1988). An ethic of caring and its implications for instructional arrangements. *American Journal of Education, 96*(2), 215–230.

Noddings, N. (1992). *The challenge to care in schools: An alternative approach to education.* New York, NY: Teachers College Press.

Noddings, N. (2003). *Caring: A feminine approach to ethics and moral education* (2nd ed.). Berkeley, CA: University of California Press.

Noguera, P. (1996). Responding to the crisis confronting California's black male youth: Providing support without furthering marginalization. *The Journal of Negro Education, 65*(2), 219–236.

Nolen, S. B., & Nicholls, J. G. (1993). Elementary school pupils' beliefs about practices for motivating pupils in mathematics. *British Journal of Educational Psychology, 63*(3), 414–430.

Norman, O., Ault, C. R. Jr., Bentz, B., & Meskimen, L. (2001). The black-white "achievement gap" as a perennial challenge for urban science education: A sociocultural and historical overview with implications for research and practice. *Journal of Research in Science Teaching, 38*(10), 1101–1114.

Normore, A. H. (2004). Ethics and values in leadership preparation programs: Finding the North Star in the dust storm. *Values and Ethics in Educational Administration, 2*(2), 1–8.

Nye, B., Konstantopoulos, S., & Hedges, L. V. (2004). How large are teacher effects? *Educational Evaluation and Policy Analysis, 26*(3), 237–257.

Nystrand, M. (1997). *Operating dialogue: Understanding the dynamics of language and learning in the English classroom.* New York, NY: Teachers College Press.

O'Connor, C. (1997). Dispositions toward (collective) struggle and educational resilience in the inner city: A case analysis of six African-American high school students. *American Educational Research Journal, 34*(4), 593–629.

O'Donnell, R. J., & White, G. P. (2005). Within the accountability era: Principals' instructional leadership behaviors and student achievement. *NASSP Bulletin, 89*(645), 56–71.

Oakes, J. (1985). *Keeping track: How schools structure inequality.* New Haven, CT: Yale University Press.

Oakes, J., & Guiton, G. (1995). Matchmaking: The dynamics of high school tracking decisions. *American Educational Research Journal, 32*(1), 3–33.

Odell, S. J. (1997, Fall). Preparing teachers for teacher leadership. *Action in Teacher Education, 19*(3), 120–124.

Ogden, E. H., & Germinario, V. (1995). *The nation's best schools: Blueprints for excellence.* Lancaster, PA: Technomic.

O'Hair, M. J., & Reitzug, W. C. (1997). Teacher leadership: In what ways? For what purpose? *Action in Teacher Education, 19*(3), 65–76.

Oldfather, P., West, J., White, J., & Wilmarth, J. (1999). *Learning through children's eyes: Social constructivism and the desire to learn.* Washington, DC: American Psychological Association.

Olivier, D., & Hipp, K. K. (2006). Leadership capacity and collective efficacy: Interacting to sustain student learning in a professional learning community. *Journal of School Leadership, 16*(5), 505–519.

O'Loughlin, M. (1995). Daring the imagination: Unlocking voices of dissent and possibility in teaching. *Theory Into Practice, 34*(2), 107–116.

Opdenakker, M., Maulana, R., & Brock, P. (2012). Teacher-student interpersonal relationships and academic motivation within one school year: Developmental changes and linkage. *School Effectiveness and School Improvement, 21*(1), 95–199.

Orr, M. T., Berg, B., Shore, R., & Meier, E. (2008). Putting the pieces together: Leadership for change in low-performing urban schools. *Education and Urban Society, 40*(6), 670–693.

Osterman, K. F. (2000). Students' need for belonging in the school community. *Review of Educational Research, 70*(3), 323–367.

Owen, S. (2003). School-based professional development: Building morale, professionalism and productive teacher learning practices. *The Journal of Educational Enquiry, 4*(2), 102–128.

Padron, Y. N., Waxman, H. C., & Rivera, H. H. (2002). Issues in educating Hispanic students. In S. Stringfield & D. Land (Eds.), *Educating at-risk students. 101st yearbook of the National Society for the Study of Education. Part II* (pp. 66–88). Chicago, IL: University of Chicago Press.

Page, R. N. (1984). *Lower-track classes at a college-preparatory high school: A caricature of educational encounters.* Paper presented at the annual meeting of the American Educational Research Association, New Orleans, Louisiana.

Page, R. N. (1991). *Lower track classrooms: A curriculum and cultural perspective.* New York, NY: Teachers College Press.

Palincsar, A., Magnusson, S., Marano, N., Ford, D., & Brown, N. (1998). Designing a community of practice: Principles and practices of the GIsML (Guided Inquiry supporting Multiple Literacies) community. *Teaching and Teacher Education, 14*(1), 5–19.

Patterson, N., Beltyukova, S., Berman, K., & Francis, A. (2007). The making of sophomores: Student, parent, and teacher reactions in the context of systemic urban high school reform. *Urban Education, 42*(2), 124–144.

Patty, D., Maschoff, J. D., & Ranson, P. E. (1996). *The reading resource handbook for school leaders.* Norwood, MA: Christopher-Gordon.

Peng, S. S., Wright, D., & Hill, S. T. (1995). *Understanding racial-ethnic differences in secondary school science and mathematics achievement.* (NCES 95–710). Washington, DC: U.S. Department of Education.

Penna, A. A., & Tallerico, M. (2005). Grade retention and school completion: Through students' eyes. *Journal of At-Risk Issues, 11*(1), 13–17.

Penuel, W. R., Fishman, B. J., Yamaguchi, R., & Gallagher, L. P. (2007). What makes professional development effective? Strategies that foster curriculum implementation. *American Educational Research Journal, 44*(4), 921–958.

Penuel, W. R., Frank, K. A., & Krause, A. (2006). The distribution of resources and expertise and the implementation of schoolwide reform initiatives. In S. A. Barab, K. E. Hay, & D. T. Hickey (Eds.), *Proceedings of the 7th International Conference of the Learning Sciences* (Vol. 1, pp. 522–528). Mahwah, NJ: Erlbaum.

Penuel, W. R., Riel, M., Joshi, A., Pearlman, L., Kim, C. M., & Frank, K. A. (2010). The alignment of the informal and formal organizational supports for reform:

Implications for improving teaching in schools. *Educational Administration Quarterly, 46*(1), 57–95.

Penuel, W., Riel, M., Krause, A., & Frank, K. (2009). Analyzing teachers' professional interactions in a school as social capital: A social network approach. *The Teachers College Record, 111*(1), 124–163.

Peterson, E. R., & Irving, S. L. (2008). Secondary school students' conceptions of assessment and feedback. *Learning and Instruction, 18*(3), 238–250.

Phelan, P., Davidson, A. L., & Cao, H. T. (1992). Speaking up: Students' perspectives on school. *The Phi Delta Kappan, 73*(9), 695–704.

Phillips, J. (2003). Powerful learning: Creating learning communities in urban school reform. *Journal of Curriculum and Supervision, 18*(3), 240–258.

Pinnell, G. S., Lyons, C. A., DeFord, D. E., Bryk, A. S., & Seltzer, M. (1994). Comparing instructional models for the literacy education of high-risk first graders. *Reading Research Quarterly, 29*(1), 9–39.

Pintrich, P. R. (2003). A motivational science perspective on the role of student motivation in learning and teaching contexts. *Journal of Educational Psychology, 95*(4), 667.

Pintrich, P. R., & De Groot, E. V. (1990). Motivational and self-regulated learning components of classroom academic performance. *Journal of Educational Psychology, 82*(1), 33–40.

Poplin, M. S., & Weeres, J. G. (1994). *Voices from the inside: A report on schooling from inside the classroom.* Claremont, CA: Institute for Education in Transformation, Claremont Graduate School.

Portelli, J. P. (Ed.). (2007, Spring-Summer). Critical democracy and educational leadership issues: Philosophical responses to the neoliberal agenda. *Journal of Thought, 42*(1), Special Issue.

Porter, A. C., Garet, M. S., Desimone, L. M., & Birman, B. F. (2003). Providing effective professional development: Lessons from the Eisenhower Program. *Science Educator, 12*(1), 23–40.

Pounder, D. G. (1999). Teacher teams: Exploring job characteristics and work-related outcomes of work group enhancement. *Educational Administration Quarterly, 35*(3), 317–348.

Powell, A. G., Farrar, E., & Cohen, D. K. (1985). *The shopping mall high school: Winners and losers in the educational marketplace.* Boston, MA: Houston Mifflin.

Powell, D. R. (1991). How schools support families: Critical policy tensions. *The Elementary School Journal, 91*(3), 307–319.

Preston, C., Goldring, E., Guthrie, J. E., & Ramsey, R. (2012). *Conceptualizing essential components of effective high schools.* Paper presented at the Achieving Success at Scale: Research on Effective High Schools Conference. Nashville, TN.

Printy, S. M. (2008). Leadership for teacher learning: A community of practice perspective. *Educational Administration Quarterly, 44*(2), 187–226.

Purkey, S. D., & Smith, M. S. (1983, March). Effective schools: A review. *Elementary School Journal, 83*(4), 427–452.

Quint, J. (2006). *Meeting five critical challenges of high school reform: Lessons from research on three reform models.* New York, NY: Manpower Demonstration Research Corporation.

Quiroz, P. A. (2001). The silencing of Latino student "voice": Puerto Rican and Mexican narratives in eighth grade and high school. *Anthropology & Education Quarterly, 32*(3), 326–349.

Raudenbush, S. W., Fotiu, R. P., & Cheong, Y. F. (1998). Inequality of access to educational opportunity: A national report card for eighth-grade math. *Educational Evaluation and Policy Analysis, 20*(4), 253–267.

Raywid, M. (1995). Professional community and its yield at Metro Academy. In K. S. Louis & S. Kruse (Eds.), *Professionalism and community: Perspectives on reforming urban schools* (pp. 43–75). Thousand Oaks, CA: Corwin.

Reeves, J. K. (1982). *Loose-coupling and elementary school social composition: The organizational copout in ghetto education.* Unpublished manuscript.

Reitzug, U. C., & O'Hair, M. J. (2002). From conventional school to democratic school community: The dilemmas of teaching and leading. In G. Furman-Brown (Ed.), *School as community: From promise to practice* (pp. 119–141). New York, NY: State University of New York Press.

Reitzug, U. C., & Patterson, J. (1998). I'm not going to lose you! Empowerment through caring in an urban principal's practice with students. *Urban Education, 33*(2), 150–181.

Reynolds, G. M. (2002). *Identifying and eliminating the achievement gaps and in-school and out-of-school factors that contribute to the gaps.* Naperville, IL: North Central Regional Educational Laboratory.

Riehl, C., & Sipple, J. (1996). Making the most of time and talent: Secondary school organizational climates, teaching task environments, and teacher commitment. *American Educational Research Journal, 33*(4), 873–901.

Riester, A. F., Pursch, V., & Skria, L. (2002). Principals for social justice: Leaders of school success for children from low-income homes. *Journal of School Leadership, 12*(3), 281–304.

Riley, K., & Docking, J. (2004). Voices of disaffected pupils: Implications for policy and practice. *British Journal of Educational Studies, 52*(2), 166–179.

Robinson, V. M. J. (2007). *School leadership and student outcomes: Identifying what works and why.* Sydney, NSW: Australian Council for Educational Leaders.

Robinson, V. M. J. (2008). Forging the links between distributed leadership and educational outcomes. *Journal of Educational Administration, 46*(2), 241–256.

Robinson, V. M. J., Lloyd, C. A., & Rowe, K. J. (2008). The impact of leadership on student outcomes: An analysis of the differential effects of leadership types. *Educational Administration Quarterly, 44*(5), 635–674.

Rodríguez, L. (2008). Teachers know you can do more: Understanding how school cultures of success affect urban high school students. *Educational Policy, 22*(5), 758–780.

Roeser, R. W., Eccles, J. S., & Sameroff, A. J. (2000). School as a context of early adolescents' academic and social-emotional development: A summary of research findings. *The Elementary School Journal, 100*(5), 443–471.

Rogers, D. L. (1994). Conceptions of caring in a fourth-grade classroom. In A. R. Prillamen, D. J. Eaker, & D. M. Kendrick (Eds.), *A tapestry of caring* (pp. 33–47). Norwood, NJ: Ablex.

Roney, K., Coleman, H., & Schlichting, K. A. (2007). Linking the organizational health of middle grades schools to student achievement. *NASSP Bulletin, 91*(4), 289–321.

Roscigno, V. J. (1998, March). Race and the reproduction of educational disadvantage. *Social Forces, 76*(3), 1033–1061.

Roscigno, V. J. (1999). The black-white achievement gap, family-school links, and the importance of place. *Sociological Inquiry, 69*(2), 159–186.

Rosenbaum, J. E. (1980). Social implications of educational grouping. In D. C. Berliner (Ed.), *Review of research in education* (Vol. 8, pp. 361–401). Washington, DC: American Educational Research Association.

Ross, S., Sterbinsky, A., & McDonald, A. (2003). *School variables as determinants of the success of comprehensive school reform: A quantitative study of 69 inner-city schools.* Paper presented to American Educational Research Association, Chicago, IL.

Rossmiller, R. A. (1992). The secondary school principal and teachers' quality of work life. *Educational Management Administration & Leadership, 20*(3), 132–146.

Roth, J. L., & Brooks-Gunn, J. (2003). Youth development programs: Risk, prevention and policy. *Journal of Adolescent Health, 32*(3), 170–182.

Roth, J. L., Brooks-Gunn, J., Murray, L., & Foster, W. (1998). Promoting healthy adolescents: Synthesis of youth development program evaluations. *Journal of Research on Adolescence, 8*(4), 423–459.

Rothman, H. R., & Cosden, M. (1995). The relationship between self-perception of a learning disability and achievement, self-concept and social support. *Learning Disability Quarterly, 18*(3), 203–212.

Rowan, B., & Miller, R. J. (2007). Organizational strategies for promoting instructional change: Implementation dynamics in schools working with comprehensive school reform providers. *American Educational Research Journal, 44*(2), 252–297.

Rowe, K. J. (1995). Factors affecting students' progress in reading: Key findings from a longitudinal study. *Literacy, Teaching and Learning, 1*(2), 57–110.

Rowley, J. (1988, May/June). The teacher as leader and teacher educator. *Journal of Teacher Education, 39*(3), 13–16.

Rudduck, J., & Flutter, J. (2004). *How to improve your school.* London, UK: Continuum International.

Rudduck, J., Chaplain, R., & Wallace, G. (1996). *School improvement: What can pupils tell us?* (pp. 17–27). London, UK: Routledge.

Rumberger, R. (2011). *Dropping out: Why students drop out of high school and what can be done about it.* Cambridge, MA: Harvard University Press.

Rumberger, R. W., & Gandara, P. (2004). Seeking equity in the education of California's English learners. *Teachers College Record, 106*(10), 2032–2056.

Rumberger, R., & Palardy, G. (2005). Does segregation still matter? The impact of student composition on academic achievement in high school. *Teachers College Record, 107*(9), 1999–2045.

Russell, J. S., Mazzarelli, J. A., White, T., & Maurer, S. (1985). *Linking the behaviors and activities of secondary school principals to school effectiveness: A focus on effective and ineffective behaviors.* Eugene, OR: University of Oregon, Center for Educational Policy and Management.

Rutherford, W. L. (1985). School principals as effective leaders. *Phi Delta Kappan, 671*), 31–34.

Rutter, M. (1983, February). School effects on pupil progress: Research findings and policy implications. *Child Development, 54*(1), 1–29.

Rutter, M., Maughan, B., Mortimore, P., & Ouston, J. (1979). *Fifteen thousand hours: Secondary schools and their effects on children.* Cambridge, MA: Harvard University Press.

Sadker, M., & Sadker, D. (1994). *Failing at fairness: How America's schools cheat girls.* New York, NY: Scribner.

Sagor, R. (1996). Building resiliency in students. *Educational Leadership, 54,* 38–43.

Samuels. S. J. (1981). Characteristics of exemplary reading programs. In J. T. Guthrie (Ed.), *Comprehension and teaching: Research review* (pp. 255–273). Newark, DE: International Reading Association.

Sanders, M. G., & Harvey, A. (2002). Beyond the school walls: A case study of principal leadership for school-community collaboration. *Teachers College Record, 104*(7), 1345–1368.

Sanon, F., Baxter, M., & Opotow, S. (2001). Cutting class: Perspectives of urban high school students. In J. J. Shultz & A. Cook-Sather (Eds.), *In our own words: Students' perspectives on school* (pp. 73–92). New York, NY: Rowman & Littlefield.

Sarason, S. B. (1990). *The predictable failure of educational reform: Can we change course before it's too late?* San Francisco, CA: Jossey-Bass.

Sather, S. E. (1999). Leading, lauding, and learning: Leadership in secondary schools serving diverse populations. *Journal of Negro Education,* 511–528.

Saunders, J., Davis, L., Williams, T., & Williams, J. H. (2004). Gender differences in self-perceptions and academic outcomes: A study of African American high school students. *Journal of Youth and Adolescence, 33*(1), 81–90.

Saunders, W. M, Goldenberg, C. N., & Gallimore, R. (2009). Increasing achievement by focusing grade-level teams on improving classroom learning: A prospective, quasi-experimental study of Title I schools. *American Educational Research Journal, 46*(4), 1006–1033.

Scales, P. C., Roehlkepartain, M. N., Keilsmeier, J. C., & Benson, P. L. (2006). Reducing academic achievement gaps: The role of community service and service-learning. *Journal of Experimental Education, 29*(1), 38–60.

Scanlan, M., & Lopez, F. (2012). Vamos! How school leaders promote equity and excellence for bilingual students. *Educational Administration Quarterly, 48*(4), 583–625.

Scheerens, J. (1997). Conceptual models and theory-embedded principles on effective schooling. *School Effectiveness and School Improvement, 8*(3), 269–310.

Scheurich, J. J. (1998). Highly successful and loving, public elementary schools populated mainly by low-SES children of color. *Urban Education, 33*(4), 451–491.

Schwartz. F. (1981). Supporting or subverting learning: Peer group patterns in four tracked schools. *Anthropology and Education Quarterly, 12*(2), 99–121.

Scribner, J. P., Cockrell, K. S., Cockrell, D. H., & Valentine, J. W. (1999). Creating professional communities in schools through organizational learning: An evaluation of a school improvement process. *Educational Administration Quarterly, 35*(1), 130–160.

Sebastian, J., & Allensworth, E. (2012). The influence of principal leadership on classroom instruction and student learning: A study of mediated pathways to learning. *Educational Administration Quarterly, 48*(4), 626–663.

Sedlak, M. W., Wheeler, C. W., Pullin, D. C., & Cusick, P. A. (1986). *Selling students short: Classroom bargains and academic reform in the American high school.* New York, NY: Teachers College Press.

Seiler, G., & Elmesky, R. (2007, February). The role of communal practices in the generation of capital and emotional energy among urban African American students in science classrooms. *Teachers College Record, 100*(2), 391–419.

Senge, P. (1990). *The fifth discipline.* New York, NY: Doubleday.

Sergiovanni, T. J. (1991a). The dark side of professionalism in educational admin-
    istration. *Phi Delta Kappan, 72*(7), 521–526.
Sergiovanni, T. J. (1991b). *The principalship: A reflective practice perspective* (2nd ed.).
    Boston, MA: Allyn & Bacon.
Sergiovanni, T. J. (1994). Organizations or communities? Changing the metaphor
    changes the theory. *Educational Administration Quarterly, 30*(2), 214–226.
Sergiovanni, T. J. (2009). *The principalship: A reflective practice perspective* (6th ed.).
    Boston, MA: Allyn & Bacon.
Shade, B. J., Kelly, C. A., & Oberg, M. (1997). *Creating culturally responsive class-
    rooms.* Washington, DC: American Psychological Association.
Shannon, S. G., & Bylsma, P. (2002, November). *Addressing the achievement gap: A
    challenge for Washington state educators.* Olympia, WA: Washington Office of
    the State Superintendent of Public Instruction. (ED 474 392)
Shapiro, H. S. (Ed.). (2009). *Education and hope in troubled times: Visions of change for
    our children's world.* New York, NY: Routledge.
Shapiro, H. S., & Purpel, D. E. (Eds.). (2005). *Social issues in American education:
    Democracy and meaning in a globalized world* (3rd ed.). Mahwah, NJ: Erlbaum.
Shapiro, J. P. (1979). The accountability movement in education: A contagious
    disease? *FORUM: For the Discussion of New Trends in Education, 22*(1), 16–18.
Shapiro, J. P. (2015). What is ethical leadership? In D. Griffiths & J. P. Portelli (Eds.),
    Key questions for educational leaders (pp. 91–98). Burlington, Ontario, Canada:
    Word & Deed & Edphil Books.
Shapiro, J. P., & Gross, S. J. (2013). *Ethical educational leadership in turbulent times:
    (Re)solving moral dilemmas* (2nd ed.). New York, NY: Routledge.
Shapiro, J. P., & Stefkovich, J. A. (2001*). Ethical leadership and decision making in
    education: Applying theoretical perspectives to complex dilemmas.* Mahwah, NJ:
    Erlbaum.
Shapiro, J. P., & Stefkovich, J. A. (2005). *Ethical leadership and decision making
    in education: Applying theoretical perspectives to complex dilemmas* (2nd ed.).
    Mahwah, NJ: Erlbaum.
Shapiro, J. P., & Stefkovich, J. A. (2011). *Ethical leadership and decision making
    in education: Applying theoretical perspectives to complex dilemmas* (3rd ed.).
    New York, NY: Routledge.
Shapiro, J. P., & Stefkovich, J. A. (2016). *Ethical leadership and decision making
    in education: Applying theoretical perspectives to complex dilemmas* (4th ed.).
    New York, NY: Routledge.
Shapiro, S. H. (2016). The importance of building community: A preschool direc-
    tor's experiences on 9/11/01. In S. J. Gross & J. P. Shapiro (Eds.), *Democratic
    ethical educational leadership: Reclaiming school reform* (pp. 49–53). New York,
    NY: Routledge.
Shear, L., Means, B., Mitchell, K., House, A., Gorges, T., Joshi, A., Smerdon, B., &
    Shlonik, J. (2008). Contrasting paths to small-school reform: Results of a 5-year
    evaluation of the Bill & Melinda Gates Foundation's National High Schools
    Initiative. *Teachers College Record, 110*(9), 1986–2039.
Sheldon, S. B. (2002). Parents' social networks and beliefs as predictors of parent
    involvement. *The Elementary School Journal*, 301–316.
Sherrill, J. A. (1999, Winter). Preparing teachers for leadership roles in the 21st
    century. *Theory Into Practice, 38*(1), 56–61.

Shields, C. (2014). Ethical leadership: A critical transformative approach. In C. M. Branson & S. J. Gross. (Eds.), *Handbook of ethical educational leadership* (pp. 24–42). New York, NY: Routledge.

Shouse, R. (1996). Academic press and sense of community: Conflict, congruence, and implications for student achievement. *Social Psychology of Education, 1*(1), 47–68.

Silins, H. C., Mulford, W. R., & Zarins, S. (2002). Organizational learning and school change. *Educational Administration Quarterly, 38*(5), 613–642.

Silins, H., & Mulford, B. (2004). Schools as learning organisations: Effects on teacher leadership and student outcomes. *School Effectiveness and School Improvement, 3*(4), 443–466.

Silins, H., & Mulford, B. (2010). Re-conceptualising school principalship that improves student outcomes. *Journal of Educational Leadership, Policy and Practice, 25*(2), 74–93.

Silva, D. Y., Gimbert, B., & Nolan, J. (2000, August). Sliding the doors: Locking and unlocking possibilities for teacher leadership. *Teachers College Record, 102*(4), 779–804.

Silverstein, B., & Krate, R. (1975). *Children of the dark ghetto: A developmental psychology.* Oxford, England: Praeger.

Singham, M. (2003, April). The achievement gap: Myths and reality. *Phi Delta Kappan, 84*(8), 586–591.

Siskin, L. S. (1994). *Realms of knowledge: Academic departments in secondary schools.* Washington, DC: Falmer Press.

Siu, W. (2008). Complexity theory and school reform. *NASSP Bulletin, 92*(2), 154–164.

Sizer, T. R. (1984). *Horace's compromise: The dilemma of the American high school.* Boston, MA: Houghton Mifflin.

Slaughter-Defoe, D. T., & Carlson, K. G. (1996). Young African American and Latino children in high-poverty urban schools: How they perceive school climate. *Journal of Negro Education,* 60–70.

Slavin, R. E., & Oickle, E. (1981, July). Effects of cooperative learning teams on student achievement and race relations: Treatment by race interactions. *Sociology of Education, 54*(3), 174–180.

Smerdon, B. A. (2002). Students' perceptions of membership in their high schools. *Sociology of Education,* 287–305.

Smerdon, B. A., Borman, K. M., & Hannaway, J. (2009). Conclusions: Implications for future reform efforts, research, and policy. In B. A. Smerdon & K. M. Borman (Eds.), *Saving America's high schools* (pp. 201–215). Washington, DC: The Urban Institute Press.

Smerdon, B. A., & Borman, K. M. (2009). Secondary school reform. In B. A. Smerdon & K. M. Borman (Eds.), *Saving America's high schools* (pp. 1–17). Washington, DC: The Urban Institute Press.

Smylie, M. A. (1996). Research on teacher leadership: Assessing the state of the art. In B. J. Biddle, T. L. Good, & I. F. Goodson (Eds.), *International handbook of teachers and teaching* (pp. 521–592). Boston, MA: Kluwer Academic.

Smylie, M. A., & Denny, J. W. (1989, March). *Teacher leadership: Tensions and ambiguities in organizational perspective.* Paper presented at the annual meeting of the American Educational Research Association, San Francisco, CA.

Smylie, M. A., & Hart, A. W. (1999). School leadership for teacher learning: A human and social capital development perspective. In J. Murphy & K. S. Louis (Eds.), *Handbook of research on educational administration* (2nd ed., pp. 421–441). San Francisco, CA: Jossey-Bass.

Smylie, M. A., Conley, S., & Marks, H. M. (2002). Exploring new approaches to teacher leadership for school improvement. In J. Murphy (Ed.), *The educational leadership challenge: Redefining leadership for the 21st century* (pp. 162–188). Chicago, IL: University of Chicago Press.

Smylie, M. A., Mayrowetz, D., Murphy, J., & Louis, K. S. (2007, July). Trust and the development of distributed leadership. *Journal of School Leadership, 17*(4), 469–503.

Smylie, M., Murphy, J., & Louis, K. S. (in press). Caring school leadership: A multi-disciplinary, cross-occupational model. *American Journal of Education.*

Smyth, J. (2006). Educational leadership that fosters "student voice." *International Journal of Leadership in Education, 9*(4), 279–284.

Snell, J., & Swanson, J. (2000, April). *The essential knowledge and skills of teacher leaders: Social stratification.* (College Board Report No. 99–5). New York, NY: The College Board.

Somech, A., & Bogler, R. (2002). Antecedents and consequences of teacher organizational and professional commitment. *Educational Administration Quarterly, 38*(4), 555–577.

Southworth, G. (2002). Instructional leadership in schools: Reflections and empirical evidence. *School Leadership & Management, 22*(1), 73–91.

Spillane, J. P., & Louis, K. S. (2002). School improvement processes and practices: Professional learning for building instructional capacity. In J. Murphy (Ed.), *The educational leadership challenge: Redefining leadership for the 21st century: Yearbook of the National Society for the Study of Education* (pp. 83–104). Chicago, IL: University of Chicago Press.

Spillane, J. P., Camburn, E., & Pareja, A. (2009). School principals at work: A distributed perspective. In K. Leithwood, B. Mascall, & T. Strauss (Eds.), *Distributed leadership according to the evidence* (pp. 87–110). London, UK: Routledge.

Spillane, J. P., Halverson, R., & Diamond, J. B. (2001a). Investigating school leadership practice: A distributed perspective. *Educational Researcher, 30*(3), 23–28.

Spillane, J. P., Diamond, J. B., Walker, L. J., Halverson, R., & Jita, L. (2001b). Urban school leadership for elementary science instruction: Identifying and activating resources in an undervalued school subject. *Journal of Research in Science Teaching, 38*(8), 918–940.

Spillane, J. P., Hallett, T., & Diamond, J. B. (2003). Forms of capital and the construction of leadership: Instructional leadership in urban elementary schools. *Sociology of Education, 76*(1), 1–17.

Spires, H. A., Lee, J. K., Turner, K. A., & Johnson, J. (2008). Having our say: Middle grade student perspectives on school, technologies, and academic engagement. *Journal of Research on Technology in Education, 40*(4), 497–515.

Spradlin, T. E., Kirk, R., Walcott, C., Kloosterman, P., Zaman, K., McNabb, S., & Zapf, J. (2005, September). *Is the achievement gap in Indiana narrowing?* [Special report]. Bloomington, IN: Center for Evaluation and Education Policy.

St. Pierre, T. L., Mark, M. M., Kaltreider, D. L., & Aikin, K. J. (1997). Involving parents of high-risk youth in drug preventions: A three year longitudinal study in Boys & Girls Clubs. *Journal of Early Adolescence, 17*(1), 21–50.

Stanton-Salazar, R. D. (1997). A social capital framework for understanding the socialization of racial minority children and youths. *Harvard Educational Review, 67*(1), 1–41.

Starratt, R. J. (2004). *Ethical leadership.* San Francisco, CA: Jossey-Bass.

Steele, C. M. (1992). Race and the schooling of Black Americans. *Atlantic Monthly, 269*(4), 68–78.

Steele, C. M. (1997). A threat in the air: How stereotypes shape the intellectual identities and performances of women and African Americans. *American Psychologist, 52*(6), 613–629.

Steele, J. M., House, E. R., & Kerins, T. (1971). An instrument for assessing instructional climate through low-inference student judgments. *American Educational Research Journal, 8*(3), 447–466.

Stein, M. K., & Coburn, C. E. (2008). Architectures for learning: A comparative analysis of two urban school districts. *American Journal of Education, 114*(4), 583–626.

Steinberg, L. (1996). *Beyond the classroom: Why school reform has failed and what parents need to do.* New York, NY: Simon & Schuster.

Stefkovich, J. A. (2006). *Best interests of the student: Applying ethical constructs to legal cases.* Mahwah, NJ: Erlbaum.

Stefkovich, J. A. (2014). *Best interests of the student: Applying ethical constructs to legal cases* (2nd ed.). New York, NY: Routledge.

Stevenson, H. W., Chen, C., & Uttal, D. H. (1990). Beliefs and achievement: A study of black, white, and Hispanic children. *Child Development, 61*(2), 508–523.

Stewart, E. B. (2008). School structural characteristics, student effort, peer associations, and parental involvement: The influence of school- and individual-level factors on academic achievement. *Education and Urban Society, 40*(2), 179–204.

Stiefel, L., Schwartz, A. E., & Ellen, I. G. (2006). Disentangling the racial test score gap: Probing the evidence in a large urban school district. *Journal of Policy Analysis and Management, 26*(1), 7–30.

Stigler, J. W., & Hiebert, J. (1999). *The teaching gap: Best ideas from the world's teachers for improving education in the classroom.* New York, NY: The Free Press.

Stinchcombe, A. (1964). *Rebellion in a high school.* Chicago, IL: Quadrangle Books.

Stinson, D. W. (2006, Winter). African American male adolescents, schooling (and mathematics): Deficiency, rejection, and achievement. *Review of Educational Research, 76*(4), 477–506.

Stoicovy, D. (2016). Maintaining a commitment to democracy (In spite of high-stakes standardized testing). In S. J. Gross & J. P. Shapiro (Eds.), *Democratic ethical educational leadership: Reclaiming school reform* (pp. 21–25). New York, NY: Routledge.

Stoll, L., Bolam, R., McMahon, A., Wallace, M., & Thomas, S. (2006). Professional learning communities: A review of the literature. *Journal of Educational Change, 7*(4), 221–258.

Stone, M., Horejs, J., & Lomas, A. (1997). Commonalities and differences in teacher leadership at the elementary, middle, and high school level. *Action in Teacher Education, 19*(3), 49–64.

Strahan, D. (2003). Promoting a collaborative professional culture in three elementary schools that have beaten the odds. *The Elementary School Journal, 104*(2), 127–146.

Strike, K. A. (2006). *Ethical leadership in schools: Creating community in an environment of accountability.* Thousand Oaks, CA: Corwin.

Strike, K. A., Haller, E. J., & Soltis, J. E. (2005). *The ethics of school administration* (3rd ed.). New York, NY: Teachers College Press.

Stringfield, S., & Reynolds, D. (2012). *Creating and sustaining secondary schools success at scale—Sandfields, Cwmtawe, and the Neath-port Talbot local education authority's high reliability schools reform.* Paper presented at the National Conference on Scaling Up Effective Schools, Nashville, TN.

Strutchens, M. E., & Silver, E. A. (2000). NAEP findings regarding race/ethnicity: Students' performance, school experiences, and attitudes and beliefs. In E. A. Silver & P. A. Kenney (Eds.), *Results from the seventh mathematics assessment of the National Assessment of Educational Progress* (pp. 45–72). Reston, VA: National Council of Teachers of Mathematics.

Sui-Chu, E. H., & Willms, J. D. (1996). Effects of parental involvement on eighth-grade achievement. *Sociology of Education, 69*(2), 126–141.

Suleiman, M., & Moore, R. (1997). *Teachers' roles revisited: Beyond classroom management.* Paper presented at the Association of Teacher Educators (ATE) summer workshop, Tarpon Springs, FL.

Supovitz, J. (2002). Developing communities of instructional practice. *The Teachers College Record, 104*(8), 1591–1626.

Supovitz, J. (2008). Instructional influence in American high schools. In M. M. Mangin & S. R. Stoelinga (Eds.), *Effective teacher leadership: Using research to inform and reform* (pp. 144–162). New York, NY: Teachers College Press.

Supovitz, J. (2010). Is high-stakes testing working? *A Review of Research, 7*(2). Retrieved from http://www.gse.upenn.edu/review/feature/supovitz

Supovitz, J. A., & Christman, J. B. (2003). *Developing communities of instructional practice: Lessons from Cincinnati and Philadelphia.* Philadelphia, PA: Consortium for Policy Research in Education, University of Pennsylvania.

Supovitz, J. A., & Klein, V. (2003). *Mapping a course for improved student learning: How innovative schools systematically use student performance data to guide improvement.* Philadelphia, PA: Consortium for Policy Research in Education.

Supovitz, J. A., & Poglinco, S. M. (2001). *Instructional leadership in a standards-based reform.* Philadelphia, PA: Consortium for Policy Research in Education.

Supovitz, J. A., & Turner, H. M. (2000). The effects of professional development on science teaching practices and classroom culture. *Journal of Research in Science Teaching, 37*(9), 963–980.

Supovitz, J., Sirinides, P., & May, H. (2010). How principals and peers influence teaching and learning. *Educational Administration Quarterly, 46*(1), 31–56.

Sweeney, J. (1982). Research synthesis on effective school leadership. *Educational Leadership, 39*(5), 346–352.

Sweetland, S. R., & Hoy, W. K. (2000). School characteristics and educational outcomes: Toward an organizational model of student achievement in middle schools. *Educational Administration Quarterly, 36*(5), 703–729.

Sykes, G., & Elmore, R. F. (1989). Making schools more manageable. In J. Hannaway & R. L. Crowson (Eds.), *The politics of reforming school administration* (pp. 77–94). New York, NY: Falmer Press.

Tate, W. F. (1997). Race-ethnicity, SES, gender, and language proficiency trends in mathematics achievement: An update. *Journal for Research in Mathematics Education, 28*(6), 652–679.

Taylor-Dunlop, K., & Norton, M. M. (1997). Out of the mouths of babes: Voices of at-risk adolescents. *The Clearing House: A Journal of Educational Strategies, Issues and Ideas, 70*(5), 274–278.

Theoharis, G. (2007). Social justice educational leaders and resistance: Toward a theory of social justice leadership. *Educational Administration Quarterly, 43*(2), 221–258.

Thompson, C. L. (2002, April). *Research-based review of reports on closing achievement gaps: Report to the education cabinet and the joint legislative oversight committee.* Chapel Hill, NC: The North Carolina Education Research Council.

Thompson, C. L. (2004). *Through ebony eyes: What teachers need to know but are afraid to ask about African-American students* (pp. 13–39). San Francisco, CA: Jossey-Bass.

Thompson, C. L., & O'Quinn, S. D., III. (2001). *Eliminating the black-white achievement gap: A summary of research.* Chapel Hill, NC: North Carolina Education Research Council. (ED 457 250)

Thomson, P., & Gunter, H. (2006). From 'consulting pupils' to 'pupils as researchers': A situated case narrative. *British Educational Research Journal, 32*(6), 839–856.

Thomson, S. (1999). Causing change: The National Policy Board for Educational Administration. In J. Murphy & P. B. Forsyth (Eds.), *Educational administration: A decade of reform* (pp. 93–114). Thousand Oaks, CA: Corwin.

Tichy, N. M., & Cardwell, N. (2004). *The cycle of leadership: How great leaders teach their companies to win.* New York, NY: Harper Business.

Timperley, H. (2005). Distributed leadership: Developing theory from practice. *Journal of Curriculum Studies, 37*(4), 395–420.

Timperley, H. (2009). Distributed leadership to improve outcomes for students. In K. Leithwood, B. Mascall, & T. Strauss (Eds.), *Distributed leadership according to the evidence* (pp. 197–222). London, UK: Routledge.

Tomlinson, J. (1986). Public education, public good. *Oxford Review of Education, 12*(3), 211–222.

Troen, V., & Boles, K. (1994). Two teachers examine the power of teacher leadership. In D. R. Walling (Ed.), *Teachers as leaders: Perspectives on the professional development of teachers* (pp. 275–286). Bloomington, IN: Phi Delta Kappa.

Tschannen-Moran, M., & Barr, M. (2004). Fostering student learning: The relationship of collective teacher efficacy and student achievement. *Leadership and Policy in Schools, 3*(3), 189–209.

Tuana, N. (2007). Conceptualizing moral literacy. *Journal of Educational Administration, 45*(4), 364–378.

Tushman, M. L., & Romanelli, E. (1985). Organizational evolution: A metamorphosis model of convergence and reorientation. In L. L. Cummings & B. M. Straw (Eds.), *Research in organizational behavior* (pp. 171–222). Greenwich, CT: JAI Press.

Tushman, M. L., Newman, W. H., & Romanelli, E. (1988). Convergence and upheaval: Managing the unsteady pace of organizational evolution. In K. S. Cameron, R. I. Sutton, & D. A. Whetten (Eds.), *Readings in organizational decline: Frameworks, research, and prescriptions* (pp. 63–74). Cambridge, MA: Ballinger.

Tyack, D. (1993). School governance in the United States: Historical puzzles and anomalies. In J. Hannaway & M. Carnoy (Eds.), *Decentralization and school improvement* (pp. 1–32). San Francisco, CA: Jossey-Bass.

Tyson, K. (2002). Weighing in: Elementary-age students and the debate on attitudes toward school among Black students. *Social Forces, 80*(4), 1157–1189.

Uhlenberg, J., & Brown, K. M. (2002, August). Racial gap in teachers' perceptions of the achievement gap. *Education and Urban Society, 34*(4), 493–530.

University Council for Educational Administration (UCEA). (2011). *UCEA code of ethics for the preparation of educational leaders.* Charlottesville, VA: University of Virginia.

Urbanski, A., & Nickolaou, M. B. (1997, June). Reflections on teacher leadership. *Educational Policy, 11*(2), 243–254.

U.S. Commission on Civil Rights. (2004). Closing the achievement gap: The impact of standards-based education reform on student performance. (Draft report for commissioners' review). Washington, DC: Author.

Useem, E. L., Christman, J. B., Gold, E., & Simon, E. (1997). Reforming alone: Barriers to organizational learning in urban school change initiatives. *Journal of Education for Students Placed at Risk (JESPAR), 2*(1), 55–78.

Valentine, J. W., & Prater, M. (2011). Instructional, transformational, and managerial leadership and student achievement: High school principals make a difference. *NASSP Bulletin, 95*(1), 5–30.

Velez, W. (1989). High school attrition among Hispanic and non-Hispanic White youths. *Sociology of Education, 62*(2), 119–133.

Venezky, R., & Winfield, L. (1979). *Schools that succeed beyond expectations in teaching reading* (Technical Report No. 1). Newark, NJ: University of Delaware.

Vescio, V., Ross, D., & Adams, A. (2008). A review of research on the impact of professional learning communities on teaching practice and student learning. *Teaching and Teacher Education, 24*(1), 80–91.

Visscher, A. J., & Witziers, B. (2004). Subject departments as professional communities? *British Educational Research Journal, 30*(6), 785–800.

Voelkl, K. E. (1997). Identification with school. *American Journal of Education, 105*(3), 294–318.

Wahlstrom, K. L., & Louis, K. S. (2008). How teachers experience principal leadership: The roles of professional community, trust, efficacy, and shared responsibility. *Educational Administration Quarterly, 44*(4), 458–495.

Walker, J. (2009). Reorganizing leaders' time: Does it create better schools for students? *NASSP Bulletin, 93*(4), 213–226.

Walker, J., & Slear, S. (2011). The impact of principal leadership behaviors on the efficacy of new and experienced middle school teachers. *NASSP Bulletin, 95*(1), 46–64.

Wallace, G. (1996a). Engaging with learning. In J. Rudduck, R. P. Chaplain, & G. Wallace (Eds.), *School improvement: What can pupils tell us?* (pp. 52–65). London, UK: Routledge.

Wallace, G. (1996b). Relating to teachers. In J. Rudduck, R. P. Chaplain, & G. Wallace (Eds.), *School improvement: What can pupils tell us?* (pp. 29–47). London, UK: Routledge.

Warrington, M., & Younger, M. (1996). Homework: Dilemmas and difficulties. In J. Rudduck, R. P. Chaplain, & G. Wallace (Eds.), *School improvement: What can pupils tell us?* (pp. 83–96). London, England: Routledge.

Wasley, P. A. (1991). *Teachers who lead: The rhetoric of reform and realities of practice.* New York, NY: Teachers College Press.

Waters, T., Marzano, R. J., & McNulty, B. (2003). *Balanced leadership: What 30 years of research tells us about the effect of leadership on student achievement.* Aurora, CO: Mid-continent Research for Education and Learning.

Waxman, H. C., Padron, Y. N., & Garcia, A. (2007). Educational issues and effective practices for Hispanic students. In S. J. Paik & H. J. Walberg (Eds.), *Narrowing the achievement gap: Strategies for educating Latino, Black, and Asian students* (pp. 131–151). New York, NY: Springer Science+Business Media.

Wayman, J., & Stringfield, S. (2006). Technology-supported involvement of entire faculties in examination of student data for instructional improvement. *American Journal of Education, 112*(4), 549–571.

Wayne, A. J., & Youngs, P. (2003, Spring). Teacher characteristics and student achievement gains: A review. *Review of Educational Research, 73*(1), 89–122.

Webb, R. (2005). Leading teaching and learning in the primary school. *Educational Management Administration & Leadership, 33*(1), 69–91.

Weber, M. (1978). *Economy and society.* Oakland, CA: University of California Press.

Wehlage, G. G., Rutter, R. A., Smith, G. A., Lesko, N., & Fernandez, R. R. (1989). *Reducing the risk: Schools as communities of support.* New York, NY: Falmer.

Weick, K. E. (1976). Educational organizations as loosely coupled systems. *Administrative Science Quarterly, 21*(2), 1–19.

Weil, M., & Murphy, J. (1982). Instructional processes. In H. E. Mitzel (Ed.), *The encyclopedia of educational research* (Vol. 2, 5th ed., pp. 890–917).

Weinstein, R. (1976). Reading group membership in first-grade: Teacher behaviors and pupil experience over time. *Journal of Educational Psychology, 68*(1), 103–116.

Weinstein, R. S. (1983). Student perceptions of schooling. *The Elementary School Journal, 83*(4), 287–312.

Weis, L. (n.d.). *Issues in education: Schooling and the reproduction of class and gender inequalities.* Buffalo, NY: State University of New York, Buffalo, Department of Educational Organization: Occasional Paper Number Ten.

Weis, L. (1990). *Working class without work: High school students in a deindustrializing economy.* New York, NY: Routledge.

Wellisch, J. B., MacQueen, A. H., Carriere, R. A., & Duck, G. A. (1978). School management and organization in successful schools. *Sociology of Education, 51*(3), 211–226.

Wenger, E. (1998). *Communities of practice: Learning, meaning, and identity.* Cambridge, UK: Cambridge University Press.

Wenger, E. (2000). Communities of practice and social learning systems. *Organization, 7*(2), 225–246.

Wenger, E., & Snyder, W. (2000). Communities of practice: The organizational frontier. *Harvard Business Review, 78*(1), 139–146.

Wentzel, K. R. (2002). Are effective teachers like good parents? Teaching styles and student adjustment in early adolescence. *Child Development, 73*(1), 287–301.

Wenz-Gross, M., & Siperstein, G. N. (1998). Students with learning problems at risk in middle school: Stress, social support, and adjustment. *Exceptional Children, 65*(1), 91–100.

Whitaker, T. (1995, January). Informed teacher leadership—the key to successful change in the middle level school. *NASSP Bulletin, 79*(567), 76–81.

Wigfield, A., Eccles, J. S., & Rodriguez, D. (1998). The development of children's motivation in school contexts. *Review of Research in Education, 23*(1), 73–118.

Wigginton, E. (1992). A vision of teacher leadership. In C. Livingston (Ed.), *Teachers as leaders: Evolving roles* (pp. 167–173). Washington, DC: National Education Association.

Williams, D. T. (2003, Spring). *Closing the achievement gap: Rural schools. CSR connection.* Washington, DC: National Clearinghouse for Comprehensive School Reform.

Wilson, B. L., & Corbett, H. D. (2001). *Listening to urban kids: School reform and the teachers they want.* Albany, NY: SUNY Press.

Wilson, B. L., & Corcoran, T. B. (1988). *Successful secondary schools: Visions of excellence in American public education.* New York, NY: Falmer.

Wilson, B., & Corbett, H. (1999). *No excuses: The eighth grade year in six Philadelphia middle schools.* Philadelphia, PA: Philadelphia Education Fund.

Wilson. M. (1993). The search for teacher leaders. *Educational Leadership, 50*(6), 24–27.

Wilson, S. M., & Berne, J. (1999). Teacher learning and the acquisition of professional knowledge: An examination of research on contemporary professional development. In A. Iran-Nejad & P. D. Pearson (Eds.), *Review of Research in Education* (pp. 173–209). Washington, DC: American Educational Research Association.

Wilson, T., Karimpour, R., & Rodkin, P. C. (2011). African American and European American students' peer groups during early adolescence: Structure, status, and academic achievement. *The Journal of Early Adolescence, 31*(1), 74–98.

Wilson, W. J. (1998). The role of the environment in the Black-White test score gap. In C. Jencks & M. Phillips (Eds.), *The Black-White test score gap* (pp. 501–510). Washington, DC: Brookings Institution Press.

Wimpelberg, R. K. (1986, April). *Bureaucratic and cultural images in the management of more and less effective schools.* Paper presented at the annual meeting of the American Educational Research Association, San Francisco, CA.

Witziers, B., Bosker, R. J., & Kruger, M. L. (2003). Educational leadership and student achievement: The elusive search for an association. *Educational Administration Quarterly, 39*(3), 398–425.

Wohlstetter, P., Datnow, A., & Park, V. (2008). Creating a system for data-driven decision-making: Applying the principal-agent framework. *School Effectiveness and School Improvement, 19*(3), 239–259.

Woloszyk, C. (1996). *Models for at risk youth* [Final Report]. Kalamazoo, MI: Upjohn Institute for Employment Research.

Wraga, W. G. (1994). *Democracy's high school: The comprehensive high school and educational reform in the United States.* Lanham, MD: University Press of America.

Wynne, E. (1980). *Looking at schools: Good, bad, and indifferent.* Lexington, MA: D. C. Heath.

Yair, G. (2000). Not just about time: Instructional practices and productive time in school. *Educational Administration Quarterly, 36*(4), 485–512.

Yodof, M., Kirp, D., & Levin, B. (1992). *Educational policy and the law* (3rd ed.). St. Paul, MN: West Publishing.

York-Barr, J., & Duke, K. (2004). What do we know about teacher leadership? Findings from two decades of scholarship. *Review of Educational Research, 74*(3), 255–316.

Young, M. D. (2014). Do standards matter in educational leadership programs? If so, how? *UCEA Review, 55*(2), 8–11.

Young, M. D., & Liable, J. (2000, September). White racism, antiracism, and school leadership preparation. *Journal of School Leadership, 19*(1), 374–415.

Young, V. (2006). Teachers' use of data: Loose coupling, agenda setting, and team norms. *American Journal of Education, 112*(4), 521–548.

Youngs, P. (2007). How elementary principals' beliefs and actions influence new teachers' experiences. *Educational Administration Quarterly, 43*(1), 101–137.

Youngs, P., & King, M. B. (2002). Principal leadership for professional development to build school capacity. *Educational Administration Quarterly, 38*(5), 643–670.

Yu, H., Leithwood, K., & Jantzi, D. (2002). The effects of transformational leadership on teachers' commitment to change in Hong Kong. *Journal of Educational Administration, 40*(4), 368–389.

Zamel, V. (1990). Through students' eyes: The experiences of three ESL writers. *Journal of Basic Writing, 9*(2), 83–98.

Zanger, V. V. (1991). Social and cultural dimensions of the education of language minority students. In A. N. Ambert (Ed.), *Bilingual education and English as a second language: A research handbook, 1988–1990* (pp. 3–53). New York, NY: Garland.

Zanger, V. V. (1993). Academic costs of social marginalization: An analysis of Latino students' perceptions at a Boston high school. In R. Rivera & S. Nieto (Eds.), *The education of Latino students in Massachusetts: Issues, research and policy implications* (pp. 170–190). Boston, MA: University of Massachusetts Press.

Zimpher, N. L. (1988, January/February). A design for the professional development of teacher leaders. *Journal of Teacher Education, 39*(1), 53–60.

Index

CORWIN

A SAGE Publishing Company

CORWIN HAS ONE MISSION: to enhance education through intentional professional learning.

We build long-term relationships with our authors, educators, clients, and associations who partner with us to develop and continuously improve the best evidence-based practices that establish and support lifelong learning.

Solutions you want. Experts you trust. Results you need.